PRAISE FOR *A FUTURE PERFECT*

"Micklethwait and Wooldridge are unusually comprehensive in their analysis."

—*The New York Times*

"One of the many virtues of this passionate and readable work is that the authors know too much about history, as well as about the world, to assume that the current situation must persist, and they take up the argument for globalization with refreshing candor and verve, ranging across continents and deep into the history of ideas. . . . Read this brilliant book."

—*The Industry Standard*

"Globalization is such a mouthful. It is a pleasure to say that *A Future Perfect*, examining its implications, soars above the indigestible noun. The authors deftly make sense of the abstract with vivid specifics we can all relate to, and it's cheering, too. This is an important book and . . . a lot of fun to read."

—Harold M. Evans, author of *The American Century*

"A timely retort to the critics of the World Trade Organization and our galloping free markets. Micklethwait and Wooldridge . . . mount an energetic defense of globalization. Their goal is to impose some order on the morass of assumption and opinion that has gelled around the concept of a global marketplace."

—*The Washington Post*

"*A Future Perfect* fills a yawning void with a magisterial case for the most powerful—and life-enhancing—force on earth: globalization."

—Tom Peters, coauthor of *In Search of Excellence*

ABOUT THE AUTHORS

JOHN MICKLETHWAIT oversees coverage of the United States for *The Economist*. He has written op-ed articles for, among others, *The New York Times*, the *Los Angeles Times*, *The Wall Street Journal*, *The Spectator*, *Fortune*, and *USA Today*. He was educated at Magdalen College, Oxford. He lives in London.

ADRIAN WOOLDRIDGE is *The Economist's* Washington correspondent. His writing has appeared in numerous publications, including *The Washington Post*, *Forbes*, *The New Republic*, *Foreign Policy*, the *Financial Times*, *The New Statesman*, and *The Times Literary Supplement*. He was educated at Balliol College and All Souls College, Oxford, where he received a D.Phil.

Micklethwait and Wooldridge are coauthors of *The Witch Doctors; Making Sense of the Management Gurus*, winner of a 1997 *Financial Times*/Booz Allen Global Business Book Award, and *The Company: A Short History of a Revolutionary Idea*. Wooldridge is also the author of *Measuring the Mind: Education and Psychology in England 1860–1990*.

A Future Perfect

A Future Perfect

The Challenge and Promise of Globalization

John Micklethwait
and
Adrian Wooldridge

RANDOM HOUSE TRADE PAPERBACKS

NEW YORK

2003 Random House Trade Paperback Edition

Copyright © 2000, 2003 John Micklethwait and Adrian Wooldridge

All rights reserved under International and Pan-American Copyright Conventions.
Published in the United States by Random House Trade Paperbacks, an imprint of
The Random House Publishing Group, a division of Random House, Inc., New York,
and simultaneously in Canada by Random House of Canada Limited, Toronto.

RANDOM HOUSE TRADE PAPERBACKS and colophon are trademarks of Random House, Inc.

This work was originally published in hardcover and paperback in 2000 by Crown Business,
a division of Random House, Inc., in different form.

Library of Congress Cataloging-in-Publication Data
Micklethwait, John.
  A future perfect : the challenge and promise of globalization / John Micklethwait
and Adrian Wooldridge.
    p. cm.
Includes bibliographical references and index.
ISBN 0-8129-6680-5
  1. Economic history—1990– 2. Globalization. I. Wooldridge, Adrian. II. Title.
HC59.15 .M53   2000   330.9—dc21   99-054251

Random House website address: www.atrandom.com
Printed in the United States of America
9 8 7 6 5 4 3

Book design by Helene Berinsky

To Ella, Tom, Guy, and Edward

For I dipt into the future, far as human eye can see,
Saw the Vision of the world, and all the wonder that would be;
Saw the heavens fill with commerce, argosies of magic sails,
Pilots of the purple twilight, dropping down with costly bales;
Heard the heavens fill with shouting, and there rain'd a ghastly dew
From the nations' airy navies grappling in the central blue;
Far along the world-wide whisper of the south-wind rushing warm,
With the standards of the peoples plunging thro' the thunder-storm;
Till the war-drum throbb'd no longer, and the battle-flags were furl'd.
In the Parliament of man, the Federation of the world.

—ALFRED, LORD TENNYSON, "Locksley Hall"

Authors' Note

THIS NOTE is being written somewhere between Los Angeles and New York City—on an American computer in an American aircraft flown by an American airline—at the behest of an American publisher. But in fact, Random House is now owned by Germany's Bertelsmann; the IBM laptop was made in Mexico; the Boeing 757 includes parts from nearly forty countries; and the future of Delta Air Lines seems to lie in its code-sharing agreements with a dozen foreign-based carriers.

On the back of the seat in front is an "airfone" that allows a passenger to telephone anywhere in the world for five dollars per minute, a price that, though extortionate, would have seemed impossibly cheap twenty years ago. Were the author more technologically competent, he could also connect his computer to the airfone's datapoint and reply to a colleague's e-mail from Thailand, which he had picked up this morning as (rather pathetically in the eyes of his wife) he used the computer to listen to Leicester City—a soccer team whose squad includes a French goalkeeper, a Jamaican fullback, a Greek midfielder, and an Icelandic striker—uncharacteristically beat Aston Villa 3–1 in Birmingham, England.

Look around you, wherever you are, and you will quickly find similar evidence that the world is becoming a smaller place. As we shall see, globalization is neither new nor complete—and it is certainly not inevitable. Listening to an obscure soccer match miles away is also evidence of how much local ties matter. At its heart, IBM is still an American company. In a truly global market, Delta would be able to take over its foreign partners rather than be forced to enter awkward alliances. But it is also clear that something fundamental has been happening to all of us.

Globalization, we believe, is the most important phenomenon of our time. It is a contentious, complicated subject, and each particular element of it—from the alleged Americanization of world culture to the supposed end of the nation-state to the triumph of global companies—is itself at the heart of a huge debate. Yet people tend to shy away from seeing the subject in the round. Economists agonize over capital movements but ignore the social and cultural disruptions that globalization brings. Left-wingers summon up apocalyptic visions of capitalism run mad, while cyberprophets indulge in utopian fantasies of a world unified by webs and wires. Businesspeople often know the meat and bones of the subject better than anyone else does—the companies and products that are drawing the world together—but they are too wrapped up in the struggle for profits to consider the wider picture.

We have tried to strike two balances that are probably impossible to maintain. The first is to write a book that engages all the fundamental arguments of the subject yet does so through examples involving real people, companies, and even religious communities. The second is to write an opinionated book in which the authors are not the main characters. The subject, the arguments, and many of the characters are substantial enough by themselves without us tacking on breathless descriptions of the hotels that we have visited, the food we have eaten, or (henceforth) the soccer matches we have heard. So let us clear up all of that right now, so we can disappear.

If nothing else, the topic of globalization offers variety for the writer. One moment you are in Paris, talking to Jeanne Moreau through a haze of cigarette smoke about the French film industry, and the next shivering on the bridge at Narva, shouting questions at embittered Russian women who think that you are an Estonian spy. One moment you are discussing global production with Jack Welch of General Electric; at the next, the same subject crops up with Steven Hirsch, the San Fernando Valley's leading pornographer. In general, we have learned far more from talking to people such as Charlie Woo, a Chinese immigrant who has revitalized some of the nastiest bits of Los Angeles, or Jackson Thubela, a gold-toothed "phone-shop" owner (who rents out time on cellular phones) in Soweto, than from political bigwigs or International Monetary Fund reports. It has taught us how small the world has become (e-mail has made it relatively easy for two people who live several thousand miles apart to write a book together) and how awesomely large it can seem: Very few of the consultants who celebrate the global village seem to have flown economy-class over long distances.

There have been two pervading sadnesses in the writing of this book. The first is that we have been forced to exclude a large number of interesting, exciting stories that we have come across around the world, for the simple reason that they are not quite as germane to our argument as we had thought. The second is that many of the most decent, admirable, and enchanting people whom we depict in these pages—whether they are favela dwellers in São Paulo or General Motors workers in Flint, Michigan—are those who have done worst by the process that we are celebrating.

But celebrate it we do. For the underlying message of this book is that globalization needs not merely to be understood but to be defended stoutly. Globalization is a subject in which the devil has tended to have all the best tunes. While supporters tend to produce ponderous examinations of trade flows, assaults on it often summon up savage, searing images of broken homes and closed factories. We do not deny these casualties. But we believe that many of them should be laid at the feet of villains other than globalization. Globalization is a savage process, but it is also a beneficial one, in which the winners far outnumber the losers.

One of the aims of this book, however, is to drag the debate about globalization away from a dire catalog of winners and losers and toward a fundamental appraisal of modern liberty. Writing this book has been a little like stepping into a time machine. Even as we have reported "forward," trying to articulate the sort of society that globalization is creating, we have read "back" to the last great global age in the nineteenth century and then back further still to the origins of modern liberal thought. It may seem odd to pick up a book that purports to be about a Future Perfect that returns often to the past tense—to Locke, Jefferson, and Macaulay, to Herder, Hegel, and Marx, to Peel, Carnegie, and Rockefeller—but we do so because they are still relevant. And the consistent message from history chimes with that from our travels and even from those IMF reports: Globalization is not an inevitable process but an all-too-human one, in which success has to be fought for rather than simply assumed.

Our acknowledgments at the other end of this book detail the many hapless, generous people on whose backs this edifice has been constructed. We cannot begin, however, without singling out two victims of our monomania. The first is *The Economist*. It would be hard to devise a better training for writing a book on globalization than the quarter century we have between us spent under its auspices. We are extremely grateful to the editor, Bill Emmott, for giving us time to research this book and for giving us permission to use some of our work for him in these pages.

The other (perhaps less tolerant) group of victims has been imposed upon even more. There are two outrageous fictions observed in the acknowledgments of books about big subjects since time immemorial. The first is that wives lovingly look forward to each fresh chapter and cheer each new trip abroad. We will simply say that we are deeply grateful—and even slightly surprised—that Fevronia and Amelia are still with us. The second fiction is that authors applaud the contribution of their children—the little tots, like the young John Stuart Mill, helpfully editing chapters about capital flows whilst nestling on their parents' knees. Ella, Tom, Guy, and Edward have, it has to be said, done everything possible to slow production of this book. On the other hand, they are all under six; they all claim that they have been shamefully neglected; and it will be their Future, perfect or not. So this book is dedicated to them.

Contents

Introduction

From Sarajevo to September 11

ON THE MORNING of June 28,1914, the world could rejoice in sixty years of extraordinary peace and progress. The first great age of globalization had made the world seem an infinitely smaller place. So great were the twin powers of technology (in the shape of the telephone, the telegram, the train, the car, electricity, the camera) and ideology (the gospel of free trade, guaranteed by the world's hegemonic power, Britain) that Edwardian intellectuals prophesized the end of all wars. Yet on that summer's day, one act of terrorism in Sarajevo—the assassination of the Archduke Ferdinand and his wife by a Serbian fanatic called Gavrilo Princip—set off a sickening train of events. The world plunged into the most horrific war in history. And even after the killing had stopped, countries everywhere renounced their previous openness, fortifying their borders to limit the movement of goods, people, and even ideas.

It would be absurd to blame all the miseries of the first half of the twentieth century on a single act of terrorism: The causes of world war and protectionist folly had been germinating for years. But those causes only became clear in retrospect. John Maynard Keynes nicely describes the typical middle-class Londoner in 1914, "sipping his morning tea in bed" while ordering goods from around the world and planning his global investments. For such a man, "the projects and politics of militarism and imperialism, of racial and cultural rivalries, of monopolies, restrictions, and exclusion, which were to play the serpent to this paradise, were little more than the amusements of his daily newspaper."[1] For such a man, and millions of others, Gavrilo Princip's two shots marked a turning point.

In the first edition of this book, published in 2000, one of the figures we chose to illustrate the backlash against the current age of globalization was another terrorist: Osama bin Laden. Drawing on research by a friend, who had interviewed bin Laden in Afghanistan, we quoted his fury against the "New World Order" that "haughty" America was imposing on the world.[2] We noted that bin Laden, like so many other opponents of globalization, had been remarkably sophisticated about exploiting the process he professed to hate, using the latest technology to promote his medieval message. And we argued that, for all its other merits, lowering borders had made the West much more vulnerable to attack. We raised the possibility of al-Qaeda using a primitive nuclear bomb to blow up the World Trade Center.

At the time, this seemed a little far-fetched. We debated shortening the section on bin Laden, lest people think we were paying too much attention to the ramblings of a marginal crank. People were far more interested in the promise of open markets and technological innovation than they were in terrorism.

The first edition of this book appeared at a dangerously heady time for supporters of globalization, particularly in the United States. The stock market continued to defy gravity. The standard indicators of globalization pointed skyward: The volume of global trade increased steadily in the decade through 2000, and foreign direct investment flows topped $1.3 trillion. Economists speculated about the birth of a "new economy" that had banished recessions for good. Gurus speculated about "Dow 36,000"—or whatever other number they plucked out of their hats. This was a time when Silicon Valley and Wall Street minted new millionaires every single day; when business-school graduates confidently expected to retire at forty and begin a new career in philanthropy; and when the first signs of liberalization seemed to be awakening parts of the third world. India and China were booming after decades of state-imposed stagnation.

Of course, there were serpents in this paradise, no less than there were in the world of Keynes's Londoner. Too many people in the developing world lived in grinding poverty. Too many people in the rich world were worried about losing their jobs. The antiglobalization movement won a huge propaganda victory when a hundred-thousand-strong army of trade unionists and students succeeded in turning the 1999 meeting of the WTO into a farce. But most people found it easy to dismiss the Seattle protests (and its successors in Washington, D.C., and Genoa) as a sideshow—cheap entertainment for students with too much money and too much time on their hands. Thousands of people might have turned out to protest against globalization. But hundreds of millions of people voted for governments that supported it.

A Definition of Globalization

How much of a reversal for globalization was September 11? To answer that question, we need to start by defining the term *globalization*. One reason for the general confusion that surrounds this subject is that people have started to use the word as shorthand for their entire philosophy of life. For highfliers in Wall Street and Silicon Valley, it is a synonym for *modernity;* for French intellectuals (as for bin Laden), it means American domination; for Ralph Nader and Pat Buchanan, it means exactly the opposite, the emasculation of their country.

Our definition of globalization is rooted in freedom. Globalization is *the freer movement of goods, services, ideas, and people around the world.* Two things about this definition are worth stressing. First, globalization is about more than just business; it is about culture and people. The Guggenheim in Bilbao is as much a symbol of globalization as DaimlerChrysler; so are the Albanian "asylum seekers" flocking into Britain. Globalization is certainly about the ratio of exports to gross domestic product. Yet it is also about the nonchalant way in which people under thirty make an international call, the cafés in Shanghai where you can get a decent cappuccino (and sometimes surf the Internet), the way that Chinese teenagers can recognize Arnold Schwarzenegger and Michael Jordan, the clothes people wear, or even the fact that in the Himalayan hamlet of Lukla people setting off for Everest are given French toast and Swiss muesli for breakfast, with American soft toilet paper to stuff in their pockets.

Second, globalization is a process rather than a fact or a structure. The forces driving globalization—the digitalization of information, falling trade barriers, even the spread of pop music—are real enough. But they have left behind an economy that is much less integrated than either the proponents or the critics of globalization admit. In some cases, observers have ignored what might be called "the undertow": the way in which the tide that seems to be bringing people together can also divide them into ever smaller groups. For instance, multichannel television has spawned not only global networks such as CNN and MTV but also countless small local "community" stations. The ease with which big-city newspapers can produce different editions for different local markets usually means that they must cut back foreign news.

People who talk excitedly about an unprecedented era of globalization

should read more history. By some measures, the world is not much more integrated than it was before Princip stepped out of the crowd in Sarajevo.
Much of the final quarter of the twentieth century was spent merely recov-
ering ground lost in the previous seventy-five years—and today's "global village" still effectively excludes billions of people. Most of the world's citizens
live on less than ten dollars a day; most don't have access to phones; four out
of every five have never traveled further than one hundred miles from their
home.

Even when you look at trade among rich countries, many markets for
products still stop at national borders. A Canadian province trades twelve
times as many goods and forty times as many services with another Canadian province as it does with an American state of similar size and proximity.[3] In the supposedly open European Union, people are still six times more
likely to trade with their countrymen than with people of other European
countries. Industries are deeply rooted in certain bits of the globe: There are
plenty of cheaper places to locate a film industry than Hollywood, but none
that has the same collection of people. A surprising number of the most
humdrum products come from local sources. Nearly all of America's lightbulbs are still made in the U.S.A., largely because transport costs are too high
to justify moving the factories elsewhere.

The uneven nature of globalization helps to explain why it is often a cruel
process. Much of this book is devoted to looking at those who have lost out
as a result of globalization: the car workers in Flint, Michigan, the people of South Korea and Russia in the wake of the "Asian contagion," the
wretchedly poor Gobetti family in a favela in São Paulo, Brazil. But these
casualties do not stop globalization from being a process worth defending.

By any economic measure yet invented, globalization has enriched the
world. Far more people suffer from too little globalization than from too
much (not least because of the barriers that the first world erects against
third world products). Once again the central issue is freedom: Any process
that increases the number of legal choices that are open to people (even if
those choices are as mundane as the right to drink Coca-Cola or surf the Internet) should command support. Indeed, it is precisely those sort of mundane freedoms that people like bin Laden detest most.

The Bin Laden Effect

Osama bin Laden changed the debate about globalization in three important
ways. First, the attacks on the World Trade Center and the Pentagon re-

vealed the soft underbelly of globalization—the way that the very tools of globalization can be turned against it. The passenger jet, which had hitherto been celebrated for bringing the world together, became a horrific weapon of destruction. Towers that were built to glorify both world trade and American power were destroyed in less than an hour; now pictures of them symbolize American insecurity. Bin Laden even bastardized some of the language of globalization. "Networks" and "cells" used to be the stuff of trendy management theories. Now they have a more ominous ring.

Second, September 11 has made it harder for goods, people, and services to cross borders. Air travel has become more bothersome, and airfreight more expensive. America's airports are currently struggling to install between two thousand and five thousand bomb-detecting devices, each costing about one million dollars.[4] America wants to force importers to "check in" their inbound containers at secure foreign ports, so that they can be cleared before reaching American waters. As for immigrants, America's system of "don't ask, don't tell," which the terrorists exploited, will surely have to be revised. In Europe, xenophobic politicians are already using September 11 as a further excuse for protesting against immigrants from North Africa and the Middle East.

The biggest question about September 11, however, is the Sarajevo one. Was the attack on the World Trade Center one of history's turning points? Are we witnessing the end of a process of global integration that has been gathering pace for decades? Many of globalization's opponents certainly think so. John Gray, one of the most intelligent globophobes, argued, just a few days after September 11, that "the era of globalization is over. The entire view of the world that supported the market's faith in globalization has melted down."[5]

Consider the case for pessimism. Bin Laden's timing could not have been better. The year 2001 produced something new in the current era of globalization: "synchronous sinking," as all the world's major economies slowed down at the same time and the major indexes of global integration stood still. World trade, which grew by 7 percent a year throughout the 1990s, remained almost stagnant. Foreign direct investment slumped from $1.3 trillion to barely half that. Almost all of this was the result of the business cycle rather than terrorism; but the coincidence was unfortunate.

The same goes for the economic crisis of 2002, which Alan Binder, a former vice chairman of the Federal Reserve, described as the biggest loss of confidence in the markets since 1929. The collapse of Enron and WorldCom, the revelations about shoddy bookkeeping, the deconstruction of the Orwellian world of stock-market analysis (where "buy" meant "maybe," "hold" meant "sell," and "sell" meant "run like hell"): All these things gave people all around the world an excuse to question shareholder capitalism, which many saw as synonymous with globalization, and to jeer at the pampered princes of America's new economy who had once lorded it over them. Suddenly, an American president, not an Indonesian one, was fending off allegations of crony capitalism. Much of this represented the continuing deflation of the dot-com bubble. But when the market loses more than a trillion dollars in a single month, as it did in July 2002, it is hard not to ask serious questions about the way the system works. And there is no doubt that there were serious weaknesses to be addressed, particularly in the auditing world.

The pain was not just in the United States. In the mid-1990s, Argentina was hailed as an example of the benefits of global integration, having opened up much of its economy to foreigners. But in December 2001, it defaulted on $155 billion of debt. The country's collapse into political and economic chaos sent the middle class into the streets banging their pots and pans. By 2002, many of Argentina's biggest states and cities were printing their own currencies. An economy that had once been one of the world's most sophisticated was reduced to something akin to medieval barter. Brazil also looked vulnerable. As for Zimbabwe, another erstwhile model, it already seemed to have fallen over the precipice.

For the pessimist, there is also much to worry about in the political core of globalization—the transatlantic alliance. Europe has yet to warm to George W. Bush, a man who before he entered office had seldom bothered to travel abroad. For his part, the new president initially seemed determined to pursue a unilateral course, shrugging off both the Kyoto Treaty and the Anti-Ballistic Missile Treaty. In the aftermath of September 11, Europe rallied round America, invoking Article Five of the NATO treaty (which holds that an attack on one is an attack on all) for the first time ever. But by 2002, the alliance was feuding over all manner of things, from the reconstruction of Afghanistan to the possible invasion of Iraq. Relations were particularly strained over the Middle East, with Europeans sympathizing with the Palestinians and Americans with Israel. Perhaps these differences can be papered over in the years ahead. But pessimists can still point to the growing strains between two powers that feel they increasingly need each other less. The Pentagon wonders about the usefulness of European troops, with their outdated equipment and "appeasement-minded" political masters; European politicians, newly emboldened by the Euro, wonder about the merits of supporting a country that refuses to listen to their advice (and that is also, they add quietly, largely to blame for its problems in the Islamic world).

This divergence is economic as well as political. In 2002, in a blatant attempt to win votes in the rust belt, George W. Bush imposed tariffs on steel imports. This calamitous decision undermined the Doha trade round, provoked threats of retaliation from Europe, and made a mockery of his professed support for free trade. If an American president couldn't stand up for his principles while his approval ratings were close to record levels, when could he stand up for them? Soon afterward Bush signed a $170 billion agriculture bill that comes close to matching Europe's Common Agricultural Policy in the harm that it inflicts on trade in general and the developing world in particular. France and Germany duly conspired to extend the CAP—and soon the Bush administration was beginning to stress bilateral trade deals rather than multilateral ones as the way forward. The main victims will be poor farmers in the third world. Despite a quarter century of globalization, the Western world now spends one billion dollars a day on agricultural protection of one sort or another, depriving the poor world of the market that it most craves.

These are real grounds for worry. Yet there are also reasons for hope. These begin with the fact that September 11 provided a bracing dose of reality. In the heady days of the 1990s, globophiles insisted that the process of globalization was unstoppable. How could people think of resisting the law of comparative advantage? And how could they contemplate putting the genie of technological advance back in the bottle? Too many Americans believed in a simplified version of Francis Fukuyama's thesis of the end of history: that the triumph of Western liberalism is inevitable; that politics no longer matters; that all they need to do to produce utopia is tend to their stock portfolios. After September 11, the Afghan campaign, and the Bali bombing, people have a renewed appreciation of nation-states and their armies and policemen. The hidden hand sometimes needs the help of the chain-mailed fist.

At the same time, the sheer horror of September 11 concealed an important fact: By most measures, Islamic fundamentalism is the weakest of all the threats that globalization has yet faced. Socialism, the main ideological opponent of liberalism for most of the past century, combined a searing analysis of contemporary injustices with a compelling promise of a better future. Whatever its defects, Marxism spoke to the genuine discontents of millions of workers. It also attracted some of the finest minds in the West—particularly during the dark days of the 1930s, when capitalism was plagued by depression and unemployment. Half a century ago, communism held sway over at least a sixth of the world's population.

Socialism also had a profound influence on plenty of democratic leaders who would never have described themselves as Marxists. In the 1940s and 1950s, European social democrats happily nationalized the commanding heights of the economy and restricted the free movement of capital; in the developing world, many leftish leaders went further and opposed free trade in goods in the name of "import substitution." The results may have been regrettable—India's domestic version of Coca-Cola was one of the most disgusting drinks invented by man—but they were the work of democratically elected leaders, with the firm backing of many economists.

By comparison, radical Islam seems a much weaker opponent. Rather than offering a futuristic workers' paradise, it looks back to the primitive world of the seventh century. The regime that came closest to embodying the radical ideal was the Taliban in Afghanistan. Even capitalism's harshest critics are unlikely to fashion an alternative out of a society that denied women education and debated whether the proper way to deal with homosexuals was to push them off tall buildings or throw them into holes and push stone walls on top of them.

This is not to say that radical Islam lacks popular appeal. Large numbers of Muslims expressed delight at the events of September 11 (and even larger numbers still argue that the atrocity was not perpetrated by Muslims). Too many Muslims in western Europe are alienated from their host societies and attracted to fundamentalism. Throughout the Arab world, authoritarian regimes try to distract popular attention from their own failures by blaming all the ills of the world on American foreign policy, especially its support for Israel.

This is a dangerous brew: It provides groups like al-Qaeda not just with a supply of raw recruits but also with a sympathetic milieu in which to hide. The continuing success of globalization depends on the willingness of the United States to stamp out terrorism and the grievances that underpin it. The war on terrorism must involve not just stepping up covert operations against al-Qaeda and disposing of Saddam Hussein but also doing more to prevent nuclear proliferation and resuming the search for peace in the Middle East.

This is a colossal challenge. Yet the threat from radical Islam is still less serious than the one posed by the Soviet Union during the cold war. Radical Islam has been relatively unsuccessful in turning itself into a coherent political force. The Taliban is gone. The mullahs are rapidly losing their grip on Iran. Iraq is a secular rather than an Islamic regime. Islam became a powerful political force because it combined three social groups: businessmen and ✓ professionals who were unhappy with their lot, the disenchanted urban young, and Islamic clerics and intellectuals. The rise of bin Ladenism has fractured this alliance: The more radicals rely on terrorism, the less mainstream Muslims are inclined to give them wholehearted support.

It is impossible to argue that the whole world faces a choice between Islam and liberal capitalism in the same way that it once faced a choice between capitalism and communism. Yet this is small comfort. As this book argues, the main threat to globalization comes from within: from Western politicians arguing about things like steel, movies, and the Middle East, and from Western workers getting tired of the unrelenting (if productive) pressure that globalization places on all of us. So far that pressure has been primarily applied to blue-collar workers, but it is now affecting the professional classes. The fuss about steel imports will be as nothing compared to the furor when lawyers, accountants, and even doctors discover that their work can be outsourced to India.

This matters because much of the time, advocates of globalization are wrestling with human nature. The steel-tariff decision perfectly illustrates how difficult it is to persuade people to care as much about the global as they do about the local. Bush backed the steel lobby for the sake of a few votes in West Virginia, Ohio, and Pennsylvania—just as, three years earlier, Bill Clinton caved in before protestors in Seattle because he was worried about shoring up labor support for Al Gore.

In his other great work, *The Theory of Moral Sentiments*, Adam Smith compared the pain that you would feel if you lost your little finger to the distress that you would feel over the news that "the great empire of China, with all its myriads of inhabitants, was suddenly swallowed up by an earthquake." You would be hugely shocked, he said. You would express your sorrow. You would reflect on the precariousness of life. You might even "enter into many reasonings concerning the effects which this disaster might produce upon the commerce of Europe, and the trade and business of the world in general." But you would sleep soundly and go about your business.[6]

The first rule of political life is that all politics is local. And people are far more easily moved by their own immediate concerns—by the state of their fingers—than they are by the fate of millions of people in a distant corner of the earth. That is why it is so easy to imagine the current phase of liberalization running out of steam. And that is why it is more important than ever for supporters of globalization to speak out in favor of the endangered process.

A Call to Arms

Too often supporters of globalization seem to be on the defensive. Public debate of the subject is largely carried out on the enemy's terms. The backdrop is usually a shuttered textile factory rather than a young African child sitting at a computer, a burning Amazonian forest rather than a young Brazilian investment banker, a scene from *Star Wars: Episode III* rather than a shot of the Guggenheim in Bilbao. At times the defenders of globalization seem crass: The Wall Street analyst on CNBC who expressed delight that the 1997–1998 Asian currency crisis was "really beginning to hurt" springs to mind. More often they are silent. In particular, the wide class of people who have gained most obviously from globalization—the people whom we dub the cosmocrats in this book—have almost made a vocation out of excluding themselves from local political debate.

The defense should begin with economics. Put simply, the more open an economy is, the quicker it tends to grow. Before 1980, globalization was largely concentrated in the rich world. Since then it has moved to the developing world, with massively beneficial results. In the 1990s, even allowing for the Asian crisis, GDP per person in the twenty-four more globalized developing countries (i.e., those with a higher ratio of trade to national income, such as Mexico and China) rose at an average rate of 5 percent a year, more than twice the rate in the rich world; meanwhile, GDP per person fell by 1 percent in the less globalized developing countries (many of which were in Africa).[7] Needless to say, literacy and life expectancy also rose in the globalizing countries, which were home to three billion people (against two billion in the less globalized ones, where poverty has increased).

Confronted with such compelling evidence that open borders help developing countries, antiglobalists usually shift their ground. They argue, first, that globalization harms the poor and, second, that it promotes inequality. The first of these arguments is dubious. Some poor people have been harmed by globalization and many more have seen disgracefully few benefits, but there is no hard evidence that the poor as a whole suffer disproportionately. Another World Bank study, of eighty countries over the past forty years, demonstrates that the incomes of the poor have risen with everybody else. The Fraser Institute also points to a more general connection between freedom and prosperity: In 2000, the income of the poorest tenth in the least free countries was a miserable $728; the figure for the poorest tenth in the freest countries was ten times as high.[8] And fewer of us are really poor: The proportion of people living on less than a dollar a day fell from 20 percent in 1970 to 5 percent in 1998.

What about inequality? There is no doubt that this has increased in many countries, but it is hard to find a specific link to trade policy. The poorest 10 percent of people in countries the world over have to make do with 2 to 3 percent of national income regardless of whether their economies are open or closed.[9] In the rich world, the rise in inequality has more to do with new technology than with lower trade barriers. One study shows that technology was five times more important than trade in widening inequality in America in the period 1973–1993.[10] In the steel industry, sleeker minimills and computerized production systems have cost thousands of Americans their jobs. Yet politicians are unwilling to risk being called Luddites by condemning technology.

These dry statistics tend to understate the human effect of liberalization. When developing countries have agreed to open up their economies—be it South Korea in the 1970s and 1980s or China in the 1980s and 1990s—the gains in well-being have been phenomenal. Deng's market reforms of the 1980s brought the biggest and most rapid eradication of poverty that the world has ever seen: Several hundred million peasants climbed out of a life that had consisted of little more than the relentless struggle to stay alive.

As we have already conceded, these aggregate figures disguise a lot of individual losers. Globalization destroys some jobs in the same remorseless way that the industrial revolution once did, but it also creates many more. Mourning the jobs lost in Detroit seems a little like regretting the departure of horse-drawn carriages (which Detroit did so much to speed). And it also forgets the jobs created in places such as São Caetano do Sul, Brazil, where General Motors has a factory and has helped push up both local wages and labor standards. There is nothing odd in this. Typically, the average wage at the foreign affiliates of multinationals is 1.5 times the local average; in the case of low-income countries, the figure is double the local domestic manufacturing wage.[11] These factories may pay less than they do in Western countries, sometimes disgracefully so, but usually they push up living standards, bring in skills, and increase the choices open to local consumers.

Time and again in debating this subject, we encounter common assumptions about globalization that are simply false. How many times, for instance, have you heard that globalization favors big companies—indeed, that it is encouraging a "silent takeover" in which companies are becoming more powerful than governments? In fact, globalization mainly favors smaller companies, because it allows them to reach markets that were previously monopolized by multinationals. In most developed economies, smaller firms have been gaining ground at the expense of larger ones. Far from being undermined by globalization, governments have grown steadily in size over the past quarter of a century. The "fact," popular in antiglobalization circles, that companies accounted for fifty-one of the world's one hundred biggest economies relies on comparing the sales of companies with the GDPs of countries. But GDP is a measure of value added, not sales. Using a measure for value added for companies, only thirty-seven multinationals appeared in the one hundred biggest economies in the world in 2000. That still sounds reasonably impressive. Yet only two companies scrape into the top fifty (Wal-Mart in forty-forth place and Exxon in forty-eighth). Wal-Mart was barely a quarter of the size of Belgium.[12] The country was certainly richer than Peru. But again, what does that mean in terms of power? Wal-Mart has no powers of coercion: It cannot tax, raise armies, or imprison people. In each of the countries where it operates, it has to bow down to local governments. [13]

Such facts need to be voiced more loudly. Yet merely choosing a better defensive position is not really good enough. Proving that globalization is, on balance, a good thing, one that has generally enriched the world economically, is certainly valuable. But the same could also be said for the lavatory or the lemon squeezer. To engender any political support, globalization needs a surer political base, a reason to believe in it rather than merely to tolerate it.

Liberty, Fraternity, Globality

To our minds, globalization is not just an economic process that can be more or less squeezed into the mold of classical liberal political theory; it marks a significant development of it. John Stuart Mill advocated the largest possible measure of individual freedom, as long as it did not involve harming others. So far, most of the battles that have been fought in freedom's name have involved combating political tyranny of one sort or another. Globalization has undoubtedly lent powerful support in that struggle—not only by helping to topple corrupt autocrats such as the Suhartos of Indonesia but also by casting light into the darker corners of the world. It is not coincidental that the pace of globalization has picked up with the spread of democratic rights; the two are symbiotic. Yet globalization also widens the concept of what the maximum degree of individual freedom might be.

Classical liberalism relies on the notion that there is a kind of contract between a government and its citizens, a contract that individuals freely enter into and may freely leave. In practical terms, that proposal has been (and still largely remains) a farce. For billions of people who live in countries that are wretchedly poor, isolated, or tyrannically ruled, there is little choice at all. But even in rich, democratic countries, most of us have faced at least two sorts of practical constraints. The first sort are all the things that make rejecting the social contract and leaving the place where you were born difficult—the rules governing where you can live; your ability to remain in touch with family, friends, even soccer teams. To the extent that globalization reduces this tyranny of place, it makes migration more likely to be a matter of choice rather than of despair; and, even if you do not move, it still provides choices where none existed before. Rather than being the worst sort of prix fixe, with only one option for every course (you will live in Germany, eat German food, shop in German shops, watch German sports), it presents a wider range of options. Thanks to globalization, a Berliner can, if he so chooses, eat Moroccan food, read *The New York Times* on the Internet, and visit Paris without changing money or producing a passport.

Put in these terms, the effect of globalization can sound a little trivial; but the underlying point is not. Globalization increases people's freedom to shape their own identities rather than assuming those of their ancestors. Of course, as communitarians point out, there are trade-offs between the comforts of community and the virtues of mobility—but those are surely trade-offs that individuals should calculate for themselves. It is hardly surprising that globalization scares authoritarians (such as Singapore's Lee Kwan Yew, who once pronounced that "to us in Asia, the individual is an ant"), not to mention wild-eyed fundamentalists such as bin Laden.

Indeed, supporters of globalization should realize that the Islamic world represents an opportunity as well as a threat. The fundamental problem in the region is more than just poverty. Remember that bin Laden inherited millions; that many of the September 11 hijackers were university graduates; that Saudi Arabia controls a fifth of the world's oil reserves; and that the Arab world has less abject poverty (defined as an income of less than a dollar a day) than any other developing region, thanks in part to Islamic traditions of charitable giving. The fundamental problem is a lack of economic and political freedom.

A report from the United Nations Development Project in 2002 ranked the Arab world lowest out of seven regions in the world in terms of freedom, with abysmal standards for civil liberties, political processes, and media independence. The wave of democracy that washed over much of the developing world (particularly Latin America) during the past decade has passed the Arab world by. The region's autocratic rulers, whether they dignify themselves with the title of president or king, only give up authority when they die. Women are denied basic economic and political rights. Not one of the Arab states that are commonly accused of spawning terrorism is a member of the World Trade Organization. All of them are dominated by intrusive states and freeloading kleptocracies, and all of them are locked in a pattern of relative decline.

This illiberalism is ruining any chance the Arab world might have of providing a decent life for its citizens, condemning the region to long-term economic decline and spawning an alienated and underemployed middle class. The non-oil-related GDP of the entire Arab world is about the same as the GDP of Finland. Between 1985 and 1998, real average income per head declined in Iran, Iraq, Jordan, Qatar, Saudi Arabia, Syria, the United Arab Emirates, and Yemen. It can hardly be an accident that the Muslim-dominated countries that have actually succeeded in offering a better life to their citizens have also been the ones that have been the most democratic and the most open to free trade. The most successful of them all, Turkey, has been a secular state since 1928.

The Lesson of a Terrible Century

None of this is meant to imply that the Western brand of globalization is a perfect model. It is not. There are clearly manifold problems—from the governance of companies such as Enron and WorldCom that allow chief executives to behave like tawdry pirates to the persistence of poverty in the developing world. Fixing all these problems requires governments to take an active role.

One of the few things that the left and the right agree on is that globalization diminishes the importance of government. They are both wrong. There is no statistical relation between the globalness of an economy and the size of its state: Sweden and Denmark are two of the most open economies in the world (with a ratio of imports to national income roughly double that of the United States), but their governments both account for more than 50 percent of GDP, way above the level in America.

The truth is the opposite: Globalization actually increases the importance of government, in at least three ways. First, markets depend on transparency and the rule of law, things that only governments can provide. The scandals now engulfing American capitalism only underline how important those rules should be. There is nothing illiberal about a government demanding that the accountants who audit companies be rotated. The same need for competent government applies in spades in the developing world: As Hernando de Soto has argued, merely giving people basic property rights—the right to own their home and the opportunity to borrow against it—could unleash trillions of dollars of capital.[14]

Second, governments have a preeminent role to play in ameliorating the downside of globalization. Like any other efficiency-producing device, globalization mercilessly exaggerates any weaknesses that it encounters. Forcing countries, companies, and people to compete with the best in the world imposes huge strains. Faulty policies—be it Brazil's push into deforesting the Amazon or Thailand's adoption of a fixed-rate currency system—are rapidly exposed in a world of mobile information and capital. The doctrine of comparative advantage is a harsh one if you possess little but comparative disadvantages. So far politicians have usually been less innovative than businesspeople in dealing with the relentless pressure to compete. Some of the necessary changes, such as making pensions in Western countries portable, pose awkward bureaucratic problems. Others, for instance changing American high schools or European universities, require a more fundamental review of the traditional role of governments. Wouldn't America's urban schools be more efficient if parents were given vouchers? And wouldn't Europe's universities be more successful if they weren't so dependent on the state?

The third area where Western governments in particular have an important role to play is in coping with third-world poverty. As we have already mentioned, Western countries could contribute enormously by opening their economies to poor-country imports. It is scandalous that agriculture and textiles, the two things most poor countries most want to export, are also the areas with the highest tariffs in the West. Yet the third world needs more than this. It has fallen too far behind.

Many nongovernmental organizations think the answer is to tilt trade rules—to make trade "fairer" by, for instance, only admitting imports produced by workers with "decent" wages. This is a recipe for hidden protectionism—for preventing the developing world from trading its way out of poverty. Instead, the simplest way to help the third world is to do so directly—by giving money and advice. Debt forgiveness could be dramatically expanded at relatively little cost to the West. Far too little thought has gone into global philanthropy.

To many Westerners, these issues might seem like a sideshow. Africa is a long way away, and there is a war against terrorism to be fought. History, however, argues that complacency is always punished—whether found in a Londoner in 1914 sipping his tea in bed or in a Californian hunched over a cappuccino in Starbucks in 1998.

We began by comparing September 11 to Sarajevo. But the underlying causes of the failure one hundred years ago went deeper—and were rooted in the complacency of the winners of the first age of globalization. A decade before Princip made his fateful move, the Salvation Army threw a dinner party at Madison Square Garden. The stadium's lights beamed down on thousands of poor people tucking into free food. The rich hired boxes and galleries to savor their philanthropy. Everybody sang "Praise God from Whom All Blessings Flow." It was hailed by the Salvation Army commander as "the dawning of a new era, the bridging of a gulf between the rich and poor."

Over the next quarter century the masses at the trestle tables turned on the elite in the galleries. The icons of American capitalism—the Rockefellers, Morgans, and Vanderbilts—were denounced as "robber barons" and "malefactors of great wealth." Even before Sarajevo, antitrust policy was being used to cut them down to size and higher taxes to narrow the inequalities they had created. The First World War provided a spur for more state intervention. The stock-market crash of 1929 (also "their" fault) led the government to interfere even more in business. Then came the Depression, which helped neither the rich nor the poor.

To avoid such a fate, the world requires better leadership. We have had many reasons to regret the title of our book since September 11. In some way a more honest title would be *A Future Contingent*. We continue to believe that globalization can produce a much better world for the vast majority of people, but it will not do so simply as the automatic result of technology. The future is contingent on the quality of our political leaders in Washington, London, and the other capitals of the world. That thought, depressing or inspiring, sets the tone for the rest of this book.

Part One

The Remaking of a
Borderless World

1

The Fall and Rise
of Globalization

IN MARCH 1906, a twenty-two-year-old Englishman who was to become one of the titans of the twentieth century took his first foreign holiday unencumbered by his parents. The trip was spent largely in Italy, a country whose food he praised but whose youth he regarded, perhaps hypocritically, as "physically repulsive." For the young traveler, the journey was a revelation of the joys of globalization. He needed no passport to visit foreign countries, and his gold sovereigns were universally convertible into local currencies at fixed rates of exchange. He found that the world was knit together by railways and steamships and that he could find comfortable hotels wherever he wanted to stay and post offices whenever he wanted to get a message back home.

At the time, Great Britain occupied much the same position in the world that the United States occupies today: that of commercial leviathan, military giant, and cultural arbiter. British goods dominated the world's markets. British money irrigated the world's businesses. British military might protected the world's trading routes. British culture was so powerful that foreigners even took to playing that most idiosyncratic of games, cricket. And most of the world accepted the British gospel of free trade and globalization.

There was no sterner defender of this creed than the young traveler, John Maynard Keynes, one of the most gilded members of one of the most gilded generations in English history. The son of a noted university administrator, he had won scholarships first to Eton and then to King's College, Cambridge. He had tried, rather precociously, to win a fellowship at King's soon after graduating, but he had been told to wait.

Yet while Keynes was a child of the establishment, he was certainly not a creature of it. A homosexual in an age when such a trait was not always appreciated, he also belonged to a generation—or rather to a clique within a generation, the Bloomsbury group—that was in more or less open revolt against the certainties of Victorian civilization. As Keynes's biographer, Robert Skidelsky, records, he spent time with the painter Duncan Grant in Paris on his way to Italy, and then with Lytton Strachey in Genoa, where the two men passed the hours, in Keynes's words, "eating omelettes and discussing ethics and sodomy."[1] Strachey later wrote the definitive Victorian-bashing book, *Eminent Victorians.*

You might imagine that Keynes rebelled against Victorian economics as well as Victorian morality. Yet at the time his enthusiasm for free trade was absolute. In his undergraduate days, he spoke out against protectionism in student debates. "I hate all priests and protectionists," he wrote to a friend, praising "Free Trade and Free Thought." In fact, free trade was arguably the only political cause that stirred the young Keynes. "We must hold to Free Trade, in its widest interpretation, as an inflexible dogma, to which no exception is admitted," he thundered. "We should hold to Free Trade as a principle of international morals, and not merely as a doctrine of economic advantage."[2]

Three great works helped persuade young men such as Keynes of the virtues of free trade: Adam Smith's *The Wealth of Nations* (1776), David Ricardo's *On the Principles of Political Economy and Taxation* (1817), and James Mill's *Elements of Political Economy* (1821). Smith's argument that the economy works best when it is left to the "invisible hand" of the market was above all a brief on the virtues of trade: Protectionism is one of the most misguided forms of state intervention. Mill reinforced Smith's argument by polemicizing against the mercantilist idea (still held widely today) that only one sort of trade—exports—is good. Mill argued, rather, that the only reason to export something is to get the money to import other things. "The benefit, which is derived from exchanging one commodity for another," he claimed, "arises in all cases from the commodity *received,* not the commodity given."[3]

For his part, Ricardo elaborated the idea of "comparative advantage," according to which free trade offers all countries, both rich and poor, chances to gain by specializing in what they do best. Sometimes these comparative advantages arise from things as basic as geography or climate (nobody took the British wine industry seriously, even then), but more often they have to do with local skills and productivity. As Ricardo argued, the most productive countries gravitate toward the industries in which they have the greatest advantage, leaving opportunities for others. As long as both the most productive countries and their less-developed peers can trade freely, both gain from this specialization. Globalization arguably comes down to nothing more than allowing this specialization to happen.

To the young Keynes, these were not merely logical arguments; they were the victors in the bloodiest intellectual battle of the previous century. Smith, Mill, and Ricardo had provided the most important battering ram against the protectionist corn laws (which protected farmers by keeping the price of wheat artificially high). That struggle—which had been won only in 1846 after Sir Robert Peel betrayed his own Conservative party and repealed the laws—had inspired people to storm out of dinner parties and even to found magazines.[4] Long after the fuss about the corn laws had died away, internationalism was more than just a way of piling up wealth for the Victorians; it was a moral duty they felt they had to the rest of humanity, a way of spreading the virtues not just of free trade but of free institutions and Christian morality.

From Keynes's perspective, Britain was the engine of a free-trading system that spanned an ever greater portion of the globe. Several economists have shown recently that the idea that the world economy was "more global" a century ago than it is today is something of a canard. There is far more trade in services today than there was a century ago, far more trade among multinational companies, and far more widely ranging capital markets.[5] But there was nonetheless an impressive degree of integration: The movement of capital and the transfer of profits were largely unhampered; governments exercised little influence over the distribution of wealth; the gold standard provided the entire industrial world and much of the developing world with a friction-free means of exchange. By 1913, the total stock of long-term foreign investment had reached $44 billion, and nearly 60 percent of the securities traded in London were foreign ones.[6]

In one vital way, the world was probably more integrated then than it is today: the movement of people. Citizenship was granted freely to immigrants, and people moved between countries without the bother of a passport, let alone a work permit. America allowed access to anybody who was not a prostitute, a convict, a lunatic, or, after 1882, Chinese. It attracted about two thirds of the thirty-six million people who emigrated from Europe in the fifty years before the First World War, usually searching for cheap land. (Even more people moved from one part of Asia to another, though many of them were indentured workers or coolies.)[7]

There were weeds in this garden, as Keynes well knew. Continental Europe, in general, was much less enthusiastic about free trade than the Anglo-Saxon world was. Between 1875 and 1913, tariffs crept up in most European countries, in part because of the "great grain invasion" from Russia and the United States. Italy, the country that Keynes was visiting, still paid lip service to the economic liberalism laid down by Camillo Benso, conte di Cavour in the 1850s. But ever since a nasty trade war with France in the 1880s, the *larghe intese* (big interests), particularly those in the steel industry, had developed a taste for the comfortable life that protectionism brought. Further, they came to rely on political influence rather than better products for their success. Meanwhile, animosity against France had led to a general fascination in Italy with all things German and the adoption of cross-shareholdings, often including banks. Protectionist economists were gaining ground at Italian universities: Four years after Keynes's trip, one of them, Luigi Luzzatti, even became prime minister.

Nor was the Anglo-Saxon world as rock solid as it might have seemed. In America, the campaign against the robber barons, initially inspired by concerns about anticompetitive practices, took on an anticapitalist hue. In Britain, Joseph Chamberlain, one of the most brilliant of the younger generation of Tory politicians, had converted to the idea of "imperial preferences," favoring goods from the empire (prompting Keynes to inform the Cambridge Union that "conservatism had died and been born again a lower animal").[8] And socialists such as Sidney and Beatrice Webb ridiculed the Victorian ideal of "the Nightwatchman State," arguing instead that the future lay with rational planning rather than with laissez-faire.

In short, it is not difficult to argue that the elements of the postwar backlash were already in place, but that is only with the benefit of hindsight. For Keynes and his friends, the first decade of the twentieth century was an Indian summer. After Joseph Chamberlain raised the scepter of protectionism in 1903, for example, Keynes's economics tutor, Alfred Marshall, sent a free-trade manifesto to *The Times* that declared confidently that no unemployment could result from an increase in imports; to think otherwise was simply to reveal your ignorance of the founding texts of economic science. One of the most influential books of the period was Norman Angell's *The Great Illusion,* published in 1911, which came close to arguing (as some American commentators on globalization were wont to do before September 11, 2001) that a major war had become an impossibility, since the world was simply too interdependent.

For Keynes, it was also a time of success. Five years after returning from Italy, he was appointed to a permanent fellowship at his old college. He began to shine not just as an economist but as a government adviser and journalist. In the summer of 1909, he moved into a suite of rooms in Cambridge over the gatehouse leading from King's Lane to Webb's Court, rooms that Virginia Woolf regarded as some of the most delightful she had ever seen.

This was the vanished world that Keynes described in his first great work, *The Economic Consequences of the Peace*. We mentioned it in our introduction, but it is worth quoting in full:

> What an extraordinary episode in the economic progress of man that age was which came to an end in August, 1914. . . . The inhabitant of London could order by telephone, sipping his morning tea in bed, the various products of the whole earth, in such quantity as he might see fit, and reasonably expect their early delivery upon his doorstep; he could at the same moment and by the same means adventure his wealth in the natural resources and new enterprises of any quarter of the world, and share, without exertion or even trouble, in their prospective fruits and advantages; or he could decide to couple the security of his fortunes with the good faith of the townspeople of any substantial municipality in any continent that fancy or information might recommend. . . . Most important of all, he regarded this state of affairs as normal, certain, and permanent, except in the direction of further improvement, and any deviation from it as aberrant, scandalous, and avoidable. The projects and politics of militarism and imperialism, of racial and cultural rivalries, of monopolies, restrictions, and exclusion, which were to play the serpent to this paradise, were little more than the amusements of his daily newspaper, and appeared to exercise almost no influence at all on the ordinary course of social and economic life, the internationalization of which was nearly complete in practice.[9]

Three Voices

You can go a long way toward understanding the history of globalization by comparing Keynes's description of the world before 1914 with many people's experience of the world today: We have come full circle. Capital once again slips round the world fairly easily. Fund managers buy and sell shares with relative impunity, despite a few moans about settlement problems in Sri Lanka. Millions of Europeans have rediscovered the joys of traveling without a passport and using a common currency. American tourists seem just as excited about boarding the Eurostar train from London to Paris as Keynes was about taking the trains in Italy.

Such a reading would be entirely accurate and entirely in tune with the current feeling that globalization is an unstoppable force. Yet it is also worth pointing out that in the intervening period, there were two world wars, the spread of communism, an interminable cold war, a great depression, several great recessions, umpteen trade wars, the nationalization of most of the world's big industries, and countless other bits of evidence that indicate that internationalism has not exactly gripped the public behavior. It is possible, of course, to dismiss all these as aberrations, but seventy years' worth of aberrations is a remarkable amount. And these aberrations have not just been the handiwork of ignorant demagogues. Throughout the twentieth century, there have been plenty of times when the most intellectually talented people turned against globalization.

Nobody illustrates this better than Keynes. An adamant free trader before the First World War, he turned to protectionism in the late 1920s and then cautiously reembraced globalization during the Second World War; even after he died in 1946, "Keynesianism" (a doctrine that, to be fair, did not always accord with his thinking) was the prevailing logic throughout the world, and it was not always that friendly toward globalization. In the remainder of this chapter, we will try to tell the story of globalization through the prism of Keynes's life. Unfortunately, even the most ingenious authors cannot make a man—or, indeed, his influence—live longer than he did. So for the final part of this chapter we will turn to three intellectuals who were well known to Keynes: Sydney and Beatrice Webb, who poured fire on him from the left, and Friedrich A. von Hayek, who attacked him (and ultimately triumphed) from the right.

By concentrating on these men and women of ideas, we do not intend to reduce history to a series of tales about intellectual life in London drawing rooms. The fall and rise of globalization, as we shall see, involves real things, such as bidets, jackboots, Trabants, and India's disgusting substitute for Coca-Cola. But ideas, we maintain, have still been crucial. The obvious example is Karl Marx, who wanted to replace capitalist globalization with a communist version. (We will look at him in more depth in our conclusion.) But the bloody enormity of Marxism should not overshadow more subtle debates that took place among thinkers gathered in England in the first half of the century. One of the ironies of the twentieth century is that, despite its gradual decline, Britain seems to have exercised an undue influence over the defining periods of globalization. And underneath it all lie both a lesson and a warning. The lesson is that we are not quite as unique as we like to think we are: Most of the problems that puzzle us today have puzzled former generations. The warning is that globalization is not a one-way process: We have gone backward in the past and can do so again.

Let Goods Be Homespun

Let us skip forward in Keynes's life to a lecture he gave at University College, Dublin, in April 1933. By then, Keynes had translated the promise of his youth into a spectacular record of achievement. *The Economic Consequences of the Peace*, a condemnation of the Allies' handling of the aftermath of the First World War, was one of those rare books that define the thinking of a generation. *A Treatise on Money* (1930) confirmed Keynes's reputation as a leading practitioner of the dismal science. Governments of all complexions looked to Keynes for advice. It is a measure of Keynes's distinction that, when he came to University College, all of Ireland's leading politicians turned up, including the new prime minister, Eamon De Valera.[10]

De Valera and his minions were nervous about what Keynes was going to say, not least because they had just embarked on a savage trade war with Great Britain. But instead of denouncing the lunacy of tariffs, Keynes used his lecture to deliver a broadside against the Victorian faith in free trade. As far as he was concerned, the future lay with national self-sufficiency.

Keynes presented four arguments. The first was that the advantages of the international division of labor were getting smaller by the day: The more countries relied on mass production, the more it made sense to bring "the producer and consumer within the ambit of the same national, economic and financial organisations." The second was that free trade—particularly free trade combined with the free mobility of capital—was much more likely to provoke war than to preserve peace. "I sympathise . . . with those who would minimise rather than with those who would maximise economic entanglement between nations," he said, in a phrase that instantly became famous. "Ideas, knowledge, art, hospitality, travel—these are the things which should by their nature be international. But let goods be homespun whenever it is reasonably and conveniently possible; and, above all, let finance be primarily national."

Keynes's third argument was that there ought to be as much variety and experiment as possible within each country. "We each would like to have a try at working out our salvation. . . . We do not wish to be at the mercy of forces working out, or trying to work out, some uniform equilibrium according to the ideal principles of laissez-faire capitalism." This brought him to his final contention: that the prevalent system of economic calculation had turned "the whole conduct of life" into a "parody of an accountant's night-mare." There were some people who thought it was justifiable to devastate the British countryside and throw the rural population from the land in order to cut a tenth of a penny off the price of a loaf of bread. But Keynes, who had turned himself into something of a country squire in middle age, did not count himself as one of them.

Keynes's conversion was not as sudden as it seemed to some of his listeners. He had been wondering for more than a decade whether democratic societies could adjust to dramatic changes in the flow of goods and capital. All the same, the speech, which, rather in the manner of a modern pop song, soon became known simply as "National Self-sufficiency," was remarkable for the degree to which it broke with the fundamental assumptions of Keynes's erstwhile heroes, Ricardo, Smith, and James Mill. How on earth had a man who had once regarded the case for free trade as established so firmly that opposition to it was evidence of some "natural malformation of the mind" become an advocate of homespun goods?[11]

In many ways, Keynes's loss of faith mirrors the course of events. The integrated economy of the prewar years did not collapse in one fell swoop but dribbled away. The aftermath of the First World War saw governments inventing a host of ingenious excuses for raising barriers of all sorts.[12] Curbs on immigration, imposed during the war, were kept in place, sometimes acquiring a racist edge. New industries that had grown up during the war needed to be protected from the shock of competition; the countries that had emerged from the wreckage of the Austro-Hungarian Empire needed to be given a fair start; and (just as in the American steel industry in 1999) industrialists in the more stable countries were pleading to be shielded from "exchange dumping"—the surge in exports from countries with seriously depreciated currencies.

Free traders made brave attempts to turn the disastrous tide. Resolutions issued from a succession of international conferences in places such as Brussels and Genoa recommended against the imposition of tariffs. In traditionally laissez-faire Britain, both the Liberal and Labor parties stuck to free trade, while the Tories sold their souls for imperial preference. And yet the protectionist tide proved far too strong. In Italy, Benito Mussolini imposed tariffs on wheat in 1925—with typical grandiloquence, he referred to this as the Battle for Wheat—and the French did the same a year later. Later, both countries added tariffs on motorcars.

In his 1928 U.S. presidential campaign, Herbert Hoover promised to raise tariffs to help farmers struggling with falling prices. In June 1930, eight months after the Wall Street crash, the Smoot-Hawley Tariff Act imposed tariffs not just on agricultural goods but on a whole range of industrial ones, too, provoking retaliatory moves around the world. The powers that later became the Axis retreated as much as possible from the world economy, sometimes trading among themselves but usually pursuing policies of autarky. The death knell of the old economic order was sounded in 1931 when the British finally embraced protectionism, imposing a 10 percent tariff on almost all goods imported from outside the empire.

Throughout this period, Keynes had himself been wavering. His initial stance could be described as one of pragmatic liberalism: He supported free trade, but he believed that there were some instances in which tariffs were necessary. In the 1920s, he worried that free trade was inappropriate for Britain, with its rigid labor market, growing pool of idle labor, and official commitment to the gold standard. In a widely discussed newspaper article in 1931, Keynes insisted that, insofar as protectionism leads to "the substitution of home-produced goods for goods previously imported, it will increase the employment of this country."[13] Keynes's belief in free trade was also undermined by events. Britain saw not one but two depressions between the wars: the depression of 1920–1922, which led to a collapse of prices, output, and employment on a scale not seen since the Napoleonic Wars, and the great depression of 1929–1932. Unemployment was stuck at about 10 percent; what had once been regarded as a product of a downswing of the business cycle now seemed like a permanent fact of life.

The failure of free-market capitalism seemed even more evident in America. In the run-up to the 1929 crash, pundits had taken to boasting that America had discovered the secret of perpetual growth, so relentless had been the rise of the stock market and so huge the country's lead in "new economy" industries, such as motorcars. But the establishment's mishandling of the Wall Street crash threatened to turn perpetual growth into perpetual immiseration. By 1933—the year Franklin Roosevelt came to power and Keynes delivered his lecture—nearly thirteen million Americans were looking for jobs, and banks across the country had closed their doors.[14]

From this perspective, it seemed only logical to Keynes that the government needed to intervene where the market had failed—to prime the pump and create demand. Indeed, this became the bedrock not just of Roosevelt's New Deal but of Keynesianism. Protectionism inevitably became part of the interventionist mix, though Keynes remained enough of a classical liberal to be nervous about it. Even now, the logic of the address in Dublin feels twisted. Can art and hospitality really remain international while manufacturing and finance are forced to become national? Do countries really have less to gain from free trade as their economies become more sophisticated? Keynes would no doubt have been disgusted if King's College bought its wine from Cornwall and expected its fellows to take their holidays in Wales.

Indeed, the new barriers being erected around national economies only helped to prolong and deepen the worldwide slump, throwing global integration into reverse. Between the early 1890s and 1913, world trade had more than doubled; between the wars it stagnated and actually declined in some countries.[15] Between 1929 and 1938, for example, the ratio of foreign trade to domestic production declined by 10 percent in Britain, by nearly 20 percent in Canada, and by 25 to 40 percent in Japan, Germany, and Italy.[16] In the six years between 1927 and 1933, international lending dropped by over 90 percent. The decline in the flow of people was almost as dramatic. From 1899 to 1914, nearly fourteen million people emigrated to the United States. In the next fifteen years, thanks to anti-immigrant legislation, the flow of people was only five and a half million; in the 1930s, it shrank to less than a million.

In short, the world that Keynes had so admired in the first decade of the century had unraveled so much that, by the time the Second World War broke out, killing seemed to be the only global business left. In June 1940, Keynes wrote despondently that "we can regard what is now happening as the final destruction of the optimistic liberalism which Locke inaugurated. . . . For the first time for more than two centuries Hobbes has more message for us than Locke." Yet in its own ghastly brutal way, the war, coupled with the economic tragedies of the 1930s, forced world leaders, including Keynes, to rethink. If the case for globalization had perhaps not been proved beyond doubt, the case for autarky had collapsed. Even before the end of the war, politicians and intellectuals began to talk about the reintegration of the world economy. Was there a way to end the beggar-thy-neighbor economic policies of the 1930s? Could the world's banking system be made more sound? How should Europe be rebuilt? One of the first people consulted was Keynes.

For He's a Jolly Good Fellow

If the speech to University College was the low point of Keynes's contribution to globalization, then the meeting at Bretton Woods, New Hampshire, to map out the world's financial future, was the high point. By 1944, Keynes had attained the sort of preeminence that is allowed to only a handful of intellectuals in each century. He was not only the inevitable choice to lead the British delegation to the conference; he was one of the reasons why the conference was being held in such an obscure location in the first place. Keynes had a serious heart condition, and it was felt that the cool New Hampshire air would be good for him. (He did, indeed, suffer a minor heart attack during the conference but soldiered on.)

The gathering at Bretton Woods was one of a stream of meetings that occurred during the closing stages of the Second World War and in the years immediately after. (There were so many conferences, in fact, that one of the World Bank's earliest memorandums complained that its people could not get their work done because they were spending all their time at international meetings.) The underlying aim was to create not a world government but a system for national governments to solve international problems by pooling their resources to prevent a repetition of a war that had left fifty-five million people dead and thirty-five million wounded. The phrase *United Nations* appeared first in January 1942 in an American-drafted treaty under which twenty-six nations pledged to overthrow the Axis powers. The UN itself finally came into being on June 26, 1945, when representatives from fifty countries, gathered in San Francisco, signed a distinctly American-sounding charter, the very first words of which are "We, the peoples."

The institutions founded at Bretton Woods were to become part of the UN system, but they were to pay only nominal fealty to the UN. And to the extent that they ushered in the postwar boom, they arguably had more immediate effect.

For Keynes in particular, the new institutions were not just a matter of financial architecture but of political philosophy and of his own legacy. Keynes's spirit pervaded the proceedings in New Hampshire. "He has throughout dominated the Conference," noted Lionel Robbins, a British delegate who had clashed sharply with Keynes when he had turned against free trade. When Keynes left the room on the final day of the conference, the delegates chanted "For He's a Jolly Good Fellow."

The unstated aim of Bretton Woods was to put Hobbes back in his box and breathe new life into "the optimistic liberalism which Locke inaugurated." Keynes proposed to do that by binding the world to his new vision of globalization, in which trade in goods should be unfettered, but capital restricted.

The 730 conference delegates at the Mount Washington Hotel debated a plan that was already the result of two years of negotiation between Keynes and Harry Dexter White, an assistant secretary at the U.S. Treasury. Keynes and White proposed removing barriers to foreign trade but at the same time imposing strict rules on the flow of speculative capital. Speculative capital could "shift with the speed of the magic carpet," in Keynes's phrase, thereby "disorganising all steady business"; the magic carpet needed to be tied down in order to provide those steady businesses with a stable environment. Exchange rates were to be fixed at agreed levels, pegged to the American dollar, and tight controls were to be imposed on the movement of investment capital.

The system would be overseen by a Stabilization Fund (later known as the International Monetary Fund), which would lend money to countries that ran into temporary financial difficulties, discipline countries that adopted irresponsible policies, and alter the exchange rates of countries that suffered permanent economic dislocations. In addition, an International Bank for Reconstruction and Development (later known as the World Bank) would help rebuild war-shattered economies and, in the longer term, finance investment into developing countries.

Keynes's direct influence over the third arm of the international economic order was minimal: He was plagued by illness in his last years and died in 1946. Bretton Woods was his bequest to the world. He would naturally have preferred a system run by decent English chaps, rather than one dominated by Washington. He even tried to put the IMF in New York to remove it from direct political influence. Nevertheless, he left behind a legacy: a system that was much more global than the prewar one, yet one in which intervention by governments was still the norm.

The attempt to create an international trade body was put off until 1948, when representatives from fifty-seven countries gathered in Havana. The International Trade Organization was based on a revolutionary principle—multilateralism—that forced all the participants in the treaty to police each other. The Americans balked, not over free trade (the United States had pointedly made Marshall Plan aid to Europe contingent on the Continent progressively lowering internal barriers to trade) but over institutional mechanics. Both Congress and the State Department disliked the idea of a permanent trade organization. Fortunately, President Truman used his executive authority to create a "temporary" organization to oversee the General Agreement on Tariffs and Trade (GATT), which twenty-three of the industrialized nations had signed in Havana. This temporary organization was to last for forty-seven years, when it became the World Trade Organization.

The end of the war and the forty-five thousand tariff concessions negotiated in the first round of GATT had ushered in a period of breathtaking economic integration.[17] World trade, which had actually contracted by 3 percent in the early 1930s, grew over the quarter of a century after 1948 at an annual rate of 7.25 percent. With many countries short of workers, migration surged, particularly in Europe. Businesses once again began to spread around the world. By the 1960s, the word *multinational* had become something of an established swearword in France. Meanwhile, the Yankee imperialist bosses of such firms fantasized publicly about their companies' becoming so global that they would have to situate their headquarters on some uninhabited island to reflect the fact that they had no real nationality.

But fantasy was all that this was. For all the increase in trade, businesses remained stubbornly national. As companies such as General Motors and Ford rebuilt their international networks, they discovered that, after years of turmoil and tariffs, their local subsidiaries had become more or less autonomous, with their own products and cultures. Cars made by Vauxhall, General Motors' British division, were aimed squarely at the middle class of Dulwich rather than that of Detroit. Meanwhile, in the developing world, the subsidiaries of American multinational giants were if anything too passive to be called global; they acted purely as distribution networks for American products, their sales merely a small bonus for the booming American market. Big European firms were arguably a little more genuinely multinational, particularly those that had dual nationality, such as Royal Dutch/Shell and Unilever. But as staff at Unilever readily admit, the firm never really thought of the world as a single market until, at the earliest, the mid-1980s; the integration of production on a worldwide basis did not really begin until the 1990s.

What kept businesspeople back? Technological backwardness is hardly a convincing answer. Postwar managers had access to technology of which the large trading empires of the late nineteenth century could have only dreamed: Imagine, for instance, what John Jacob Astor might have achieved with a telephone. Rather, the two barriers that held back the reintegration of the global economy were both political. (Commerce is rather like water: It will flow wherever it is allowed.) The more obvious barrier was the Iron Curtain, behind which one third of the world's population had been consigned to regional autarky. But the second barrier was equally obstinate: the postwar consensus in the West that stressed state intervention.

For at least the first forty years after the Second World War, most governments outside the United States (and many critics would include the United States as well) refused to leave business alone.[18] In adopting this interventionist consensus, nobody imagined that they were contradicting the spirit of the Bretton Woods settlement, which had been designed to free the world trading system only in a carefully controlled way. (Besides, it was thought,

Bretton Woods was the brainchild of the world's most famous intervention-ist.) Governments wanted to provide better lives for the people who had sac-rificed so much in the war, and most of the intelligentsia told them that measured state intervention was much better at generating prosperity than was the free play of global markets. For that they had to thank not just Keynes but also Sidney and Beatrice Webb, whose ideas fused with those of Keynes to provide much of the backing for the postwar consensus.

The Curse of the Fabians

The Webbs, the spiritual parents of British socialism, were much more parochial figures than Keynes. A rather odd couple—she was a renowned beauty; Sidney quite the opposite—they were known in intellectual circles for a seriousness that went well beyond humorlessness. Dinner with the Webbs often consisted of a few sprigs of lettuce washed down with water. Trade unionists were dismissed not just as "nitwits" but also "boozers." The Webbs inevitably disapproved of the Bloomsbury group. (Keynes did admit to having a "deeply spiritual" lunch with Beatrice in 1913, but he did not re-peat the experience until 1926.) Despite these social handicaps, the Webbs' Fabian Society still managed to gather in many of the most influential writ-ers of the first part of the twentieth century, including George Bernard Shaw and H. G. Wells.

If the Webbs stood for anything, it was the assumption that "government knowledge" was superior to market knowledge—that dispassionate experts (most of them sitting in national capitals) were much better at allocating goods and services than self-interested businessmen and shortsighted con-sumers. Capitalists were myopic oafs, the Webbs argued in a series of books including *The Decay of Capitalist Civilization* (1923); the best chance for eco-nomic efficiency lay in handing decisions to intelligent and benevolent peo-ple like themselves. (Beatrice once described herself as "the cleverest member of one of the cleverest families in the cleverest class of the cleverest nation in the world.")[19] They created the London School of Economics to supply these experts and helped to form Britain's Labor Party, to put their ideas into practice.

Some of the events of the 1930s—not to mention the unfolding night-mare behind the Iron Curtain—might be expected to have turned Europeans against socialism. Yet from the perspective of many Europeans in 1945, re-cent history had conclusively vindicated the Webbs. The Wall Street crash had destroyed faith in the rationality of markets. The Soviet Union, which the Webbs idolized in *Soviet Communism: A New Civilization*, had enjoyed both double-digit growth rates and full employment. During the war, governments had seized control of basic industries, demonstrating to many people's satisfaction that the state could run things more efficiently than the private sector could. One wartime best-seller, James Burnham's *Managerial Revolution* (1941), proclaimed that "the capitalist organization of society has entered its final years." And the experience of the war itself, which involved everybody pulling together for the national good, created widespread hope for the creation of a more just and egalitarian society.

Fabian political ideas chimed well with Keynesian economics, which quickly became orthodox in the West's universities and finance ministries after the Second World War. Keynes himself had always been sympathetic to the Webbs' stress on experts ("We have little faith in the average sensual man," Beatrice decided. "We do not believe that he can do much more than describe his grievances.")[20] After the war, Keynes's followers, expanding his notion that government could have prevented the interwar disaster by spending more, generated the idea that economies needed to be micromanaged, with "expert" economists pulling appropriate levers. The Keynesians also leaned toward national rather than international solutions. Nation-states, they believed, played a crucial role in saving the capitalist system from itself, and anything that threatened to shift power too far away from national governments needed to be treated with the greatest suspicion.

Indeed, economic nationalism soon became another pillar of the postwar consensus. While the war discredited the virulent nationalism of the Axis powers, it also justified the benevolent nationalism of the Allies. Across Europe, governments nationalized "strategic industries" so that they could be run for the benefit of the nation as a whole rather than that of international speculators, just as they also took control of the burgeoning broadcasting industries so that they could prevent national identities from being diluted. The New Jerusalem of the Labor government, which swept Winston Churchill out of power in 1945, was built on nationalizing the coal industry, which provided 90 percent of the country's energy needs, as well as the steel industry, the utilities, and the railroads. Nationalization, the Labor leadership argued, would give these industries the scale that they needed to be competitive in the modern world, and it would replace shortsighted bosses with professional managers and also make good the government's promise of full employment.

It was hardly surprising that many governments—particularly in the third world—assumed that the right to shelter chosen industries was an integral part of the Keynesian legacy. Countries such as India, Brazil, and Argentina argued that they stood chances of progressing from raw-material providers into fully fledged industrial powers only if they protected their "infant industries" from competition with established multinationals. Such protection was always presented as a temporary measure, to be abandoned when the time came to be reconnected with the international economy. But somehow the time was never quite right, and protectionism, particularly in the developing world, became—alongside nationalism and the divine intelligence of government bureaucrats—the third pillar of the postwar consensus.

Bidets and Jackboots

This makes it sound as if the consensus was a disaster from the start. Far from it: Handing control of what Lenin called "the commanding heights" of the economy to the state seemed to work extremely well. Certain liberal economists have tried to rewrite the history of the postwar miracles in Japan and Germany to downplay the roles of the states. But both contained hefty dollops of statism, nationalism, and protectionism. Similar ideas lay behind France's *trente glorieuse* (thirty glorious years) from 1945 to 1975, when many French people saw spectacular changes in their living standards. At the end of the war, Paris was a dump: From lavatories (normally courtyard privies, shared between several apartments) to lightbulbs (more than a couple of which could blow a building's fuse), it had barely advanced since the turn of the century.[21] The dirigiste bureaucrats from schools such as the École Nationale d'Administration changed all this, giving their citizens not just better electricity and sanitation but modern roads, railways, telephones, a welfare service, and cheap cars.

Dirigisme spread quickly around the world, taking on the peculiar hues of each host country, from jackbooted militarism in Latin America to fussy paternalism in India. Some governments, such as South Korea's, were relatively clever about using their resources to build export industries and relatively ruthless about dropping businesses whose products could not hack it overseas. But most focused more on defense rather than on attack. Jawaharlal Nehru, India's first prime minister after independence, introduced a fully fledged system of national planning, in which elite mandarins devoted their talents to telling lowly businesspeople what to do. They treated international trade as the devil incarnate, partly because it threatened their power and partly because it threatened India's hard-won independence.

In Latin America, a generation of economists developed something called "dependency theory," which held that, far from being an engine of prosperity, international trade was a tool of oppression. The rich world treated the poor one as a source of cheap commodities while keeping all the higher, value-added jobs for itself. The only chance the poor world had of freeing itself from perpetual commodity-producing servitude lay in allowing their governments to use tariffs and licenses to steer trade. Dependency theorists not only exercised a Svengalian influence over Latin American politicians from Juan Perón to Salvador Allende but also managed to turn parts of the United Nations into propaganda vehicles for their theories.

The late 1960s and the 1970s saw antiglobal ideas sweep all before them in the developing world. Hirsute ideological descendants of the Webbs argued that the third world was engaged in an anticolonial struggle against its imperial masters, and the 1973 oil crisis suggested that the struggle was finally being resolved in favor of the formerly colonized. From Chile to Kuwait, third-world politicians expropriated foreign-owned companies on a massive scale, especially in the oil and mineral sectors, and created nationalized companies to protect their economies from multinational predators.[22] In the developed world, most of the big economies started to tighten their immigration rules and created national champions in computers, aerospace, and nuclear power to safeguard these "strategic sectors." Harold Wilson, who won four British elections in the 1960s and 1970s, blamed his woes on "the gnomes of Zurich" and praised nationalization as a way "to render accountable to the public the power of those increasingly anonymous, unidentifiable, often faceless, more often soulless corporations, national and multinational."[23]

Gradually, however, the tide began to turn—and not only with the ascensions of Margaret Thatcher and Ronald Reagan. After winning the French presidency in May 1981 on an antiglobalist platform, François Mitterrand proceeded to nationalize thirteen of the country's twenty largest corporations and most of its banking system. But he could not contend with the economic chaos this created. Rather than suffer further humiliations at the hands of international currency speculators, he pegged the franc to the deutsche mark and France's fate to the integration of Europe. The postwar consensus had finally begun to collapse.

The Road from Serfdom

State intervention, despite its early successes, was plainly not working. The most extreme example was in Eastern Europe. The Soviet Union's command economy gradually ground to a halt, its infertility symbolized by the dying Aral Sea, once the fourth-biggest freshwater body in the world, now polluted beyond repair by state factories producing substandard cotton, for which there was no market other than the one mandated by bureaucrats. Eventually, by increasing military spending, Ronald Reagan threw down a challenge that the Soviet Union was simply incapable of meeting. But long before the Berlin Wall crumbled, the sheer wretchedness of the communist world had become obvious to most people in the West. By the 1970s, the West Germans might still have been jealous of East Germany's (pharmaceutically enhanced) athletic excellence at the Olympics, but they took considerable consolation from the tawdry tracksuits and leisure wear of their rivals. "How do you double the value of a Trabant?" West Berliners, smug in their BMWs, joked: "Fill up the gas tank."

Outside Eastern Europe, people who had previously welcomed the postwar consensus began to worry whether it represented only a less virulent strain of the Soviet disease. Far from picking up the slack created by inadequate private investment, Keynesian demand management crowded out private investors; far from smoothing out the economic cycle, it stoked up recurrent inflation-driven crises. Governments ate up a growing proportion of national incomes, borrowing what they could not squeeze out of taxpayers, and yet they were still unable to fulfill their obligations. From Madrid to Madras, nationalized industries became poster children for inefficiency. Well into the 1980s, Indians, on account of government policy, had access to only their own version of Coca-Cola (a concoction so foul that its American equivalent tasted comparatively like the nectar of the gods), drove around in old Austin cars that had ceased being produced in Britain in the 1950s, and watched their well-trained young science graduates stream overseas to find jobs.

History had repeated itself, albeit in a much gentler manner. Just as the Second World War had been the final, bloody proof of the futility of the economic policies of the previous two decades, the stagflation, social discord, and crummy products of the 1970s were all evidence of the bankruptcy of the postwar consensus: The old Austins on the streets of Bombay and the wave of strikes and demonstrations across Europe were all signs of a system in terminal decline. But what was the alternative?

One rather graphic answer was provided by a young woman at a meeting at the Conservative Party's research department in Smith Square, just around the corner from the Palace of Westminster.[24] A staff member was arguing that the Conservative Party should adopt a middle way between left and right—very much the conventional wisdom of the time—when Margaret Thatcher, who had recently been elected leader of the party, interrupted him brusquely. There was no future in resuscitating the Keynesian consensus, she said, and reached into her briefcase to produce a copy of Hayek's *The Constitution of Liberty*. "This is what we believe," she said, flourishing the book.

Friedrich von Hayek was born in Vienna in 1899, the son of a distinguished botanist and second cousin to the philosopher Ludwig Wittgenstein. A tall, austere intellectual, he served as a gunner during the First World War—an experience that turned him into a socialist. Yet as he returned to his studies, he went through a slow, painful intellectual conversion, eventually emerging as a fervent supporter of free markets. His fervor drew its force from two sources: the collapse of the Austro-Hungarian Empire, which left him with a low view of politicians; and the influence of his mentor Ludwig von Mises, the leading figure in the Austrian school of economics, who taught that the market system is a self-adjusting order that is far more intelligent than any caste of experts. In 1931, Hayek took up a professorship at the London School of Economics, where he announced his presence by writing a savage review of Keynes's *Treatise on Money*.

Thus began an odd relationship. Hayek and Keynes got on very well in private life, corresponding about mutual enthusiasms, such as antiquarian books. Hayek was certainly not immune to Keynes's intellectual charms and wrote approvingly of "the magnetism of the brilliant conversationalist with his wide range of interests and bewitching voice." Keynes also went out of his way to be generous to his opponent, arranging for him to move from London to Cambridge during the Blitz and proposing him for a fellowship of the British Academy. But their academic exchanges could be sulphurous.

Hayek regarded Keynes's influence on economics as "both miraculous and tragic." The two parted company most violently over the recession of the 1930s. Keynes regarded public investment as the only way to save capitalism from itself; Hayek argued that it would simply perpetuate the economy's fundamental maladjustments. Keynes described one of Hayek's books, *Prices and Production* (1931), as "one of the most frightful muddles I have ever read." He went on: "It is an extraordinary example of how, starting with a mistake, a remorseless logician can end in Bedlam." On the draft copy of another article he scribbled, "The wildest farrago of nonsense yet."[25]

Hayek became hopelessly marginalized as the Keynesian revolution unfolded. Established opinion praised Keynes as the genius who had saved capitalism from itself and dismissed free-market purists as a bunch of right-wing nuts. But Hayek was nothing if not persistent. His *Road to Serfdom*, published in the year the Bretton Woods conference was held, sounded a clarion call to everyone who was uneasy about the growing power of the state. After Keynes's death, Hayek began to organize the opposition in earnest. He convened a regular meeting of the Mont Pelerin Society, a group of thirty-six fellow travelers, including the young Milton Friedman, who mutually supported each other. In 1950, Hayek moved to join Friedman at the more sympathetic environment of the University of Chicago, though notably as a professor of social and political sciences rather than as a member of the economics department.

The central tenet of the postwar economic consensus was that markets were much more prone to failure than governments were. In his stream of books and papers, Hayek argued the opposite: Yes, markets can fail, but they remain much more subtle and efficient than bureaucrats, who usually could not even understand what was going on around them, let alone predict the future. They drove out productive enterprises through taxes and intervention. Even the most benign form of government intervention—regulation—was prone to "producer capture" as regulators repeatedly became the tools of vested interests. Free trade was an important part of this new heretical creed. Hayek argued that countries needed to lower tariffs in order to subject their industries to the bracing effects of competition, and he repeatedly celebrated places such as Hong Kong, where lenient regulation had turned a barren rock into a mighty regional entrepôt.

Other academics were unconvinced. Even when Hayek was eventually awarded a Nobel Prize in 1974, it was for work done in the 1920s and 1930s, and many economists were openly outraged by the decision. The first country that consciously put Hayek's arguments into practice was an international pariah, Chile. Following Augusto Pinochet's coup in 1973, the dictator turned to a group of "Chicago boys" for advice. At first, Hayek's disciples made some damaging mistakes, selling off state companies too cheaply. But their overall program of reform—privatization, deregulation, and the embrace of global markets—eventually began to work. Chilean family businesses prospered as a result of their links to the world market; previously state-owned companies were forced to shed excess labor and adopt more innovative policies. Chile's economy grew by more than 6 percent a year from the late 1980s onward.

By that time, however, two other politicians had already brought Friedman, Hayek, and others to the world's attention: Ronald Reagan and, even more emphatically, Margaret Thatcher. Never exactly a consensus politician, Thatcher seemed only to gain strength from the hysterical opposition of the British establishment—at one point, 364 economists took the trouble to write to *The Times* to urge the government to change policies. Thatcher believed firmly that Britain could regain its former greatness only if it opened its economy to global competition. One of her first acts was to abolish controls on the flow of international capital. A succession of privatizations opened industries that had once been regarded as national champions to foreign ownership. Thatcher argued repeatedly that Britain's success in attracting investment, notably from the Japanese, was a sign of the country's vitality.

As Thatcherism and then Reaganism began to work their often cruel magic, other governments liberalized their economies, even when it seemed to go against their most ingrained instincts. In China, Deng Xiaoping genuflected to Marx but struck deals with the multinationals. Having swept over such an easy target as Beijing, Thatcherism even crashed through the portals of Paris. (The French did not embrace privatization, but they did at least air-kiss it.) A growing number of emerging economies followed suit. In 1989, the Argentines elected a messianic Peronist named Carlos Menem, who seemed to want to nationalize everything and print money; once in power, he sold off state businesses and introduced a currency board that remained the centerpiece of the country's economy up to the peso crisis of 2002.

Like an invading army finding a small breach in a fortress, businesspeople poured through the gap opened up by the politicians. The value of imported and exported manufactured goods, which had been $2 trillion in 1986, ballooned to $5.2 trillion just a decade later.[26] By the early 1990s, the number of transnational corporations as measured by the United Nations Conference on Trade and Development (UNCTAD) had increased to about thirty-seven thousand from seven thousand in the 1960s.[27] Multinationals started acting like integrated global organizations rather than like loose affiliations of national companies that happened to share the same name. In the 1970s, the various national branches of Xerox had so little in common that they almost regarded each other as competitors. But in the 1980s, Xerox decided that its only chance of defeating the competition lay in acting as a single integrated organization. Meanwhile, falling trade barriers and improvements in communications made it much cheaper to establish and manage international production systems. Microsoft, for example, became an international force without moving many of its resources from its "global campus" near Seattle.

More generally, a symbiotic relationship developed between politicians keen to form free-trade areas and businesspeople keen to exploit them. There were almost one hundred regional trade treaties by the end of the 1990s, up from fewer than twenty-five in 1990. The newcomers included the ASEAN Free Trade Area (or AFTA), which was launched in January 1993 in order to reduce trade barriers in Asia and prevent member countries from cutting each other's throats by competing for foreign direct investment; Mercosur, a treaty between Argentina, Brazil, Paraguay, and Uruguay established in 1991; and the North American Free Trade Agreement (NAFTA), which brought together the United States, Canada, and Mexico in 1994.

But perhaps the most notable of these was the European Union's single market of 1992. The single market, like the single currency that followed on its heels, came into being only because the political leaders of France and Germany regarded it as an essential part of "the European project." Yet much of the momentum was provided by the Continent's business elite. "1992" was used as the rationale for countless takeovers and reorganizations, as well as for all too many tedious conferences. Businesspeople also bullied governments to loosen their grips on industries, so that they could have greater freedom to compete. The decade after 1985 saw a host of "national champions" either wholly or partially privatized, including Volkswagen, Lufthansa, Renault, Elf Aquitaine, ENI, and Deutsche Telekom. The nightclubs of London filled with Gucci-wearing "Eurotrash" financiers—many of them working for American and Japanese firms that were no less keen on treating the Continent as a single unit.

Hope Floats

We could happily fill the rest of this book with examples of globalization spreading through the 1990s and early 2000s: privatizations in Ulan Bator; American firms setting up *maquiladoras;* Asian patriarchs sending their oldest sons to America to set up research arms. In the next section, we will look at the way that three "nonpolitical" forces—technology, capital, and management—are pulling the world together. Yet at the beginning of the twenty-first century, it is still hard to answer the question "Which John Maynard Keynes won?" On the face of it, the young Keynes who visited Italy triumphed. Globalist ideas are once again in the ascendancy. There are plenty of impressive statistics to show how the world is getting smaller. But there are also some very big things that would have delighted his later, more interventionist self. Despite all the talk about the death of big government, the states' shares of GDPs are at levels about which Sidney and Beatrice Webb might only have dreamed. Nor would they have been that unhappy with many parts of those regional trade agreements, which have often had the paradoxical effect of cementing barriers to further globalization. Europe's single market, for example, has left the infamous Common Agricultural Policy in place. Immigration controls persist everywhere.

More generally, politicians from Bombay to Bonn remain at best fair-weather friends of economic liberalism. Like their equivalents in the Italy that the young Keynes visited, they support free trade in principle but can always find a reason to make temporary exemptions for people with political connections, whether they are French film producers, Midwestern farmers, or Indonesian timber merchants. In America, for example, support for free trade ebbs at the first sign of a trade deficit. The late 1980s saw an outbreak of Japanophobia in America and a lot of guff about the virtues of managed trade. George W. Bush, who had seemed an instinctive free trader, still rushed to protect America's steel industry with tariffs in 2002, in order to win votes in the rust belt.

In 1997 and 1998, various developing countries reacted to the gathering crisis in Asia by retreating from planned reforms. Indeed, at one point—following the imposition of capital controls in Malaysia, Russia's default, and the government of Hong Kong's decision to intervene in the stock market (to frustrate evil "speculators")—the chattering classes rushed to declare the death of laissez-faire capitalism. Osama bin Laden sent another jolt through the international system when al-Qaeda felled the World Trade Center in 2001. That year also saw world trade stall and border controls increase. The collapse of Argentina and the brutal "reelection" of Robert Mugabe in 2002 each showed how far the developing world had to catch up.

In the next few chapters, we will turn to the forces that are pushing the world closer together. These forces are indeed profound, enough to turn some surprising people into friends of globalization. But as we gaze at the might of the capital markets or the distance-destroying magic of modern technology, it is important to remember the young traveler to Italy in 1906, when the internationalization of the world was "nearly complete in practice," and to remind ourselves that, given the frailty of human nature and the complexity of human affairs, the world can roll backward as well as forward.

Part Two

The Three Engines
of Globalization

2

Technology as Freedom

WHAT DRIVES GLOBALIZATION? The gradual decision by politicians to step out of its way since the end of the Second World War has allowed a wide variety of commercial forces to come to the fore: the Internet, the foreign-exchange market, mergers, and foreign direct investment. Some people would argue (rightly but unhelpfully) that these gusts are all part of the same all-devouring hurricane called modern capitalism. We have chosen to cluster them and others under three headings, each of which we will address in the following three chapters: technology, the capital markets, and management.

Each of these forces is powerful enough in its own right, but what has given them their apparent invincibility in recent years is the fact that they all fit together so neatly. Free-flowing capital makes it easier for companies in even the most out-of-the-way places to buy new technology. New technology makes it easier to move capital to similarly obscure places. And management—by which we mean the spread of common management methods, the growth of the management industry of consultants and business schools, and the development of a new cadre of professional multinational managers—alerts companies to the clever ways in which they can use capital and technology. Companies that organize themselves better than their rivals do soon expand beyond their national borders, and in so doing put pressure on less cosmopolitan companies to follow suit or risk annihilation. And so the circle continues.

The Bolton Wanderer

To most Britons, the name Ferranti is bound up with the past rather than the future. For much of this century, the Ferranti family was Britain's preeminent electronics dynasty. But in the 1970s, the firm had to be rescued by the British government, and eventually it collapsed anyway, after an accounting scandal. To a visitor, the family photographs in Marcus de Ferranti's house in the Boltons seem to confirm this backward-looking picture. Family photographs show a predictable journey through the British establishment, from Eton school days to skiing parties. Until recently, the only visible piece of technology was a computer in Ferranti's study: Its screensaver image is of a small, deserted Scottish island where Ferranti wants to build a house. As for Ferranti himself, he has the easygoing charm of somebody who has never had to try too hard for anything. Play tennis against him, and, despite having spent a small fortune on trying to improve his game, he laughs when he loses.

In fact, Ferranti's career has always been slightly unconventional and is now downright revolutionary. On leaving the University of Edinburgh in 1982, he became a fighter pilot—a worryingly meritocratic profession for lazy Etonians because it rejects nine out of ten applicants. He then spent two years working in a software subsidiary of GEC—the British defense giant that, ironically, had swallowed the rump of the Ferranti family business—before being offered a surprising assignment: a year in a unit set up by the Conservative government to deregulate British industry.

At first, Whitehall's strange ways amused Ferranti. But he soon found his job frustrating. The Tories, already unpopular, were scared to take further moves to increase competition. Yet as Ferranti saw it, deregulation, particularly in telecommunications, had not gone far enough. Whenever he asked why the old monopolist, British Telecom, remained firmly in control, he was told that he was naive. And didn't he know the Tories were going to lose? In November 1996, six months before the Tories fell, Ferranti left the unit and went to join his brother, an entrepreneur.

In June 1997, a friend named Richard Elliott came around to the Boltons for a drink after tennis. Another tall public-school boy who had always wanted to start his own business, Elliott had drifted into the army and then into the City of London. Ferranti pestered him about the inefficiency of various markets—in particular, why it cost so much to call overseas. Why was there no market on which people could trade telephone time? Ferranti sketched out an idea for an Internet-based exchange where telecommunication firms could post offers anonymously to buy or sell minutes of calling time between any two locations. Elliott, still imagining a building with traders in it, asked how on earth Ferranti would find the money to start a commodities exchange. Ferranti, the Pimms taking hold, explained that there did not have to be any bricks and mortar: All the exchange really needed was some software and a website. By the end of June, Elliott had handed in his resignation to his bemused bosses at Kleinwort Benson, and Band-X had set up shop in Ferranti's study.

In retrospect, one of Band-X's biggest assets was its founders' ignorance about telecommunications. Two experienced executives from the industry whom Ferranti consulted before he set up the business both told him to give up immediately. Yes, the experts conceded, it was pretty simple nowadays to switch calls from carrier to carrier; and, yes, many big carriers did have excess capacity. But most international telephone calls were still governed by rates set by complicated international treaties; only around 10 percent of them were sold at market rates. Ferranti, having done the sums, replied that there was still a sixty-billion-dollar market. Yes, the executives admitted, but it was a fuss to sell such time: You could do it, but only through special brokers who took 20 percent commissions. Ferranti replied that his exchange would charge just 1 percent, and, since all parties could see the bids or offers, each would know that they were getting the best price. "Really, you are so naive."

In fact, Band-X grew quickly precisely because it was so simple. By August 1997, the exchange had collected two hundred members, and it had shown how far prices could fall in a free market. A minute between New York and London was being traded for about seven cents—a sixth of what British Telecom charged and about the same cost as a local call in London. The differential in the prices on more exotic routes was even bigger. A succession of telecommunications bosses filed through the Ferrantis' drawing room (the head of one public-sector Scandinavian company was forced to play with the children while he waited). In June 1998, having amassed three thousand members, including firms from Bosnia to Bangladesh, Band-X became even more like a stock exchange when it bought its own switch in Telehouse, a central exchange in London, allowing it to settle its deals as well as arrange them. It also made it much easier to do spot trading—selling excess minutes when you have them rather than in advance.

The extra business generated by the switch means that Band-X has finally had to quit Ferranti's study, and in 1999 they raised eleven million dollars from a Chicago-based venture capitalist in a deal that valued Band-X at more than thirty million dollars. Like many Internet-related businesses, Band-X had to cut back its operations in 2001, but the company's core business is growing. More important, the two Englishmen can claim at least a small role in the phenomenon that Frances Cairncross of *The Economist* has dubbed "the death of distance."

Even before sans-culottes such as Ferranti began to challenge the old ways, the cost of a telephone call from New York to London in 1996 was only a couple of dollars, compared with around three hundred dollars (in 1996 prices) in 1930. Already if you wander around India you will find cheaper hands, eyes, voices, and brains doing plenty of surprising things: processing insurance forms, running Swissair's back office, talking to General Electric's American credit-card users, even guarding office buildings in California (the security pictures are simply sent by satellite). Now, thanks to a mixture of technology and deregulation, there is the tantalizing prospect of having the cost of making a call fall to practically nothing.

That revolution might be a little farther away than people hope. There are also plenty of more famous figures than Ferranti and Elliott. But even their effect is noticeable. Already consumer groups around the world are using Band-X's revelations of the true cost of telecommunications in order to attack the old monopolies. And the cleverer brains in the industry are still convinced that a proper derivatives market in telecommunications time will evolve, despite Enron's abortive push into the market. Needless to say, Ferranti and Elliott remain unperturbed about Band-X's role in this revolution. The success of Band-X has ruined their social lives, they complain. The idea that they deserve any credit for reducing the cost of telephone time, let alone "killing distance," genuinely amuses them. "It was obvious," says Ferranti, gazing a little mournfully at his screensaver. "Some naive idiot was bound to have done it sooner or later."

On the Waterfront

Band-X's story should be read as a rebuff to two sets of people. The first is all those technodeterminists who think that it is merely enough for a gadget to exist for its effect to be universal. For example, Andy Grove of Intel has stated that "technology change and its effects are inevitable. Stopping them is not an option."[1] But Band-X's story is a complicated, accident-plagued one in which things like Pimms count more than bytes and in which the big idea is still some way from realization. The notion that the progress toward a "friction-free world" is as simple as the traffic lights changing in Palo Alto just seems downright wrong. It might be merely an expression of Luddism (we remain the sort of journalists who often spend longer trying to transmit a story back to London than we do writing the thing in the first place), but the world is littered with examples of how hopelessly messy and sometimes contradictory the link between technology and globalization can be.

The second group of people contains all those crusty old liberals who still equate technology with Big Brother and the restriction of individual freedom; machines, for them, are a way to trap data about people, to coerce them, even to spy on "enemies of the state" from the sky. In fact, it is exactly the chaotic, unpredictable way in which technology spreads around the world that makes it so subversive. Technology gives entrepreneurs such as Ferranti the freedom to challenge giant companies and to break up concentrations of power. Technology gives people the power to weave connections all over the world. Technology allows people to escape from the tyranny of place.

When most people think of the impact of technology on globalization, they think of computers and telephones. Arguably, much more mundane inventions have had even greater effects: Few things have done more to allow people to escape from the tyranny of place, for example, than the air conditioner. Although the first air-conditioned home was built by a Minneapolis millionaire in 1914, the gadget did not begin to have a real effect on society till after the Second World War. In the United States, several people have claimed that air-conditioning had as much impact on integration in the South as the civil-rights movement did. As history professor Raymond Arsenault has put it, "General Electric has proved a more devastating invader than General Sherman."[2]

And what is true for Savannah is also true for São Paulo, Seville, and Shanghai. "Historically, advanced civilizations have flourished in the cooler climates," argues Lee Kwan Yew, Singapore's senior minister. "Now lifestyles have become comparable to those in temperate zones and civilization in the tropical zones need no longer lag behind."[3] Air-conditioning is the reason why offices and hotel rooms—those two staples of business life—feel pretty much the same everywhere. Meanwhile, air-conditioning also paved the way for the much derided theater of placelessness, the shopping mall. Stand in Pacific Place in Hong Kong or the Metrocentre at Gateshead, and it is not just the names of the shops—Benetton, The Body Shop—that are the same, but also that cool, dry, slightly lifeless atmosphere.

Something that has had an even greater effect on globalization is really no more than a twenty-foot-long metal box. In most big cities, a fair propor-

tion of the male workforce used to work down at the docks, loading and un-
loading things, first from trucks into warehouses and then from warehouses
into ships. In 1956, a hauler from Cape Fear, North Carolina, named Malcolm McLean offered shippers space on the *Ideal X*, a vessel sailing from
Newark, New Jersey, to Houston, which he had converted specially so that it
could carry trailers. Soon shippers realized that it was unnecessary to include the wheels. Within a decade, ships with detachable containers were
plying the Atlantic routes, and the life celebrated in *A View from the Bridge*
and *On the Waterfront* began to disappear.

Rather than hundreds of dockworkers, these containers (which soon became known as longshoremen's coffins) needed just a handful. And because
the goods were better protected, manufacturers became much more likely to
import complicated, small parts. (It is hard to imagine Marlon Brando muttering about being a contender while tossing compact-disc drives into the
hold of a ship.) At the beginning of the twentieth century, 40 percent of
America's imports and exports were made up of "crude food" and "crude materials." Now nearly 80 percent of exported goods are manufactured goods.[4]

By 2002, the world's fifteen million containers carried 90 percent of its
traded cargo. This seaborne revolution prompted similar changes on land.
Led by America in the 1970s, governments began to relax the rules with
which they had shackled their freight and postal industries, allowing trucks
to pick up containers at ports as well as drop them off and giving more freedom to private postal services. Haulers responded by teaming up with railways and even airlines, and as a result container transportation became
genuinely intermodal, with boxes being switched rapidly from one sort of
carrier to another. The typical ship now spends just twenty-four hours in a
port, rather than three weeks. On land, the cost of rail freight in America fell
by about a quarter between 1986 and 1996. Every day, FedEx alone delivers
three million packages around the world.

Once again, this can sound fairly anodyne. But it has changed many
manufacturers' perspectives on the world. Cheaper, quicker transportation
opened up new markets, encouraging even small firms to go global, and allowed companies to "source" components from the other side of the world
and to experiment with "just in time" manufacturing methods. No longer relying on huge factories and warehouses, manufacturing has become a
leaner business, with companies outsourcing their supply systems to logistics specialists. For example, FedEx runs most of National Semiconductor's
distribution system; in Malaysia, it coordinates the assembly of Dell PCs and
deals with all the customs work.

Almost every form of innovation in transport seems to help globalization, often in fairly subtle ways. Faster planes (not to mention fewer rules about who can fly them and when) mean that no factory is more than a day and a half away, thus restricting even the most independent local manager from defying the head office. Meanwhile, people are more willing to be posted abroad if they know that they can get back home quickly. How many reluctant spouses have been persuaded that a place is not as far away as it seems? Twenty years ago, the idea of flying from New York to London for the weekend to attend a friend's wedding would have been considered the height of decadence. Now secretaries and plumbers do it.

The Holy Trinity

The computer, the telephone, and the television are not the whole technological story, but they are the three things that stand out the most. That is partly because they are attracting the most investment. Back in 1980, only about a tenth of the equipment budgets of American firms was spent on information technology; now it is close to half. But these three items are also the cornerstones of the information age (if we can take the liberty of mixing a preindustrial metaphor with a postindustrial cliché). The effect of television on globalization is the subject of chapter 10. That leaves the computer and the telephone. To what extent are they driving globalization?

Neither device is exactly a spring chicken. The telephone is more than a century old. The computer is older still, if you take Charles Babbage's counting machine as the first computer; and even if you think the computer age did not begin until the Altair 8800, the first mainstream personal computer, the PC is rapidly approaching middle age. Arguably, both instruments went global only in the 1990s. By 2002, there were more than three hundred million PCs with web browsers on the planet—roughly one for every twenty-four people—and although about 40 percent of them are in America, that proportion is falling. As long ago as 1998, some local surveys reckoned that as many as one in ten families in Shanghai and Beijing had a PC.[5] (The machines cost around half a year's pay, but the Chinese tend to be big savers and their children—the bossy little emperors—are notoriously demanding.)

This ubiquity would mean very little without two things: digitalization in general and the Internet in particular. Nowadays, virtually everything—voices on telephones, pictures on screens, even management decisions—can be converted into ones and zeroes and then stored or transmitted. Indeed, if there is such a thing as a universal language, it is not English but binary: A Chinese computer speaks exactly the same language as a Spanish one, as well as the same one as a Spanish digital phone.

In 1990, only a few academics had even so much as heard of the Internet; by 1999, 200 million people were using it. The World Wide Web not only allows people to access a vast storehouse of information from almost anywhere in the world but also allows all sorts of businesses to become borderless. In 1998, John Chambers, boss of Cisco Systems, summarized the potential power of the Internet to Congress:

> The Internet will change how people live, work, play and learn. The Industrial Revolution brought together people with machines in factories, and the Internet revolution will bring together people with knowledge and information in virtual companies. . . . It will promote globalization at an incredible pace. But instead of happening over 100 years like the Industrial Revolution, it will happen over seven years.[6]

It is at this point that skepticism starts to intrude. Only seven years before Chambers spoke to Congress, other technoenthusiasts were talking excitedly about the way that every home would soon have video on demand. Today, people continue to fork out small fortunes for overdue rented videotapes. The fact that more than half the users of the Internet live in one country—the United States—means that its role as a global medium is limited. Even in the United States, the Internet is not changing business as radically as the likes of Chambers imagine. If consumers want to buy books, computers, or even some shares, they may well use the Internet, but many businesses still think of the Internet as something of a toy.

One immediate reason for caution is that there is still a shortage of the bandwidth necessary to deliver many services. Other hangups have as much to do with regulation and corporate psychology as with technology. In 1996, for example, the American government deregulated its local communications market. But instead of building fiber-optic networks or launching cable-television systems, the so-called Baby Bells spent most of the next few years buying each other up. It was only once AT&T bullied its way into the market by buying most of America's cable-television systems that there were some signs of movement. Even now the final mile to the home remains largely unbuilt.

These glitches seem particularly glaring when considering how far ahead America is of most of the rest of the world. Europe has its strong points: Finland has the highest Internet penetration in the world. But in general, the Continent (like Japan) spends less on technology than America does. In 1996, there were only fifty-two PCs for every one hundred European white-collar workers, barely half of the proportion in America.[7] In many parts of the developing world, there is a chronic shortage of telephones, let alone computers. Only about one in ten Brazilians and one in three hundred Africans has a fixed-line phone. There are fewer telephones in sub-Saharan Africa than in Manhattan and precious little infrastructure. A call from Lagos to Abidjan has to go via Europe.[8] For most people in the world, the World Wide Web is just another unobtainable American toy.

The Inevitability of Gradualness

Things are not going to change as quickly as the technologists hope. But change they will. Arthur C. Clarke argued that in general people exaggerate the short-run impact of technological change and underestimate the long-run impact.[9] This is what happened with the spread of electricity, and it could well happen again with the Internet.

Thomas Edison built his first power station in 1882. Yet by the turn of the century, only 3 percent of America's factories used electric motors to drive their machinery, and by 1919 that figure had risen only to a third. The standards war between alternating and direct current was partly to blame, but the bigger problem was that manufacturers, such as Maytag, a pioneering washing-machine maker, did not use the technology properly: Electricity typically turned just a single steel shaft on the production line with various belts running off of it. It was only once they worked out how to use the new source of energy to power individual machines—something that Maytag undertook only in the mid-1920s—that productivity took off. In their book *Prosperity*, Bob Davis and David Wessel point out that a Maytag worker in 1926 made 48 percent more machines than his counterpart in 1923, and profits also soared.[10]

In the long term, the Internet will triumph through a mixture of technology and momentum. As communications keep improving—already a pair of fibers no thicker than a human hair can carry all the voice traffic passing across the Atlantic at any one moment—the pressure on incumbents to do something will mount. Increasingly, rather than going from switch to switch, packets of digital or voice data float through connectionless networks based on Internet protocols, with the only charges being ever-smaller access fees. For the telecommunications companies, that model not only means making huge new investments but also embracing a completely new profit structure. Yet it is beginning to happen. In America, the Baby Bells talk about the need in the long term to turn themselves into "universal players"—big, integrated communications companies—or face extinction. In France and Germany, consumer choice is at last appearing.[11] Meanwhile, most developing countries have relieved their postal companies of responsibility for phone lines, and many of them are leapfrogging the rich world into the wireless future.

The other thing that is happening—again, slowly—is that the Maytags of today are beginning to embrace the Internet. General Electric, for instance, can certainly be accused of spotting the potential of the Internet late. But in 1999, Jack Welch hurled his whole company at what he calls the "biggest change I have ever seen." Under the heading "destroyyourbusiness.com," a flurry of memos, speeches, and e-mails has carried one characteristically blunt message: Change your business model, or somebody else will.

GE started buying some of its supplies via on-line auction. A host of other items—aircraft-engine instruction manuals, color charts for plastics—all followed on-line quickly. But the real challenge is to use the Internet to reinvent rather than merely to streamline businesses. Many of GE's first ideas involve reaching out to consumers much more directly. GE Power Systems, for instance, wants to become a "home aggregator." That means it offers consumers a domestic, Internet-based version of the same sort of electricity-management service that it offers utilities: It will buy electricity for your home at the cheapest rate and also at the cheapest time of the day, remotely monitor your appliances (alerting you when your refrigerator needs checking), and allow you to turn things on and off via the Internet.

All this can only hasten globalization. One obvious feature of the Internet, as with many previous technological innovations, is its capacity to reduce the importance of geography. An early instance of this came when Netscape managed to "export" its software around the world without ever leaving California; another came when Amazon.com became a national bookseller without setting foot outside Washington State. Most of the clients of Infosys, one of India's largest software firms, are in the United States. At the end of its working day, the office in the United States simply e-mails Infosys's office in Bangalore with customer problems, and the company's technicians solve them while the Americans slumber. What might happen when Hollywood studios use the Internet to distribute their films to cinemas for almost nothing? Or when schools begin to teach across borders? Britain's Open University, which specializes in educating adults who have missed out on regular universities, runs Europe's largest business school, thanks partly to the Internet. Craig Barrett of Intel argues that the Internet will create "a seventh continent"—a world of one billion connected computers.[12]

One of the most important effects of the Internet will be on prices. There are already a few substances, such as gold and oil, for which there are established global values. The chances are that far more things will follow as the Internet spreads. At the very least, the Internet allows people to compare prices across borders, as they go window-shopping for Amazon's books or the Gap's khakis; at best, it allows them to buy from the best source anywhere in the world, gradually squeezing overpricing and inefficiency out of the market. The Internet does not even have to become ubiquitous for the law of "one price" to begin to assert its power. In the United States, only a small fraction of people buy their cars or shares from virtual dealers, but they use the prices offered on the Internet to demand lower rates from the dealers' real-life equivalents.

The Conquest of Location

The Internet has so hogged the headlines that it has tended to obscure another spin-off from the telephone-television-computer triumvirate that might end up having a greater effect on globalization: the mobile phone. (This could simply be because the United States leads the world in computers but lags horribly in mobile phones.) If the drop in telephone prices and the development of the Internet is all about the death of distance, then the spread of mobile phones might be said to herald "the conquest of location."

Until recently, one of the worst things about the tyranny of place was that, in an age of information, you lost power every time you left your house or office. You became like the idiot in Woody Allen's *Play It Again, Sam* who, on entering a restaurant, immediately called his office to tell them where he was. Now companies such as Nokia talk about people being able to live in "a personal bubble" of data that they can take from place to place. Even more excitingly, people in the emerging world are using mobile phones to escape from isolation and perhaps even from poverty. Mobile phones started out as yuppie toys, but they are arguably doing more than any other device to provide poor people with chances to plug into the global marketplace.

None of these lofty concepts seems to be on the minds of the people milling outside Yodobashi Camera, in Tokyo's frenetic Shinjuku district. Some of the people are ogling the store's flat-screened televisions and sliver-thin laptops. But most of them are staring at phones, which come in a rainbow of colors, from pearl (the schoolgirls' favorite) to silver (preferred by salarymen) to camouflage green. There are cheap and cheerful "power carrots" for people who want to do nothing more than chat. There are "pocket boards" for people who want to swap short messages. And there are "smart phones," such as the I-mode, that allow you to organize your life (address books and schedules are the least of it), consult the Internet, and check your e-mail.

Most of the people who crowd around the displays already have mobile phones: The salarymen carry them in holsters hanging from their belts, while many of the schoolgirls wear them around their necks. ("My phone is an extension of myself," says one, giggling.) But some of them are interested in upgrading to the newest model—or at least dreaming about it—while others simply want to personalize the phones they have. The shop also boasts a melody machine that allows you to change your dial tone to, for instance, the latest popular song: "Girls Be Ambitious" by True Kiss Destination was a particular favorite in 1999.

The Japanese are ardent fans of their mobile phones, but they are not unique. The Germans talk about their "handies"; the Singaporeans call them "prawns," because a popular model looked like one when opened; the Finns call them *kännykkä* or känny, meaning an extension of the hand. In eight countries, more than one third of the population owns mobile phones, with the figure reaching almost 100 percent among Scandinavian men in their twenties. In Hong Kong, the industry is already pushing the idea that any well-presented person has to have different mobile phones for different occasions. A decade ago, there were only around ten million mobile phones. By 2002, there were more than one billion of them, and their number would soon overtake that of wired phones.

Increasingly, the mobile-phone industry is going not just digital but high-speed digital with Internet access. The next few years will see the matings of three devices—mobile telephones, computers, and personal organizers—in order to create a single handheld device. As the number of wireless devices with Internet access increases, such devices might have a dramatic effect on the expansion of the Web in places such as Japan. Despite the slow transmission speeds, tiny screens, and inconvenient keyboards of many current devices, a surprising amount of mobile traffic is already data rather than speech. Finnish teenagers communicate as much by short messages (which are extremely cheap) as by talk. In Japan, the airwaves clog up at 10 P.M. with teenagers sending good-night messages to one another.

Smart phones are already allowing users to change how they use locations. Because such phones know where you are, they can provide you with information about that place. Go into a shopping center in Hong Kong, and your phone can inform you where to get the best deals on everything from meals to Gucci loafers. Go into a bar and it will tell you—provided you have signed up for the dating service—whether there is anybody there matching your requirements. Soon, such products will be offered globally.

On balance, there is more reason to be gung ho about mobile phones than about the PC-based Internet. Yet technodeterminists should also note that the field is equally prey to government interference. Of course, the gadgets have over time become smaller, cheaper, and more useful, but Japan's love affair with them, for example, dates from the 1994 removal of an absurd law that forbade Japanese from owning cellular handsets, forcing those who wanted them to rent them for a prohibitive thousand dollars a year instead. The spread of mobile phones is also usually linked to the amount of competition. In Asia, six of the nine biggest markets have at least five cellular firms. In much of Latin America, by contrast, cellular prices are as much as ten times those of local landline calls because governments have been reluctant to take on the established monopolies.

If you want an indication of how much regulation can hold globalization back, look no further than the United States. America is the world's largest single market for mobile phones, with eighty million subscribers at the end of 1999, but as a proportion of the population (30 percent), this is low. Americans have to put up with abysmal service (particularly in big cities at peak times) and exorbitant "roaming" charges, and (this really causes a laugh in Helsinki) they even have to pay for incoming as well as outgoing calls. The world's technological powerhouse is anywhere from two to four years behind the sluggards in Europe—something underlined in 2000 by the record-setting merger of Britain's Vodafone and Germany's Mannesmann.

The blame for this lies in a series of bizarre decisions. Congress took years to auction off digital spectrums in the first half of the nineties. Rather than uniting around one digital standard, such as Europe's GSM, America has several competing ones. Most other countries issue national cellular licenses, but the Federal Communications Commission (FCC) carved out 734 cellular markets the first time it auctioned off spectrum and 544 more the second time.

All this implies that Arthur C. Clarke has been proved right again: The conquest of location is some way off, but it will still happen. Iridium, a global satellite-based phone service, may have been one of the great business disasters of the 1990s, but the vision that inspired the company—allowing people to remain in contact wherever they go in the world—is not that far from realization. Already the industry is pushing for a common "third-generation" standard for digital phones that can be used everywhere. In fact, it is probably only a matter of time before the term *mobile phone* becomes redundant, because there won't be any other sort around. Many young people already see no point in paying for a fixed line when their lives are so peripatetic; as the price differential between fixed and cellular services disappears, this inclination will spread to the rest of the population, too. The time is not very far off when people will find it hard to understand why you ever had to call a place to talk to a person.

Let Them Eat Wireless

In the meantime, wireless technology is allowing the world's poorest people to plug themselves into the global economy, with huge benefits to their standard of living. Four-fifths of the world's mobile-phone subscribers still live in the rich world, but by far the fastest growth in mobile-phone ownership is in the developing world. By 2002, the mobile boom had finally helped push the least developed countries above the threshold of one phone subscriber per one hundred inhabitants.

In the rich world, people tend to use mobile phones because they are convenient. In much of the developing world, they use them because they are the only types of phones available: There are forty million people currently waiting for fixed-line telephones. In places such as Russia and Moldavia, the average wait is ten years; in isolated areas, the wait is an eternity, because it makes no economic sense for any company to lay fixed lines to serve only a handful of people. Not that long ago, hardly anybody in China had access to a phone. Now China is the world's second-biggest market for mobile phones. The average Chinese subscriber spends four hundred minutes on the phone each month, three times as much as the average American. In April 2002, a GSM wireless system was launched in Afghanistan.

Unlike landline firms, cellular operators do not have to dig holes in the ground and lay expensive copper wire to get to poor or isolated customers. "You simply put up the masts and you are in business," says Nape Maepa, South Africa's head telecommunications regulator. In Argentina, it took Lucent Technologies just five months to install eight hundred base stations in some of the remotest bits of the country—enough to bring telephone service to half a million previously isolated people. Foreign telecommunications firms have also been prepared to invest in other countries that are not rated by investment services, such as Cambodia, the Democratic Republic of the Congo, and Rwanda.

Mobile phones are also easier to tailor to poor lifestyles. Rather than employ the standard fixed-line process of issuing monthly bills, wireless companies often work with prepaid cards. The price of a mobile handset is still steep, of course, but its cost and the service-connection fee is lower than the installation charge for a new fixed line in many developing countries (assuming you can get one). And mobile costs—like those of all things digital—are coming down all the time.

Bangladesh is a telephone desert: There is only one fixed-line phone for every 275 people (compared with one for every fifty in neighboring India), and about 90 percent of the country's sixty-eight thousand villages have no access to a phone whatsoever. This is changing thanks to a new breed of entrepreneur: "phone ladies" who rent out time on mobile phones. The ladies buy state-of-the-art cell phones for as much as $375 using loans made available by the Grameen Bank, a private firm that specializes in microlending. Since it started in 1997, the program has supplied three hundred villages with phones. In five years' time, everybody in the country should be within two kilometers of a mobile phone.

For Bangladeshi farmers, the phones provide liberation from middlemen. Rather than having to accept a broker's price, Bangladeshi farmers go to the phone ladies to find out the fair value of their rice and vegetables. The cocoa and coffee farmers of the Ivory Coast used to sell their products to middlemen in Abidjan and Yamoussoukro at a fraction of their market value, because isolation and illiteracy meant that they knew no better. Now they club together to buy mobile phones so that they can check the current prices of cocoa and coffee on the London commodity markets and get a better deal.

Wireless Is Tireless

It might be a stretch to claim that all the technological elements that are bringing the world together are present in Jackson Thubela's phone shop in Soweto, but most of them are there in some form or other. To begin with, the phone shop itself is that quintessential symbol of globalization, an old shipping container. Though Thubela, a gold-toothed twenty-year-old who often wears an Adidas tracksuit, cannot muster an air-conditioning unit, there is at least an electric fan; and the pictures of rappers such as Tùpac Shakur and Wu-Tang Clan might make some Americans feel that they were in a teenager's bedroom. For some reason, many of the customers who throng Thubela's shop are neatly dressed flight attendants—reminders of the importance of transportation. And, of course, tethered with a chain to each of the makeshift cubicles is the shop's main product: a mobile phone.

Soweto contains a remarkable number of phone shops, which rent out time on the phone. Thubela used to have landline phones, but they kept breaking down—largely because thieves made off with the copper wire— and the old landline monopoly, Telkom, did not bother to send people to fix them. The mobile phones, he insists, are much better. After school hours, the lines can be ten people long. The phone business provides Thubela with a reasonable living (which he supplements by selling loose cigarettes) and also attracts a number of other businesses. A cobbler has set up shop just outside the container. Next to him, a man in Muslim dress sells individual sweets.

When the previous South African government licensed two firms, Vodacom and Mobile Telephone Networks Holdings (MTN), to provide digital service in 1993, it insisted that they install thirty thousand pay phones in underserved areas over the following five years. Vodacom estimates that in the process it has created as many as five thousand jobs in local communities. The companies have even installed phones in areas that are so remote. that the devices have to be powered by car batteries and solar energy.

Soweto has not only a vast network of phone shops (one of the best kept is just opposite Nelson Mandela's first house) but also a growing number of black South Africans who have bought their own mobile phones. Pratty Mphuthi is not a rich woman. She has raised four daughters on her own and now runs a sports bar and catering business. But she has a mobile phone of her own (a tiny Motorola), as do three of her four daughters, including her nine-year-old. "A mobile phone is a necessity if you are a busy person," she explains. The phone not only allows her customers to contact her when she is on the move but also means that her nine-year-old can tell her if she has to stay late at school for extra lessons.

Plenty of people who are much poorer than Mphuthi is also have phones. In many areas of Johannesburg, the streets are lined with homemade signs offering basic services such as housepainting or gardening that include cellphone numbers. Often, several poor people club together to buy a phone and a phone card. Even after the card runs out, they can continue to receive incoming calls for nothing.

It is a very long way from Soweto to Marcus de Ferranti's house. In Soweto, horses and cows still wander nonchalantly down the side streets, and most of the expensive cars are being carted off to chop shops to be torn apart for spare parts. Yet Ferranti and Thubela are part of the same revolution. Indeed, Ferranti's customers include not just phone firms from the third world but also the Western world's closest equivalent to phone shops: small companies, based in immigrant-rich cities such as Bradford, that offer special phone services and calling cards for people to phone home.

More fundamental, both Ferranti and Thubela have found that they can acquire a remarkable number of customers by going with the grain of modern technology and against the telecommunications establishment. Both see themselves primarily as entrepreneurs, working from home or a trailer in the street, rather than loyal company men. And both men are using technology, in their different ways, to make the world a much smaller place.

3

The Dirty Dollar

VISITING SOUTH KOREA at the end of 1998 was rather like visiting a once-proud friend who has suddenly been engulfed by a profound identity crisis. Eighteen months previously, South Korea had boasted one of the world's most admired economies, and its big industrial conglomerates, the *chaebol*, were being hailed as new models of corporate development. By the end of 1997, in the wake of the collapse of the Thai baht, the value of South Korea's currency (the won) had been halved, the *chaebol* were pleading with bankers for credit, and the government had been forced to beg fifty-eight billion dollars from the IMF. Throughout 1998, the misery continued: The economy contracted by nearly 8 percent, some of the country's best-known companies went bankrupt, and industrial production suffered its biggest drop since the Bank of Korea started keeping statistics in 1953.

The most dramatic place to see the effects of the resulting identity crisis was on the border with North Korea. The South has long reserved its bravest face for the border. The road from Seoul to the demilitarized zone is one of the finest in the country—a many-laned highway that is meant to symbolize both the South's economic might and the belief that the country will eventually be unified again. The air at the border is filled with the sounds of jaunty pop songs doing battle with the North's martial hymns. One giant billboard proclaims the South a "land of opportunity." Another reads simply, "ten million cars."

Even in December 1998, few of the South Koreans who visited the DMZ seemed tempted to heed the invitations from Kim Jong Il, broadcast every few minutes over loudspeakers, to "come join us in paradise." Yet the face that South Korea turned northward was not as brave as it once had been. A guide to the border zone admitted rather shamefacedly that his country had just taken down a billboard that had boasted of a national per-capita average income of more than ten thousand dollars. The young soldiers admitted that they were worried about their futures. After military service and university, many could have expected a safe billet in one of the *chaebol*. Now they thought their best chances lay in getting jobs with foreign companies. Several had friends who were suffering from a fate that had been unknown in their country a year previously: life on the dole.

This identity crisis was evident throughout the country. One moment you were shown the sparkling new financial district; the next, Seoul Station, a granite edifice that is home to a growing number of homeless people. The air was thick with disturbing stories: The staff of one hospital in Seoul, for example, turned up to work only to find that the place had gone bankrupt and everything—including the beds—had been removed by creditors. Ordinary people alternated between vainglory and humility, between foreigner bashing and foreigner worship, with disconcerting rapidity. Koreans sometimes blamed their misfortunes on foreigners, particularly foreign currency speculators and bankers. But on the other hand, they thought that foreigners held the keys to solving their country's problems. The number of children enrolled in language classes had shot up since the economic crisis began.

One foreign institution attracted the most angst. An easy way to meet an untimely death in Seoul would have been to wander into a bar late at night and casually mention that you work for the International Monetary Fund. When the IMF first put its rescue package in place, huge crowds of strikers—some of them wearing bandannas emblazoned with the slogan IMF = I'M FIRED—packed the streets of the big cities. One television program was about "IMF orphans"—children who were being brought up in state orphanages because their parents had either committed suicide or abandoned them in the wake of the crisis. (The number has reportedly trebled.) Journalists dub the recent period of national humiliation "the IMF era." Pop psychologists diagnosed a condition called "IMF phobia."

On the other hand, even in 1998, the Koreans had plainly begun to take to heart the institution that has brought them so much misery. It seemed as if every other restaurant and shop in Seoul was festooned with a banner on which the only roman letters were *IMF*. "IMF menus" were the cheapest menus. "IMF shopping" meant discount shopping. An "IMF meeting" was a cheap date, on which the partners "go Dutch." One of the restaurants opposite Seoul Station had simply changed its name to IMF.

Even an outsider had to admit that the country's schizophrenia was actually fairly logical. South Korea had every reason to think that it had been kicked in the teeth by its friends in Western finance. In 1960, the country had a per-capita GDP equivalent to that of Algeria and its third-largest export was wigs. In the following decades, it had become the world's eleventh-largest economy, with an income per head equal to Portugal's. South Korea had been admitted to the Organisation for Economic Co-operation and Development (OECD), the rich person's club. Throughout the mid-1990s, the IMF repeatedly sang the country's praises, and the World Bank went into ecstasies about its educational system. The international money markets gave it a higher credit rating than they gave to IBM.

From this perspective, the only thing that changed in 1997 was that another Asian country, Thailand, got into trouble, and the foreign bankers who had once fallen over each other to lend to the *chaebol* panicked. The underlying economy did not change; nor did the *chaebol*. The previously heralded economic tiger became a symbol of "crony capitalism" for no better reason than that the markets suddenly changed. The *chaebol*'s long involvement in political corruption, previously barely mentioned in the glowing IMF reports, suddenly obliterated in importance all the figures lauding per-capita income and record microchip production. Suddenly, South Korean companies that had been able to cover their debts easily were asked to pay back twice as much (because the won had been halved). How, asked South Koreans, could any firm survive in such conditions?

The markets' attitude was not just fickle but downright hypocritical. Look, argued the South Koreans, at Long-Term Capital Management, an American hedge fund that was bailed out by its friends on Wall Street, while decent Korean firms were allowed to go the wall. The IMF's policies only exacerbated the crisis and also paved the way for Western firms to swoop in and buy cheap Korean ones. Meanwhile, as 1999 dawned, both the stock market and the currency began to recover—proof, if any was needed, that the international capital markets had briefly lost their heads.

Many parts of this story are, indeed, hard to contest. The markets plainly exaggerated first Korea's might, then its weakness. The IMF also deployed its tactics badly. But it was also clear, even to South Koreans in late 1998, that foreign capital markets were not solely to blame. The financial crisis had also revealed that much was rotten in Korea. Many South Koreans had long been uneasy about the country's social contract, under which most citizens traded a certain amount of political and economic liberty in exchange for security, guaranteed by a slightly corrupt oligarchy. In December 1998, the realization grew that this oligarchy was not just hopelessly corrupt but also not terribly clever.

South Korea's leaders had tried to buck the system—to get half pregnant, as several observers put it. The country had opened up its markets to foreign capital yet refused to regulate them according to foreign standards or to let foreign banks take over domestic ones. In 1996, South Korean banks showed bad-loan ratios accounting for just 1 percent of the country's lending, forcing outsiders to guess how much higher the true figure was. The *chaebol* had used their political connections to bully banks into lending them far too much cheap money. They had diversified into far too many unrelated activities—what exactly is the connection between building offices and making underwear, for example?—and their enthusiasm for endless cross-subsidies meant that even the healthiest companies could be dragged down by their sick subsidiaries. Entrepreneurial young firms had never had room to grow.

A fair if brutal self-examination was led by Kim Dae Jung, a longtime dissident who two decades before had been sentenced to death but who had been elected president at the same time that the reverberation from Thailand struck South Korea. Kim possessed a Thatcherite commitment to root-and-branch reform. He denounced the "collusive link between politicians and businessmen"; lamented "government influence over finance"; and promised to end the system of "government-controlled economic growth." He led a wide-ranging campaign for economic liberalization. A welcome mat was put out for foreign companies. State-owned industries were privatized. The *chaebol* were ordered to concentrate on their core businesses through a sort of giant swap meet. Small businesses were encouraged. For Kim, openness to foreign capital was a matter not just of money but of democracy.

Some Like It Hot

The South Koreans were not alone in their plight. Some of the most memorable images of the past decade have been provided by people grappling desperately with the harsh logic of "the markets." In Britain on September 16, 1992, an ashen-faced Norman Lamont, Chancellor of the Exchequer, emerged from the Treasury looking rather like a hunted badger and explained that the global capital markets had driven the stately pound out of the European Monetary System. On January 12, 1999, the president of Brazil took refuge in a public lavatory at the São Paulo airport, took out his mobile phone, and told the governor of the central bank to run up the white flag: The country's currency was to be devalued the next morning. In 2002, Argentines rioted in angry frustration at the collapse of the peso.

The best piece of street theater was provided by Vladimir Zhirinovsky during Bill Clinton's visit to Moscow in September 1998. As the Clintons prepared to go to bed, the reactionary Russian appeared outside their hotel to denounce them. After a few earthy remarks about Monica Lewinsky, Zhirinovsky shouted to the jet-lagged president, "Your dollar is dirt, and this dirt is all over the world." He then produced a dollar and demanded that his entourage burn it. They duly did.

Everything about global capital markets seems to be breaking records these days. The amount of capital in circulation is greater than ever before. The speed of movement is faster, the ratio of capital to traded goods bigger, and the consequences of a mistake more devastating. But, as the experience of South Korea shows, figures probably underestimate the impact of the capital markets on the world. The markets are not just wiring economies together and altering the structures of companies but changing entire political systems. How new is this phenomenon? How complete is it? And is it something that we should fear or praise?

Of course, it has long been possible to trade goods, but being able to move billions of dollars around the world at the touch of a button is new. Technology has revolutionized capital markets more dramatically than almost any other part of the economy. News programs may still illustrate their reports on the money markets with scenes of hollering traders, but most transactions take place silently, at the touch of a computer key. Indeed, one reason for the wave of mergers and acquisitions that has swept through the banking industry arises from the need to pay for all the high-tech equipment that modern finance demands, as well as for people who can understand it. If you want to find a world-class mathematician nowadays, you might find him at Goldman Sachs sooner than at MIT.

Inevitably, financial firms are now among the world's most global organizations. Most traders and bankers spend more time on the phone to people they have never met on the other side of the world than they do speaking with their spouses. This internationalization has not always been a comfortable experience: Deutsche Bank lost a fortune because of one misguided fund manager in its London office, and the Baring family lost their bank because of another in Singapore. But such events seem to have only stiffened the resolve of their peers.

The "masters of the universe" often assume that the globalization of finance is inevitable. In 1998, when Citibank and Travelers Group merged to form Citigroup, their minds were on access to financial consumers in Asia, Latin America, and Europe as much as on those in the United States. During the merger discussions, one of the bankers asked aloud, "Can anyone stop us?" There was a long pause, and then somebody ventured, "NATO."

In a world where even *The People's Daily*, the organ of China's Communist Party, carries a weekly financial supplement, this sort of chutzpah is understandable. But in fact the liberalization of the capital markets is both relatively recent and incomplete. At Bretton Woods, national economies were linked together by trade in goods, while capital flows were limited to those necessary to finance that trade. After the war, many governments erected two sorts of barriers: *capital controls*, a term that strictly speaking refers just to things that affect a country's capital account in its balance of payments, such as foreigners buying businesses or shares in the country; and foreign-exchange controls, which affect how an exporter uses the foreign currency that his exports earn.

Worse, as we have seen in South Korea, many countries added a third barrier: a set of controls, either formal or informal, on their own banking system. The postwar social consensus relied on financiers following the national will. Bankers acted more like court treasurers than masters of the universe. In return for being protected from foreign competition, they agreed to act as instruments of national policy. In Japan and its Asian imitators, bankers plowed money into export-related industries; even in the United States, banks were far more interested in national than international affairs. In 1960, for example, only eight of the 13,126 banks in the United States had their own permanent foreign operations.[1]

This world, in which people needed to have their passport stamped if they carried foreign currency, lasted a long time. Some countries got rid of trade-related foreign-exchange controls in the 1960s, and financiers managed to elude other controls by setting up Euromarkets in which banks took deposits and made loans in foreign currencies. But even after the fixed-exchange-rate system broke down in the early 1970s, many rich countries did not loosen their capital controls for another decade—at about the same time that Latin American countries, responding to their debt crises, reapplied them. According to the IMF, 144 countries still had controls on foreign direct investment in 1997, and 128 imposed rules on international financial transactions.[2]

Meanwhile, barriers against foreign financial institutions are even more plentiful. South Korea was only one of a number of countries that spent the

1990s greedily eating up foreign capital yet restricting the role of foreign banks in its domestic markets. Thailand and Indonesia pursued exactly the same policy. In the mid-1990s, foreign-owned banks accounted for roughly one in twenty of the loans made in those countries—about the same as in India. In Japan, the proportion was even lower. Even after the disasters of 1997 and 1998, when their financial systems were desperate for foreign support, many Asian governments found that their regulations prevented them from allowing foreigners to take over banks and brokerages.

An Investor's Dream

How does all this add up? From an economist's point of view, there is no single, integrated global capital market. Even during the 1990s, only 10 percent of investment in emerging countries was financed from abroad. Indeed, some economic historians use current-account statistics to argue that capital is less mobile today than it was one hundred years ago.[3]

From a trader's point of view, there are also gaps. Foreign exchange is now an extremely liquid market, at least as far as the major currencies are concerned, and the international debt markets are not that far behind. But the market for equities is still often frustratingly illiquid: Prices are volatile, information murky, and transactions difficult to clear. Even the Asian contagion took some time to earn the accolade "global." Despite all those twenty-four-hour markets, it took a whole year for the tremors from the currency devaluation in Bangkok in July 1997 to cause the earthquake in Moscow, and another year and a half to affect Brazil.

These, however, are demanding standards. From the point of view of a businessperson, investor, or politician, the trend is fairly clear: Capital now moves around the world much more easily than it ever has before. "The electronic herd," as Thomas Friedman of *The New York Times* has dubbed the market, may not be able to run quite as freely as he and other optimists believe—there are still fences, even a few regulatory canyons, that either restrict or slow its movement—but the area it can trample (or productively graze upon) has definitely increased.

One reason for this is that financial regulators have discovered that, in the rich world at least, he who takes down his fences fastest prospers most. Throughout the 1980s, pressure mounted on the City of London to follow Wall Street's lead and embrace deregulation, known as "Big Bang." Many old-school types forecast ruin if the City got rid of its traditional distinction between brokers and jobbers; they also regarded electronic trading floors as an unpleasant American innovation. In fact, Big Bang proved to be a bonanza both for the old partnerships that scrambled to sell themselves to outsiders, often foreigners, at outrageous prices (the Home Counties saw a tidal wave of swimming pools built on the profits) and for the City. London consolidated its grip not just on the foreign-exchange market but also on international equities. The value of international share trading on the stock exchange is rising toward two trillion dollars a year, a third more than the turnover in British shares. Now Continental exchanges have rushed to imitate this success; indeed, for a while Frankfurt stole a march on London in options trading.

Even Japan has caught the deregulatory bug. "Something finally changed in the mid-1990s," argues Yoshihiko Miyauchi.[4] Miyauchi, a scholarly-looking, bespectacled figure, is a good example of a species found in financial markets around the world: a liberal who owes much of his success to the fact that his country's financial establishment has not listened to him. During the 1980s, at the peak of Japan's success, Miyauchi was one of the few businesspeople to chafe about the country's "semisocialist" taxation policy and the insular nature of its financial establishment. The upstart company he built, Orix, pioneered leasing and consumer finance in Japan— an area neglected by the big banks and securities houses. By remaining outside Japan's financial club, Orix had to contend with all sorts of anomalies, such as not being able to issue commercial paper to finance its loans. Rather, its success has been largely a matter of attitude and flexibility: It was one of the first companies in Japan to introduce share options for managers, and it is one of the few Japanese financial institutions listed on the New York Stock Exchange.

As markets have loosened up, Miyauchi has moved into more areas, snapping up a banking license by buying part of the defunct Yamaichi Securities and starting a telephone-sales operation to sell life insurance. Increasingly, his rivals are not Japan's somewhat stodgy banks and securities houses but foreigners with the same punchy attitude as Orix, such as GE Capital, Fidelity Investments, and Merrill Lynch. These are powerful names, but Miyauchi seems unconcerned. He regards the arrival of the foreigners as a good thing in principle. (Indeed, as the head of the government's new deregulation committee, he has campaigned for it.) He also thinks that Japan's financial market still remains extraordinarily underdeveloped. Only one in ten Japanese firms uses lease finance. And most Japanese still keep their savings, which total some ten trillion dollars, in bank accounts that yield only slightly better interest rates than stashing the money under the bed. "There is," Miyauchi notes dryly, "some room for improvement."

The Freedom of Mutual Funds

This points to the main force behind the growth of the international capital market: the investor. In places such as South Korea, concepts such as "popular capitalism" and "shareholder democracy" might ring a little hollow, but throughout the developed world, an increasing number of relatively poor people have been buying shares and liking the results.

When waitresses ask, as they put down your cappuccino, whether they should short Dell, it is tempting to abandon all faith in capitalism. But whatever the madness of day traders brings in the short term, buying shares is now both cheap (a trade now costs only about three cappuccinos) and easy. Which would take you longer, buying one hundred shares of IBM on-line or programming your VCR?

In America, mutual funds now have more money in them than either pension funds or insurers and roughly the same amount as banks. In Europe, where people are gradually getting used to the idea that they will have to save for their retirements themselves rather than rely on an overextended welfare state, there is a growing interest in equities, which have delivered the best long-term results. America's stock-market capitalization is roughly one and a half times its GDP; in Europe, each stock market is worth around half of its country's output. One in two American households owns shares or mutual funds. In France, the figure is 15 percent; in Italy just over 10 percent; and in Germany even less.[5] Even if the number of shareholders on the Continent merely increases to British levels, where about one in four people own shares, the capital markets will expand hugely.

And, in time, this should bring the world closer together. Even with the memory of the financial turmoil of 1997–1998 still lingering, it seems likely that investors will gradually put more of their money outside their country's borders. The long-term prospects for growth in South Korea and its neighbors still comfortably outstrip those for America or Europe. Before the new Eurozone came into being at the start of 1999, investors in the four main European countries kept at least 85 percent of their money at home. As a result, most German investors had no shares in the oil industry, just as most Dutch people had no shares in the car industry; now they are more likely to buy Royal Dutch/Shell and Daimler-Benz respectively. Flemings, a British investment bank, reckons that it could take two decades for the new pool of money (which it puts at nine trillion dollars) to be fully Europeanized.

A Capital Democracy

From the perspective of somebody sitting in, say, SBC Warburg Dillon Read's sixty-five-thousand-square-foot trading floor in Stamford, Connecticut, the deregulation of Western financial centers and the growth in the number of international investors add up to a single unstoppable force. But in many parts of the emerging world, there are plenty of people who feel far less gung ho about liberalization, and there are also a surprising number of critics in the temples of Mammon. "Instead of acting like a pendulum," George Soros testified to Congress, "financial markets have recently acted like a wrecking ball, knocking over one country after another."[6] So our final argument for why the capital markets will continue to bring the world closer together is also the most controversial: Basically, they work—even in places such as South Korea.

The arguments about capital flows are complicated, but they usually come down to balancing one clear advantage against several disadvantages and qualifications. The advantage of financial liberalization is clearly efficiency. Countries that get rid of capital controls and liberalize their banking systems see more efficient investment because markets allocate money better than bureaucrats do. Research by the Milken Institute has demonstrated that economies fare best when capital is cheap, plentiful, and, just as important, allocated fairly.[7] The institute ranked emerging markets in terms of the openness of their capital markets. The top three places went to Asian countries that survived the financial crisis with the least damage done: Singapore, Taiwan, and Hong Kong. The bottom four places went to Indonesia, South Korea, Russia, and Bulgaria, all of which, with the exception of Bulgaria, were devastated by the crisis.

Nevertheless, the case for the free flow of capital is much less straightforward than that for free trade in goods. Markets for goods and services are reasonably predictable; financial markets are horribly volatile. Much depends on the amount of information in investor's hands, and even well-informed decisions are often motivated not just by economic fundamentals but by what investors imagine other investors will do—in other words, by a herd instinct. It is all very well to argue that South Korea recovered very quickly, but that only prompts the question of whether it needed to go through quite so much hell in the first place. Chile is often cited as a paragon of free trade that nevertheless has some controls on short-term investment. China, too, has seen substantial growth without loosening its capital controls.

It is notable that although it is hard to find any respected economist who opposes free trade, several—notably Dani Rodrik of Harvard University

and Jagdish Bhagwati of Columbia—are much more skeptical about the
benefits of the free movement of capital.[8] There is also a fairly large group
of people, including Paul Krugman, who think that capital controls can be
an attractive temporary cure for countries that get into a currency crisis.
Such controls can give a country time to fight off recession by loosening its
monetary and fiscal policies, without setting off a huge flight of foreign
money.

On balance, we disapprove of capital controls, especially as a long-term
policy—but it is an awkward case to make. Capital markets (rather like the
postcrisis South Koreans) suffer from something of a split personality. In one
guise, capital is splendidly, even ruthlessly, rational. Gregory Millman has
nicely compared traders such as Andy Krieger and investors such as George
Soros to the bounty hunters of the Old West, "who enforce the law, not for
love of law, but for profit" and who administer "economic justice."[9] As Walter Wriston, the former chairman of Citibank, puts it, "Money goes where it
wants and stays where it is well treated." Watching Black Monday in Britain
or the collapse of the peso in Argentina was like watching a *Terminator* film:
The machine could not tolerate human weakness.

Yet, at other times, this same relentlessly robotic creature can be just as
neurotic as any character yet invented by Woody Allen. Only the most Pan-
glossian free-marketeer would deny that capital markets can sometimes get
things wrong. The history of markets is dotted with speculative manias from
the Dutch tulip mania of the seventeenth century to the frenzy that preceded
the 1929 crash. A century ago, Wall Street was arguably as prone to crashes
as emerging Asia is today. The gold standard that lasted from 1870 to 1914
came under repeated speculative attacks from investors.

The markets have repeatedly misjudged emerging economies. The capital
that poured into Seoul (just like the money that flowed into Moscow and
Bangkok) spurred the construction of a lot of extravagant buildings and
convinced an army of company managers and government bureaucrats
that they could get away with borrowing short-term money. In Argentina,
the currency board continued to be seen as a boon long after it had in fact become a threat. At the same time, emerging economies are feeble things when
set beside the might of the global capital markets. Paul Volcker is fond of
pointing out that the entire Argentine banking system in the mid-1990s
was worth less than the third biggest bank in Pittsburgh.

Many of the wildest gyrations of the past five years have been blamed on
the financial world's most ineptly named institutions: hedge funds. There
are about four thousand such funds, most of which exist in unregulated off-

shore markets. They control a total of four hundred billion dollars in equity—which allows them to borrow four or five times that amount—and concentrate for the most part on short-term transactions. Their activities have posed a threat not just to the stability of emerging economies—one fund supposedly had a short position in the bhat that was equivalent to a fifth of Thailand's reserves—but even to the economy of the United States itself. The collapse of Long-Term Capital Management, whose gambles were based on underlying assets worth more than one trillion dollars, caused such a panic in Wall Street and in Washington that a consortium of big banks, egged on by Alan Greenspan, the chairman of the Federal Reserve Board, clubbed together to bail it out.

David Hale, the chief economist for the Zurich Group, points out that this sort of highly leveraged speculative fringe is new to the global capital markets. There were certainly currency crises and financial panics in the nineteenth century, but money could not be flicked across borders at the touch of a button, and international investment, which was driven by about twenty-five thousand European families, was usually longer term and usually based on real assets.[10] On the other hand, singling out hedge funds is unfair. The fallout of the scandal made it clear that many of Long-Term Capital Management's practices were not unique to the world of hedge funds; banks and securities houses all around the world were speculating almost as heavily through their proprietary trading (i.e., gambling) operations.

This is frightening stuff. But in the fog of panic that can surround the discussion of financial markets, it is easy to miss several important distinctions. For instance, it is misleading to treat all the money flowing in and out of emerging markets in the same way. "Foreign direct investment" (i.e., people building new factories) undoubtedly helped to contribute to Asia's economic overexpansion, and the resulting overcapacity is the underlying reason for the deflation that haunts the region. It is also true that "foreign portfolio investment" (i.e., buying shares) helped blow up the Asian bubble by inflating local stock-market prices. But the chief cause of Asia's woes was the third source of capital: debt.

Asian companies borrowed too much short-term money, most of it denominated in foreign currency, in financing their various long-term projects. When banks got nervous about declining foreign-exchange reserves in the lending countries and refused to roll over the loans, the crisis began. Equity investors, by contrast, could not ask for their money back; all they could do was sell, which many did at a loss. The people who actually turned off the tap were bankers, who did so in much the same boring way that they have for

centuries: writing letters and serving notices about clauses in their contracts. With both South Korea and Long-Term Capital Management, banks'
credit-control systems tended to be based on the bear-outside-your-tent
strategy (derived from an old joke: Two people are inside a tent when a bear
begins to shake it. One of them starts putting on his sneakers. "You can't
outrun a bear!" observes the other. "I don't need to," the first replies. "I just
need to outrun you"). Each bank thought that it could get its money out
faster than its rivals could.

Do open capital markets encourage imprudent lending? In essence, there
are two opposing views. One school thinks that capital has become more
dangerous because it has been overprotected. The assumption that the IMF
would bail them out encouraged banks to lend to South Korean companies;
and the U.S. government's deposit insurance encouraged American consumers to deposit their money without checking whether a bank was lending to South Korea. This approach has the advantage of intellectual purity,
but it seems both ill suited to the real world (why should Aunt Agatha with
her savings account know about South Korea?) and slightly blasé about the
prospect of systemic failure.

On the other hand, there is plainly a temptation to go too far in the opposite direction and start constructing all sorts of new financial orders. Many
of the problems with imprudent lending could be solved if, rather than regulating different risk levels, governments embraced the concept of narrow
banking and forced banks to separate the insurable deposit-taking part of
their business from the riskier things that they do. In many cases, a decent
set of accounts would have alerted them to the danger. Long before Enron, a
devastating report on auditing practices in Asia by UNCTAD criticized
Arthur Andersen and other big accounting firms for putting their names to
audit reports that clearly failed to meet international standards. One badly
burned banker in Russia puts it simply: "No Western audited accounts; no
Western money." But this presumes the audits will be accurate.

For many developing countries, better banking and accounting standards would be very helpful, but they are not enough. First, such concern
shows that the rich West is preoccupied with hanging on to its dirty dollar
(and rightly so: a banking collapse in California, let alone Japan, is much
more dangerous to the global financial system than the disintegration of the
entire Malaysian economy). Second, standards alone do not answer developing countries' fundamental grievance: that they opened up their markets
and got slapped in the face for their efforts.

This second point is as mistaken as it is emotionally appealing. Rather than surrendering to the rule of the market, most of the countries were engaged in elaborate attempts to buck it: sticking to unsustainable exchange-rate policies; borrowing too much; refusing to change inadequate standards of accounting and supervision; and, crucially, not opening up their local financial systems to outsiders. Markets need openness, and too much went on behind closed doors. Markets need competition, and too much was decided by collusive cliques. Above all, markets need information, and too little of it was available. Would Thailand or Argentina have collapsed if it had not stuck to its exchange-rate policy? Would South Korea be in such a mess if it had not (staggeringly) discriminated against long-term foreign capital? Would Russia have hit the rocks if it had not handed its government to kleptocrats? We think not.

The travails of 1997–1999 do not invalidate the claim that the most open countries have usually been the most successful. India and China are often cited as successes because they avoided the Asian flu, but they have suffered from much more debilitating diseases instead. As Alan Greenspan pointed out to Congress in September 1998, even the most badly savaged East Asian economies only lost about a sixth of their per-capita growth over the past decade, and their average incomes were still two and a half times those in China and India. Without foreign money and foreign know-how, economies grow more slowly. Chile has always coupled its capital controls with openness to foreign financiers and a transparency in its financial sector that contrasts strongly with the situation in the Asian countries. More than half of Chile's banks are foreign owned.

That still leaves the question of whether temporary capital controls can work in a crisis. The answer is that they can. But a lot depends both on how cleverly the policy is enforced and what exactly the word *temporary* means. It is noticeable that Chile lowered its controls when the Asian contagion was whistling around the world. When Malaysia decided to put Krugman's thesis into action, the economist, far from celebrating this rare triumph for the dismal science, promptly distanced himself from the decision, arguing that controls must be "an aid to reform not an alternative."[11] Not only is there a great danger of cronyism in the short term (if people cannot take their money out legally, they will do so illegally), there is the problem of the long-term impact on foreign investors. Even now that Malaysia has lifted its controls, few investors of any sort are likely to forget that they were trapped—and there are plenty of other places to invest.

In Defense of the Gunslinger

This leaves the argument that capital markets are generally a force for openness. Open markets go hand in hand with open governments and open societies. That does not mean that capitalism automatically favors democracy: Given a choice between a stable authoritarian regime and a crisis-racked liberal one, those greedy young men at the trading terminals would probably put their money on authoritarianism. The same markets that punished President Suharto in 1997 had showered him with gold for years. But in general, as Suharto found out, openness and political stability tend to go together. Open systems of corporate governance discourage managers from making foolish decisions. Open systems of politics prevent a ruling clique from amassing too large a share of the nation's resources. Above all, open systems generate the one thing that markets require to work properly: information.

The capital markets can take some of the credit for several blessings that are now common in most developed countries: low inflation, low interest rates, and (notwithstanding George W. Bush's huge tax cut) shrinking government budget deficits. As well as punishing governments that stray off course, the capital markets also reward the ones that stay on the straight and narrow. For instance, when Sweden's budget deficit reached almost 13 percent of its GDP in 1994, yields on government bonds rose to almost 12 percent. When the government attacked the deficit, the interest rate demanded dropped by about half. Asia shows not only that the capital markets are becoming ever quicker to turn against people but also that they are quicker to forgive. Latin America spent most of the 1980s trying to recover its reputation. By contrast, South Korea was able to issue bonds worth billions of dollars within months of going to the IMF.

More generally, when people think about the capital markets, they usually focus on dealing rooms. But much of their magic is worked in boardrooms. Corporate governance provides the best method we have for holding bosses accountable for their actions. It makes it easier to sack the real duds. It prevents managers from treating a company's money as their own. (Pay may still be out of control in the United States, but the good ol' boys of the boardroom are awarding themselves fewer perks.) In general, it lets a little daylight into what could easily be a completely secret world.

Demands for accountability have even more explosive implications outside the United States. Even in relatively advanced markets, such as France and Germany, old elites have suddenly had to explain what they are doing with other people's money. Nearly two out of three German investors would prefer to have global (i.e., American) corporate governance standards.[12] In France, thousands of ordinary investors have signed up to take courses at a traveling "École de la Bourse" to find out more about their money. In places such as South Korea, the idea of asking the *chaebol* or their equivalents to justify their performance remains a revolutionary concept. To see this struggle at work, let us return to Seoul.

Sweet Seoul Music

Even by the dismal standards of economics departments, Korea University's concrete bunker stands out in its ugliness. Jang Ha Sung, a preppie-looking figure in blue blazer, club tie, and button-down shirt, seems out of place—like a classicist who has been forced to join the squalid world of numbers as part of a bizarre academic experiment. As he works, opera burbles in the background; *The New Harvard Dictionary of Music* nestles next to *Financial Theory and Corporate Policy* on his shelves.

If Jang makes an unlikely economics professor, he makes an even less likely agitator. Yet that is what he is. At shareholder meeting after shareholder meeting, Jang gets up and shouts questions at the *chaebol* chiefs, while supporters from his People's Solidarity Movement taunt the corporate leaders from behind him. Jang also has to put up with boos and hisses from the *chaebol*'s henchmen, but that seems a small price to pay. Not long ago, shareholder meetings were about as rowdy as a party congress in the communist North; often the entire agenda was wrapped up in only a few minutes. Now Jang and his allies regularly keep the business elite onstage for hours on end.

For Jang, the movement to open up Korea's businesses is part of a broader movement to open up its political life. Company chairmen, he complains, act like kings, plundering company property to enrich their families, transferring resources from one company to another, and making idiotic decisions without fear of reprimand. Many suspect that Jang has long-term political ambitions: He comes from a family of politicians, and People's Solidarity is backed by several leading reformers. But Jang thinks that political reform is impossible without corporate reform.

As a student of finance at the Wharton School, Jang learned that the purpose of public companies is to increase shareholders' return on their capital and that the purpose of corporate governance is to hold managers accountable. In 1994, he helped to form People's Solidarity, a group two hundred strong that campaigns for liberal reform. At the time, this seemed an impossible cause. Corporate law required that shareholders own 3 percent of a company before they could bring a motion at a shareholders' meeting—a huge hurdle in a country dominated by giant conglomerates. The *chaebol* tried to intimidate Jang, spreading the rumor that he was bent on selling the country's assets to foreigners. People's Solidarity found it so hard to track down shareholders of one of its first targets, the Korea First Bank, that members took to walking the streets with placards asking shareholders to come forward.

Helped by foreign investors, Jang won a few early skirmishes, notably a struggle to force SK Telecom to appoint an independent auditor. But the arrival of the Asian crisis gave him a welcome burst of publicity. The World Bank invited him to speak at its annual meeting; professional shareholder activists started asking him to their conferences; Bill Clinton even invited him to join a discussion group when he visited South Korea in November 1997. Meanwhile, President Kim changed the law, making it easier for foreign shareholders to invest in South Korea; he also changed the regulatory environment. Now Jang needs a stake of just 0.01 percent to bring a motion, and public companies must appoint one quarter of their directors from the outside.

In one way, Jang has already won the war. "Punish conglomerate chiefs!" has become the rallying cry for the huge crowds of Koreans that regularly gather outside the *chaebol*-dominated Federation of Korean Industries. The chiefs themselves have become symbols of profligacy, inefficiency, and nepotism. Capital markets are now open to foreigners. More than a dozen *chaebol* have gone bankrupt. Mighty Daewoo, the second biggest of them all, has been broken up.

Yet the forces ranged against reform are huge. There is no shortage of bureaucrats who think that the creation of what Kim calls a "democratic free-market system" will deprive them of not just their power but also their job security. The big trade unions are nostalgic for the old world. Both trade unionists and bureaucrats are suspicious of the foreigners in whom Kim puts such faith. Kim's government, South Korea's first experiment in coalition rule, is a fragile affair.

Worse, many reforms have proved to be either synthetic or counterproductive. Foreign financial institutions have often been frustrated in their attempts to buy Korean firms. For instance, HSBC's attempt to take over Seoulbank, nationalized in 1998, ran aground because Kim's government refused to have the bank's loans assessed according to international standards. Meanwhile, the attempts to force banks to tighten up their credit control have paradoxically helped the *chaebol*. The banks concentrated their resources on their best-connected clients, convinced that the government would never allow them to go under, while small and medium-sized businesses went bankrupt by the thousands. And, wily as ever, the *chaebol* moved to defend themselves by buying stakes in life insurers, asset managers, and a new class of "merchant banks," which specialize in short-term corporate loans (of just the sort that you might need if you had a slightly dodgy subsidiary that needed cash fast).

All this leaves the visitor to Jang Ha Sung's office with a worrying conclusion for the new century: From a long-term perspective, South Korea—and Asia in general—may have bounced back too quickly. Far from suffering from years of depression and stagnation, the region's stricken economies recovered at a remarkable pace, none more so than South Korea's; indeed, South Korea's GDP in 2001 was nearly a quarter bigger than in 1996. Some of this recovery was due to reforms pushed by people such as Jang, but the biggest contribution came from that buyer of last resort, the American consumer—who cannot buy forever. Even today, South Korea seems to be trying to buck the capital market, welcoming money but still insisting that it plays by the rules of the *chaebol*. Unless that changes, there is always a risk that the crisis that almost sank the country in 1997–1998 will repeat itself, and the national schizophrenia will never go away.

4

The Visible Hand

IN THE LATE 1970s, the General Motors plant in Fremont, near the southern tip of San Francisco Bay, was a symbol of everything that was wrong with the American car industry; it was a perennial victim of slowdowns, sickouts, and strikes. The workers hated the bosses, the bosses despised the workers, and the two had as little to do with each other as possible. Absenteeism ran at 20 percent. The company's parking lot became a bazaar, featuring hookers, drugs, and barbecued food; the factory was so full of marijuana smoke that you could get high just by doing your job. One GM worker recalled,

> There was shit all over the place. The parking lot was covered with broken glass. It looked like a diamond field in the morning sunlight. Busted beer and whiskey bottles all over the place! It looked like pigs lived [t]here. People would sit wherever they wanted and read books, eat, and play radios. I remember working on a car that was full of chicken bones left over from a guy's lunch. Nobody cared.[1]

In 1982, GM's managers finally gave up the struggle, closing down the four-million-square-foot plant and throwing its employees on the dole. Yet two years later, the plant was back in business with a new name—New United Motor Manufacturing, Inc. (NUMMI)—and a new ethos. General Motors had decided to use the plant as a laboratory for the introduction of Japanese manufacturing techniques into the United States. It formed a joint venture with Toyota and gave the Japanese company a free hand to introduce the same "lean production" methods that it had used to such astonish-

ing effect at home. Toyota divided the workers up into teams, requiring them
to check their own work rather than leaving oversight to the quality department; it forced managers to work on the floor; it cut back the huge inventory
of parts, switching to suppliers that delivered just in time.

The result was a dramatic increase in productivity. By 1994, the plant
was producing the same number of cars that it had produced in 1982 but
with just 65 percent of the workforce. And this time the cars worked. J. D.
Power rated the factory's Geo Prism as one of the best American cars ever
built. NUMMI exported more than four hundred million dollars' worth of
cars, including twenty-six thousand Corollas to Taiwan, as well as seventy-
eight million dollars' worth of car parts to Japan. It acted as a magnet for
dozens of parts suppliers, anxious not only to get its business but also to
learn "lean production." As Detroit began to restructure (Ford and Chrysler
each closed roughly 40 percent of their American capacity in the 1980s;
General Motors axed 25 percent), surviving factories copied Toyota's ideas.
Nowadays, every car factory carries NUMMI's imprint in one way or another—so much so that when you visit Fremont, it no longer feels particularly special.

But this is only the beginning of the story. From Britain to Thailand, Toyota has acted as a schoolmaster to the world's car industry. It is hard to think
of a big manufacturer anywhere in the world that has not studied the Japanese carmaker in depth, as have scores of service companies and public-sector
organizations. And the standards are always getting higher. Toyota itself
has recently turned to Ford to learn how to improve relations between its engineers and its shop-floor workers, and to Chrysler to learn about "value
engineering," a new method of speeding up production by using interchangeable components in different models.

Nor is it just a matter of Japan and America: Arguably the most advanced
car manufacturing country in the world is Brazil. At first sight, GM's factory
in São Caetano do Sul on the outskirts of São Paulo, looks quaint rather than
revolutionary. The factory is an old one, with an attractive main office. But
as its proud managers point out, it is one of the most efficient in the world,
for which they credit the fact that most of the local bosses come from
NUMMI. Everything is done to NUMMI standards, indicated by small yellow
triangles with which the workers label their products and record their
progress. Charts around the factory display a seemingly endless array of
lines sloping upward from the time the plant began to introduce Japanese
methods. It used to take 103 minutes to prepare a new set of dies in the
stamping plant; now it takes just four—a standard other GM plants use as a

benchmark. Workers can win six thousand reals for suggesting useful improvements. And so on.

The Brazilians are not just running the NUMMI system better than their peers, they are changing it. In Brazil, GM's outside suppliers now assemble many more of the parts before delivering them to the assembly plants, hugely reducing the number of people it needs to employ to produce each vehicle. The firm is even changing the shape of its factories, replacing the typical American squares with L or T shapes, so that there are more loading docks from which external suppliers can deliver parts directly onto the production line. GM found that it could introduce new midsize cars in just two months in Brazil, compared with seven months in Kansas.[2] GM is also at work on a new plant, called the Blue Macaw project, that will reportedly require even more of the car to be assembled by outside suppliers.

These innovations have had an effect in Detroit and throughout the industry. GM is now run by Richard Wagoner, an American who made his name in Brazil. (However, his attempts to Brazilianize GM were one reason why American workers went on strike in the summer of 1998; see chapter 13.)

The Third Force

The ideas and people that make up this busy trade in management are the third force behind globalization, linking the world together just as surely as the international trade in capital and information does. To be sure, management ideas are arguably just another form of technological know-how, and much of the pressure on companies to adopt them has come from the capital markets. But the internationalization of business practices now has its own momentum, and it is also accelerating. Ideas that were hit upon only in the 1990s, such as reengineering and "economic-value added" methods for analyzing corporate performance, are already practiced worldwide by organizations as diverse as the British Treasury, Universal Studios, Thai Farmers Bank, and Siemens.

This is in part on account of deregulation: Privatization and the elimination of protective rules has forced once-cosseted companies to modernize. At the beginning of the 1990s, there were still some big companies in Continental Europe that disdained "American" fads. Now there are not. Far from being insulted by being labeled "Neutron Jürgen," on account of his ruthless methods, Jürgen Schrempp at DaimlerChrysler has generally taken it as a compliment to be compared to "Neutron Jack" Welch of General Electric.

When Paolo Fresco was plucked out of General Electric to be Fiat's chairman, the Italian company's chief executive, Paolo Cantarella, was asked what his new boss's main contribution would be. He replied, "Fresco's experience from General Electric." If anything, small European companies are even more taken with Yankee capitalism.

Most institutions—both private sector and public—are now fairly ecumenical about the sources of their management ideas: They do not care if a business method was invented by a Canadian management guru such as Henry Mintzberg (who spends half the year teaching at Insead, a European business school) or a Taiwanese computer maker such as Acer. All that matters is that it works. While this could imply that companies are becoming homogeneous, a distinctive culture can be an important source of strength. Nevertheless, an increasing number of routine business operations follow the same patterns just about everywhere, and an increasing number of managers speak the same hideous if efficient language of BPR, TQM, and JIT.

One example of this convergence that is not to everybody's taste concerns executive pay. Notwithstanding the howls of protest in Germany when Chrysler's managers picked up close to one billion dollars when their firm was bought by Daimler-Benz, European and Japanese companies are in general adopting American pay schemes, with hefty share-option packages. This may just be corporate greed, but it reflects the fact that in many industries there is now a global market for talent. In Japan, 160 big companies now have option plans. In Britain, salaries for run-of-the-mill chief executives in large companies now often reach the equivalent of five million dollars, with options and bonuses (still only a quarter of what their American peers might make but an unimaginable figure only a decade ago). Perhaps inevitably, compensation consultants refer to American-style packages as "global pay deals." An alternative view is expressed by Graef Crystal, America's best-known pay expert: "The virus is now spreading around the world."[3]

The Four Horsemen

There are four main disseminators of Crystal's management virus: multinational companies, management consultancies, business schools, and management thinkers.

We have already seen a good example of the first in Toyota and GM. In a knowledge economy, multinational companies are essentially machines for transferring ideas across borders. The United Nations estimates that 70 percent of all international royalties involve payments between parent companies and their subsidiaries. The same is probably true for management ideas. It is common for critics of globalization to argue that multinationals are driven, above all, by the pursuit of cheap hands. Yet even companies that pursue such a crude strategy usually export at least some management know-how. And the most successful multinationals (which are increasingly concentrated in highly skilled areas such as pharmaceuticals and computers) are more interested in access to the world's brains than its hands. The subsidiaries of Japanese firms in the United States typically outspend their American rivals on training.

This sounds a little, well, frivolous, but it is becoming the raison d'être of multinational firms (see chapter 7). Nowadays, they cannot rely on sheer size alone. The arrival of freer capital markets and powerful desktop computers has made it easier for small companies to compete with their bigger rivals, and the march of free trade means that start-ups can break into markets without setting up expensive offices or cultivating cozy relationships with local politicians. But multinationals have at least one advantage over their smaller rivals: They can easily mix and match ideas from around the world. Indeed, the best multinationals are arguably turning themselves into knowledge brokers, skilled at bringing together people who might not otherwise meet: Italian designers and Japanese computer nerds, for example, or Taiwanese advertisers and German chemists.

One of the main ways in which management ideas whip around the globe is through training. European companies such as Nestlé have exported their apprenticeship system to Latin America. A particular favorite model is the in-house "university." Motorola's university has several campuses, including one in Beijing. Nestlé's training center, Rive-Reine, in La Tour de Peilz, trains people from sixty different countries.

Perhaps the most famous of the 1,600 corporate universities in America sits in a pretty stone building by a lake in Oak Brook, Illinois. Laugh, cry, faint: It is hard to imagine how the average cash-starved headmaster or university dean would respond to Hamburger University, with its gleaming lecture halls, new computers, and faculty-sized team of interpreters, ready to translate the lessons into twenty-six languages. The university, which has trained sixty-five thousand "bachelors of hamburgerology," now boasts twenty-five professors and teaches seven thousand students a year. It also sits at the heart of a huge network that includes five overseas campuses and more than one hundred training centers and arguably reaches down into every restaurant. The moment anyone joins McDonald's, he or she is trained in something. By the time they reach Oak Brook, restaurant managers, whether they are from Sri Lanka or Southampton, should have had at least two thousand hours' training.

A lot of the teaching at Hamburger University is of the slightly mundane "And don't forget the fries and Coke" sort. Historically, HU has also focused largely on instructing rather than learning—with all the commands coming from the United States. However, HU's current dean, Rafik Mankarious, an Egyptian turned Australian who is the first non-American to hold the post, is under orders to change that. McDonald's now realizes that its future relies on its foreign restaurants coming up with ideas rather than just being well-disciplined burger-distribution points. Mankarious encourages his students to air their complaints and to swap ideas. McDonald's boss, Jack Greenberg, talks enthusiastically about the time he spends answering questions at each HU course as the "best way of getting information from the field" on everything from the firm's new ten-second toasters to his recent restructuring.

Much of the globalizing drive and energy of multinationals is provided by the management industry: the business schools, consultancies, and gurus. The job of management consultants is to give their clients access to the best business thinking that is currently available worldwide. The past decade has seen consultancies turn themselves into thoroughly global organizations. This transformation is exemplified most clearly by the fact that two of the most venerable American consultancies now have non-American bosses: McKinsey is run by an Indian, Bain by an Israeli. When Rajat Gupta joined McKinsey a quarter of a century ago, the firm he now heads had fifty consultants; now it has four thousand, and its fastest-growing office is in his native India. Bigger still, Accenture (as Andersen Consulting is now called) employs forty thousand people, and has 152 offices in 47 countries. Accenture's training center in Saint Charles, Illinois, which mass produces the famous "Andersen androids" who consult all around the world, is the largest customer of Chicago's O'Hare Airport.

As this implies, consultancies are doing more than just leading thinking on globalization. They are producing a cadre of people who live the global lifestyle more thoroughly than any other modern businesspeople. Consultancies have access to a good proportion of the brightest people that universities are producing. Inevitably, they hire an enormous number of business-school graduates—around a third of the total. But consultancies are so avaricious that they are also scouring Ph.D. programs, medical schools, and even art courses. They then encourage their recruits to become somewhat harassed citizens of the world, or cosmocrats (see chapter 12). Young consultants relocate their families (if they have had time to acquire them) at the bidding of their employers and spend an unenviable portion of their lives on airplanes. But the rewards for this peripatetic lifestyle can be enormous.

Like consultancies, business schools are essentially American inventions. But there is a growing number of good European ones, including Insead, IMD, and the London Business School. And the American schools have tried desperately to internationalize themselves, recruiting more foreign students, forming alliances with foreign universities, and even setting up outposts abroad: The Harvard Business School has numerous tentacles around the world; the University of Chicago Graduate School of Business has a campus in Spain; and MIT's Sloan School has close links with Hong Kong University.

The third engine of the management industry is the gurus themselves—the rock stars of globalization. They provide consultancies and business schools with their best thinking and travel the world peddling their ideas and seeking new ones. The guru with the longest global track record is Peter Drucker, an Austrian-born polymath who internationalized himself early in his career by moving to the United States. Drucker's first management book, *Concept of the Corporation,* a study of General Motors that argued for many of the reforms that were later implemented at NUMMI, turned him into a sage in Japan. Drucker cleverly used his access to Japanese business to popularize Japanese business methods in the United States.

Drucker has since found many imitators (if no peers), an increasing number of whom come from outside America. There are now Japanese business gurus such as Kenichi Ohmae (who explains Japanese business methods to foreigners and foreign business methods to the Japanese) and English business gurus such as Charles Handy (who preaches a gentle style of socially responsible capitalism). Even black South Africans have got in on the global boom with "*ubuntu* management," which blends Western ideas with African traditions such as tribal loyalty.

Worth the Wait

Much as with the capital markets, management theorists will continue to increase in power because, basically, they work. Making this case, however, is controversial. Many leading businesspeople still like to think that most successful management strategies are all their own work. In 1998, Bill Gates reflected that most management books "that try to tell people about the future are really pretty bad." He then cited one of the better management books of the past decade, *Competing for the Future*, which was published in 1994. "The authors are two smart guys. They're probably as good as there is in the field. So what examples did they pick? General Magic. Yeah, they understand the future. Apple Computer? Every example they gave, with the exception of Hewlett Packard, was a total joke."[4] Rupert Murdoch puts it slightly differently: "Guru? You find a gem here or there. But most of it's fairly obvious, you know. You go to [a bookshop's] business section and you see all these wonderful titles and you spend $300 and then you throw them all away."[5]

Such complaints are common. Many of the fads that companies try are misguided; virtually all of them are oversold by the management industry. On the other hand, there are plainly nuggets within management theory that either give real competitive advantage or have become an essential part of remaining in business. Successful management ideas are not just bits of local knowledge, fixed by culture and circumstances; they can travel and, suitably modified, can be used to reproduce that success in other countries and industries; perhaps they can even be melded into a discipline of management that holds lessons for all organizations. The methods that Toyota introduced at NUMMI clearly made a difference, and they are now regarded as the bare operational minimum for an international car factory.

This suggests that the problem with management theory is not that it has turned into a giant industry—with all the attendant problems of overblown fads—but that it has not spread far enough. Nowhere is the danger of building a modern economy without sufficient management science clearer than in developing Asia.

The region has a voracious thirst for management ideas. (Where else can you find earnest young men on a bus, avidly reading magazines with titles such as *Supply Chain Management Review*?) But there is still a dramatic shortage of trained managers. Even before the crisis of 1997–1998, there was talk of Asia needing a million more managers if it was to stay competitive. Now that looks like an underestimate. There are undoubtedly examples of excellence in developing Asia, such as in hotels and airlines. Yet many of the mistakes Asian businesses made, such as borrowing too much short-term money or ignoring currency risks, are the sort of thing that business schools caution against in their first few months.

This reflects a deeper problem: The region's two dominant business models look out of date. The weaknesses of the *chaebol* are well known, though

China's leaders have nevertheless tried to introduce a similar system. The other Asian model, business networks created by the overseas Chinese, is in some ways impressively modern: The free-flowing networks it uses are immaculately virtual. But in general the wealth created has been built largely on connections rather than on new products or better services. It is hard to name an overseas Chinese business that has the organizational capacity to build a modern car.

This may change, thanks to two developments. The first is a determined attempt to build Asian versions of Wharton and the Harvard Business School. One aspirant to this throne is the China Europe International Business School, which, as its name and sprinkling of European staff implies, has had help from the European Union. The building itself is an unprepossessing place, about an hour from the center of Shanghai and surrounded by Japanese-owned factories. On the other hand, it buzzes with ambition. Some of this aggression comes from the Chinese government, which wants to train two hundred thousand managers every year, but this is more than matched by the drives of the students themselves. There are typically eighty applicants for each place, and admissions interviews are exhibitions in single-mindedness that would make Bill Gates or Larry Ellison shudder.

Another effort, the Indian School of Business in Hyderabad—or "Cyberbad," as some would like it to be known—only produced its first year of graduates in 2002. It starts, however, with the advantage of being backed by both Wharton and the Kellogg Graduate School of Management—two of America's best business schools—a blue-ribbon list of Indian business leaders, and an impressive quorum of international managers, including Jürgen Schrempp of DaimlerChrysler and Martin Sorrell of WPP. The project has been largely the brainchild of a group of successful Indians living in America. Rajat Gupta of McKinsey talks with unexpected passion about the school becoming not only the best in Asia but also a rival of the existing American and European schools. Whether this dream-team approach works remains to be seen: India has a habit of tripping up grandiose schemes. But the signs so far are that the school means business. Its first 126 students received 190 job offers. When Bombay, the original choice for the school, began to demand special favors, such as places reserved for "native sons" (read: "sons of local ministers"), Gupta and his colleagues simply moved the site to Hyderabad. The message could not be clearer: The school will follow international standards, not Indian ones.

Producing more managers will count for little if the businesses that they join still rely purely on their connections and give key jobs to family members. Fortunately, a revolution also seems to be at least beginning in the upper reaches of Asia's family-run companies, led by people such as Patrick Wang Shui-chung.

Wang's World

You do not have to be a very astute student of Chinese culture to finger Patrick Wang as the eldest son of a self-made tycoon. His suit is exquisitely tailored, his thick black hair is neatly combed, and he speaks impeccable Harvard Business School English. His company, Johnson Electric, the world's second-largest maker of electric motors, feels like a business-school case study dumped into the sulphur-scented hell of Hong Kong's grimy Tai Po Industrial Estate. By the time you arrive at the building, you feel as if you have smoked a pack and a half of Gitanes, and one of the first things you see is that staple of Chinese business, a bust of the family patriarch, in this case Wang's father. But the quiet office is on a thoroughly open plan, and everywhere you look there are signs of management ideas in action—from the cabinets stuffed full of boring-looking awards for manufacturing efficiency, awarded by partners such as Kodak, Texas Instruments, and Black & Decker, to the ubiquitous posters inviting workers to spend exciting evenings learning about transformational leadership, e-commerce, and conflict resolution.

For Wang, management theory is not some arcane subject. "We are now in a new world," he says. In the past, national barriers could keep second-rate operations in business. Now, everybody "is just a click away." Like so many Hong Kong companies, Johnson had its roots in the toy business. Wang senior started his career making tiny motors for toy cars in the 1950s. Nowadays, micromotors are used to drive all sorts of things that have come to seem like necessities in our pampered times, including car seats, overhead projectors, blenders, electric knives, and can openers. Johnson employs more than fifteen thousand people and does business with more than twenty countries.

Johnson long ago outsourced most of its manufacturing to China and Thailand (hence the quiet). It has also established research, development, and marketing facilities in Germany, Switzerland, and the United States. Johnson's biggest customers—global car companies—want global suppliers, not to mention ever lower prices and ever higher quality. Wang recalls Michael Porter's argument that companies can beat the competition in one of two ways—by being cheaper or being better—with a wistful sigh. Here, "the great man is wrong." Johnson has to do both at once if it is to have any chance of staying alive.

Porter's name is frequently on Patrick Wang's lips. The air outside may be foul with every kind of chemical, and the world's most fearsome gerontocracy may be only a couple of hours away in Beijing, but Wang's heart is clearly on the banks of the River Charles. Wang has been a regular at Harvard's executive-education program since the early 1990s. He reads the *Harvard Business Review* "religiously." Management theory is the "brains trust for the business world," he argues, and the best way to learn the secrets of the world's most successful companies. "Even if I lived for three hundred years," he says, "I would not be able to study all these companies."

Wang took some time to reach that conclusion. As a young man, he had studied electrical engineering at Purdue University, a "dry and serious place" whose non–Ivy League status clearly embarrasses him. For a while, he thought he would be able to learn all the management he needed from business magazines—a belief that was reinforced by the fact that his "maths genius" father did not even finish high school. But by the early 1990s, Wang was fed up with being pestered by twenty-something stock-market analysts about things like EVA (economic value added) and worried by their presumption that family firms merely wanted to hive that EVA for themselves. He enrolled himself at Harvard Business School and on his return brought in consultants from McKinsey and the Thomas Group.

Consultants have plenty of defects, but one clear advantage of hiring outsiders for hierarchical family businesses is that they are more willing to tell people like Wang the harsh facts. McKinsey revealed that Wang's customers were unhappy with the firm's slowness. (Wang had been under the impression that their love knew no bounds.) Thomas told him to modernize his production processes and to reduce clutter so as to keep inventory to a minimum. ("We use the sea as our warehouse," he boasts today.) Since then, Wang has led his company on a trail of permanent revolutions of reengineering, cutting costs, and pushing quality. Credit Suisse First Boston now praises Johnson as "one of the few companies globally that can deliver defect-free motors." In 1999, it took over Lear's electric-motor division for $310 million.

As Wang breathlessly explains how McKinsey's work on "the war for talent" has set him on reconsidering his recruitment policy and then mentions the interesting paper he saw on "disruptive technologies," he seems to have drunk perhaps a little too deeply from the management-theory spring. But it is also clear that embracing all these ideas has given him a psychological edge. In Chinese business, size has usually been a token of esteem. But management theory has taught Wang to fire as well as to hire, and labor now accounts for only 3 percent of the company's costs. An even more important lesson has been humility. Most Chinese princelings make Tom Wolfe's masters of the universe look as if they have inferiority complexes. Not Wang. "I'm just the CEO," he says, in what might strike many of his peers as an oxymoron, "I'm not omnipotent."

He thinks that Dilbert has it right: The higher you go in an organization, the less you understand what is really happening. Although there are other members of the Wang family in the company, Wang boasts that Johnson is "flat" and "unhierarchical," organizing its people in "cross-functional" teams and getting them to communicate regardless of national boundaries. He himself is merely a middleman who takes the wisdom of the Charles and translates it so it can be understood on the Yangtze. He holds "drumbeat" meetings in his Chinese factories as often as possible in order to communicate his latest ideas to his employees. Instructions should be simple. Examples should be concrete. Feedback should be frequent. And measurement should be relentless. "Management is not rocket science," he says. "Most of it is just common sense."

The Sun Also Rises

If Asia provides one example of the globalizing effect of management, then America provides another. Although most of the ideas that the new schools in India and China will drum into the heads of their pupils will be well-established Western ones, it is wrong to associate business excellence solely with the United States. Management science is in a constant process of evolution, and that evolution works best when it is open to ideas from all over the world.

One of the most feted management thinkers in the United States at the moment is a mild-mannered Japanese professor with thick glasses and a taste for talking about epistemology: Ikujiro Nonaka. Nonaka has been given a chair at the University of California, Berkeley, and he is regarded as the doyen of a fashionable new area of management science: how companies create and use knowledge. One consultant—himself a "chief knowledge officer"—calculates that about three quarters of large American companies either have "knowledge initiatives" in place or are about to launch them. There are many books with the phrase *intellectual capital* in the title, proving, if nothing else, that the gurus' emphasis on creativity and communication does not extend to their own book titles. And the market for "knowledge-management services" is already in the billions.

Nonaka's acolytes (who include some of Silicon Valley's finest) like to ascribe his preeminence in this burgeoning field to his taste for rigorous philosophizing. His book *The Knowledge-Creating Company* is profound stuff compared with most management tomes. Yet people no more buy management books for their insights into epistemology than they read *Playboy* for the short stories by John Updike. The real value of Nonaka's approach to knowledge management is that it is very different from the one that prevails in the United States.

The first difference is Nonaka's relative lack of interest in information technology. Many American companies equate "knowledge creation" with setting up computer databases. Nonaka argues that much of a company's knowledge bank has nothing to do with data but is based on informal on-the-job knowledge—everything from the name of a customer's secretary to the best way to deal with truculent suppliers. Many of these tidbits are stored in the brains of middle managers, exactly the people whom big reengineering projects in America replaced with computers. Nonaka argues that Japanese companies are past masters of tapping into the tacit insights and hunches of employees; he also argues that companies that cut their workforces too radically or too cavalierly risk getting rid of a store of tacit knowledge that might never be replaced.

The second thing that makes Nonaka stand out is his insistence that companies need plenty of slack to remain creative. Allow employees time to pursue harebrained schemes or just sit around chatting, and you may come up with a market-changing idea, he argues; force them to account for every minute of their day, and you will be stuck with routine products.

Looking to Japan for insights on management might seem odd at a time when that recession-bound country has become known for its bloated companies and bankrupt banks. Moreover, Silicon Valley works by decidedly different rules from those laid down by Nonaka: Institutional memory is weak and middle managers rare, knowledge generation appears to be split between individual entrepreneurs and the Valley's collective intellectual infrastructure. But America's interest in Nonaka demonstrates just how ecumenical the search for good management ideas has become. Some of the best companies in the Valley clearly take his thinking very seriously.

In other words, America can still learn from Japan. In fact, Nonaka fits into an elaborate game of "pass the parcel" that has been taking place across the Pacific pretty much since the war. The first time the parcel was passed was when the Japanese seized on the ideas of W. Edwards Deming. The next was when Toyota sent back its system of lean production. Since then, the process has become something of a blur, with each side picking up the other's ideas, changing them, and sending them back. In time, somebody—perhaps Nonaka himself—will give his ideas an American spin and fling the parcel back across the Pacific. The game will stop only when somebody invents a perfect parcel—and that, despite all the outrageous promises of ultimate and immediate satisfaction found on the shelves of business-book shops, is unlikely to happen soon.

5

Sex, Death, and
the Welfare State

HOW MUCH HAVE political liberalization, technology, capital, and management already turned the world economy into a single, integrated system? There have been so many extravagant claims about the depth and breadth of globalization that it is hard not to dismiss all the rhetorical froth as pure globaloney. But globalization is a continuing process, and a complex and convoluted one at that. Globalization moves at different speeds in different parts of the planet and in different sections of the population.

We should thus be on our guard against taking our skepticism too far. The world economy *is* becoming more integrated. Activities that were once fairly isolated *are* being woven into a worldwide web. We want to illustrate this point by looking at how three businesses associated with activities that have hitherto seemed quintessentially local or at most national—sex, death, and the public sector—are being globalized. This is not, we hope, just an exercise in commercial prurience. All three activities show the power of the engines of globalization, and all three show how globalization is affecting the deepest feelings and anxieties of a growing number of people on the planet. If globalization can reach these areas, it can reach anywhere.

The Van Nuys Experience

Van Nuys is an area of the San Fernando Valley that has clearly seen better days. "The town that started right" (as its motto has it) is beginning to run to seed. Many of the small bungalows that dominate the area look worn. Groups of Latinos hang around on street corners, waiting for people to give them jobs. Giant car lots give the main streets sepulchral airs. The California sun struggles in vain to confer a touch of glamour on the shopping malls.

The San Fernando Valley is rapidly becoming the capital of one of the world's saddest and, until recently, least global industries: sex. The business, which *Forbes* reckons is worth fifty-six billion dollars a year, stretches from the oldest profession on earth to the most complicated forms of interactive video.[1] It also has many faces, from the harmless to the unspeakably evil. Porn is no longer a ghetto. Adult movies account for more than a quarter of all videotape sales and rentals. Wholesome hotel chains, like Hilton and Sheraton, present their visitors adult entertainment, beamed into their rooms by NASDAQ-listed companies such as On Command Corporation and LodgeNet Entertainment. Virtually every Western investment bank in Moscow takes clients to prostitute-packed nightclubs. AT&T happily connects people to expensive phone-sex numbers. *Cosmopolitan* needs sex as much as *Playboy* does. Howard Stern, Jerry Springer, and the E! channel feature porn stars, who have themselves become industries: Ron Jeremy (known in the industry as "the hedgehog") has managed to get his fat, hairy face on cigars, beer, T-shirts, and, of course, a sex toy modeled on a certain part of his anatomy.

"Silicone Valley," home to fifty out of the top eighty-five porn companies, grinds out more sex films than any other area on the planet, and it follows a business model much like that of other industrial clusters. Alongside the filmmakers there are talent agencies such as Pretty Girls International; strip clubs such as Bob's Classy Lady; sex-toy emporiums; some sixteen hundred leading stars; and film-production sets such as Trac Tech, a gigantic affair with permanent sets made up to look like a hospital, a bar, and a restaurant, as well as the inevitable bedrooms. In all, it employs some twenty thousand people; at one point in 1999, one out of every five films in production in Los Angeles was a porn film.[2]

The most eloquent guide to the globalization of this business is Steven Hirsch, the president of Vivid Video, the largest porn studio. From a collection of low buildings in a residential bit of Van Nuys, Vivid produces about ninety sex films a year. In one building, a team of ten postproduction specialists, using state-of-the-art dubbing machines and digital editing suites, churn out films twenty-four hours a day seven days a week; in another, teams of technicians perfect Vivid's Internet site. Vivid distributes its films on five continents, via video stores, mail-order houses, the Internet, and cable and satellite television. Vivid produces 80 percent of the content of the Playboy Channel. It is also the world's largest provider of adult films for hotels and motels. The company employs some 150 people and had sales of about sixty million dollars in 1999.

The tanned and aerobicized Hirsch looks like a foot soldier in that vast army of Californians who divide their time between the gym and the beach. But, oddly, he sounds as if he has just graduated from a high-powered business school. He talks fluently about diversifying the company, segmenting the market, integrating vertically, and rethinking distribution channels. Indeed, if one ignored his somewhat conspicuous display of Adult Video News Awards (in 1997, Vivid won no fewer than fifteen of these adult Oscars, an all-time high), one could be forgiven for thinking he was one of the more technologically astute studio moguls.

Like a lot of people in Hollywood, Hirsch grew up around the business. His father made his name producing eight-millimeter films back in the days when they were called stag movies. He worked in the warehouse of his father's company while attending the University of California, Los Angeles; later, he signed on as the national sales manager at Cal Vista, one of the largest distributors in the business. (His sister, Marci, another graduate of the warehouse, also works for Vivid, overseeing production.) In 1985, he co-founded Vivid with David James, a barrel-chested Welshman who sports tattoos and a walrus mustache. James, whose previous careers include spells as a coal miner and as a member of the antiterrorist unit of the British army, now runs Vivid's new-technology division, focusing on digital video discs. DVD, he claims, is the reason why "I've gone from the coal mines to the gold mines."

Hirsch never consciously planned to turn Vivid into a global powerhouse. The business that he entered was an amateurish affair, not much given to thinking about the next month, let alone the long term. In his early years, he was more interested in getting his products across state lines than across national frontiers; some states have much tougher laws on obscenity than others do. The company set up a small foreign division to handle its overseas rights ten years ago. Now that division accounts for a fifth of Vivid's revenues, with the Internet becoming an important distribution service. Certainly, the era of state troopers searching trucks for smut is over.

Porn is a nasty industry, run by ugly characters. All the same, if you hold your nose tightly, it is possible to see how Vivid has been driven by the three engines of globalization: management, technology, and, to a lesser extent, capital. The management bit has been simple enough. Hirsch has simply imported the best practices (or, at least, not-bad practices) into an industry where such things were nonexistent. In the past, the standard way to get rich in porn was either to rip off your customers or to sell them the sleaziest product imaginable. Now that anyone with a handheld video camera and a few willing bodies can make a porn film, the market is being saturated. By the end of the 1990s, there were thirty new hard-core titles, around a quarter of them homemade, hitting the market every day.

Hirsch has pushed Vivid relatively upmarket. Vivid's flagship products are the thirty feature-length films that it makes each year, shot on film rather than video and with budgets of about two hundred thousand dollars, an unheard-of sum in the porn world. Vivid employs its own in-house director, Paul Thomas, to give its films a consistent "Vivid feel." (Thomas, himself a veteran porn actor, appeared as the apostle Peter in *Jesus Christ Superstar.*) Most Vivid films feature presentable sets and exotic locations rather than grimy bedrooms and moldering hot tubs. And most feature something that is surprisingly rare in the porn business: beautiful women.

Hirsch managed to get a lock on the prettiest girls in the business by reviving an old entertainment practice: the studio system. Vivid made its first big star, Ginger Lynn (Hirsch's erstwhile girlfriend) into its first "Vivid Girl." There are now nine Vivid Girls, who have typically signed one- to three-year contracts to appear in about six films a year. In exchange, they get some kind of security; a guarantee of exactly what they will and will not do on camera (don't ask); and heavy promotion by Vivid's powerful publicity machine through fan clubs and websites. (Kobe Tai's hobbies, we learn, are "singing country music and Disney tunes"; Tia Bella likes to spend time with her five adopted pets.)

Most porn girls harbor secret dreams of crossing over into the mainstream world; their chances of doing this, though pretty small, are probably higher with Vivid than with anyone else. Vivid Girls, who are encouraged to wear a special Vivid necklace at all times, have had cameo roles in proper films and have appeared, clothed, in various advertisements. Vivid's publicity agents, who tend to have backgrounds in the music business, are also good at introducing them to rock bands. In the meantime, while they wait for the phone call from Warner Bros. asking them to step in for Meg Ryan, the girls can command a premium on the lucrative stripping circuit, earning as much as twenty thousand dollars a week. There is even a certain amount of camaraderie attached to being a Vivid Girl. Hirsch and many of his girls are vocal supporters of the hard-line animal-rights group, People for the Ethical Treatment of Animals.

In terms of "thinking global but acting local," Hirsch is arguably ahead of the mainstream studios. The most that respectable Hollywood does in the

way of fine-tuning its films for different markets is beeping over a few words
and employing, for example, Asian rock bands to compose local anthems.
Vivid recuts (and sometimes reshoots) its footage to produce hard- and soft-
core versions of the same film for different markets. It also allows foreign
partners to edit its films for local content. The Japanese, for example, still
have a prohibition on showing pubic hair. The result, according to Hirsch, is
that Vivid uses its footage even more thoroughly than the Plains Indians
used the buffalo.

The other thing that stands out about Hirsch is that he understands the
importance of technology. It is one of the oddities of the consumer-
electronics industry that the snazziest products often have their origins in
the world's oldest profession. The porn industry's embrace of the videocassette helped guarantee the technology's commercial success. Today, it is
doing the same for DVD and the Internet. Vivid is not only cranking out
DVDs faster than any other studio but also blazing trails in using the
medium's special capabilities, such as allowing a viewer to watch a single
scene from several angles. Internet peep shows allow cybervoyeurs in one
country to give instructions to models sitting in another. Vivid, a pioneer in
the questionably named field of cyberdildonics, has even designed an electronic suit that allows couples in different countries to "interact" to their
mutual satisfaction—perhaps the final delocalization of sex. "You always
want to expand your business," enthuses Hirsch. "You always want more."

Porn sans Frontiers

With its DVDs and vertical integration, Vivid is perhaps an extreme example,
yet even at its most basic level the sex business has been profoundly transformed by globalization. Take the growing ease with which people and businesses can cross borders, either legally or illegally. In poorer countries,
international tourism and business travel is making prostitution spectacu-
larly rewarding: Women in Russia and Eastern Europe can earn several
times the average weekly wage for a night's work in an exclusive hotel. Indeed, sex was one of the first industries to feel the effect of the fall of the
Berlin Wall. In many parts of Eastern Europe, industries that had been
buried underground came bubbling to the surface. In the meantime, the
Western European sex markets were flooded by Eastern European sex workers, driving down wages. In Kiel, Germany, the standard price for a prostitute
remained fifty marks (thirty dollars) from 1992 to 1998, a substantial drop
in real terms.[3] At the other end of the market, rumors abound in Manhattan

of a group of former KGB women, trained for "honey-trap" activities, who have now aimed their charms at some of the city's wealthier citizens.

It would be an exaggeration to say that the price of prostitution is being fixed by a global labor market, though it is certainly having an effect. Besides, the ease with which people can now cross borders is as nothing compared with the ease with which goods can. Sex entrepreneurs have rushed to outsource and to take advantage of the standard laws of comparative advantage. China has become the world's biggest producer of sex aids. Most Western European producers of sex videos use Eastern European actors for the simple reason that "they will do more for less." Budapest has become the biggest center for the production of pornography in Europe, eclipsing such old stalwarts as Amsterdam and Copenhagen. Scott Stein, the head of SMS Promotions, based in Playa del Rey, California, offers something called XXX-treme vacations, which promise, among other things, a ringside seat at the making of porn films in some exotic location or other.

The industry may be about to be given a big push by yet another powerful force: the global capital markets. Several porn firms, including America's New Frontier Media and LodgeNet Entertainment and the Barcelona-based Private Media Group, are listed on American exchanges; Germany's Beate Uhse, one of the world's biggest sex-store chains, is listed in Frankfurt. Hirsch is coy about whether he will take Vivid public. He argues that Wall Street will have little patience for an undiversified pornography company, particularly as videotape faces such an uncertain future. But he is devoting a lot of effort to making sure that Vivid diversifies itself.

In the end, however, the biggest force driving the current hectic globalization of the sex industry remains the Internet. Forrester Research of Cambridge, Massachusetts, calculates that the Internet porn business is already worth one billion dollars a year and is set to get much bigger. The medium removes at a stroke the two biggest obstacles to selling sexual images and services: shame and ignorance. Anyone planning a business trip need only look at the World Sex Guide, an Internet site, to find detailed reviews of brothels, escort agencies, and nightclubs in hundreds of cities around the world. It also makes it possible for people to bypass regional censors, getting access to images from anywhere on the planet. The girls on the Vivid site who cavort at their customers' pleasure are based in Amsterdam.

What is the result of all this? From a consumer's point of view, globalization is simple enough: You can get more of what you want when you want it than ever before. But the impact on producers is rather more mixed. While the upper end of the porn business is consolidating, the seamier parts of it seem to be fragmenting. Low barriers to entry mean that there is an ever-changing group of new players. Even more than in other walks of life, in the sex industry globalization seems to be driving a wedge between the successful and the unsuccessful. In the prostitution business, some women (particularly good-looking ones in poorer countries) are making quick killings. Others, however, are being forced to perform ever more degrading acts for ever less money. Some of the newest pimps in the business—particularly the Russians—have reputations for astonishing violence and brutality.

Many other critics would go further, arguing that globalization is the ugly stepmother both of child-porn sites on the Internet and even of AIDS, a truly global plague. Yet it is plainly not all bad. Even with sex, globalization increases transparency and helps spread generally tolerant standards. The sad truth seems to be that the nastier customers of the sex industry have always been prepared to travel, and national boundaries have often provided them with protection. For Western child molesters, places such as Bangkok and Manila have long been areas where you can get away with murder (or its nearest equivalent). Now they stand a much higher chance of being exposed by authorities cooperating across borders.

At the other end of the scale, globalization has helped force governments and society to rethink their attitudes toward adult sex, usually in ways of which most liberals would approve. Intolerance toward homosexuals is still needlessly prevalent in various parts of the world, but legal discrimination is becoming rare; bigotry against your own citizens is hard to uphold when you are trying to sign a trade deal with an openly gay minister from another country. Similarly, globalization is one reason why several Western countries have finally begun to discuss legalizing prostitution, bringing it off the streets, where it is often dangerous and unhealthy, to safer, cleaner, licensed brothels. If, for instance, Sheffield in Britain starts to license massage parlors, with the permits being subject to medical checks on the masseuses, it will be partly because cities in the Netherlands and Germany have done the same, with a general improvement to all concerned.

The Global Way of Death

There is every reason to think that the death business is more immune to globalization than the sex business is. Different cultures deal with death in profoundly different ways. Ireland has its alcohol-fueled wakes, New Orleans its brass bands and wailing women. In India, funerals can be a riot of noise and color. In England, they tend to be muted affairs, with the bereaved hopelessly embarrassed about their emotions. Death is an occasion not just for meditating on ultimate things but also for celebrating what binds us to our kin and kind. Nobody—not even the most dedicated champion of globalization—wants to be buried by an anonymous global corporation.

Those corporations are colonizing death nonetheless. The biggest of these is Houston-based Services Corporation International (SCI), the largest provider of "death care services" in the world. SCI spent the mid-1990s expanding aggressively, taking over France's largest funeral chain and two of Britain's largest chains. At its peak in 1998, SCI owned some 3,420 funeral-service locations, 433 cemeteries, and 191 crematoriums in twenty countries and on five continents. The empire includes both the funeral parlor that buried Elvis and the one that buried Sir Winston Churchill, suggesting that globalization has an odd way of uniting the dead as well as the living.[4] In 1998, SCI performed 11 percent of all the funeral services in the United States, 14 percent of those in Great Britain, 25 percent in Australia, and 28 percent in France, a country that is normally highly resistant to American corporate imperialism.

Others followed SCI's lead. By the same year, the British Columbia–based Loewen Group owned far more funeral homes and cemeteries in the United States than it did in its native Canada. It also operated in Puerto Rico and in the United Kingdom. Stewart Enterprises, from New Orleans, relied on its operations in Latin America, Europe, and Australasia for a fifth of its profits.

In a few cases, this Americanization of the graveyard has come about through the construction of new parlors, but for the most part it has been through acquisition. There is no point in saturating one of the world's most mature markets. Acquisition also allows foreigners to overcome the two biggest barriers to entering new markets in this business: heritage and tradition. The death business has traditionally been dominated by small family businesses that have put down roots in a community over several generations. Customers would find powerful consolation in the fact that the same family that buried their grandfather was now burying their father. It is also a nice, safe business to be in. Dun & Bradstreet calculates that the average business failure rate in the funeral industry in 1995 was thirteen per ten thousand, compared with eighty-two per ten thousand for American business as a whole.

In some cases, parlors have been driven to sell by the need to solve their own problems with succession or estate planning. Others have simply been tempted by the possibility of making, so to speak, a quick killing. The big firms have been willing to pay above the market rate, too, because they think that they can reap economies of scale through "clustering." Learning from an idea pioneered by McDonald's, which centralizes its food production and management, SCI and its competitors first buy up a carefully chosen selection of funeral homes, cemeteries, flower shops, and crematoriums in a given metropolitan area. They then cluster everything that goes into making a "fulfilling death experience" into a central depot: hearses, limousine drivers, dispatchers, embalmers, marketers, and a small army of clerical workers.

Clustering does more than just allow firms to control costs: It allows them to endure fluctuations in the local death rates, which often swamp smaller companies, and to plan for the future by marketing prearranged funeral services. Further, SCI does not sacrifice the local roots that took so many years to establish. When SCI buys, for example, Johnson's Chapel of Eternal Rest, Jessica Mitford noted in the final edition of her classic *The American Way of Death*, it keeps not only the name "but also Johnson himself, now installed as salaried manager, thus ensuring continuity of recognition and goodwill."[5]

This is not to say that the corporate owners leave local traditions untouched. Their technique is to persuade other countries, imperceptibly but relentlessly, to embrace the American way of death. Jessica Mitford quoted an anonymous British informant about how SCI gradually rearranged a business after taking it over. For six months, nothing really changed. But then all the employees were invited to a smart Kensington hotel, where a new range of coffins was unveiled and the arts of salesmanship explained. The goal is to steer people away from cheaper options such as "typically English-looking, pleasant coffins" and cremation (a more popular option in Britain than in the United States) and persuade them to go for more expensive options.[6]

Just as in other industries that are globalizing, it is an uneven process. The big groups got carried away with their own rhetoric. The race between SCI and the Loewen Group to snap up assets turned into a disastrous bidding war, fueled in part by a bitter personal rivalry between William Heiligbrodt, SCI's boss, and Raymond Loewen. Both men were eventually forced out after SCI's shares plunged and Loewen filed for chapter 11 bankruptcy.

Yet there is every reason to think that this is nothing but a pause in a longer-term trend toward a more global industry. The five publicly traded companies still account for only 20 percent of the death-care industry. And clustering does offer genuine economies of scale. Loewen has been reborn as the Alderwoods Group; SCI is back on the acquisition trail, albeit in a less aggressive way. And Stewart Enterprises—which was much more cautious than its competitors in the heyday of consolidation, refusing to pay more than eight times operating earnings for a funeral home at a time when SCI was happily paying nine—is now buying again. The postwar baby boomers are rapidly approaching the ages at which their minds begin to turn to funeral plots rather than new sports-utility vehicles. It would be appropriate if the members of the generation that has led the current wave of globalization made their final trips in the company of a few multinational corporations.

Globalizing Compassion

One good indication of how little the welfare state has had to do with globalization lies in the way that the concept means completely different things to different people. For the Swedes, virtually everything the public sector does is part of the welfare state; Americans tend to think of it as merely providing food stamps for the poor. In our discussion here, we will use the British definition, under which the welfare state involves four basic social services: health care, unemployment pay, pensions, and education.

In its many incarnations, this four-headed monster and miracle has been the antithesis of global capitalism, provided by governments rather than by businesses and bound up with the process of building nation-states. Most people would probably like to keep things that way, just as they would like to keep "the people who buried Elvis" out of their local funeral parlors. But the logic of globalization is beginning to affect the provisions of welfare nonetheless.[7]

Otto von Bismarck, the architect of modern Germany, pioneered nationalized compassion when he introduced state pensions in 1889. Thereafter, citizens increasingly looked to their governments to provide them with "social insurance"; governments, conversely, increasingly used social insurance to endear themselves to the newly enfranchised masses. Before the First World War, the British Liberal government that Keynes so admired introduced such programs as free school meals for needy children and old-age pensions. In the 1930s, America's Social Security, a product of the New Deal, served similar aims. Schools also came to be seen as some of the most powerful instruments of nation building. Governments coopted or forcibly nationalized many of the voluntary organizations that had provided education in the past. They then regulated what was taught in schools with the goal of creating properly educated national citizens.

The provisions of the welfare state are so enormously popular that prudent governments regard them as the third rail of democratic politics, too dangerous to touch. But such systems are enormously expensive, too, eating up the bulk of government spending throughout the OECD and lurching from one crisis to another. These crises have been so severe that politicians now are trying to halt the seemingly irreversible expansion of governments into every aspect of social welfare. Further, they are beginning to question whether personal security must inevitably be the responsibility of national governments rather than prudent individuals and global markets.

There are three reasons for this outbreak of apparent radicalism. The first is that the welfare state was designed for a world that no longer exists. When Bismarck invented the state pension, with a retirement age of sixty-five, the average life expectancy was forty-five. Now, in the OECD, it is seventy-six and rising, and yet the labor-force participation of men between sixty and sixty-four has declined from over 80 percent in most rich countries in 1960 to 50 percent in America and below 35 percent in Germany, Italy, and France. When most welfare states were created, a large proportion of the population was poor and uneducated. Now most people are relatively affluent, and most are educated enough to look after themselves and can make life's major decisions for themselves rather than have them made for them by their rulers. The welfare state was designed for a world in which women stayed at home, families remained together, and unemployment carried a huge social stigma; in other words, a world we have lost.

The second reason behind the shift is that most welfare states have failed to eliminate many of the problems they were established to tackle. R. H. Tawney's prediction that under a welfare state it "would cease to be the rule for the rich to be rewarded, not only with riches, but with a preferential share of health and life, and for the penalty of the poor to be not merely poverty, but ignorance, sickness and premature death" has not been borne out. There are enormous inequalities in both health and educational performance between the rich and the poor. Indeed, it is arguable that the welfare state is actually worsening some of the problems that it was supposed to solve. In countries such as Germany, high social-security contributions are a severe tax on jobs.

The third force behind the shift comes from the fear national governments have of being swamped by the swelling tide of inherited obligations. William Beveridge, the architect of Britain's postwar welfare state, estimated no real increase over time in the cost of health and rehabilitation services because a healthier population would make fewer demands on services. In fact, spending rose astronomically and is continuing to rise. Populations in rich countries are aging rapidly as the baby-boomer generation heads toward retirement and the birthrate declines. While today's ratio of working taxpayers to nonworking pensioners in the developed world is 3:1, in thirty years, without reform, the ratio could fall to 1.5:1 or even lower, costing an extra 9 to 16 percent of GDP to finance benefits for the elderly.[8] To provide established entitlements, governments will have to make a grim choice: They will either have to raise tax rates dramatically—undermining economic competitiveness and threatening to unleash a generational war as the young refuse to impoverish themselves in order to indulge the aging children of Woodstock—or they will have to enlist the help of the private sector.

By turning to the private sector, as most governments are now doing, they usually end up "denationalizing" the public sector in more than one sense. No sensible government wants to enlist the support of an incompetent private-sector operation to run the welfare state. Fairly soon, however, they discover that the most competent private-sector organizations are usually global ones. For instance, the British government originally turned over nursing homes to local family operators; now that industry, not unlike the funeral business that it supplies, is clustering into bigger, professional multinational companies. When governments outsource the administration of unemployment pay, it is now nearly always to big global firms such as Accenture and Electronic Data Services. It is no accident that Chile, which has led the way in introducing private retirement accounts, is also one of the places where foreign fund managers are most welcome. The headlong assault on Europe's financial-services industry by large American firms is inspired by the idea that sooner or later most Europeans will rely on their state pension less and their own portable pension far more.

Letting foreigners run boring computer systems that pay your unemployed is one thing. But globalization is now touching a much more sensitive part of the public sector: education. For many nationalists, schools and classrooms are the smithies where national identity is forged. Perhaps unsurprisingly, America—the country least wedded to the idea that education is part of the welfare state—has produced companies that are beginning to sell education around the world.

Reading, Writing, and Enrichment

Driving to the Sylvan Testing Center in Johannesburg provides a lesson in the perils of the new South Africa. The journey takes you past carefully tended rugby fields and elaborately fortified houses. An "all-hit" radio station advertises itself with the slogan "more police"; a poster demands "no mercy for criminals." The only obvious reference to education is a newspaper billboard on a lamppost: PRINCIPAL SHOT IN HIJACK. It comes as something of a relief that at the testing center, you have to report to a uniformed guard with a truncheon and a military bearing.

Sylvan Learning Systems is a Baltimore-based company founded by two university dropouts. Its most profitable business is the administration of computer-based versions of the standardized examinations that regulate admission to everything from universities to professional organizations. It also provides coaching for children with schoolwork problems and for those of any age who just want to steal a march on their contemporaries. In the United States, it is hard to enter the middle class without paying a toll to Sylvan; if the company gets its way, the same will become true in much of the rest of the world.

In Africa, Sylvan has decided to concentrate on examining people rather than teaching them. Some fifteen thousand students there take Sylvan-administered exams, a number that is growing fast and would be much higher but for the strength of the dollar. The exams differ widely in difficulty—some are designed to test basic command of English, others to divine a grasp of sophisticated medical knowledge—but they are all multiple-choice. Sylvan does not create the examinations itself; its contribution to the proceedings—apart from the tight security—is a computerized system that makes administration and marking easy. The computer adjusts automatically to the candidates' abilities so that strong candidates are given the hard questions that carry the highest marks.

Once you get past the guard, the Johannesburg test center could be literally anywhere in the world. Sylvan centers are all built to a formula that is a far cry from the echoing examination halls that people of a certain age still remember from their childhoods. All the centers are divided into regulation-sized cubicles, each containing a Compaq computer. A regulation-sized window allows a supervisor to look in, as do regulation-sized mirrors and standard-issue video and audio equipment.

The distinguishing quality of Sylvan, argues the test center's boss, Lyn Van Haght, is that it always combines a global product with local roots. (A tall, blond Californian, Van Haght herself took this policy a little literally: She met her future husband three days after first arriving in South Africa.) Some African universities now require candidates to take Sylvan-administered tests for English proficiency, as does the Nigerian civil service. But Van Haght points out that most of Sylvan's customers are trying to get into an American university or a South African one that is running a joint course with an American one.

American universities enjoy huge status in South Africa, to the extent that the newspapers are full of advertisements for fly-by-night American institutions (the University of Harvard in Beverly Hills and the like) offering "internationally certified degrees." (Oxford and Cambridge are still highly regarded in South Africa, but otherwise British universities seem to have lost their former luster, despite the fact that many leading figures in the African National Congress were educated at the University of Sussex.) The most popular American degree by far is the M.B.A., which South Africans have long seen as a ticket to the top in their best companies. They thus naturally assume that the world's most powerful business culture also provides the best business education. At the other end of the popularity scale are niche subjects that are simply not available on the African continent, such as equine dentistry.

In South Africa about half the university candidates are black and half are white; in the rest of Africa, most are black. Many of the white candidates disappear to the United States, never to return. But for the most part, the Sylvan Testing Center is being used to handle African issues rather than to provide an escape route for a disaffected minority. African governments and big South African companies (who are desperately trying to increase the number of blacks in senior management) both use the tests to select highfliers, many of whom are then sent on to American business schools. Similarly promising black athletes—including devotees of that very un-American game of rugby—regard an American sports scholarship as their best way into the middle class and thus pay particular attention to Sylvan tests.

Schoolmasters of the Universe

Sylvan is only one in a crowd of mainly American companies that are determined to turn education into a global business. Michael Milken, the former junk-bond king, is quietly putting together one of the world's biggest education companies, Knowledge Universe. Kohlberg Kravis Roberts, a firm that strikes fear into managers the world over, also owns an education company, KinderCare. Various billionaires, including Warren Buffett and Paul Allen, have invested heavily in education, as have companies from a wide range of more conventional industries, including computers (IBM, Sun Microsystems), software (Microsoft, Oracle), telecommunications (MCI), entertainment (Sony), and publishing (*The Washington Post*).

There are at least two reasons why so many American companies are particularly attracted to this market. The first is the sheer size of the domestic market. The U.S. Department of Education estimates that the country spends $635 billion a year on education—more than on Social Security or defense—and predicts that spending per pupil will grow by 40 percent over the next decade. Private companies currently have no more than a seventh of the market, and that mostly in the training sector.[9]

The second impetus comes from the fact that the American public sector has made such a hash of keeping pace with either public expectations or international standards. The United States spends a higher proportion of its GDP on education than most other countries do, but it achieves results that are nothing more than mediocre. More than 40 percent of American fourth graders cannot pass a basic reading test, and forty-two million adults are functionally illiterate. Part of the reason for this dismal performance is that as much as half the $6,500 spent each year on each child is eaten up by "noninstructional services." While the public sector fumbles this basic job, demand for extra services is rising. As the income gap between high-school and university graduates grows, so does parents' determination to get their children into college. And the latest research on intellectual development, which stresses the overwhelming importance of the first three years of life, is leading to a craze for "smart" kindergartens.

Most of the private-sector activity in education so far has been focused on providing supplementary services to established schools. Some school boards that have contracted out peripheral services have been so impressed with the results that they are beginning to apply the principle to teaching itself. So companies such as Sylvan are venturing gingerly into what could be the biggest market of all: running public schools. The barrier between the public and private sectors is eroding. The country's growing number of charter schools are often free to experiment with private management without losing their public funding. There is also a growing number of "educational management organizations"—modeled on health-maintenance organizations—that promise to reduce the administrative costs of running public schools while producing better results.

In some ways, the arrival of the education companies signals a "back to the future" approach. One of their hallmarks is a Victorian enthusiasm for testing that Dickens's Mr. Gradgrind might have appreciated. These companies have to prove that they are delivering results not just for their pupils but also for their shareholders. Sylvan offers free tuition in its classes if its students fail to meet specified targets and offers both students and teachers generous prizes if they can improve their performances. Another hallmark is a focus on individual customers and on personal tuition in particular. The Apollo Group, a private university that specializes in educating working adults, has tried to update the function of the family governess: It goes to meet its pupils and locates its classrooms near major freeways, the better to serve busy commuters. The Edison Project insists that the homes of all its pupils above the third grade have computer links to the school.

All these firms believe that they are selling a global product. Sylvan, which bought Europe's largest training company in 1994, now has learning and testing centers in 105 countries. About a quarter of its revenues comes from outside the United States. Knowledge Universe is built on Milken's idea that the global "intellectual capital" market is as ripe for revolution as the financial capital market was in the 1980s; further, he wants to create a gigantic education company that can provide its customers with cradle-to-grave service around the world. By 1999, he and his partners—his brother Lowell and Larry Ellison, boss of Oracle—had put together an education empire worth an estimated four billion dollars, stretching from an American educational-toy company to Britain's largest training company.

The Half Monty

Even more than with sex and death, this is an uneven process. Education is a redoubt not only of public-sector trade unions but also of the professional middle classes. Witness such job-creating notions as that British teachers have to go back to school to be able to teach in America and vice versa. Unscrupulous politicians have accused potential reformers of local education systems—who, for instance, introduce experimental voucher schemes so parents can choose their own schools—of plotting to break the social contract, apparently motivated by a desire to preserve existing jobs.

Such cronyism aside, there are also good reasons to be careful about introducing the profit motive into the education system. What happens if firms such as Sylvan and Knowledge Universe "cherrypick" the better students and the safer schools? When the privatization—and hence globalization—of the welfare state happens, there are usually important roles for government, as a regulator, to make sure that private companies do not abuse their positions, and as a provider of last resort, to make sure that there is still a safety net for people who do not have the resources to look after themselves.

The global classroom, like the global pension and the global hospital, is even farther off than the global graveyard and the global peep show, but that is the way that globalization works. Some industries are racing toward it; in others, the movement is glacial; and in many, there is an undertow, with parts of an industry localizing while the main market globalizes. There are plenty of other difficult businesses being affected. One is the law, where huge cross-border mergers between law firms became common only in the late 1990s. Another is gambling, where an industry that has always relied on its relationship with local regulators, such as the Nevada Gaming Commission or the Hong Kong Jockey Club, now finds itself in competition with Internet bookmakers and virtual casinos operating out of places such as Antigua.

Indeed, the overall trend, even with the welfare state, is fairly clear. Who would have imagined that a British Labor government would sell off nearly all its unemployment offices to a consortium led by Goldman Sachs, with the result that some of the richest people on Wall Street now own the places where *Full Monty* types go to pick up their weekly benefits? And who would have believed that an American conglomerate in Johannesburg would help create the black middle class that the continent needs so desperately? Lyn Van Haght and Steven Hirsch might be somewhat unusual soul mates, but they are part of the same uneven but relentless process.

Part Three

One World:
The Business of
Globalization

6

The Five Myths
of Globalization

DRIVE INTO DOWNTOWN Los Angeles from the coast and you are confronted
by a wall of shimmering skyscrapers, monuments to the city's dream of itself
as the Manhattan of the Pacific Rim. Within this citadel of quartz, built
mostly with Japanese money, bankers, oil executives, and lawyers toil for
multinational companies. Drive a little further, however, and the first world
dissolves. The buildings become dingy and dilapidated; whole blocks have
been boarded up. A stretch of Fifth Street now hosts denizens of the lowest
rungs of the underclass—amputees delivering drug-crazed lectures to the
empty sidewalk, beggars begging from each other.

H. G. Wells once predicted that mankind would mutate into two species,
the effete Eloi and the subterranean Morlocks. Downtown Los Angeles
would seem to be clinching evidence that the harsh economics of globalization have brought his vision into reality. Spend a little longer on Fifth Street,
however, and you begin to realize that the situation is rather more complicated. The local warehouses, crumbling with disuse just a few years ago, are
being renovated, the dingy tenements turned into makeshift shops and offices. The city is even having trouble regulating parking in an area that was
once synonymous with desolation. Early in the morning, the local streets are
jam-packed with trucks; on the weekend, they fill up with shoppers looking
for bargains.

For this, Los Angeles has to thank a cluster of roughly four hundred toy
companies and wholesalers that collectively employs four thousand people
and sells more than one billion dollars' worth of toys, half of that outside the
United States. The two or three biggest companies each employ almost five

hundred people, but most of the firms are one-warehouse operations run by ethnic Chinese, Mexicans, and Koreans. Many of the shops have mirrors hanging outside to deter evil spirits from entering; inside, next to the piles of toys, stand shrines to ancestral gods.

The architect of this urban regeneration is an affable Hong Kong immigrant in his late forties named Charlie Woo. The last few years have clearly been good to Woo: His stomach droops over his belt, and his face is so pudgy that it pushes up against his large glasses. But he has all the energy of a much younger man, talking rapidly, laughing loudly, and waving his arms about to illustrate his many enthusiasms. The overall impression of vitality is such that it is easy to forget, until he gets up to pull down a toy, that a childhood illness has left one leg paralyzed and that movement is painful for him. His office is a combination of thoroughfare and storehouse: His employees rush through his office to reach a loading bay in the back of the building; stacks of Darth Vader masks threaten to tumble over and submerge him. An endless succession of Chinese men, most of them apparently cousins, drop in for tea. His fearsome secretary, who has failed to master the intercom he bought for her, announces each new visitor with a piercing scream of "Charlie! Charlie!"

This informality conceals respect, even awe. Woo is known locally as the king of Toytown, and he takes his regal duties seriously. Anybody who braves the beggars to visit him is treated to an enthusiastic tour of his kingdom. Despite his handicap, he repeatedly stops his car (a specially modified Mercedes) to walk around or swap gossip with one of his competitors. As he wanders around, Woo points to houses that were once crack dens or storerooms that contained more rats than products. He contrasts the desolation of Fifth Street when he first arrived not just with the present but with an even brighter future, when thousands of new businesses will bring work to everyone in the area. It is only when he looks to the gleaming towers down the road that his habitual optimism departs. Businesses no longer need a huge superstructure of managers, he argues: The skyscrapers are Potemkin towers, 80 percent empty. But there will always be places for entrepreneurial businesses such as his own—small companies that actually make things.

Woo came to America in 1968 to embark on a Ph.D. in physics at UCLA. He was a promising student, but his family wanted him to make money, and he reluctantly dropped out to spend several years running a Chinese restaurant in Laguna Beach. Then he flirted with the rag trade before dismissing it as too fickle. Finally, pondering the sorry state of the local toy market, he saw an opportunity.

At the time, the American toy business was really two industries. One was a relatively high-quality affair, dominated by multinationals such as Mattel. The other comprised cheaper, fly-by-night firms, often selling their tawdry products through flea-market hawkers. Woo calculated that he could undercut the likes of Mattel by importing cheap but not flimsy toys from Hong Kong. Woo started his first business, ABC Toys, in 1979, drafting his father and three brothers from Hong Kong to help him; a decade later, he spun off Megatoys, the business that he runs today.

Downtown Los Angeles proved to be a better place for a toy business than even Woo imagined. The people who owned the buildings around Fifth Street were so keen to get rid of them that they all but gave them away. There were plenty of immigrants willing to do the grunt work. The proximity of the giant twin ports of Los Angeles and Long Beach meant that Woo could import toys from the Far East much more cheaply than his rivals in other parts of the country could. And, to his surprise, his market was not limited to the United States. Mexican retailers, who lacked the connections to import toys directly from Hong Kong but who had a huge market in their child-obsessed homeland, started beating a path to his door. Other toy makers joined Woo's little cluster, and Toytown appeared.

For most of his career, Woo's biggest headaches have been political rather than commercial. He spent years trying to get something done about the street people who harassed his staff and customers by day and broke into his buildings at night. But left-wing city councillors treated him like a sweatshop owner, and the city's conservative establishment was too busy building its gleaming towers to pay any heed to a manufacturer of fluffy toys. Woo won some friends by employing street people as cleaners and security guards and becoming heavily involved in local charities. Meanwhile, many of the big companies that once promised to populate the region's skyscrapers were gobbled up by out of towners. Woo, who only a few years ago was unable to get the lowest local dignitary on the phone, is now inundated with invitations to civic functions.

The Myth Factory

For Charlie Woo, globalization is simply a fact of life—or, perhaps more accurately, it is a set of facts about suppliers, customers, and workers. It does not matter to him that many aspects of Toytown seem to contradict common perceptions about how capitalism affects society. He does not use the word *globalization* except in sales pitches. In this he is not unusual. Businesses of all sorts have discovered that globalization is a good excuse for everything from closing plants to buying a new private plane for the chairman. In Tom Wolfe's novel *A Man in Full*, the hero, Charlie Croker, calls his Atlanta real-estate firm Croker Global mainly to justify the private jet that he uses to commute to his estate for quail shooting. Meanwhile, governments use globalization to justify everything from defending fixed exchange rates to not having the cash for school reform.

Endowed with equal amounts of emotion and imprecision, *globalization* has thus joined that list of turbocharged words—others include *family*, *fairness*, and *community*—that usually tell us more about people's underlying attitudes to the world than they do about what is actually going on in it. For most cultural conservatives, *globalization* is a code word for everything that perturbs them about the modern world, from broken homes to ubiquitous pop music. For people in high-tech industries, by contrast, it is one of those words that prove that you "get it."

Turbocharged words inevitably generate myths. Here, we will single out what we regard as the myths that need particular scrutiny: (1) that globalization is leading to the triumph of big companies; (2) that it is ushering in an age of global products, from Coca-Cola to Marlboro; (3) that it has ended the traditional business cycle; (4) that globalization is a zero-sum game (in which some people have to lose so that others can win); and (5) that it means that geography does not matter.

Exposing such globaloney is more than just an exercise in intellectual housekeeping. The myths associated with globalization, no less than other uninformed prejudices, lead to actions that can have dismal effects on the lives of millions of people. The idea that companies must be big or products global leads to pointless mergers. Investors pile money into absurdly valued companies, convinced that a "new economy" has obliterated the rules of economics. The idea that countries are engaged in a struggle for a limited number of jobs—in which one side will inevitably come out the loser—fuels the fires of protectionism and gives succor to more benign illusions, like the idea of "fair trade." The idea that firms are now rootless pushes governments to spend millions to dissuade a company from moving.

The First Myth: That Size Trumps All

Charlie Woo's office in the shadow of Los Angeles's skyscrapers is a good place to sit and ponder the first of our myths: that a handful of global megacorporations will carve up the world between them. The "faceless multinational" crops up in screed after screed about globalization. Coca-Colonization; Disneyfication; McJobs; the Nike economy: Such slurs are by-words for the process in which the small guy gets crushed. The onrush of mergers in the past few years—there were some $2.4 trillion worth in 1998 alone—seems only to add to this image. With each new deal—Daimler-Benz mating with Chrysler, Vodafone with Mannesmann, America Online with Time Warner—we are told that the reason has to do with the need for "scale" in the global economy.

But the idea that the big are getting bigger is an old myth that seems to get statistically more inaccurate each time it is repeated. More than thirty years ago, in *The New Industrial State*, John Kenneth Galbraith predicted that the world would be run by huge corporations: "With the rise of the modern cor-poration, the emergence of the organization required by modern technology and planning and the divorce of capital from the control of the business, the entrepreneur no longer exists as an individual person in the mature indus-trial enterprise." Ever since then, of course, American corporate history has been dominated by entrepreneurs of one sort or another, whether corporate raiders ripping apart the old monsters or young tycoons simply outsmarting them. The proportion of American output coming from big companies rose gradually from 22 percent in 1918 to 33 percent in 1970, but it did not change between then and 1990 (and surely, given the arrival of the technol-ogy industries, it must have fallen since then). In Germany, Japan, and Britain, the proportions all fell pretty dramatically between 1970 and 1990.

Big companies have never been particularly good at remaining on top. USX was once America's largest company; J&P Coats was once Britain's biggest manufacturer.[1] The title of world's biggest bank changed hands at least six times in the twentieth century. As Robert Samuelson has pointed out, an American president who wanted to talk to corporate America once needed to talk only to J. P. Morgan. Now he would need a small amphitheater. Industry after industry has fragmented. In the 1970s, America's roads were ruled by just three companies (Ford, Chrysler, and General Motors), its air-waves by three (NBC, ABC, and CBS), its telephones by AT&T, and most of its technology industry by IBM.[2] Nowadays, whatever you think of Microsoft, it remains just one of nearly ten thousand software companies. And even in industries where there has been obvious consolidation, such as banking, globalization and deregulation have created opportunities for competitors from all sides.

There are plenty of ways in which globalization reduces the power of big firms. True, national champions find it easier to spread their tentacles around the world, but they have tended to encounter other giants spreading their own rubbery arms. In Woo's own industry, Mattel and Hasbro have run into Lego, Sony, and Nintendo; Toys "R" Us has been losing market share to discounters such as Wal-Mart, and now it has to contend with Internet toy firms. Small firms have few of the fixed costs of their bigger rivals, such as bloated head offices and waffling middle managers. The deregulation of the capital markets has made it easier for such firms to borrow money; the avail- ability of information technology has made it easier for them to do the sort of number crunching that was once the preserve of the giants; and the declin- ing cost of transport has turned the entire world into their marketplace. Consider many of the characters we have already met—not just Woo but also Patrick Wang, Marcus de Ferranti, and Jackson Thubela—and it is not hard to see why small firms feel less cowed than they once did.

So why are so many large companies trying to become even larger ones? There are clearly some markets in which size has always mattered: aero- space, for example. There are others where it is beginning to matter more than ever. The rising cost of designing new cars means that carmakers are dividing into two tiers: Half a dozen global giants are prospering while their smaller rivals are treading water or going under. But in many big mergers, companies are pursuing size out of weakness rather than as part of some megalomaniacal scheme of world domination. The world's biggest oil com- panies have been driven to merge by their own fatalism about a long-term decline in the price of oil and also by the difficulty of finding more of the stuff. Many big mergers, including both Daimler-Chrysler and Exxon-Mobil, are intent on reducing costs in industries that have too much capacity.

These sound like good reasons. Yet the only thing more certain than a continuing rise in the number of mergers is that most of them will be fail- ures. A relentless series of academic studies has come up with the same con- clusion: Roughly two out every three mergers do not work; the only winners are the shareholders of the acquired company, who receive for their shares more than they are subsequently proved to be worth. The obvious reason for this preponderance of failures is that companies overpay. In the heat of bat- tle, ego often triumphs over logic. (See, for example, Bryan Burrough and John Helyar's *Barbarians at the Gate.*) One delicious study points out that the size of the overpayment is linked to the number of magazine covers graced by the acquiring boss prior to the deal.

But the faults in the big-is-better arguments go much deeper than just price. Diversity is not a sufficient condition for a successful merger. South Korea's *chaebol*, for example, managed to diversify into a dizzying range of activities, from shipbuilding to hair care, but rarely became world-class in more than one. In other cases, buyers cite mythical synergies, such as the hardware-software argument that lured Sony and Matsushita into Hollywood. Rather than correct weaknesses, upsizing can often exaggerate them. Most American bank deals have been done in the name of cost cutting. Yet when Anthony Santomero, a finance professor at the Wharton School, examined the cost-cutting performance of retail banks in America, he found that the wise virgins had usually cut costs faster than banks that had gone through the sweaty distraction of mating.

Above all, there is the difficulty of welding an empire together. Many a promising fit has been undone by the presumption that computers like each other. Boeing and McDonnell Douglas were left struggling with 450 incompatible computer systems. The marriage between Union Pacific and Southern Pacific in 1996 was supposed to deliver seamless rail service; instead, it produced a logistics nightmare, with at one point ten thousand train cars stalled throughout Texas and California. Even worse than incompatible machines are incompatible people. Look behind any disastrous American deal—AT&T's acquisition of NCR (bought for $7 billion in 1991; spun off in 1995 for $3 billion) or Quaker Oats' takeover of Snapple (bought for $1.7 billion in 1994; sold for $300 million in 1997)—and one word always appears: culture. People never fit together as easily as flowcharts. After one large American merger, for example, the two companies had a row over the annual picnic: Employees of one company were accustomed to inviting spouses, the others were dead set against the idea. The issue was resolved only by agreeing to allow spouses in alternate years.

Global mergers are even harder. It is even more tempting to start counting which side is winning if the other firm is from another country. In Japan, foreign banks that have bought local firms, such as Merrill Lynch, have had to cope with employees who would not dream of refusing to lend friendly clients money just because their business was obviously tanking. The link between Swedish Pharmacia and American Upjohn in 1995 was supposed to be driven by cost cutting and by complementary drug portfolios. But plenty of time was wasted on rows about "American" practices, such as banning alcohol at lunch. Even worse, Pharmacia had not properly integrated an Italian acquisition. The new company thus started with power bases in Stockholm, Milan, and Kalamazoo. After a botched attempt to make everybody report to a new office near London, the firm eventually moved to New Jersey. At BP-Amoco, what was billed as a merger of equals rapidly became a British takeover. "How do you pronounce the company's name?" went one joke. "BP: the 'Amoco' is silent."

Similar stories emerged from DaimlerChrysler, arguably the most "global" merger ever and one that is proving a case study in how (or how not) to reconcile different management cultures. One immediate issue was compensation. Chrysler's boss, Robert Eaton, who pocketed at least seventy million dollars as a result of the takeover and is used to earning up to five million dollars a year, had to report to the more modestly rewarded Jürgen Schrempp. Similar discrepancies still occur throughout management. If Chrysler were to cut pay to German levels, then its managers might defect to Ford and General Motors. But the egalitarian Germans also dislike the type of pay disparity that is common in American firms. One Daimler man shudders to think of his reputation in the small town where he lives if, say, it were reported that his pay had tripled.

The Second Myth: The Triumph of Universal Products

The sister myth to the triumph of size is the triumph of global products, the idea that an elite group of powerful brand names, supported by mighty marketing machines, will end up conquering the world. The clearest statement of this view is to be found in "The Globalization of Markets," a classic article by Theodore Levitt, a marketing guru at the Harvard Business School. Levitt argued that technology was producing "a new commercial reality—the emergence of global markets on a previously unimagined scale of magnitude." Global companies that ignore "superficial" regional differences and exploit economies of scale by selling the same things in the same way everywhere would soon sideline not only small local companies but also the old sort of multinational company that spent much of its time trying to be "respectful" of local quirks and peccadilloes. "The earth is round," argued Levitt, "but, for most purposes, it's sensible to treat it as flat."[3]

But is it? There are a few upmarket products—*The Economist* is one—that happily inhabit Levitt's "flattened world," many of them selling to the cosmocratic class. But most people have begun to realize that in marketing, just as in navigation, treating the world as if it is flat can have drawbacks. In the broader consumer market, there are only a handful of truly global brands that sell everywhere to everybody, and even these giant names do not mean the same thing in Beijing (where they are status symbols) as they do in Boston (where they are far from cool). Asked to name how many truly global brands there are, one of the top people at Coca-Cola mentions McDonald's, Mercedes-Benz, BMW, and Sony, "and that is about it."

Even Coca-Cola finds it hard to live up to its "Always Coca-Cola" slogan. The bottlers who bring the magic liquid to the world's consumers are independent contractors rather than company employees—so independent, in fact, that one Coke chieftain was reduced to pleading to a group of them at a company conference in Mexico, "Please paint your trucks red."[4] The company is also far more responsive to local tastes than it likes to pretend. Coca-Cola's biggest-selling product in India, for example, is not Coke but Thums Up, which outsells "the real thing" by a margin of four to one in some markets.[5]

Coca-Cola is not alone. McDonald's sells *bulgogi* burgers in South Korea and offers teriyaki sauce in Japan. "I do not know how a global firm could not be decentralized," says Jack Greenberg, McDonald's boss. Asked to define the consistent element in a McDonald's experience, he replies, "An excellent fresh meal in a clean restaurant." Budweiser produces a superstrength lager in Japan and even boasts about the brew's intoxicating qualities in its advertisements, something that would be inconceivable in prudish America. In the Middle East, Pillsbury puts lamb in its toaster strudels rather than jam, as in America; in China it uses pork and dough, so that they have a dim-sum taste. Naturally, local products sometimes have unexpected global markets: Pillsbury started making green-tea ice cream for the Japanese, but other people like it, too. But those companies that fail to take into account local differences are bound for trouble, as General Motors discovered when it tried to sell its Chevrolet Nova in Latin America without changing the car's name. (*No va* means "doesn't go" in Spanish.)

Indeed, in recent years, marketing departments have become obsessed with segmenting customers rather than bundling them together. Companies err if they treat entire countries as single markets, let alone the whole world. In Europe, companies that consolidated their marketing operations in anticipation of the birth of the Euro are rediscovering the importance of national differences. In the United States, where blacks, Latinos, and Asians have a collective purchasing power of about nine hundred billion dollars a year, marketing to "hyphenated Americans" is a booming business.[6] And there is probably more room to divide markets geographically. In 1997, McDonald's split its approach to the United States into five regional divisions to reflect the fact that different areas have different climates and different sets of competitors and customers. Car firms already vary their pitches around the country. Now the art of television programming—traditionally a Los Angeles and New York affair where honchos like to boast that they "program for the people they fly over"—might also soon take a local direction. Research shows that American viewers rate stations by the quality of their local news, not by which network they are attached to.

Charlie Woo's own industry appears to be symptomatic. Even "global" toys are carefully localized by their manufacturers. In Japan, Barbie has smaller breasts than she does in America. Despite the extra cost, Woo is always fiddling with packaging and designs so that his Latin American toys look different from the American ones. Indeed, for students of the nature-versus-nurture debate, the toy industry offers plenty of insights that are potentially politically incorrect. Why is it that, even at a young age, German children are notably more organized than their unruly American peers and thus more likely to buy complicated building toys? Why do black American children like some sort of toys and their Asian peers others? Woo does not care about the psychological insights; like everybody else, he just changes his products to fit.

The Third Myth: That Economics Needs to Be Rewritten

Put to Charlie Woo the idea that he is part of some new economy and all you get is a wry chuckle. Far from assuming that the business cycle is dead, he talks at length about the prospect of another downturn, like the one in the early 1990s. As for inflation, it is indeed low; in fact, deflation seems to have gripped some parts of the toy industry. But Woo's main fears are still about rising costs, particularly for labor. He is always squabbling with his workers about pay raises. His environment certainly seems to be changing a little more quickly than before: Globalization means that competitors can spring up anywhere. But the underlying rules of how to make money are the same as always.

This is not a view that Peter Schwartz shares. Schwartz, an affable man with a neat beard and habit of saying "absolutely," is the driving force behind the Global Business Network. GBN specializes in a rarefied form of consultancy: mapping the future. Nearly one hundred clients—ranging from blue-chip firms such as IBM and AT&T to the government of Singapore—pay thirty-five thousand dollars each to belong to GBN's intellectual community. For considerably more money, GBN also provides them with bespoke maps of the future. Schwartz has a good record as a cartographer, particularly in his earlier career as a scenario planner at Royal Dutch/Shell. In 1982, he speculated that oil prices might collapse to sixteen dollars a barrel. Shell piled up cash to prepare for that eventuality and was not caught short, as its rivals were.

Schwartz lent his authority to a view of the future that won widespread applause in Silicon Valley in the late 1990s: A mixture of globalization and technological innovation was all but abolishing the business cycle. He laid out his case in richest detail in "The Long Boom," an article he cowrote in 1997 for the country's leading organ of high-tech boosterism, *Wired*, and later turned into a book of the same title. A brief quote conveys both the essence and the tone of the argument then common:

> We are watching the beginning of a global economic boom on a scale never experienced before. We have entered a period of sustained growth that could eventually double the world's economy every dozen years and bring increasing prosperity for—quite literally—billions of people on the planet. We are riding the early waves of a 25-year run of a greatly expanding economy that will do much to solve seemingly intractable problems like poverty and to ease tensions throughout the world. And we'll do it without blowing the lid off the environment.[7]

Schwartz was on the extreme end of the scale, but the idea that we were entering a new economy that was governed by fundamentally different rules from the old one gained a remarkable amount of influence in the 1990s. Silicon Valley treated it as gospel. Kevin Kelly, executive editor of *Wired*, wrote a book called *New Rules for the New Economy*. *BusinessWeek* was an early convert. Alan Greenspan flirted with the phrase. On Wall Street, brokers cited the new economy as an explanation for why old expectations about how quickly profits can grow were invalid—and pumped up a stock-market bubble. Meanwhile, even those few Americans who had not piled their life savings into Amazon.com seemed to be caught up in the grip of what Nathan Myhrvold of Microsoft once dismissively (and perhaps ungratefully) called "technomania." ("If *The Graduate* were to be made in the late 1990s the single word of advice imparted to Benjamin would be 'information.'")[8]

The new economy is difficult to define, largely because it encompasses three things. The first, now fortunately gone for good, had to do with the stock market in the 1990s: that it somehow justified crazy equity prices. But the other two things have survived the bubble. The second has to do with the organization of business: the idea that corporate life, particularly in America, is being transformed by the Internet and by Internet companies. This seems very hard to quarrel with. The third, most complicated debate has to do with macroeconomics and how much its laws and assumptions need to be rewritten in the light of all this new technology and, to a lesser extent, globalization.

For most of the 1990s, the basic argument that technology had revolutionized productivity and changed the speed limit at which the American economy could grow looked weak. Yes, American firms had poured money into technology, and inflation had stayed low, but there were plenty of other things holding down prices, including cheap commodities, a strong dollar, and even the aftereffects of the savage restructurings at the beginning of the decade: Scared workers restricted (inflation-causing) wage demands. Worse, despite a colossal investment in technology in the last two decades of the twentieth century, American productivity growth bounced along well below the postwar average of 3.4 percent a year for most of the 1990s. Some people wondered whether the gains in productivity were limited to just a few high-tech industries; others even whispered that technology might not be quite as productive as people claimed. As Stephen Roach has pointed out, the hours that we all spend trying to tap into office networks from hotel rooms often stretch workdays without achieving much.[9]

On the other hand, throughout the 1990s, most of the anecdotal evidence from the real economy indicated that something had happened. It was almost impossible to visit an American company in the 1990s without discovering more evidence that productivity was increasing and that technology (and to a lesser extent globalization) had played a role. Inventories were being tracked, parts being automatically ordered when they were needed, workers reminded that factories could be relocated to cheaper countries. And by the early twenty-first century, the statistical evidence had begun to move a little: The annual speed limit at which the American economy could grow safely appeared to rise from around 2.25 percent to 2.75 percent. That was a long way from the revolution that Silicon Valley preached but not insignificant.

Both sides of the new-economy debate have tended to characterize their opponents unfairly.[10] But even if the American economy's speed limit has increased, some pretty strange ideas seem to have been embraced in its name. One clear area has been stock-market valuations: The astronomic changes in stock valuations, still evident in 2002, are well above historic norms and anything that could be explained by improvements in corporate earnings (even if the numbers are actually correct, which scandals like Enron and WorldCom have cast doubts over). Another is the idea that economics needs to be rewritten. Most of the ingredients of the new economy are actually fairly old. Deflation, for instance, is not a new threat, and there is a fairly simple way to cure it: loosen monetary policy. And the idea that the new economy will look after inflation all by itself seems extremely unlikely.

On balance, we are skeptical about whether the Internet marks the same paradigm shift as the introduction of electricity and the arrival of the combustion engine. (Whenever you meet somebody from Silicon Valley who talks about how the World Wide Web will revolutionize your business "like never before," ask yourself whether the improvements it is bringing will really be as life changing as the ability to keep on working easily after dark was for businesses one hundred years ago.) And even if the change does prove to be as large, that does not mean that the economic cycle has gone, let alone that it justified the idea of "Dow 36,000" in 1999.[11] Globalization shows that the old economy is being quite as inventive as ever; there is no need to invent another one.

The Fourth Myth: Globalization as a Zero-Sum Game

Tell the story of Charlie Woo to many American trade unionists, and they react with disapproval. Far from creating jobs, they argue, Woo has been stealing them. By employing cheap immigrant labor and importing Chinese-made goods, he has undermined the good middle-class jobs that Mattel and Hasbro used to provide. This accusation certainly contains some truth. Both Mattel and Hasbro have cut jobs as they have outsourced manufacturing. More than two thirds of the world's toys are made in China or Hong Kong. The toy industry has also been caught out repeatedly for making toys in deplorable conditions in the third world. Yet even if Woo's opponents can marshal a few honest facts, their accusation is still based on a much bigger, dishonest myth: For some people to profit from globalization, others must lose to an equal degree.

The idea that economic integration is a zero-sum game underpins antiglobalist thinking about everything from "fair trade" to jobs to wages to the relationship between rich countries and poor ones.[12] Ross Perot expressed this belief most vividly when he warned that NAFTA would produce a "great sucking sound" as jobs went south of the border. Other politicians—including Pat Buchanan and Dick Gephardt in America, Oskar LaFontaine in Germany, and just about every French leader you have ever heard of—have peddled the same line. Allow low-wage workers to compete head-to-head with high-wage workers, they maintain, and the high-wage workers will end up on the dole. Allowing Germans to buy foreign-made lightbulbs means fewer lightbulbs made by German workers. Allowing German companies to move their plants abroad means more jobs for foreigners and fewer for Germans. This is why even supposed supporters of free trade, such as the Bush administration, announce each reduction in American tariffs as if it were a concession. There is, it seems, only so much employment and so much trade to go round, so the primary job of a government should be to hang on to its share of the pie.

In some cases, this myth is pathetically easy to expose. For instance, NAFTA seems to have had a negligible effect on jobs in the United States: American direct investment in Mexico has increased since the agreement, but only from $2 billion a year to $3 billion, still a small figure compared with the more than $700 billion that American firms currently invest in their home country. However, in most cases, the zero-sum myth falls into the small-truth/big-myth category. Of course, some first-world workers lose as a result of foreign trade or foreign direct investment. Just ask a steelworker or a coal miner, if you can find one. But globalization also creates jobs. If Buchanan were right, the United States, with one of the most liberal trading policies in the world, would be losing jobs by the million. Instead, it has generated twenty million additional jobs in the past decade alone.

In most places outside Paris and Havana, the zero-sum myth has been thoroughly debunked. This may explain why its partisans have recently shifted their focus from the quantity of jobs to the quality. Free trade, they point out, forces workers from rich countries into head-to-head competition with workers from poor countries. Companies can then move jobs to low-wage countries in order to reduce their payrolls—or at least they can threaten to move there if domestic workers refuse to accept "realistic" wage levels. This pressures the first-world worker into either accepting low wages or following the steelworkers-cum-strippers of *The Full Monty* into dodgy jobs in the service sector. Marx, exponents of this scenario imply, was right: Capital profits at the expense of labor; that is why American companies did so well in the 1990s and also why wages in the United States have risen more slowly since 1973 than they did during the "less global" period before then.

This argument has plenty of statistical problems and two big conceptual ones. The first statistical hitch is that relatively few American workers are in direct competition with workers from poor countries: Most of them are engaged in producing goods or services for industries in which there is little cross-border competition, such as health care or construction. (Immigration has a much more direct impact on American wages than trade does.) Second, most American manufacturing jobs are in industries in which the most direct competition comes from other rich countries rather than poor ones. Third, low-skilled workers seem to be doing even worse in industries that are little affected by trade than in those that are greatly affected by it. This suggests that something else explains their fate, and most economists suspect it is technological change.

The first conceptual problem is that labor costs are best measured not just by wages but also by productivity. It makes perfect economic sense to pay high wages to people who are highly productive—and since first-world workers are more productive than their third-world counterparts, thanks to better education, management, machinery, and infrastructure, they can compete in the open market without getting poorer. So why have wages grown more slowly since 1973 than they did before then? Once again, productivity provides the answer. The rate of growth of pay has slowed over the past decades because, as we have already noted, the rate of growth of productivity slowed (at least until recently).

Tellingly, many third-world Pat Buchanans seize on the issue of productivity in order to preach a more or less opposite version of the same myth: Globalization is helping productive, capital-rich countries profit at the expense of poor ones. Mexican trade unions complain that America is more productive just as American trade unions moan that Mexican workers are cheap. In fact, the evidence is that the current system has helped them catch up. In 1960, the average wage in developing countries was just 10 percent of the average manufacturing wage in the United States; in 1992, despite all that terrible globalization, it had risen to 30 percent. The reason lies in the second concept that the antiglobalists cannot handle: Globalization helps the whole pie get bigger.

Toytown provides an example of this. Sales of toys in America have grown pretty steadily since Woo founded Toytown. To be sure, Woo has replaced some jobs, but many of those that he has created are new ones. In America, his toys helped create a new niche in the market—below that of Mattel but above that of street vendors. In other markets, notably Latin America, Toytown has helped broaden the choice available to an emerging middle class. But it is not just a matter of price: Toytown has created new products, increasing the pie. Typically, innovation is not usually thought of in terms of a scarier Darth Vader mask, but in Woo's world it can be.

Two fundamental principles show why he is right. The first is Adam Smith's principle of the division of labor: The more people specialize in what they do best, the more productivity is improved—and the bigger the market, the more refined the division of labor can become. The second is David Ricardo's principle of comparative advantage. The whole point of engaging in trade is to allocate resources to the country that can use them best, even if that activity is linking Chinese hands with American consumers. This process is never painless. Some workers are forced to move to new lines of business. Some are forced to take a reduction in pay. But in the long run, the process creates far more winners than losers. Consumers obviously benefit from cheaper prices and more choice, but producers also benefit from doing what they do best rather than from what can be done better by others.

Why then does the zero-sum-game myth persist? One reason is that some supporters of globalization have sometimes tried to beat the pessimists in the exaggeration game. To Ross Perot's taunt that NAFTA would produce a great sucking sound, they frequently retorted that, on the contrary, it would produce a great sound of job creation (which, given the fact that tariffs were pretty low anyway, was never going to happen). Another reason is that the costs of globalization are far more visible than the benefits. The costs tend to fall on identifiable people, such as steelworkers. The benefits are spread through the whole of society, but they do not come with a label that screams globalization. Workers who make products sold abroad often fail to understand that their jobs depend on their country's willingness to import as well as its capacity to export. People contributing to a pension fund seldom realize that the value of their investments is sometimes boosted by the fund's ability to invest abroad.

The area where the zero-sum-game myth is most pernicious is trade policy. Each reduction in the volume of world trade means higher prices and fewer choices for consumers, scarcer jobs for producers, and less opportunity for people such as Charlie Woo to innovate. Nevertheless, trade policy even in America is based on the peculiar belief that giving consumers the chance to buy cheaper, better products is a great sacrifice. Thus, in 1999, the American government made a great show of reacting to the European Union's refusal to open its banana market by imposing huge tariffs on various European imports such as cashmere sweaters and Gucci handbags. Even leaving aside the questionable symmetry of these actions—not to mention the financial contributions to the Clinton administration by America's biggest banana-grower—the decision still seemed like a scene from an economic version of *Dr. Strangelove.* "The Europeans are punishing their banana eaters," one can imagine the dialogue, "so let's make American sweater wearers really sweat." Three years later George W. Bush outdid even that farce, screaming bloody murder at foreign steel mills for "dumping" their products on the American market, thereby criminally forcing down prices for American industry.

In fact, *unfair trade* is usually an oxymoron. Frédéric Bastiat, a French satirist, once argued that the sun offered unfair competition to candle makers. Why not, he suggested, board up windows so that there would be more jobs for them? In America, every time the trade deficit swells, so does use of the phrase *fair trade* and then, in turn, calls to use Section 301, the part of

U.S. trade law that allows America (probably in contravention of WTO law) to take retaliatory action against anyone whose trade policies are unreasonable. In the 1980s, the unfair traders were the Japanese who were unreasonably exporting cheaper, better products to America. By 2002, the charge seemed to be shifting to China and the Europeans, who were apparently not doing enough to jolt their economies into life and thus forcing those reluctant "consumers of last resort," the American people, to buy cheap goods.

As numerous economists, notably Jagdish Bhagwati, have pointed out, this is piffle of the first order. People generally gain from trade regardless of what their trading partners do. Perhaps the most cruel use of "fair trade" comes when it is tied to issues such as labor conditions and environmental standards. For instance, the goal of eradicating child labor is a noble one, but when it has been linked to trade, it has nearly always been for protectionist reasons (step forward, the American textile industry) and has often had disastrous consequences for those it has tried to help. It would be better if poor children in Pakistan did not spend their days stitching together baskets rather than going to school, but close down their factory and they will merely enter less appetizing professions. Two solutions suggest themselves. The first is labeling and publicity: Witness both the success of "dolphin-friendly tuna" and the way that multinational companies rapidly drop suppliers who are found to breach labor standards. The second is direct help for the people concerned: If the United States, which gives a pathetic amount of money to the third world, and the European Union, which gives only slightly more, put as much effort into helping poor children directly as they do into discriminating against their products, the effect could be dramatic.

The use of "fair trade" in this context is particularly galling because the single thing that the developed world could do to help the third world most would be to remove its own deeply unfair barriers to trade. The children flocking to third-world cities go there in part because the local farms have so few export markets. Removing the rich world's restrictions on agricultural imports would give the poor world a huge new market. Additionally, much of the money that the West spends supporting manufacturing (some sixty billion dollars a year within the European Union alone) goes to the sort of basic industries that could represent a step up the development ladder for poor countries. Rich countries' average tariffs on manufacturing imports from poor countries are four times higher than those on other rich countries. One estimate by UNCTAD reckons that by 2005 the developing world could add seven hundred billion dollars a year to its exports if the rich world lowered these barriers.[13] That would be much "fairer."

The Fifth Myth: The Disappearance of Geography

Wandering around the warehouses and factories of Toytown, you get the distinct feeling that they should be somewhere else. Isn't this just the sort of low-tech manufacturing that should be based in, say, India or China rather than downtown Los Angeles? The idea that in a global economy "geography does not matter"—that business will inevitably migrate to where it can find the cheapest hands—is such a staple of the debate about globalization that it seems strange to point out that this is by no means always the case. Los Angeles certainly has a powerful array of high-tech and service industries; its biggest business, by far, is entertainment. But as Joel Kotkin, a local economist, points out, three of the city's biggest industries are furniture, food processing, and clothing. The last of these, thanks to a new generation of Asian, Middle Eastern, and Latin American immigrant entrepreneurs, is now probably bigger than defense.

This is not unusual. Far from relocating overseas to benefit from cheap labor and lax regulations, most of low-tech America seems to be staying put. For every ballyhooed high-tech manufacturer such as Intel or fashionably "virtual" company such as Nike (whose sneakers are assembled across Asia), there are plenty of humdrum manufacturers spinning out such mundane but essential products as plastic chairs, cutlery, toys, tape measures, and T-shirts. Overall numbers are hard to come by, but a crude index measuring most of the above products shows that they held their own in terms of both output and jobs from 1992 to 1996.[14] Many of America's "millionaires next door," celebrated in the best-selling book of that title, are small family firms. In some cases—notably, textiles and virtually anything to do with agriculture—these local heroes are protected by trade barriers. But many more of them are earning their keep in fairly open markets, making fairly basic things.

Wages and fringe benefits per manufacturing worker in the United States average about eighteen dollars an hour. Many low-tech manufacturers undoubtedly pay their workers (both legal and illegal) much less, but hourly rates in America are more than a day's pay for workers in many developing countries. So why do the companies stay?

One reason why geography still matters is that in a global economy, business clusters are important—something Woo has always appreciated. Rather than trying to discourage competitors, as most businessmen do, he spread the word about his success around Hong Kong and also helped local entrepreneurs. He felt strongly that a business that was surrounded by other similar businesses had much more of a chance to succeed than one that sat in splendid isolation. The number of customers would increase, he reasoned, because each new business would bring its own clients, and people would be more likely to brave the horrors of downtown if they had hundreds of outlets from which to choose. And there would be more opportunities to contract out work to nearby specialists. "It is much better to make friends out of your fellow businessmen than enemies," argues Woo, before adding, with a smile, "and I make a healthy living out of renting my warehouses to newcomers."

As a result, Toytown contains a set of skills that would be difficult to match elsewhere. Of course, Woo's kingdom does not compare with the entertainment cluster in Hollywood or the technology one in Silicon Valley (which is the subject of chapter 11). But Toytown has helped consolidate southern California's hold on the toy industry: Around 60 percent of America's toys come through the region. If you look at other low-tech clusters—South Carolina's furniture makers, for instance—you find the same sort of economics at work. They are always threatened by globalization, but it also offers them new markets.[15]

However, even when low-tech firms are not linked in some cluster, there is another, much broader set of reasons why they can survive, as should become apparent from a consideration of Osram Sylvania's factory in Maybrook, New York. America's electronics industry usually conjures up images of semiconductor workers in Dr. No suits, not people in T-shirts checking lightbulbs. The machinery is more than a decade old and the technology involved in lightbulb making has not changed greatly in half a century. But the 210 workers at Maybrook still manage to churn out some twenty-two million fluorescent lights a year, and their parent company has the biggest share of the American market for compact fluorescent lights.

Osram Sylvania is owned by Germany's Siemens. No doubt it is a caring concern, but it is hard to imagine that Siemens would think twice before moving production elsewhere if it made economic sense to do so. But there are sound reasons for staying put. In the lightbulb industry, the key factor is transport costs. Importing a fifty-cent lightbulb from overseas might cost twenty cents.

Look around low-tech America and you will find plenty of other companies with particular reasons to stay put. Foamex International, the world's biggest supplier of urethane foam (which goes into car seats and mattresses), has sixty-seven different factories and distribution outlets in the United States because transporting a product that is 95 percent air is not economical.

Time is often more important than price. Rubbermaid could make many of its basic plastic household products more cheaply in Asia, but in order to keep fussy retailers such as Wal-Mart happy, it has to keep an enormous inventory of its products on hand, so it might miss the chance to ramp up production quickly if a new product or promotion proves especially successful. More than 90 percent of Rubbermaid's sales in America are of products made there. In the clothing business, oscillating fashions, promotion schedules, and seasonal offerings require suppliers to be flexible. Nike's decision to make its shoes in Asia has forced distributors to order months in advance and is contingent on fashions changing relatively slowly. When American teenagers lost some of their appetite for Nike in 1997, the system clogged up with unsold sneakers.

Even old-fashioned prejudices can play a part. It might be cheaper to can soup in Laos rather than Los Angeles, but the product would be a tough sell in Des Moines. One South Carolina furniture distributor says that furniture made in many Asian countries does not look "American enough": So far, globally, he has got what he wants only from a factory in the Philippines, so he buys the rest from domestic manufacturers. Some even suggest that patriotism comes into play. There is no evidence that Nike has lost any sales by making its shoes abroad, despite widespread criticism of its working practices there. But two shoe companies, New Balance and Red Wing, maintain that "a certain segment" of their customers care a lot about their "Made in the USA" stickers.

Perhaps the most important reason why America's low-tech industries have been able to defy globalization, however, is because they have fought like hell. At Maybrook, the story has not been an easy one. Three years ago, despite its relative efficiency, the plant was barely breaking even. Now, having introduced a blizzard of quality-related programs and other new management methods, Dick Brace, the plant's manager, boasts that the factory is one of the group's most profitable in the world. Labor accounts for only 20 percent of the cost of each fluorescent light; nevertheless, the firm works relentlessly to keep costs down yet maintain quality. And it is always looking for little competitive edges. One of the problems with fluorescent lights is that they heat up as they burn out, often expanding so they get stuck in their fixtures. Maybrook has just started adding small drops of titanium hydride that will put the light out when it gets too hot, giving the company a (probably fleeting) advantage over its competitors. Brace insists that his lamps are better than others'. "You can't just train people to make lamps overnight," he says indignantly, pointing out that new competitors from places such as Asia always run into problems with quality.

Osram Sylvania recently closed down another light factory near Boston, moving the work to factories in Kentucky and Canada. Brace also noticed at a recent trade show that the quality of lights made by cheap overseas firms is getting better. He also faces an internal challenge: New equipment at an Osram Sylvania factory in Bari, Italy, is faster than Maybrook's. Brace may have to cut back the line that makes the same "S-type" lights as Bari (which currently accounts for a third of Maybrook's output). But he also thinks that Maybrook can take over some work from a German factory, which will let it expand its share of another part of the American market. In the meantime, he is pushing through other changes, such as a new profit-sharing scheme that will include all the workers at the factory, as well as a new computer system. As long as the factory keeps on changing faster than its competitors, it will be some time before the lights go out in Maybrook.

Woo's World

Although Maybrook demonstrates how companies can defy globalization, Dick Brace's gyrations—and subsequently those of his workers—still show how much his life is affected by it. One thing about myths is that even if they are wrong they often contain substantial fragments of truth. The only one of the five key myths that seems to be wholly dishonest is the zero-sum-game one. But there are some good big companies that have prospered by getting bigger; there are some global products; the old economy has not become a new one, but it is being changed by globalization; and although geography is certainly not dead, it matters less. The point is that globalization is potent enough on its own account; it is not necessary to exaggerate its effects.

Charlie Woo is as aware of those effects as Brace is. Despite his achievements and his bursts of optimism, Woo is not content. He has a nagging fear that the same forces that created his kingdom could destroy it. He worries that relying on *guanxi*, or connections, alone will leave him vulnerable to even cheaper competitors. He frets that some of Toytown's most successful companies are now diversifying into products such as kitchenware and sunglasses. Meanwhile, the toy business itself is getting more complicated. In 1998, the traditional toy industry failed to grow in America. Instead, parents poured their money into educational and entertainment software. Mattel decided to redefine itself as a "global children's products company" and bought The Learning Company, an educational software company, for $3.8 billion. In Hong Kong and Shenzhen, Charlie Woo's spiritual offspring are starting firms such as actionace.com, which sells toys across the Internet.

As a result, Woo is forcing his kingdom upmarket. His own business has employed a small team of trendy designers, packagers, and advertising people. He has also organized a course in toy design at a local college to give him an entrée to young talent and has started a manufacturing and design center so that his fellow entrepreneurs can improve their products. Woo also plans to get around this threat by extending his network and plugging Toytown into Tinseltown. Hollywood, he argues, increasingly defines children's dreams around the world; to thrive, a toy maker needs to be part of the dream machine. Woo no longer mocks Mattel for producing overpriced products but instead praises them for employing six hundred designers and smooching with studio chiefs. The studios are pumping out a growing number of film-related products, he notes, and he wants to get in on the action. The unreturned phone calls that irritate him now are to Hollywood producers rather than to politicians.

Globalization may not be dividing the world into the people who live in glass towers and those who sleep on the streets, but it is undoubtedly forcing even the humblest businesspeople to keep improving their products and to look for alliances, like the one Woo is trying to forge with the film industry. The Darth Vader masks above Charlie Woo's desk that his secretary keeps warning him will one day topple down on top of him also hold the key to Toytown's future.

7

Managing in a Global Age

IF A MEMBER of the Académie Française had to define hell, it might well be as the McDonald's outside the Animal Kingdom in Orlando, Florida. The smart new burger joint is a themed Walt Disney World restaurant—the theme being McDonald's ubiquity. The staff wears special Disney-approved uniforms showing McDonald's characters. On the wall, there is a list of battle honors: "1993: Saipan, Israel, Iceland, Slovenia . . . 1996: Fiji, Liechtenstein, Lithuania." A video screen displays various McFacts ("Which country has a Maharajah burger?"). In the middle of the store, an oversized bottle dispenses Coca-Cola.

If our Gallic intellectual did a little more research about the ties between Disney, McDonald's, and Coke, he might be even more horrified. These three icons of Americanization form not just a cultural triumvirate but also a commercial one, linked through a series of partnerships and alliances. McDonald's relationship with Coca-Cola goes back to the 1950s. Although Coke sells drinks to other restaurants, its involvement with McDonald's goes far beyond that of a mere supplier. It has helped McDonald's set up new operations around the world. When Roberto Goizueta, Coke's chairman, died, flags flew at half-mast at McDonald's around the world. Meanwhile, Coke has been the sole provider of soft drinks at Disney theme parks since 1955, and McDonald's has had a formal alliance with Disney since 1997. Mediocre Disney films such as *Flubber* have been helped by tie-ins at McDonald's, which has also sold a lot of Disney Happy Meals.

This is the sort of image that most ordinary people have of "managing in a global age": It is just an easy affair of extending well-known brands around the world and doing deals with your friends. In fact, globalization is incredibly difficult to manage, and for most managers it is usually more a source of fear than of excitement. For every McDonald's, Coke, or Disney, there are countless smaller firms fighting to avoid getting run over by these global juggernauts. And even the three giants have hardly had easy times recently. Disney's magic dust has lost its sparkle, as profits have stalled and the company has failed to make any sense out of its acquisition of Capital Cities/ABC. Coke's growth also stalled at the same time that it ran into an embarrassing series of health-related and legal disasters in Europe. And after complaints that Burger King does indeed "just taste better," McDonald's has had to revamp its menu and even retreat from some countries.

Any manager will tell you that his or her job has become much more difficult. In some cases, these challenges are self-inflicted. (Disney's Michael Eisner seems to be unusually good at falling out with his senior managers.) But there is also a universal feeling that every manager now faces a world in which the old certainties have been replaced by a string of unpleasant surprises and in which strategy has devolved from long-term planning to simple panicking. Globalization is not the only reason for this uncertainty, but, with the possible exception of technological innovation, it is the main destabilizer of the management psyche.

One way to understand the full horror of global management is to look at the process in slow motion and with the benefit of hindsight. At the beginning of the nineteenth century, Britain was the world leader in textiles, thanks to its water-driven looms. The machines, blueprints, and so on were carefully guarded secrets. An aristocratic American, Francis Cabot Lowell, managed to finagle his way into the factories and talked to the workers about the machines they used. By the time he left Britain in 1813, the textile barons were on to him. Customs officials searched his baggage twice and discovered no drawings. But Lowell had memorized the designs. Built on the back of the Cartwright power loom, the town of Lowell (named after him posthumously) became not just one of America's first industrial centers but also a thorn in the side of Britain's textiles industry. But before you get too distraught about the poor old British, it is worth remembering Manaus. By the 1870s, the Brazilian jungle city had become one of the world's most advanced. (It had an electric tramway and an opera house.) Then another resourceful entrepreneur, a Briton named Henry Wickham, managed to smuggle out some rubber-tree seeds, cultivated them in Kew Gardens, and then shipped them out to British colonies in Asia, such as Sri Lanka and Malaysia. Rubber prices collapsed, and so did the fortunes of Manaus.

The sort of things that happened to Lancashire and Manaus over decades happen to businesses today in months and sometimes even just days. Suddenly, competitors leap out of nowhere; prices start falling; seemingly impervious products are suddenly upstaged; if you don't get your idea around the world quickly enough, somebody else will.

In a growing number of industries (cars and computers are the most obvious examples), there is simply too much capacity around the world, so globalization keeps pushing down prices. To keep track, some companies then squeeze their workers. Firms such as BMW have pointed to the labor practices its American workers are prepared to accept in order to bully its German and British workers into doing the same.

New products have to be thrown around the world rapidly to make profits. Gillette used to unveil its razors around the world gradually. The Mach 3 razor it launched in 1998, by contrast, was available in one hundred countries within eighteen months of its release. Developing the technology to justify this sort of launch gets ever more expensive, even for something as cheap as a razor. You can buy a Mach 3 razor for $1.35; the razor cost 550 million times that to bring to market (and even if you factor in the exorbitant cost of replacing the blades, the multiple still runs into the millions). Worst of all, there is no guarantee even then that you can control the market: Despite Gillette's patents, a British supermarket had produced a similar three-bladed razor by the summer of 1999.

This sort of dog-eat-dog world might at least be tolerable if we could rely on the world behaving as a single market. But another complication for managers is that the world is not quite as global as it seems in places like Orlando. As we have seen, the triumph of global products is a myth. Razors are one of the very few global products, and even with them there are plenty of questions about pricing ($1.35 is a lot of money in many parts of the world) and advertising. Consultants at McKinsey estimate that only about 20 percent of world output—or $6 trillion out of the world's GDP of $28 trillion—is produced and consumed in global markets; the rest is still in places where products are delivered "primarily through local or national industry structures." If you make aircraft or semiconductors, you are fighting in a global market; if you make beer or sell life insurance, you are, for the most part, fighting local battles.[1]

Companies forget their local markets at their peril, yet they have no choice but to think about globalization. As we have already seen (chapter 5), even the most stubbornly local industries are being caught up in the maelstrom. Beer and life insurance might still be local, but international brands, companies, and standards are emerging. In even the most hole-in-the-corner service (office cleaning, for instance) there is at least one multinational (such as International Service Systems of Denmark) sniffing around. Within thirty years, McKinsey reckons that a market worth seventy-three trillion dollars—or 80 percent of its forecast for world GDP—will be globally accessible. The trend toward global integration is accelerating relentlessly. A decade ago, there were only about two thousand cross-border deals a year; now the total is more than six thousand. More than twenty thousand alliances were formed worldwide between 1996 and 1998, the vast majority of them involving the entering of new markets.

This means that the only chance even the most obscure company has to survive in the global age is to concentrate on producing the best product or service in its class—and, as soon as it has achieved that, to go on producing another and then another. This does not necessarily mean "going global," but even in national markets global standards are increasingly taking hold, albeit with products tailored to local quirks. Business has become a series of short-term sprints: Once you have won one race, another one begins immediately, but this time with different rules and tougher terrain. That is one reason why the premium that the stock market is prepared to pay for firms that can consistently outinnovate their peers has risen: The rewards have become much greater.

This raises the daunting question of how to build an organization that can keep on producing world-class products and services. Here, we will study the ways that three very different companies have taken to globalization. The first is a tiny family-owned perfumery that has never left the bazaar in Tangiers. The second is Nokia, a Finnish telephone company, which has been one of the great success stories of globalization. And the last is General Electric, until recently, the world's most admired company—and one that is just beginning to realize how much globalization is going to change it.[2]

The Six Principles of Global Management

Management writers usually resort to case studies when they do not really know the answer to a question. We plead half guilty to that charge. Put simply, there is no model for how to design a global company. For much of this century, there was a fairly clear model of what a good company should look like: the hierarchical, multidivisional firm invented by Alfred Sloan of General Motors. But this basically American model broke down in the 1970s and 1980s, as it was in short order humiliated by lean Japanese firms such as

Toyota, outinnovated by the T-shirted people in Silicon Valley, and in general found to be far too inflexible to deal with the sort of uncertainty that is the signature of globalization. Since then, management theory has fragmented.

Globalization defies hard and fast rules. For every general principle there are so many glaring exceptions that it is tempting to forget about management theory and just go by the seat of the pants. For example, marketing appears to be exactly the sort of task that should be left to local managers of global brands. But when Nabisco ran a jovial advertisement on Peruvian television that showed a group of African cannibals preparing to tuck into some tasty white tourists—but then having second thoughts when offered Nabisco's Royal Pudding—it immediately ran into a storm of protests in its home market. Racism helps sell in some parts of South America (a Peruvian ad by Goodyear compared the thickness of their tires to a black man's lips), but it is the sort of thing that turns a company's reputation to mud in the United States: An embarrassed Nabisco had to centralize control.[3] Prophets of globalization invariably urge companies to recruit their senior figures from as wide a range of countries and backgrounds as possible. But one of the reasons why Iridium, the satellite consortium, came crashing to the ground was that its famously multicultural board (which included the son of an American presidential candidate and the brother of Osama bin Laden) was impossible to manage. The board's twenty-eight members spoke multiple languages, turning meetings into mini-UN conferences, complete with headsets translating the proceedings into five languages. Cultural squabbles and misunderstandings were commonplace.

Though hard rules are impossible to find, we will nonetheless dare to put forward six general principles. The first is that management matters, particularly when it comes to corporate culture. Take, for instance, General Motors. Today, the big car companies have pretty similar arrays of factories and access to talent; their cars are also distressingly similar. Yet in 1998 General Motors spent twice as much money on labor per car as Toyota did. GM was also about a third less efficient than Ford. The simple fact was that GM had not been as well managed. Take the bullet train to Toyota City, and you are immersed immediately in one of the world's great management machines— a company town where even the humblest workers seem to spend their days conjuring up new ways to make manufacturing slightly more efficient.

This ties into the second point: Size complicates. According to John Stopford of the London Business School, half of the firms that operate internationally employ fewer than 250 employees.[4] For most small companies, globalization is essentially a matter of looking for as many opportunities to sell their wares as possible. With multinationals—ironically the very firms that were set up to exploit global opportunities—there is a much more diffi-cult challenge of persuading people to think together. A small firm can man-age to replicate many of the advantages of a big firm by forming alliances and so on; it is often much harder for big companies to replicate the advan-tages of small ones by remaining lean and entrepreneurial.

A big global company is nearly always caught between two admirable goals: its need to make the most out of all its ideas, bring forward local talent, and become more multicultural; and its need to remain true to the (often strongly nationalist) culture that often is central to why it became a big com-pany in the first place. Many companies do not want particularly to shed their national identities. As Michael Porter has argued, if everybody can make the same product everywhere, then a firm's distinguishing mark is often its geography—the "Californianness" of a software firm or the "Ger-manness" of a machine-tools firm.

The third principle is that, in general, the very things that define good na-tional management also define good international management, only more so. It is possible to write treatises on the virtues of things such as trans-parency, clear lines of command (Peter Drucker likes to point to the Roman proverb that "a slave who has three masters is a free man"), and "flat" man-agement structures (another Druckerism: "Every relay doubles the noise and cuts the message in half"), but these lessons have long applied to man-agement of all sorts.[5] One of the problems about globalization is that even the best companies can leave their brains behind when they go abroad. When it went to Hollywood, Sony forgot even the first principle of account-ability. The result was a series of huge losses culminating in a $2.7 billion write-off in 1994. A new boss, Nobuyuki Idei, introduced a new manage-ment team with specific responsibilities. He also made a point of visiting America once a month. By 1997, a unit that lost $1.7 billion in 1995 made $3.4 billion. Had the film studio been based in Osaka, the problem would likely never have occurred.

The fourth principle is perhaps just an extension of the third: It pays to behave ethically. Many companies pay lip service to corporate ethics—most American business schools now teach courses on the subject, some of them compulsory. Most of the obvious abuses have stopped: It has been some time since a multinational got caught running a sweatshop itself, for instance—but they still sometimes subcontract work to firms that do. And there is still a tendency for firms to behave like vacationers abroad and assume that the usual rules of good behavior do not need to be observed so strictly. A 1998 study of local newspaper employment ads in Thailand, Malaysia, and Singapore by two researchers from the University of Illinois found that 13 percent of American firms placed ads specifying males only, and another 11.5 percent specified females only; the companies included Cargill, Bank of America, and, perhaps inevitably, Nike.[6]

Ethical capitalism makes sense for several reasons. It forces companies to remember their constituents back home. It also forces them to play to their own strengths rather than to exploit their host society's weaknesses. Multinational companies are seldom successful purely because they cut corners or bribe officials. Above all, in a world where a growing number of assets are intangible, a company's reputation can be its most prized asset. Reputation helps companies to recruit the most ambitious and motivated people. (Drucker argues that one of a company's most important jobs is selling itself to potential employees.) Reputation also helps companies earn the goodwill of the wider community. Companies that have lost that goodwill, such as Nike, find that their every mistake is pounced on; those that have reserves of goodwill, such as The Body Shop, find that even their shareholders will forgive them a few lapses.

The fifth point might sound like one of those vague generalizations that trips off management gurus' tongues without really meaning anything. But in fact it gets us as close to the heart of the matter as anything: Global management is really about how you husband human capital, knowledge in particular. In a world that is characterized increasingly by uncertainty, it is important to have the right people to cope with it. "Intangible" assets (which usually means what those outside accountancy refer to as "people") make up at least half of the market value of most American firms; they become ever more important as tangible assets such as capital and resources become available to all. Countless surveys show that managers think that talent is their most important resource.[7] Yet anecdotal evidence suggests that multinationals still think that their best talent is Californian or, at a stretch, Catalan, rather than Colombian, or Congolese. There is no shortage of big companies prepared to say that by 2010 as much as a third of their profits will come from India, Brazil, and China; but how many of them are prepared to recruit the same proportion of their top managers from China, India, and Brazil?[8]

The sixth principle is that, far from dissipating the effect of personality, globalization has made leadership even more important. No company has put more effort into trying to develop a broad management team than General Electric. Yet its immediate future is dominated by the fact that its boss,

Jack Welch, retired in 2001. One part of Welch's cult was purely skillful public relations, and there have been questions raised about General Electric's auditing methods. But all the speeches, phrasemaking, and appearances at GE's training center had an effect precisely because Welch had a personality big enough to somehow reach across borders. Despite being worth several hundred million dollars, Welch was still seen as one of the grunts.

From Cortés to Rue Sabou

If any single group of companies looks particularly exposed to globalization, it is big, established ones from emerging markets, which account for only two of the top one hundred transnationals. While Western multinationals have years of experience in moving into new markets, these flabby organizations, particularly the ones that have grown up behind high tariff barriers, tend to be about as well prepared for contact with foreigners as the Aztecs were for the arrival of Cortés.[9] By the time that they adapt to the new, foreign standards, their empire has been "colonized." It is certainly difficult to feel sorry for local champions such as Indonesia's timber barons, who have thrived purely on account of their skills at winning connections. But even when globalization sweeps away such corrupt empires, its victory is often pyrrhic. Foreign takeovers are not depicted as victories for local consumers or as injections of capital but as assaults on the patriotic heartland. (It is worth remembering the storm in America just a decade ago when, as *Newsweek*'s cover put it, Sony "invaded" Hollywood.)

The oligarchs sometimes do not disappear outright, but they often modify their methods and can become invaluable contacts for foreign businesses trying to push into the country. In this changing of their guises they resemble other small companies that fight back against globalizing forces.

Sit around a table in Shanghai with a group of local businesspeople, and they all begin by moaning about how difficult life is. Then a quietly determined young woman from Shanghai Jahwa, China's oldest cosmetics firm, explains how her firm has met the challenge of invading Western firms by upgrading its manufacturing, training its saleswomen, and, in particular, refining its marketing. Jahwa concentrates on Chinese potions, which it now exports to Chinese communities around the world. Many Chinese people believe that human organs such as the heart and liver are internal spirits that determine the health of the body. Jahwa has launched several highly successful products that are meant to cure ailments such as prickly heat by appeasing these "six spirits." After the woman finishes, the other businesspeople tell similar stories. Connections are involved, of course, and there are plenty of rules in China that tilt markets toward local firms, but many of these local companies have found legitimate ways to compete with foreign multinationals.

At the moment, most of China's better companies concentrate on subcontracting. Only one mainland Chinese brand—Tsingtao Beer—made it onto a list of the top fifty non-Japanese Asian brands. But mainland firms are beginning to find niches overseas, making things under their own names; and they are not just sticking to products like perfume and beer for which preferences are largely matters of taste. Walk into an American appliance store and you may well find a small refrigerator made by a German-sounding company called Haier; in fact, it is a state-owned Chinese firm that started selling abroad only in 1997 but now claims 20 percent of the American market for small fridges and a smaller share of that for air conditioners. It is now building a factory in South Carolina. Haier's products will soon be joined on the shelf by those of its local rival, Guangdong Kelon, which already makes and designs Wal-Mart's Magic Chef refrigerators. Meidi, another Chinese firm, is also pushing into the American air-conditioner market.[10] Legend, a Chinese computer maker, which has managed to fend off companies such as IBM and Compaq at home, might also soon start appearing overseas.

In fact, there are quite a lot of firms in low-tech industries in emerging markets that have shown that they can surge to the top of world markets, as Mexico's Cemex has in cement and India's Reliance and Ispat have in bulk chemicals and steel. Niraj Dawar and Tony Frost, one of the few management teams to consider globalization from the local firm's perspective, point out that even when local champions are on the defensive, one of their biggest problems could be overestimating the invaders' strength.[11] When India's market opened up, Bajaj Auto, India's leading scooter maker, considered forming an alliance with Honda. But then it realized that many of the supposedly invincible Japanese firm's strengths, such as its cutting-edge technology, did not matter in India. What Indians wanted were cheap bikes that they could take to a local dealership if anything went wrong. So Bajaj's nationwide distribution system proved much more valuable than Honda's mechanical knowledge. Jollibee Foods, a family-owned fast-food company in the Philippines, matched McDonald's cleanliness and then trumped the invader by localizing its menu more: Jollibee's hamburger seasoned with garlic and soy sauce, for example, captured three quarters of the country's burger market. Now Jollibee is establishing restaurants near large expatriate populations in Hong Kong, the Middle East, and California.

And even if the largest companies in emerging markets have to be on their guards, the opportunities that technology and globalization offer for small businesses can be breathtaking. Consider the way that globalization has gradually brought the world to the door of a family business in northern Africa that has barely changed for centuries.

Entering the Madini family's tiny perfume shop on rue Sabou in the old town of Tangier, it is hard to think of anything more local. The shop is really no more than a tiny counter with small glass bottles containing the different essences that go into making a perfume. The Madinis grow most of the flowers that are crushed to make the essences themselves. The little cylindrical vials are just wide enough for a few drops to be shaken out each time. (The essences are fairly powerful, so they are not the sort of thing you splash all over.) The skill comes in knowing how to mix them. Bubka and Suleiman Madini are the fourteenth generation of the family to be in the business; they each spent more than a decade learning their art from their father, Sherif Ibrahim Madini.

Madini means "one from Medina." For as long as anybody can remember, the members of the Hariri family were perfumers in the city of Medina. When one of them married a Moroccan sultan at the turn of the century, some of the family moved to Tangier and took the name Madini. Sherif Ibrahim Madini soon built up a reputation in Tangier's expatriate community for being able to copy the favorite scent of the day for a fraction of the going price. Buyers were told to take a walk around the Kasbah, and when they came back the perfume would be ready. In the 1960s and 1970s, hippies discovered the tiny store as a place to buy patchouli and musk. As flights became cheaper and Tangier more accessible, the Madinis' shop became an occasional stop on some tourist routes. In 1997, after Suleiman had taken over the business, the family opened another, more modern (though less atmospheric) shop in the new part of town.

The Madinis' first attempt to go global came through Dulce Roppenecker, a Cuban-born housewife-cum-entrepreneur who had come across the store in 1969 and become a friend of the family. When her husband's employer sent him to New York State, Roppenecker was "appointed" the family's international agent and set up a small shop called Talisman to sell the oils in Woodstock. The shop was fairly popular with hippies, but most of the business was either mail-order or wholesale, with an increasing number of customers coming from overseas. So in 1997, when her husband was transferred to Seattle, Roppenecker closed down the shop to concentrate on the wholesale business, mail-order, and the Internet. A slightly rudimentary website had been set up a year before in lieu of rent by David McCarthy, a student of Tibetan Buddhism who lived in a cottage owned by the Roppeneckers.

This pleasantly serendipitous approach to expansion has worked a treat. The Madinis have an aversion to precise numbers, but they say that their cottage industry is shipping tens of thousands of bottles every year. Around 40 percent of their bottles are exported (in all, they serve one hundred countries), and a fifth of their customers order their oils via the Internet. One of the Internet's charms for a small business is that, compared with other distribution systems, it costs so little to set up. Another particular saving is in marketing. Rather than shipping a catalog, the Madinis can simply ask their customers to download it. There are fiddly things to do with customs and so on, but as Roppenecker says, "We now realize that we can reach and sell to just about anyone."

None of this has changed life greatly on rue Sabou. The two brothers are still reluctant to use the Internet themselves. They prefer to talk about the fact that they have just discovered that their rose oil is used to perfume the shroud of the Kaaba stone in Mecca. Ask about future plans and you are told, "We can never know what we cannot see around the corner." And already they are concentrating on training the fifteenth generation. Even though he can barely see over the counter, Bubka's young son, Aman, is already beginning to serve his apprenticeship.

To the Finland (Base) Station

If the Madinis represent an almost accidental success story of globalization, then Nokia is a much more determined example of how a local company can convert itself into a global industry leader. In 1998, the Finnish company roared past Motorola to become the world's biggest manufacturer of mobile phones, selling 41 million of the 163 million phones sold around the world.[12] This success has made it far the biggest company in Finland, accounting for about 10 percent of the country's GDP and more than half the value of its stock exchange. How on earth has a small Scandinavian conglomerate—previously known only for its skill at making things such as toilet paper and rubber boots in a country where the top tax rate is a distinctly unentrepreneurial 60 percent—beaten the world in one of the most competitive high-tech areas around?

The answer is really a story of how clever management exploited what at first seems to be a relatively small cultural advantage. Finland's low population density has long made telephony popular there. The Finns were using telephones only a year after Alexander Graham Bell tested the first one in 1876. Some even argue that the telephone has a psychological allure. "For Finns, it is easier to talk on a mobile phone than face-to-face," says Janne

Vainio, vice president of mobile communications for Sonera, Finland's largest telephone company, an observation that is amply confirmed in restaurants by the groups of diners who break their collective silence only to answer calls on their mobile phones.

This natural affinity for such devices has been strengthened enormously by benign regulation. The Finnish national telephone company never had a monopoly in the way that, say, British Telecom had: There were more than 850 private telephone companies battling for survival in the 1930s. Then, in the early 1980s, Finland made the farsighted decision, along with Denmark, Norway, and Sweden, to form the Nordic Mobile Telephone Group, an alliance that then helped turn GSM into the common standard for Europe and much of the rest of the world. From the very beginning, Nordic telephone companies were thinking internationally.

Nokia was fairly late to spot this advantage. In the late 1970s, the conglomerate bought a couple of telephone companies as part of a general diversification strategy. In 1982, it manufactured its first "portable" phone. (The Nokia Senator weighed twenty-two pounds.) But until the mid-1980s, the mobile division was nothing more than an outer satellite of the Nokia empire. Then three things happened. The company's boss, Kari Kairamo, committed suicide; the Soviet Union collapsed, taking a big chunk of the Finnish economy (and Nokia's business) with it; and Jorma Ollila, the hard-driving head of the company's mobile-phone division, was appointed to run the company.

Ollila set about doing two things: focusing Nokia ruthlessly on mobile phones and turning it into a global company. The result was a startling transformation that has lifted Nokia's market value 200-fold. Ten years ago, telecommunications accounted for only 10 percent of Nokia's net sales of 2.3 billion Euros. Now, phones account for virtually all its 13.3 billion Euros. Ten years ago, Finland accounted for 30 percent of the company's net sales; today it accounts for just 4 percent of the company's much larger net sales.[13] Altogether, Nokia is now in 140 markets—about the same number as McDonald's. The company's expansion has been so fast that the trickiest management problem facing it is handling its own growth, as well as recruiting large numbers of people without losing its distinctive identity.

This explosion in value can be explained partly by the popularity of mobile phones in general and by Nokia's devotion to technology; its managers never seem happier than when they are pulling mock-ups of new products like videophones out of their briefcases. But Nokia has also succeeded plainly because it has thought about globalization much more deeply than its opponents have. Nokia's roots in a country where three quarters of the population have mobile phones—the highest percentage in the world—help it to keep on the cutting edge of fashion. But it is also constantly looking for input from elsewhere. Advised by a British advertising agency, it has developed a "segmentation model" of its target customers. The four most important groups are "poseurs," "trendsetters," "social contact seekers," and "highfliers"; once you have conquered these, argues Nokia, then the phones spread inexorably to the rest of the population. Nokia is the antithesis of the ugly multinational. It is a company that bends over backward to tailor its products to every local quirk, from the Chinese need to have long-lasting batteries (because the phone system eats up power) to the Japanese enthusiasm for dialing by voice. Indeed, one of the keys to Nokia's success is that it was the first phone company to think like a consumer-products manufacturer, introducing several new models every year, changing colors according to fashion—two-tone and aluminum have been particular favorites recently—and encouraging people to customize their phones with clip-on covers.

Almost as important as how it has tailored its products is how Nokia has tailored its people by relentlessly preaching the virtues of transparency and humility. Visitors to the firm's modernist headquarters are reminded constantly that "there are no dark corridors in Nokia." To prove the point, the building is transparent to the sky and nearby water and covered with twenty-six thousand panes of glass.

Finland still supplies about half the company's forty-four thousand workers and the majority of its senior management. But Jorma Ollila has gone to unusual lengths to encourage a resolutely global mind-set, from making English the company's official language, to naming meeting rooms after the world's greatest cities, to expecting senior managers to spend some time working abroad. Moreover, Nokia does more than half its research and development outside its home country—something that immediately sets it apart from its rivals. That may be simply a matter of necessity (Nokia employs far more engineers than Finland can train), but the company also makes a point of consulting knowledgeable outsiders—particularly people from the media and information sciences—about the future direction of markets. The R and D division has a system of "internal start-ups": People who come up with a good idea are expected to produce a business model and then move from the laboratory to a business unit to try to turn it into reality.

This willingness to deal with outsiders is becoming increasingly important as the wireless and computer industries converge. For several years, the Holy Grail of the wireless industry has been an omnipurpose handheld de-

vice that can combine the qualities of a personal computer, a personal organizer, and a phone. But creating such a device forced the phone companies to
learn how to handle something that they had not needed to handle before:
data. They were also confronted with a series of daunting problems: How do
you get access to the Internet without all the palaver about wires and complicated protocols? How do you create an operating system that is sophisticated enough to work like a computer but robust enough to provide phone
users with reliable service? How do you get PCs and smart phones to communicate with each other so that people can synchronize vital information
such as address books? All this required a formidable amount of cooperation
not just between different companies but also between different industries.

Nokia is one of the central players in two of the most important alliances
in the wireless industry: the Open Mobile Alliance (OMA) and Bluetooth.
The OMA, an alliance of hundreds of companies, has developed common
protocols to allow people to get Internet content from their mobile phones.
Bluetooth, an alliance of more than five hundred companies, is finding ways
to allow various wireless devices to talk to each other via radio waves so that
people can synchronize the information stored in their various electronic
servants. Nokia is also one of the founding members of Symbian, an alliance that is trying to turn the operating system that runs the Psion personal
organizer into the standard operating system for smart mobile phones—
something that throws it up against Microsoft's Windows CE system.

Taking on Bill Gates is not always sensible. Psion is a slip of a thing compared with Microsoft, and it is losing out badly to Palm Pilots. But Gates is
clearly worried: In a memo to employees in 1998, he singled out Symbian as
one of the greatest threats to his empire. The fact that Nokia, which thought
during the glory days of *glasnost* that its best hope for the future lay in the
Russian toilet-paper market, has become such a thorn in the side of the
world's richest man gives hope to us all.

The House That Jack Built

"Ein Nod: Bodlonrwydd Llwyr I Gwsmeriaid" is not perhaps the snappiest
business slogan to someone who does not speak Welsh. Nevertheless, the
banner hanging inside General Electric's aircraft engine–servicing department in southern Wales—"Our Goal: Total Customer Satisfaction"—is not a
bad description of what GE has been up to in Nantgarw since it bought the
engine shop from British Airways in 1991. Back then, nearly all the shop's
$250 million worth of revenues came from the airline, which off-loaded it to

GE as part of a deal in which it bought various GE engines. Many people in Wales, a nation not known for its optimism, expected the plant to be gradually phased out. Yet in 1999 its sales topped $900 million (with British Airways providing less than half that). Some 98 percent of its 1,600 workers are shareholders in GE. And everywhere you can hear the strange sound of Welsh voices talking in GE-speak, boasting about "delighting customers" or about the fact that the plant now has three hundred green belts and eighteen black belts in GE's "six sigma" quality-management program.

Several thousand miles away, on the streets of Tokyo, strange, unmanned "automated loan kiosks" have begun to appear. Looking from the outside like high-tech public lavatories, the kiosks, which are located in shopping districts, allow any Japanese consumer with a driver's license to have their credit checked, sign a loan contract, and get cash within half an hour; a television camera allows the borrowers to talk to human beings if necessary. The loan kiosks are owned by Lake, a Japanese finance house and one of a score of Asian firms bought by GE Capital, the American firm's finance unit, in 1998 and 1999. In the early 1990s, GE made a killing on the acquisition trail in (then depressed) Europe. Now it claims to have discovered an even larger gold mine in the East, in the wake of the Asian contagion.

Wherever you live, the chances are that today you will use a General Electric product. Open your fridge or turn on your lightbulb and you might see GE on them; in some parts of eastern Europe, there are even GE bank branches. But you probably will not notice GE's generators providing your electricity, its trains taking you to work, or its plastic enclosing your PC. Pay with a store charge card at Harrods or Home Depot, and you are really paying GE Capital. Turn on your television and gaze greedily at the "money honey" on CNBC or chuckle at *Friends* on NBC, and you are watching GE employees in action.

If this implies a slight lack of focus, that is because General Electric is a conglomerate, with ten product groups. But this lineup is not entirely random. GE tends to stick to businesses in which size is still important. (It spent one million dollars a day for four and a half years to design the GE 90 aircraft engine.) It is also rigorous about either remaining in one of the top two worldwide slots in each field or getting out. But even though there is more synergy between the different products and services than you might expect, most of them have as little in common as, well, the cast of *Friends* and your fridge. Nevertheless, the sprawling global conglomerate is held together by a cadre of managers, a pervasive relentlessness, and (at least until he handed over control to Jeff Immelt in 2001) Jack Welch.

For nearly two decades, the intense, combative Irish American was the Princess Diana of business journalism, appearing on covers wherever he went. His various revolutions—like six sigma—were detailed lovingly in countless books and newspaper articles. That reputation has since been battered both by a slump in GE's share price and by a messy divorce. Our guess is it will recover somewhat as people reassess the changes that Welch pushed through. One of the longest lasting will be the fact that he globalized the firm. Soon, half of GE's sales and most of its workforce will be outside America. Walk into any part of GE, and you will be told about a string of acquisitions or new factories overseas, often accumulating at a remarkable rate. The loan kiosks, for instance, are part of GE's non-American consumer-finance operation. Its chief, David Nissen, started with three people in 1993. Within six years, he had twenty-three thousand people and a loan book of thirty-four billion dollars.

In one way, Welch had no choice but to look for foreign markets. If GE had not expanded abroad, its profits would have been flat in the 1990s. Besides, as Welch put it, "there is no point in being big without being global." His ambition was to get all the dots on the map to work together "the GE way." Yet in doing so Welch exacerbated the ever-present danger that an already large group will become still less controllable. Even the peripatetic Welch did not get around to visiting the engine shop in Wales. For Immelt, the group's size must seem daunting.

That challenge is also increased by the need to preserve the culture that has on the whole made GE so successful.[14] Rosabeth Moss Kanter once observed that businesses are the only sort of social organization that allows men homosocial reproduction. GE hires a particular sort of people, eschewing Ivy League types for graduates from lesser schools or the armed forces, whom it picks more for their competitiveness and capacity for hard work than for their exam results. Despite a gradual increase in the number of women managers, most parts of GE remain emphatically male worlds, where soft handshakes are rare, where a senior manager discussing the merger of two competitors can quip, "tying two cripples together doesn't mean that they can walk," and where people who "don't get it" are forced out early.

On the other hand, it is very hard to think of any other large company where people are quicker to admit they know nothing about something or where other people's ideas are accepted more quickly. In 1999, a London manager in GE Capital told Welch how the unit was using young people to teach older employers about the Internet. Within days, the order went out that every senior manager at GE, from Welch down, should spend a couple of hours a week being bossed around by an Internet mentor, usually a generation younger.

Plenty of other firms also claim idea-sharing as a cultural trait, but at GE the culture has structural roots. Pay and promotion, for instance, are tied to "boundaryless behavior," particularly for the three thousand managers. Crotonville, GE's famous training center that Welch used to attend monthly, is used to spread the message. And the notion of sharing ideas has been embedded in most of GE's management revolutions. Thanks to six sigma, people whose businesses have nothing in common (and who often speak limited English) suddenly start telling war stories in the same ugly vernacular. Christopher Bartlett, a professor at Harvard Business School (and one of the best writers on globalization) argues that GE has got around the traditional objection that a conglomerate cannot allocate capital better than the market can. Capital, he points out, is not a scarce resource, but knowledge is. GE's success is rooted in the way that it circulates more ideas and management talent faster than smaller specialists ever could.

Whether this still holds true was being tested by the stock market in 2002: GE was trading at a discount to the value of its assets. And the cultural changes remain. The company was built by a very specific kind of American: no-nonsense engineers who delighted in getting the job done and in outcompeting those foppish Ivy League types. Can the company find similar types of people as it expands abroad? Can it maintain its cultural cohesiveness even as it transforms itself into a multicultural organization? Or will globalization eventually dissolve the glue that holds GE together and turn it into just another collection of unrelated businesses that would be better broken up?

Jack Be Nimble

There are arguably four stages to being a big global company. The first was corporate colonialism, under which companies either used foreign outposts as "dumb terminals" to distribute domestic goods or, through either laziness or a desire to be local, let those outposts develop lives of their own. During the First World War, for instance, Fiat supplied the Italian Army, but its Austrian subsidiary supplied the rival Austro-Hungarian Empire. The second stage, which most big companies had already passed through by the 1980s, might be described as the cheap-hands stage, in which big companies integrated their manufacturing along global lines but often did not bother to adapt them too much to local needs. The third stage might be described as the transnational one, when companies begin to use their foreign subsidiaries for ideas as well as production; they also tailor global products to local needs. The fourth stage has less to do with structure than state of mind: Businesses become genuinely multicultural multinationals in which the nationality of employees ceases to matter.

GE is somewhere around stage three on this continuum. One of Welch's first changes was to force all the operating units into global product groups, with regional managers typically left to coordinate things such as acquisitions and local public relations. This global attitude toward products is now being matched by a global attitude toward resources. GE has redoubled attempts to outsource production to cheap hands, as well as to cheap voices and cheap minds. If you live in Texas and get a strange-sounding person asking why your credit-card payment is late, it is probably because that voice is coming from India. (The operators, who assume Western names such as Janet, reportedly pick up some of the twang of the region that they call.) Much of the software that provides the brains for GE's medical scanners comes from Bangalore. GE's Tungstram plant in Hungary is now its center for excellence in various lighting technologies.

True to GE's model, ideas also whip backward and forward. For instance, most of the new technology for GE Capital's consumer-finance business still comes out of America, but most of the sales and marketing gimmicks (like the loan-toilets) develop in the rest of the world. The clever bits of GE's new six-hundred-million-dollar plastics factory in Cartagena, Spain, were designed by a multinational team, composed principally of Japanese and Dutch scientists. A new flexible manufacturing technique invented in New Zealand was transferred to Canada and then to America.

And yet even while it searches for these ideas, GE also has to impose its own values. Every foreign company that GE buys goes through a process of GE-ification. This involves immediately adhering to a series of hard rules, typically having to do with supplying financial information, embracing six sigma, and so on. ("Joining GE is like taking a drink from a fire hose" is a typical complaint.) On the other hand, the newly acquired companies usually keep their own names, their own marketing strategies, and, at least to begin with, their own chief executives. Any of the latter suspected of not "walking the talk," though, are quickly ejected.

The same process also takes place at new facilities. At the new plastics factory in Cartagena, a deeply unlovely part of Spain that rivals southern Wales as one of Europe's most backward areas, GE has GE-ified everything from the local architecture firm it used (which it introduced to three-dimensional computer-aided design) to the workforce (which has completed a collective thirty-six thousand hours of training). The process, according to the plant manager, has been "less about building a site than building a culture."

Welch claimed to us that his "boundaryless" company had long since outgrown any idea that American is best: "It is a badge of honor to learn something here—no matter where it comes from." GE is also prepared to compromise its culture a little. In Japan, for instance, it has tried to allow consensus-based decision making. Yet for Welch, GE's fundamental values—meritocracy, dignity, simplicity, speed, a hatred of bureaucracy—are universal values, not American ones, and "if some pompous horse's ass wants to behave in such a way that the work experience will not provide those things, then they are out."

Whether these values really are global is a moot point; Welch's way of proclaiming them, however, was as American as General Patton—and so was the heart of the company he bequeathed to Immelt. All GE's product divisions are still headquartered in America and run by Americans. With Paolo Fresco gone to Fiat, all of Welch's senior lieutenants were American. By most measures of multiculturalism, GE is less global than some of its European competitors, Asea Brown Boveri in particular.

On the other hand, precisely the same meritocratic values that Welch trumpets were slowly but relentlessly de-Americanizing GE. In most of its divisions, there is a growing layer of non-American managers in their thirties and forties. Immelt himself hails from Cincinnati, but ten of the twenty-one people who used to report to him when he ran GE Medical Systems in the late 1990s were foreigners (and all but five of the Americans had worked abroad). Of the twenty-three thousand people in consumer finance at the same time, fewer than two hundred were American, and every national consumer-finance business bar one was run by a local.

This demographic switch leaves an awkward balancing act for Welch's successor. On one side, Immelt needs to make full use of all those dots on the map to justify GE's size and to keep the ideas flowing. Yet a core part of GE's competitive edge is its Americanness. It would be hard to imagine a British company putting up a big banner in Welsh about total quality management or pushing the people in the Welsh aircraft-engine factory as hard as GE does. Indeed, far from being satisfied with what is going on in places such as Wales and Cartagena, GE still wants more: In Cincinnati, the people responsible for maintaining quality standards in the airplane engine division still bridle at the idea that other sites are further ahead in applying six sigma and worry about the head office seeing the numbers. An "un-American" GE would be a toothless beast.

Hard Days' Night

General Electric is an interesting example precisely because it is ahead of the pack. Most multinationals still have two thirds of their employees and their sales in their host countries. Despite claims that capitalism is converging on a single model, as a rule American, Japanese, and German firms are still structured, financed, and motivated in fundamentally different ways; and, unlike Nokia, they do most of their R and D at home. Even pharmaceutical and computer companies, long in the forefront of the charge toward globalization, continue to perform the bulk of their most sensitive research in their home countries.[15] Most big companies have set up global supply and distribution systems, but they have been less active with things such as human resources. When they talk about knowledge management, it is usually about assembling big computer systems rather than getting the best out of their employees.

All this gives rise to a heretical thought: The idea of a company—particularly a big company—needs to be redefined even further than it already has been since the passing of the Sloan model. Plenty of traditional corporate walls are falling, as even the biggest firms are pushed into cooperating with each other (remember the web of ties binding together Coke, McDonald's, and Disney), but big firms can find it very difficult to achieve anything from their alliances. The most interesting thing about many new management models is that they tend to favor small, specialist firms, particularly once those firms start to form networks of their own.

At the same time, presenting Jack Welch as the last of a dying breed—a man who made an impossible structure work—also seems wrong. There will always be a place for a company like GE, as long as it can keep its ideas flowing and maintain that relentless edge and those relentless people. One of the firm's more recent recruits is Antonio Espinosa, a young engineer who has joined the Cartagena plant. Having come from a more leisurely local rival, he moans that GE is always looking for perfection, but he likes the performance pay and the training (which in his case has already included visits to America and the Netherlands). Asked where he wants to be in five years, Espinosa points at the back of the plant manager and says, "In his office." A quarter of a century ago, another young engineer, when asked a similar question in an evaluation, cockily put "Chief executive officer of General Electric." His name was Jack Welch.

Part Four

The Politics of Interdependence

8

The Strange Survival
of the Nation-State

ON A BRISK autumn day, the junction of Friedrichstrasse and Zimmerstrasse can seem like just another Berlin construction site. On one side, there is a billboard for Cheez Ums; on the other, a banner for an Internet company proclaims the merits of "least-cost routing." People and cars move by regardless. Yet until recently, Checkpoint Charlie was a monument to "highest-cost routing"—the place where East Germans seemed willing to pay any price as they dug, bullied, jumped, tricked, or charged their way across the border. Some two hundred died in attempts at various points along the wall.

From a table at Café Adler—once at the gateway to freedom, now just another Berlin bar—you cannot help but feel that the march toward a "borderless world" is proceeding briskly. Thanks to the Schengen agreement between the countries at the heart of the European Union, you could drive your Mercedes from here to Seville without a border guard so much as looking at you and pay for your petrol in Euros. Europe is not alone. In North America, politicians are talking about building borderless trade corridors "from Murmansk to Monterrey." Even in Asia, the bamboo curtain around China is gradually parting. And as we have already seen, money and power now leap across frontiers at touches of buttons.

But is the view from the Café Adler correct? Take your cup of coffee about five hundred miles northeast to the somewhat shabby office of Ants Limets, the town manager of Narva. A polite but harassed bureaucrat of the sort that Chekhov might have depicted, Limets's life is now dominated by the magnificent, windswept bridge just around the corner that links Narva to Ivangorod. A decade ago, the two predominantly Russian-speaking towns were part of the same country, sharing the same schools and hospital. Now Narva is a frontier town of Estonia, a fiercely independent Baltic republic.

Narva is not only in a different time zone from Ivangorod but also in a different economic one, with a much higher cost of living. The few things the towns still share—such as water and electricity—are the subjects of interminable disputes. Every day, hundreds of elderly Russian-speaking Narvans cross the bridge to go shopping in Ivangorod's shabby market. They look tired and defeated: Most were dumped in the region by Stalin. The windy trek, moan the old ladies, is necessitated by the small pensions the Estonians pay them. One purchases only a jar of honey, which costs just seven Estonian crowns in Ivangorod, a fifth of the price in Narva. Narva is a Russian town, they all insist, though they do not want it to be Russian at the moment. When will this all be alleviated? "As soon as Boris Yeltsin lies under these waves," spits out one crone, pointing to the torrent below.

The Estonian border—or, as some Estonians like to call it, the future eastern border of the European Union—sometimes has a quaint, *Tintin*-like feel. In some of the rural border guard towers, the cash-strapped Russians parade only crude mannequins dressed up in soldiers' uniforms. In Moscow, politicians claim that the border crossings are thoroughfares for drugs and guns. Not so, says Georgy Kusnitsov, the head of Ivangorod's border guards: All they have found is the odd ounce of marijuana. Nevertheless, the sleeper from Saint Petersburg to Tallinn often wastes four hours at the border as guards and dogs pick through the train, opening suitcases. Near the border in 1998, Russian troops carried out a war game in which they simulated taking over a small country; it was called "Operation Return." Russian miners periodically threaten to block the border at Narva if Estonia does not buy their oil shale.

In Narva, people like Ants Limets still think of the land beyond Ivangorod as their own. In Moscow, Alexei Mitrofanov, a leading nationalist, complains that the border was created by trickery, and its barring of Russia's access to the Baltic Sea is like "taking away the gates to your own home." Mitrofanov is careful to talk about referendums, integration on a bilateral basis, and the importance of persuasion. But the Estonians and Russia's other neighbors are justifiably jumpy. Most of Russia's leaders have made hostile noises about their Baltic borders. Kusnitsov, who used to run across the bridge to play with friends as a boy, thinks that Narva is a Russian town. "All a country's problems end up at the border," he laments, "We are the sharp edge."

The Wounded King of the Jungle

Borders are arbitrary abstractions, economic impediments, and surprisingly ineradicable. A feeling of unfairness hangs around borders almost as often as uniformed guards such as Kusnitsov do. All the same, borders are the best place to begin any discussion about the nation-state because they represent something relatively solid in a debate that is often irritatingly fluid. Arguments about the extent to which globalization is weakening national identities tend to end up in a splurge of unprovable generalizations; Café Adler and Kusnitsov's office, by contrast, are tangible. Nations can exist without states (the Palestinians) or between states (the Kurds or the Catalans). A state can contain many nations (Austro-Hungary), a part of a nation (Ireland), or no nation (the Vatican). A single nation can also be divided into two states (the two Koreas). But however many nations are involved, without a border you can have no state at all.[1]

The thickness of any particular border provides an immediate metaphor for the distance a particular state wants to keep between itself and the outside world. Anybody caring to find out about Enver Hoxha's Albania needed only to know that border guards occasionally took potshots at Italian bathers. More generally, the average thickness of borders around the world is a good guide to the strength of the nation-state in general. Ever since the Roman empire, with its detailed delineation between *civitas, provincia,* and *regio,* the ability to maintain a border has been a test of political power and will. One of the first signs of the rebirth of European nation-states during the Renaissance and the Enlightenment was the introduction of borders. Since then, the nation-state has been the basic unit not only of modern politics but also of identity and culture.

Now globalization stands accused of destroying the nation-state, not to mention national identity, the power of governments to set policy and protect their citizens, high culture, and the Barcelona Football Club. In our next three chapters, we will show that this is not so. Yes, globalization is wearing away at the edges of these things. Yes, it does restrict the power of governments to do some things. Yes, it imports "foreign" ideas and "foreign" soccer players, and not all of them are welcome. Yes, most definitely, it is changing our world and us. But globalization is fundamentally a democratic process, driven by individual choices, and what most people still want are senses of culture, place, and nationality. National politicians are not powerless, history is not ending, and the basic substance of foreign policy is, for better or worse, little different from what it was a century ago.

The Great Debate

Once again, the debate about the nation-state itself shows some of these differences between nations. Although millions of Americans died in faraway places throughout the twentieth century because of disagreements about lines on maps, there is still a surprising lack of interest in the United States in the theory that those lines might not mean much any more. In most of the rest of the world, it is at the forefront of political debate.

Some groups have always hated nation-states. Religions tend to be against temporal borders; the papacy once disliked nationalism just as much as official Islam does today. So are classical economists and, in principle, communists. Nowadays, the idea that the nation-state is facing its Götterdämmerung is pretty common. Academics like to point out that the nation-state has not been with us forever. Eric Hobsbawm, the doyen of Marxist historians, has argued that it is a legacy of the French Revolution and a peculiarly bloody one at that.[2] Ernest Gellner, a British anthropologist, argues that it is the invention of self-serving elites. Benedict Anderson, an American cultural critic, insists that it is nothing more than an "imagined community."[3] Others are keen on showing that it is incompatible with today's androgynous, multicultural, postpatriotic society. "The old model of nationality is outmoded in this globalizing world," says Aiwa Ong, an anthropologist at the University of California at Berkeley. Kenichi Ohmae, a management guru, argues that the natural engines of growth are not "dysfunctional" states but cross-border regions such as Tijuana–San Diego and Hong Kong–Shenzhen.

The general notion behind these arguments is that the nation-state is both too small to deal with the vast forces of the global economy and too big to connect with the lives of ordinary people. According to its critics, the nation-state is a little like a badly wounded lion: Rendered powerless by hunters' spears, it now has to watch other beasts gradually steal its territory. The hunters are the different forms of global capitalism—pimply currency traders, subversive technologists, arrogant businessmen, and so on. The beasts come from two different directions: from above, where a whole alphabet of acronyms from APEC to the UN and the WTO are gradually sucking sovereignty out of the nation-state; and from below, where cities, counties, and tribes, such as the Scots and the Quebecois, see no need to keep up their loyalties to arbitrary centers, such as London and Ottawa.

The devastating thing about the lion's predicament is that its assailants compliment each other. Each time the money markets humiliate a national government, there are more calls for regional cooperation. Each time power is ceded to a body like the European Union, it increases the separatists' case that "their" people can look after themselves.

In general, the people who herald the end of the nation-state do so in tones of triumph. However, even as they celebrate the removal of the old order, many, particularly on the left, are struck by a nasty second thought: The end of the nation-state could mean the end of the welfare state. Governments will have no choice but to cut taxes, reduce social benefits, and lighten regulations if they are to have any chance of attracting mobile capital. Globalization is threatening not just the nation-state but also the benefits that it provides.

The Running Dogs of Capitalism

The conclusion that globalization is destroying the nation-state is an awesome one. But is it true? Consider first the idea that the nation-state has been fatally wounded by the slings and arrows of outrageous capitalism.

Some of the ways in which commerce eats away at political divisions are as old as the hills. While Greek Cypriot guards in Nicosia helpfully point out that to the north lies a land of murderers and rapists, and while Turks over the border have painted a Turkish Cypriot flag hundreds of meters across on a mountainside simply to irritate their Greek neighbors, one of the worst-kept secrets in Cyprus is that Greek and Turkish farmers meet regularly along deserted parts of the Green Line to trade goats and other animals. Governments have lived with such casual treachery for centuries. The difference now is that rather than merely cheating the state, capitalism seems to be intent on usurping it.

In part, it is a matter of style. Business heroes command respect that modern politicians only dream about. When Bill Gates visits Davos, the crowds gather around him, not the prime ministers. But it is also, many politicians complain, a matter of raw power. During the past two decades, there has been a fairly dramatic change in the balance of power between national governments and international markets. The most extreme example of this is Russia, where the state has shrunk from almost monopolizing economic activity to controlling barely a quarter of the GDP; a centrally planned economy has given way to anarcho-capitalism or even raw theft.[4] But in much of the rest of the world, governments have divested themselves of responsibilities and gradually accepted the rule of the market.

Naturally, some of this power has been given up voluntarily, through privatization and deregulation, but not all of it. When the currency markets won their battle with the British government over sterling's membership in the European exchange-rate mechanism in 1992, they not only destroyed a particular government's credibility but also challenged the credibility of any government that took on the world's trading rooms. When Asia's governments fell foul of the same process in 1997, plenty of people complained about the result, but nobody considered the defeat unusual. And even the United States has to bend its knee: When asked in what form he would want to be reincarnated, James Carville, Bill Clinton's sidekick, said he wanted to be reincarnated as the bond market because it was more powerful than God.

Nor is it just a question of money markets. Politicians complain that *industrial policy* is now a meaningless term. Governments no longer drive growth. In the 1960s, government spending accounted for about 15 percent of America's growth, almost the same as private-sector fixed investment; but in the 1990s boom private investment contributed more than 30 percent of the growth, while government spending accounted for only 2 percent.[5]

Rather than taking their orders from governments, multinational companies, according to their critics, have begun to treat their homes as hotels—places where they stay by choice and can leave if they don't like the view. Ericsson has threatened to leave Sweden if the government fails to lighten its onerous tax burdens. Foreign firms hold American state governments to ransom, only locating their factories where they are offered irresistible tax breaks. Companies such as Rover and Chrysler were once national champions that had to be kept British or American; now they are both German. Meanwhile, smaller entrepreneurs publicly thumb their noses at the whole system. What, one wonders, would Jean-Baptiste Colbert, the *grandpère* of dirigisme, make of Oliver Cadic, a young French entrepreneur who not only moved his own computer company, InfoElec, to Britain because it offered lighter taxes and regulations but also founded a pressure group to encourage other French people to do likewise?[6]

The information age has added another challenge. Until the 1980s, governments around the world controlled a good proportion of radio and television bandwidth; outside America, there were relatively few commercial channels, and most of them were heavily regulated by the state and tended to model themselves on the public channels. Now, technology has multiplied the number of commercial channels to a point where they are making public-sector channels such as the BBC nearly irrelevant. Media entrepreneurs such as Rupert Murdoch now have power in a plethora of national markets. The Internet seems almost impossible to police. When the French government tried to ban a book that revealed that François Mitterrand had suffered from prostate cancer for the last fourteen years of his life, curious citizens simply read the offending text via the Internet.[7] And just as Europeans can buy books from American booksellers, they can also invest in the Chilean stock market, gamble in Antigua-based casinos, or patronize South American art dealers—all beyond the purview of their political masters.

Remember Sherman McCoy?

Certainly, some think that forcing governments to cede ground on industrial policy and censorship is no bad thing at all. But regardless of one's ideological bent, there are fairly good factual reasons to question the idea that the state is in headlong retreat. Yes, it may have ceded ground in some areas, but its capacity to maul businesspeople remains pretty much unchecked. Rupert Murdoch, for instance, may frighten some politicians, but he is also plainly frightened by others: Witness his attempts to keep the Chinese government happy. Like those of most media barons, Murdoch's empire is defined not just by his ambitions but also by rules about where he can own television stations, where he can own newspapers, and what he can show to his customers. The "global citizen" still had to become an American one to own Fox.

Or consider Joel Klein. At times when talking to the slender, balding lawyer during his stint as the boss of the Department of Justice's antitrust division under Bill Clinton, you were reminded of another (albeit fictional) litigator from the Bronx: Larry Kramer, the hardworking and underpaid district attorney who brought down Sherman McCoy in Tom Wolfe's *Bonfire of the Vanities*. Although Klein was a classier, more upright act than Kramer, he plainly lived a completely different life from the global business leaders whom he policed. The musty corridors of the Department of Justice are as far from the average executive suite as Kramer's cardboard-walled apartment was from McCoy's Park Avenue co-op. All the same, the list of corporate titans that Klein brought crashing to the ground is a long one. Northrop Grumman and Lockheed Martin assumed that their merger would get the go-ahead from Klein; so did KPMG and Ernst & Young. In both cases, Klein demanded savage concessions, and what would have been the world's biggest defense and accounting firms never came into being.

But the person Klein will always be associated with is somebody whom most people would have picked as the modern master of the universe: Bill Gates. Leave aside the rights and wrongs of the antitrust case against Microsoft, and two things are already apparent, both of which make nonsense of the idea that capitalism can run roughshod over government. First, by the time he left Justice, Klein had done more damage to Gates than any mere businessman could. Only the government could force Gates to give hours of cripplingly embarrassing video testimony and thus speed his transformation from guileless geek to Rockefelleresque ogre. Indeed, Klein changed the whole company. The difference is tangible to any regular visitor to Microsoft: Despite a warmer response from the Bush administration, there is a touch of defensiveness about everyone at the firm, even Gates.

The second point is that Klein did this by expanding the scope of antitrust actions. Until the Microsoft case, competition policy was founded on existing abuses rather than potential ones. But Klein maintained that the measure of competition in technology industries should be not just market share (at the time he launched his case, Microsoft's browser share was much smaller than Netscape's) or price increases (Microsoft had consistently reduced prices and was giving away its browser) but also the whole industry's ability to innovate. He launched the case against Gates to protect not just Netscape but also a host of Netscapes as yet unborn. This was in line with fashionable economic thinking about "network effects" in high-tech markets. But it was also plainly new territory—an example of government expanding its reach rather than retreating.

The Microsoft case also indirectly proves another point: Companies are much less mobile than people believe. One reason why the federal government can harass Microsoft is because it knows that the computer company will not move elsewhere. Microsoft's fixed assets may be modest and its workforce small, but it cannot afford to divorce itself from American universities and other American computer companies. Removing itself from America's high-tech cluster would be suicidal.

Further, there is always a lag between government mistreatment and any sign of resistance from businesspeople. Despite France's habit of loading taxes onto its employers, rebels who are prepared to vote with their feet like Cadic are few. Similarly, Ericsson is still in Sweden. Given a choice between putting up with a tax hike and abandoning a multimillion-dollar factory, most sensible companies tolerate the tax hike, at least for some time. It takes a great deal for a large company to uproot itself, and both businesspeople and their regulators know that.

Globalization Is Good for Governments

If globalization is supposed to be killing big government, it is doing a remarkably slow job of it. In 1900, government spending in today's industrial countries accounted for less than one tenth of national income. In the United States, it accounted for less than 3 percent. Today, in the same countries, it accounts for an average of one half. Even relatively restrained countries such as the United States and Japan devote a third of their GDP to public spending. Bill Clinton's proclamation that "the age of big government is over" was no more truthful than his finger wagging about Monica Lewinsky. While the number of Department of Defense workers has been cut since the cold war, if you exclude them America's civil service is twice the size it was in 1960.[8]

Individual attempts to slow down spending have barely scratched the surface. Between 1979 and 1997, a succession of British Conservative governments labored mightily to tame the leviathan and endured a relentless stream of complaints that they were "cutting" essential services and "persecuting the poor" in the process. They succeeded in reducing public spending from 43 percent of GDP to 42 percent. Since 1994, most European countries have tried hard to reduce their budget deficits in order to meet the Maastricht criteria for setting up the Euro, but they succeeded in reducing public spending only from an average of 51 percent of GDP to 50 percent, and even this fall owed more to accounting tricks than to fiscal restraint. The only dramatic example of a state reducing spending is provided by Sweden, which succeeded in reducing its share from an absurd 71 percent in 1993 to a merely preposterous 65 percent three years later.

Cutting the state in any significant way is not likely to get any easier in the future for at least three reasons. The first is that the middle classes do remarkably well on account of public spending (far better than the poor, who are supposed to be its main beneficiaries). Julian Le Grand, an economist based at the London School of Economics, has studied the way that public spending was distributed between the rich and the poor in Britain in the 1980s. In health care, the wealthiest fifth of the population received 40 percent more public spending than the poorest fifth did; in secondary education, they received 80 percent more; in university education, five times more; and in rail subsidies, ten times more. Second, public-sector workers make up a powerful force within the electorate. They not only command a lot of votes in their own right but are exceedingly good at identifying themselves with the public interest, not least because so many of them are involved in delivering services that command universal approval, such as health care and education.

The third constituency is probably the most powerful. The aging of the population in most rich countries is both pushing the cost of pensions relentlessly upward and also providing a voting bloc to defend the larger state needed to dish out that money. Some form of social-security reform is necessary in virtually every country, but the vast constituency of elderly voters that will do anything to hang on to "their" money means that dramatic change is unlikely. Rootless capitalism can trample over many sorts of people, but a retired couple of registered Democrats in Florida is not one of them.

This is not to say that globalization is doing nothing to change the state's role, only that it is changing it less dramatically than many people imagine. States may not be surrendering many of their core functions to the markets, but they undoubtedly have to rethink most of those functions in the light of globalization. Is it better to try to pick industrial winners or to put more money into education and training? Is there a way to tax the relatively mobile rich without scaring them away? How should it restructure social insurance? Should it try to establish a monopoly over social services (including education and training), or should it contract out some services to the private sector? These are questions that we will return to in chapter 15. All that needs to be stressed for now is that they are questions, not ultimatums made to a dying form of government.

Power Goes Up . . .

It is tempting at this point to conclude that the argument is over: Capitalism is not destroying government. But that still leaves open the question of whether the nation-state is yielding power to other sorts of government. Once again, nobody denies that this is happening; the questions are how much and to whom.

States seem to share just about everything, beginning with physical infrastructure. Virtually every country in the world seems to be building a bridge, a road, or a tunnel to its neighbor. The French, German, and Swiss cities of Mulhouse, Freiburg, and Basel share the EuroAirport (which has a Eurobar, where the currency one uses depends on which side you are being served on). Proud young Estonia wants to improve its railway to Russia and to build a "Via Baltica" linking it to Finland and Latvia.

Bureaucrats are also building bridges. After Enron and WorldCom, accountancy regulators in Washington and London now compare their work. Sports ministers agree on common standards for drug testing. Fishery ministers squabble about the numbers of cod in the North Atlantic. Telecommunications officials try to set international-call rates. The past two decades have seen an outbreak of transborder networking between different branches of nation-states—courts, regulatory agencies, various bureaucracies, and legislatures—as they have struggled to deal with problems that seep across borders, such as pollution, illegal drugs, and terrorism.

This creeping "transgovernmentalism," as Ann-Marie Slaughter has dubbed it, encompasses everything from the citation by German courts of precedents from American law to the decisions of the Basel committee on banking standards and is confined largely to the more developed states.[9] An influential argument put forward by Robert Cooper, a British diplomat, holds that since the death of traditional balance-of-power politics in 1989, the world has divided into three sorts of states: premodern ones such as Somalia, the Congo, or North Korea, which are in states of chaos not dissimilar from that in medieval Europe before the rise of nation-states; modern states such as Iran, Brazil, Indonesia, and China that still want to flex their nationalistic muscles; and mature, rich, postmodern ones such as the members of the European Union, which have grown past such concerns about sovereignty and for whom the distinction between foreign and domestic affairs is fading fast.[10]

Yet nation-states remain much more than mere cogs in some global machine; even the most postmodern of them can and do opt out. Indeed, at times it seems that French diplomacy ever since Charles de Gaulle has been built upon that privilege. This independence becomes much more noticeable in the more formal supranational organizations, such as the UN and the EU. By and large, governments have not ceded sovereignty to such bodies as shared it with them on the basis of carefully defined rules that are packed with out clauses. They treat international organizations as instruments of national policy rather than harbingers of some misty new world order. They join lots of different organizations—military alliances as well as economic ones, regional trade organizations as well as global ones—rather than handing power to a single omnipotent body.

This helps explain why the putative organs of world government such as the United Nations and the IMF are such messes. It is certainly true that some power has seeped up to such global institutions (see chapter 9), but it is a patchy affair; national governments have tended to hold on to the most important areas of sovereignty. For every Republican congressman who worries about the UN's black helicopters spying on him, there are several million dollars' worth of UN initiatives that lie stillborn because Congress has not bothered to pay its dues in full.

By contrast, governments have been much freer in ceding sovereignty to regional bodies. Every continent bar Antarctica now has its own frontier-lowering trade pact. In most cases, these pacts have led to other sorts of integration, too. For instance, thanks to Mercosur, children in Rio Grande do Sul, Brazil's southernmost state, now have to learn Spanish, and there are even a handful of Argentines who now admit to being Latin Americans. Meanwhile, organizations that have long just been talking shops have begun to extend their reach. The Association of South East Asian Nations, traditionally little more than a brief annual golfing holiday for local leaders, has begun to talk—albeit in fairly elaborate code—about regional problems such as Indonesia's penchant for burning down forests (and thus shrouding its neighbors in smog).

The foremost regional economic organization, of course, is the European Union. For a decade now, there has been a single market among its members that allows people from one state to work in others. At the beginning of 2002, eleven European countries took this a step further when they gave up their own currencies, replacing them with the Euro. Their monetary policy is now set by the European Central Bank. The Maastricht Treaty speaks loftily of "ever closer union" between countries, and some in Europe will not rest until they have created a United States of Europe.

But will they get their way? Some Benelux countries seem happy to merge their national identities in a wider regional identity. In the Netherlands, long more dependent on trade than bigger European countries, signs tend to be in English, French, and German as well as Dutch.[11] The Belgians seem to think that turning themselves into Europeans will help resolve long-standing ethnic hatreds between the Flemish and the Walloons (and also provide Brussels with a huge economic stimulus).

But these are the exceptions. Even the most enthusiastic devotees of the European project are haunted by nationalist passions. The Dutch do not mind ceding power to Europe, but they still harbor deep resentments against the Germans. A recent Belgian film called *The Wall* fantasized about building a Berlin Wall–type structure between the Flemish and the Walloons. The French threatened to wreck the final stages of preparation for monetary union if a Frenchman did not become head of the new European Central Bank at the earliest possible opportunity. Unsurprisingly, opinion polls show no great enthusiasm for the bureaucrats in Brussels; the only Europeans who say they identify strongly with the European Union are those trying to join it, such as the Czechs and the Hungarians.

European states often hang on to much of their sovereignty. For instance, while the signatories of the Schengen agreement have surrendered some frontier controls, they have looked for ways to replace them, such as increasing the number of spot checks on trucks behind borders. And further attempts to integrate or expand the union might meet greater resistance. One well-placed Eurocrat reckons that the union's coming attempts to harmonize external immigration policies could present "the next big row after the Euro." In Austria, whose main cities are within commuting reach of five million foreign workers, calls for strong borders have become rallying cries for the right.

. . . and Power Goes Down

Arguably, the most serious challenge to nation-states is not from above but from below. After all, the former Soviet Union reluctantly disintegrated into its constituent republics; it did not dissolve into Comecon. The federal government in the United States has willingly handed power (notably over welfare programs) to individual states. Spain is deliberately trying to turn itself into "a nation of nationalities." Great Britain has given the peoples of Scotland and Wales their own regional assemblies. The Quebecois have succeeded in maintaining a francophone enclave in anglophone Canada, and many would like to go further and create a separate nation-state.

This independence is not just limited to tribes. Around the world, cities and states have started to develop economic policies of their own, often in direct competition with other parts of their countries. In the European Union, cities and regions have taken to lobbying multinational companies directly, in order to get around EU rules that discourage nation-states from indulging in such special pleading. Many American states have even imposed their own sanctions on bits of the world that they disapprove of, with Massachusetts far outscoring Washington, D.C., in self-righteousness. Meanwhile, cross-border economic clusters in places such as San Diego–Tijuana seem to ignore national boundaries.

Nongovernmental organizations (NGOs) are invading areas that used to be reserved for national politicians. Some NGOs, such as the Soros Foundation, Amnesty International, Doctors Without Borders, and Alert International, already command resources that dwarf those available to the states in which they operate; and the imbalance is likely to get bigger still, particularly given the fact that first-world activists are rather more technologically savvy than third-world bureaucrats.

Many NGOs have also become enthusiastic converts to the ancient idea that universal human rights are more important than national sovereignty, adding their voices to the growing clamor for the expansion of the role of the International Criminal Court. The highly contentious case of the former Chilean dictator, Augusto Pinochet, who spent months trapped in England, the subject of a tussle between various NGOs and the Chilean government, not only suggests that international law is gradually moving in a direction that undermines national sovereignty; it also raises the possibility that bizarre coalitions of international civil servants, professional human-rights activists, and international lawyers will increasingly set the agenda for national governments.

In America, there is a particular fear that recent immigrants are becoming harder to assimilate, at least in the old, uncompromising way. Many of the Irish and Italians who came to America in the late nineteenth century never saw their native countries again. Nowadays, Mexican immigrants can frequently visit their motherland. Cheaper air travel and telecommunications mean that immigrants can keep in close touch with their homelands; the proliferation of Spanish-language television channels allows immigrants to entertain themselves without leaving their linguistic ghetto; and the ever-expanding range of ethnic products in the supermarkets means that they do not have to change their diet, either. Add to this the official fashion for multiculturalism and you have a recipe, at the very least, for cultural pluralism.

This is giving rise to a new class of Americans who might be dubbed not hyphenated Americans (Mexican-American) but ampersand Americans (Mexican & American). In 1998, Mexico started allowing its nationals to hold American passports and even allowed naturalized Mexican Americans to reclaim their Mexican passports. About five million Mexican Americans are eligible to vote in Mexican elections—a development that has turned Los Angeles into one of Mexico's most important political stamping grounds. At the same time, a growing number of native-born Americans of European descent are acquiring a second passport, often in an attempt to acquire the privileges that go with European Union citizenship. In 1998, a retired federal employee, Valdas Adamkus, was elected president of his native Lithuania.

The resurgence of identity politics—what Karl Popper called "the return to tribe"—would appear to be antiglobal. After all, there are today 192 independent nation-states, compared with 74 in 1946.[12] But, in recent years at least, political separatism has been nevertheless linked to globalization, at least to the degree that a world so fluid and fast moving encourages some people to take comfort in local identity. There is also a direct link between the relative success of regional institutions such as the EU and NAFTA and the renewed vigor of separatist movements in places such as Scotland, northern Italy, Flanders, and Quebec. For example, now that power is seeping from Rome to Brussels, many Venetians see the opportunity to create an independent city-state. Conversely, the EU habitually bypasses national governments in making regional grants to relatively deprived areas such as Wales or Barcelona. These deprived regions respond by agitating for more EU intervention.

But how far will this process go? When their prospects are laid out by a good critic such as the late Raphael Samuel, even the most ancient nations can seem doomed. For example, Samuel argued that the British Isles, far from being a permanent United Kingdom, were unified for fewer than two hundred years—from the battle of Culloden Moor in 1746 to the Irish treaty in 1921. As the Celts leave the English, "the word 'Britain,' " Samuel concluded, "may become as obsolete as 'Soviet' is in post-1989 Russia."[13]

This is alluring rhetoric, but there seems to be a limit to how far nation-states are prepared to stretch. Limited devolution for Scotland enjoys considerable support on both sides of Hadrian's Wall. But giving too much power to the Scottish parliament risks provoking the "West Lothian question": Why should the Scottish MP for West Lothian be able to vote on English issues if English MPs cannot vote on issues that affect West Lothian? In another instance, California, despite its Hispanification, voted recently to ban teaching in Spanish as a first language—a change that many immigrants supported, some because they want to be Americans and others because they do not want to be put at a disadvantage by speaking a different language than most. Even in Canada, the nation-state has turned nasty. If Canada is divisible, Canadian federalists argue, so is Quebec. About fifty municipalities, representing about one in twelve of the rebel province's citizens, have gone to the trouble of saying that they would rather stay Canadian.

Indeed, the modern nation-state is usually very hard to break down. While states may be blurring a little at the edges, they only collapse when the relationship between the state and its nation or nations is untenable. Both the USSR and Yugoslavia were federations. For all its arbitrary borders, Africa has seen remarkably few secessions, largely because of the difficulty of redrawing the map. Dividing up Rwanda between the Hutus and Tutsis would be even bloodier than the present arrangement. The same applies to Kurdistan. Despite all that Serbia has done to the inhabitants of Kosovo, countries as far afield as China have worried about the precedent that an independent Kosovo would set. The general presumption remains that borders, like rivers, tend to stay in their places yet do the most damage when they wander.

Lines That Matter

In the end, many of the debates about the future of the state come down to a simple battle between common sense (often economic, sometimes humanitarian) and emotion (anything from nationalism to fear of the unknown). The citizens of a particular country might be better off if they did not see their economic interests in national terms. In some cases, they would surely live much more peaceful lives if they were prepared to yield ground to either minorities or their neighbors. But they do not, and it is best to act accordingly. The best place to see this obstinacy in action is where we started: the border.

Far from fading away, borders are still fought over. Virtually every region of the world has a border dispute of some sort or another, often over territory that is economically meaningless. In the Middle East, Saudi warships opened fire on a Yemeni island in the Red Sea in 1998, killing three people; the two countries have been having border disputes since the Treaty of Taif in 1934. Most of the main borders in Asia—including those between China and Russia, India and Pakistan, and the two Koreas—are disputed. In Latin America, Argentina nearly went to war with Chile in 1978 over its southern tip and actually did with Britain in 1982 over the Falklands. Peru and Ecuador came to blows in 1995 over their disputed territory. Most of the disputes about Bosnia come down to different ideas about where lines on the map should be drawn.

In many cases, people's idea of their territory has its roots in centuries past. Saddam Hussein came up with some excuse having to do with the Ottoman Empire when he grabbed Kuwait; some Israelis maintain that the west bank of the Jordan is theirs because the Bible says so.

Nevertheless, many Westerners claim that in "advanced countries" borders are disappearing. This is correct only up to a point. Consider the two borders of the most advanced country in the world, the United States. The Mexican-American border has certainly been made easier to cross by NAFTA, as long as you are inanimate or heading south; Mexicans still have a problem. The United States has already built a "tortilla curtain" along more than sixty miles of the Rio Grande. Guards in "hot" areas such as Tucson-Nogales now wear bulletproof jackets. The Border Patrol's budget has been rising steadily, and the events of September 11 will only increase the level of security.

Far from destroying the border, NAFTA has often reinforced it by creating a community that relies on it. The number of people living along the Mexican-American border has increased from 3.5 million in 1980 to 12 million. Some four thousand *maquiladoras* employ nearly one million workers in Mexico, contributing seven billion dollars to the local economy (the second biggest sector after oil). Although many of these factories are becoming relatively high-tech affairs, they exist because wages remain highly sensitive to the border: Mexican workers cost about a quarter of their counterparts in America. The border also matters to a surprising extent within the cross-border towns themselves. Take El Paso–Ciudad Juárez. El Paso certainly has a more Latin feel than, say, Houston, but it also feels different than Juárez. The Mexican side is much poorer (two million people, no sewage system), but the attitude is what most sets the two towns apart: El Paso is a backwater; Juárez feels like a boomtown.

This could be an unfair example: After all, Mexico and the United States are in different economic leagues and have different principal languages. Neither of these distinctions applies to America's northern boundary. After retreating to Canada following the battle of Little Bighorn, Sitting Bull noted dryly that "the meat of the buffalo tastes the same on both sides of the border." People have been holding the Canadian-American border up as a model of compatibility for years. In 1939, Churchill hailed it as "an example to every country and a pattern for the future of the world."

At first sight, that border does indeed seem to be disappearing. Nowadays, one billion dollars in goods and services flow over it every day. The city of Buffalo, which long kept its gaze focused southward at the rest of the United States, is now beginning to look at itself as the southern tip of a golden horseshoe stretching around Lake Ontario to Toronto. The customs and immigration chiefs from both sides greet each other as old friends.

Yet the numbers still show that boundaries of mind and habit persist. John Helliwell, a professor at the University of British Columbia, has made a thorough study of trade across the Canadian-American border.[14] He found that a Canadian province in 1996 was twelve times more likely to trade merchandise and forty times more likely to trade services with another Canadian province than with an American state of similar size and at comparable distance. Interprovincial immigration was one hundred times more likely, after adjusting for income difference and population sizes. Helliwell's research shows that the Free Trade Act, which came into effect in 1989, did have an impact: The ratio for traded goods had been higher, about twenty to one. But the level has held steady since. (Although the figures are less reliable, Helliwell also estimates that "trade densities" within countries in the European Union are around six times greater than those between those countries.)

There are also political frictions. In the past few years, Canada and the United States have scrapped about, among other things, lumber, potatoes, electricity, magazines, steel, salmon, and BC Bud, a particularly potent form of marijuana grown by British Columbian hippies. The Canadians are furious about the effects on them of American border laws that were aimed first at Mexico and now at Arab terrorism. For example, one idea is for American officials to check all its visitors out of the country as well as in, so that rather than being waved through checkpoints, Canadians would be stopped.

Even though Americans are throwing up most of the obstacles along the border, the most fundamental barrier is on the Canadian side. Canadians are

keen to integrate their economy with that of the United States, but they are
equally keen not to become American. Canada's health system and its cultural protectionism are popular even with its businessmen. "Yes, I want to
see more economic integration," says one. "But I also happen to think we
have a better society, and I never want to lose it."

The Continuation of History

Nation-states may thus prove surprisingly endurable, though it would be
odd if under pressure from globalization borders did not get thinner. Not
only is there room for much freer trade, but there are also problems that are
difficult to solve on a national basis. For instance, it might eventually be logical for European voters to let the European Union decide, say, transport policy. And there is even the desperate hope that logic will triumph over
emotion. In the past, borders have tended to be knocked down by force. Perhaps, as people discover the economic benefits of lowering borders peace-
fully, they will agree to changes in more democratic ways.

That would be nice. But diplomacy is not about niceties, and conducting
foreign policy on that basis seems not only naive but dangerous. If the continued importance of borders presents one nasty, unpleasantly real challenge to the canard about the end of history, then an even nastier one is
provided by armies. Despite globalization and transgovernmentalism, there
is no getting away from the fact that the nation-state preserves a monopoly
on the legitimate use of force.

To be sure, the European Union is talking about creating a common military and foreign policy, but it remains to be seen if that will work. And the EU
is a long way ahead of any other regional grouping. There are as yet few
signs that America's Joint Chiefs of Staff are about to hand control of their
troops over to the Secretariat of NAFTA. Every now and again there has been
some blithe talk about giving the United Nations a standing army (actually,
not a bad idea). It still has to rely on nation-states.

Of course, national armies will come together in alliances and coalitions,
just as they always have. NATO is fifty years old. The two "global" wars of the
1990s—against Iraq and Serbia—were fought by coalitions of the sort that
the Duke of Wellington might well have recognized. The administrative hell
described by the American general of coordinating forces in Kosovo sounds
no different than the British negotiations dealing with the Prussians before
Waterloo. And the Iraq and Kosovo coalitions would have come to nothing if
one nation-state, the United States, had not decided to act.

Far from creating a need for a new sort of foreign policy, globalization has not changed the fundamental rules and aims of diplomacy. Globalization garners one mention in the index of Henry Kissinger's mammoth *Diplomacy*—and rightly so. Nation-states remain the most important actors on the world stage, and the issues that concern them most will be the same as they have always been: protecting their interests and preserving a balance of power.

This is most definitely not a plea for isolationism. If only out of its long-term self-interest, the United States needs to stay involved abroad, championing the mainly global ideas that it believes in, preserving the stability that its companies require, establishing relationships with potential enemies, and cementing alliances with friends. But that is not substantially different from the brief that Kissinger himself followed, or that Lord Palmerston and Fürst von Metternich employed in the nineteenth century.

If globalization does not change the basic rules of the game, it does change the tempo at which it is played. The sheer complexity of some foreign-policy questions probably forces the United States to rely on ad hoc coalitions rather than formal alliances. In both business and politics, self-sufficiency is giving way to mutual interdependence, command-and-control management to touchy-feely alliance building. Just as managers are expected to team up not only with suppliers but also with competitors, it makes sense for America to wait to attack even a tinpot dictator like Saddam Hussein until only after an interminable amount of resolution passing.

There are also likely to be more occasions when humanitarian issues come to the fore, not least because mass communications make atrocities in distant parts of the world so difficult to ignore. But even here there are limits. The war against Serbia was touted as the first "third-way war," a new sort of conflict in which the Western powers were willing to forget the principle of sovereignty in the name of humanity. But there has long been a moral dimension to most wars, particularly ones involving the United States. And the allies did not take their alleged enthusiasm for this third way as far as invading Serbia and deposing its leader.

Under George W. Bush, American foreign policy has managed to leap forward and backward simultaneously. The war against terrorism has given diplomacy a new purpose. Americans once again care about the abroad. The president has proved much fiercer than Bill Clinton, who tended to meander from crisis to crisis while mouthing fashionable nostrums about protecting democracy. Advancing global humanitarian causes is certainly a legitimate concern of foreign policy, but the accent should be on prevention rather than cure. If a cause is just, then it is worth expending blood in its pursuit. Unfortunately, this new involvement has far too often been on a unilateral basis. Bush made scant use of his allies in Afghanistan, despite having the whole world on his side. On a series of diplomatic questions, America has snubbed either its allies or multilateral organizations (or both). Even if many of America's individual stances have been defensible, the overall effect has not been.

Meanwhile, the repeated emphasis on the war against terrorism, "the axis of evil," and so on may mean that America will neglect the real strategic issues that revolve around questions to do with nation-states. Yes, Osama bin Laden is important; but is he as important as, say, preventing China from destabilizing Asia? Ever since the Thirty Years War, crusaders who have wrapped their foreign policy in one global moral flag or another have tended to cause many more deaths than Machiavellian balance-of-power types.

As Brian Beedham has argued, foreign policy comes down partly to a question of how people define the first-person plural. For the moment, when people think about *we*, they think about nation-states.[15] Borders and nation-states are usually about more than just administrative logic. Their force is evident from the fact that even when they did not have a country, most Estonians knew the name of their national bird and the tune of their national anthem; or the fact that a routine meeting with Estonia's transport minister to discuss infrastructure begins with his declaration, "We are not Russian. . . . We have never been so."

Fundamentally, nationalism is not particularly rational, and its costs and benefits are not often counted up. In the same issue of *Foreign Affairs* in which Ann-Marie Slaughter put forward her theory of transgovernmentalism, Peter Drucker pointed to the long list of people—Immanuel Kant, the liberals of Austro-Hungary, and Mikhail Gorbachev—who have argued that economic interdependence would prove stronger than nationalist passions. In many cases, right was on their side. "But whenever in the last 200 years political passions and nation-state politics have collided with economic rationality, political passions and the nation state have won."[16]

Certainly this conclusion is borne out by the life of Osama bin Laden. It is also borne out in Narva. On the last day of 1998, Ants Limets, the somewhat harassed but kindly city manager of the Estonian town, decided that enough was enough and cut off the water supply to Narva's Russian twin, which had not paid its bill for months. Ivangorod retaliated by dumping its sewage—four hundred thousand gallons a day—into the river through a pipe just next door to Georgy Kusnitsov's border post. The old ladies still cross the bridge to do their shopping, but the stench is reportedly unspeakable.

9

The Failure of
Global Government ✓

THE JOB OF secretary-general at the United Nations is rather like that of a
medieval pope. In one sense, you are the leader of Christendom. Yet at the
same time, your power is limited: You have no battalions of your own (all
those peacekeeping troops are only on loan); your organization is a hodge-
podge of feuding bishoprics, most of which owe their first loyalty to their
temporal rulers; and you are normally broke. It is a frustrating business in
which much depends on character and momentum and in which the smallest promise of glory means that you are apt to get carried away.

Early in the 1990s, Boutros Boutros-Ghali, then the UN pontiff, proclaimed that "the victor of the end of the cold war would be the democratization of international relations, the new role of the United Nations." Those
words seem foolhardy now. But at the time, the idea of world government
was a surprisingly fashionable one: George Bush senior had proclaimed a
"new world order" and led his crusade against Iraq under the banner of the
UN. Around the globe, blue-helmeted soldiers were keeping the peace. The
UN was establishing itself as the natural forum for policy debates of every
variety, hosting an earth summit in Rio de Janeiro in 1992, followed by ones
on human rights, social development, and women. The General Assembly of
the UN, previously just another sparring place for the two superpowers,
seemed to be a little closer to the "Parliament of man" envisaged by Tennyson in "Locksley Hall."

Meanwhile, the other organs of world government seemed to be flourishing. The high priests of the IMF and the World Bank preached "the Washington consensus"—the idea that more open markets, freer trade, and larger

international flows of capital were necessarily good. Their young appren-
tices swaggered around the treasuries of eastern Europe, "teaching" capitalism to the natives. The World Trade Organization was established as a
permanent replacement to the "temporary" GATT. There also seemed to be
an outbreak of what might be called "bottom-up globalism": People deserted
petty national political parties to join global nongovernmental organizations such as Greenpeace.

Today, talk about the "democratization of international relations," let
alone a Parliament of man, seems like a pipe dream. Rather than lead a new
world order, Boutros-Ghali lost his job in 1996, ousted by the United States.
In Bosnia, Somalia, Angola, and the Congo, the UN retreated ignominiously
while bullies such as Jonas Savimbi and Slobodan Milosevic waved blood-
stained fists at it. In the hills of Kosovo, babies froze to death. In Africa, UN
people talk about the "well-fed dead"—refugees that it can feed but not protect. Politicians around the world have made the IMF and the World Bank
the whipping boys for the Asian contagion. Under George W. Bush, the
United States has rejected the test-ban treaty, the World Court, and the Kyoto
Protocol. Its use of the UN against Saddam Hussein seemed tactical rather
than strategic.

But should we be so quick to deride global institutions just because they
are global institutions? Although Boutros-Ghali was proved humiliatingly
wrong in practice, his diagnosis was correct: The end of the cold war and the
integration of the former communist countries into the world economy have
only bolstered the case for globalism as a political creed and economic practice. The very challenges that have humbled the multilaterals—the Asian
contagion, Rwanda, Bosnia, even Osama bin Laden—were also plainly outside the capabilities of national governments.

In a few cases this economic and political interdependence has found an
institutional framework through which countries have been willing to cede
sovereignty for the common good. But for the most part, the international
institutions have been found wanting. The main reason why should be obvious from chapter 8: The nation-state remains alive and kicking. But even
with that proviso, organizations such as the IMF and the UN have degenerated into a collection of unaccountable committees that oscillate between
casual arrogance and well-meaning inefficiency. The leaders of the organizations claim that they are restrained from introducing dramatic reforms by
the tightfistedness of their member governments; the member governments
reply that they would be more forthcoming if they saw some sign of reform.
As a result of this impasse, responsibility disappears into the political ether,

and change retreats to the margins. And nobody asks the fundamental questions: What are these institutions for? And can they be made better?

The Road So Far

The first thing to do is to look back and then to lower our expectations. "The sad truth seems to be that the only time that you have a chance of constructing global organizations that might work in peace is during a war." Such a conclusion would be mildly depressing from any observer. But from Sir Brian Urquhart, a former undersecretary-general of the UN who has devoted much of his life to multilateralism, it seems especially discouraging. For the past 150 years, there has been a constant, growing tension between the demand for some sort of multinational responsibility and the tug of national sovereignty. The development of global institutions has been a strange mixture of ad hoc pragmatism and utopianism. Only once, during the 1940s, has there been a brief moment of pragmatic utopianism, and it took a depression and a world war to achieve that oxymoronic state.

The idea of multiple states forming pacts that apply equally to each of them goes back to the second half of the nineteenth century. In 1856, forty-nine countries signed the Declaration of Paris on maritime law, concerning how warring parties should treat neutral shipping. Nine years later, the International Telegraph Union (now the International Telecommunications Union) was set up to regulate the international flow of telegraphs, and it was soon followed by other standard-setting bodies to govern things such as postage and weights and measures. These institutions were kept deliberately small; the aim was to produce precise rules that national governments could enforce. Gradually, however, things became more utopian. In 1899 and 1907, there were Hague Peace Conferences, the second one attended by forty-four nations, that sought to prevent war. The machine guns of the Somme and Ypres made a mockery of that idea, though the same meetings did produce the Hague Convention rules concerning how wars could be fought.

Even before the First World War, the three most important lessons of multilateralism had already been learned: Commonly agreed-upon standards tend to be more useful than institutions; all the great powers must be part of global endeavors; and specific small goals are much better than vague lofty ones. Unfortunately, with the foundation of the League of Nations in 1920, all three rules were ignored. For all its noble ideals and promises to curb state aggression, the league had no mechanism to prevent or counter state aggression, a failure on which Adolf Hitler, among others, capitalized.[1] And without America as a member, the league became increasingly irrelevant, finally disappearing during the Second World War.

That second catastrophe sparked the foundation of the United Nations and the Bretton Woods institutions, with most of the important lessons of the previous half century finally learned. The UN, for instance, was deliberately set up in the world's most powerful nation, the United States—and if its goals were unabashedly lofty, its procedures were boringly detailed. The Security Council was not only designed to be inclusive (the great powers of the time were all permanent members) but also given a fairly streamlined set of rules of engagement and decision making that it still follows today. On the economic side were formed the IMF to oversee the system of fixed exchange rates, the GATT to oversee trade, and the World Bank to promote development. It was, in short, a job well done—a fact echoed by the way that reformers often call for a new Bretton Woods or for the UN to return to the ideals of its charter.

Yet even as you admire the construction of this bright, shining city, you are forced to accept Urquhart's gloomy conclusion. The city could rise only from the rubble of war. The sheer horror of what had happened—not only the war but the economic depression that had preceded it—concentrated the minds of politicians "to save succeeding generations from the scourge of war which twice in our lifetime brought untold sorrow to mankind"[2] and also presented a *tabula rasa* for its architects, such as John Maynard Keynes and Harry Dexter White. And because the Allies—or the United Nations as they became officially known—won the war, they also won the right to impose their order on the world.

Subsequent events have only underscored the uniqueness of that moment. The world has changed, and the multilaterals, shorn of that special set of founding circumstances, have been unable to change enough. The UN soon found itself having to deal with new problems—such as drugs and nuclear proliferation—that it had never foreseen. In a few cases, notably decolonization, it rose courageously to the task. But in general, its response to the changing world has been both lazy and self-indulgent: It has spread and sprawled, giving every problem a new committee and every committee member an inflation-proof pension.

On the economic side, the ad hoc nature of institutional change has had mind-boggling effects. Once the system of fixed exchange rates broke down in the 1970s, the IMF was technically without a job. An official Committee of Twenty debated whether to construct "a new Bretton Woods." Instead, the oil shocks and then the Latin American debt crisis gave the IMF a pretext to expand one of its subsidiary roles—providing temporary resources to deal with countries balance-of-payments problems—into a new identity as an international lender of last resort for poorer countries. In so doing, it assumed a role for which it lacked the most important qualification—the ability to print money—and relied on lending limited amounts of money. But the driving force behind the IMF's "mission creep" was not just job preservation. Most national finance ministers liked the idea of a halfway house that could provide some help to countries in need but that would also have to rely on them to bail it out.

Since then, the fiddling has continued. The UN, for instance, has added the World Court. The IMF now sees itself as a kind of financial overlord. The GATT has become the WTO. And new multilateral institutions have sprung up, such as the G5 (now the G8), the Basel Capital Accord (which sets minimum standards for banking health), and the International Accounting Standards Committee. But the growth of multinational organizations has been most pronounced in the private sector, with the multiplication of both multinational companies and NGOs. In 1990, the *Yearbook of International Organizations* had six thousand international NGOs; by the end of the decade the figure was twenty-six thousand. And that does not include the far wider universe of local groups. The Worldwatch Institute, itself an NGO, reckons there are two million NGOs in the United States alone and one million in India. Visit any of the big, old-fashioned multilateral organizations and you will find that it is surrounded by NGOs (there are 1,700 clustered around the UN in Geneva); that an increasing amount of its work is being done by them (more than half the World Bank's projects in 1998 involved NGOs); and that its agenda is often being set by them: Witness the way that NGOs, through a mixture of passion, technology, and downright media savvy, took control of the WTO's disastrous meeting in Seattle in 1999.

The Multilateral Paradox

Three easy answers to the multilateral muddle immediately present themselves. The easiest is to call for the abolition of multilateral organizations and to rely on the self-interests of states and companies to solve things. Get rid of the IMF, we are told, and borrowers and lenders will begin to watch their steps. Dismiss the UN, and the money will be put to better use by Save the Children.

Unfortunately, obliteration is simply not practicable. No sooner had you pushed the IMF out of Washington than finance ministers would begin to talk about the need to have some body to oversee the world's financial system. Dismiss the United Nations and the foreign ministers of America, Russia, and China would soon suggest annual meetings. Within years, there would be permanent committees, followed fairly soon by an institution similar to the UN's Security Council. Interdependence is a reality even for big countries. In the United States, polls show that three quarters of the population want to share power internationally; under 15 percent want America to throw its weight around as the sole superpower.[3] This reality requires some sort of institutional framework.

The second answer—"the new bright, shining city argument"—is a little more practical but still unachievable and thus appeals to national politicians the world over. It accepts the need for some layer of multilateral institutions but argues that the current set of organizations is out-of-date. What is needed is a completely new system, comprehensive, modern, and high-tech. George W. Bush and Tony Blair, for example, have taken to calling for "a new architecture of global finance" (though their fondness for architectural metaphors does not extend to providing detailed building plans). Some of their proposals make sense, but their arguments remain disingenuous for two reasons.

The first is that existing institutions cannot be simply wished away. It is more than a little dishonest for politicians who have made little headway in modernizing their own national bureaucracies to call for instantaneous revolutions at bodies over which they have even less control. The second is that all the splendid blueprints tend to provide national politicians with excuses for ignoring what is arguably the most important thing about global governance: There is no perfect system. There will always be a tension between national sovereignty and international responsibility, and national sovereignty will generally prevail.

Examine any multilateral institution, and you will soon find that it is caught in some kind of global catch-22. American politicians want an efficient, impartial global political body to take problems, such as peacekeeping and refugees, off their hands; but they also want to control it, overrule it, and even use it to spy on their enemies. The French periodically talk about building up multilateral institutions as a bulwark against American power, but then they perform unilateral nuclear tests. Asian countries want the World Bank to be their champion in the West but resent it when it tries to apply the same standards to them. Everybody believes in the WTO when it is prying open foreign markets but not when it is prying open domestic ones.

This is all the more depressing because, as a rule, the easiest place to make changes is at the national level. The best way to prevent another Thailand or Brazil collapse is not to redesign the IMF; it is to redesign Thailand and Brazil. The outside world has spent more than one billion dollars over the past decade trying to alleviate the suffering of the Sudanese people, with some success. But the only thing that will stop the suffering is if the country's leaders agree to a lasting truce. Even in medieval chaos, the best solution is better national government, not global government.

From this perspective, multilateralism begins to seem like a cruel joke. The world needs multilateral institutions yet also dooms them to be failures. Such a conclusion, unfortunately, leads to the third easy solution, which is to do nothing at all. "It is an impossible job, but somebody has to do it" could be the grumpy motto of almost any multilateral worker. Yet even if you accept the limitations of a world where nation-states still rule the roost, there are still plenty of ways to make global institutions better. If world government had only two purposes, they would be the prevention of financial meltdowns and unnecessary bloodshed. Yet as we start a new century, both seem as likely as ever.

A journey through all the multilateral institutions would make a subject that already seems to fall into the "important but dull" category even less negotiable. We have thus decided to concentrate on the two institutions that should sit at the heart of any new world order: the UN and the IMF.

Back to the Drawing Board

Sit and watch the East River from Kofi Annan's glorious office at UN Plaza and you can feel both at the center of the world and at its extreme. The slight Ghanaian, who succeeded Boutros-Ghali as secretary-general, returns to the subject of globalization frequently and adamantly, as if it were a religion. Indeed, the papal image suits Annan much better than it did his bombastic predecessor. He often holds his hands together as if in prayer. A man with an almost priestly calm, he rarely raises his voice, except to laugh; some critics claim his laugh is the last African thing left in an impeccably cosmopolitan man. Educated in America, married to a Swedish artist, Annan has spent most of his life serving in the curia of the UN bureaucracy.

Indeed, listening to Annan, you begin to wonder whether his unabashed globalism is just a case of a man ascribing his own qualities to the world. The UN is usually involved in the world's most momentous debates: What should be done in Iraq, East Timor, and Afghanistan? Should peacekeepers also be peacemakers? But the world seldom returns the compliment and discusses the future of the UN. National governments make policies that relate to individual parts of the UN system: Their health ministers talk to its health agencies; their foreign ministries complain about the composition of the Security Council or the policy on Israel. But—with the exception of a few Republicans who want to abolish the whole thing—nobody has a UN policy. And there is no debate about whether the world needs a new global political architecture to match its financial equivalent. There should be.

The UN is an enormous organization that, among other things, buys half the world's children's vaccines, protects twenty million refugees, hosts 7,500 meetings a year in Geneva alone, and is the world's biggest purchaser of condoms. At times—wandering around the tunnels under the UN's offices in Geneva, for instance, or navigating the escalators in its New York headquarters—you can feel as if stuck on the set of a 1960s futurist film. It also boasts a structure that bewilders even its own staff. It is fairly easy, for instance, to find officials in Geneva who believe that the WTO is part of the UN. (It is not, though its staff participates in the pension plan.)

There are at least five big UN centers—New York, Geneva, Vienna, Rome, and Nairobi—and countless smaller ones. The operational side of the UN is a mess of competing funds, programs, and specialized agencies, stretching from the United Nations Children's Fund (UNICEF) to the IMF, the World Bank, the World Health Organization, and the World Meteorological Organization. Most of the subsidiaries raise nearly all their money from outside sources, have their own governing bodies, and regard their membership in the UN as accidental. They all meet twice a year at something called the Administrative Committee on Coordination (ACC), at which, as one member points out, "discussing issues like the security of UN personnel in war zones is a little lost on the man from the World Intellectual Property Organization."

Kofi Annan has done more to streamline this structure than any of his predecessors. He has introduced cabinet-style government at the top of the UN and set up UN houses in various countries to bring together numerous agencies and programs. Boutros-Ghali never appointed a deputy for fear that he (never mind she) would elbow him out of his job; Annan appointed a woman, Louise Frechette, to the job. And he has begun the slow task of introducing the United Nations to the private sector, bringing in business leaders, such as Percy Barnevik, to secret summits at the Rockefeller estate near New York City. He has also persuaded some notable capitalists to give the UN money: It is hard to imagine Ted Turner pledging one billion dollars to any of Annan's predecessors. Add in Annan's occasional diplomatic coups—notably his success in averting a second war in Iraq in 1997—and it is not hard to see why he has been hailed as the most successful secretary-general since Dag Hammarskjöld, the Swede who was perhaps the only outstanding leader the UN has had.

While Annan's achievements are real enough, so are his limitations. His curia dispatch his encyclicals, and leaders come to genuflect, but the UN feels like a sideshow: Even when it comes to an issue like Iraq, the real decisions are still made by national politicians, particularly in Washington. The UN remains a place where a senior official can compare the bureaucracy unfavorably with that of the old Soviet Union; where discord between "the South" (as less-developed nations are known) and "the North" paralyzes decision making; where America can decide unilaterally to cancel several hundred million dollars in dues; where a combination of budget cuts and jobs-for-life has created a gerontocracy, with an average age in the Secretariat of nearly fifty; where the 1998 budget was agreed to only after a demeaning haggling session in which favored Secretariat posts were auctioned off by a moderator using a can of potato chips as a gavel.[4]

Annan's reforms have only really affected the thin sliver of the organization that he actually runs. Worse, he has not always been successful. The General Assembly scotched a proposal by Annan to set sunset dates for new committees.

Look around the whole UN, and you find a haze of duplication among the manifold funds, programs, and agencies. Even when set alongside national governments, it seems bloated: Its aid budget is ten times that of Britain's Department for International Development, but it employs thirty times as many people. In the field, the agencies remain choosy about which UN projects and UN houses they join and how much money they devote to them. The fact that the half-dozen agencies that deal with AIDS in one African country finally have fairly regular meetings is an achievement, but as one participant admits, "They all go their separate ways once they leave the door—and take their money with them."

This is not always pure bloody-mindedness. The agencies in question have usually raised money for specific purposes: Why should they let other people spend it? UNICEF insists that one of its strengths is its *esprit de corps*, and its workers thus resent being bundled in with other, less effective bodies, such as UNESCO. But the plain fact is that much of the UN's work is duplicated if not triplicated. Why should Rome play host to no fewer than three separate food agencies? Why should both the World Bank and the UN have a development program when the two do increasingly the same thing? The UN is a 1960s-style governmental organization that devotes most of its time and around three quarters of its money to development, when, in the real world, development is driven more and more by the private and voluntary sectors. Usually leaner and more dynamic, NGOs not only compete for dollars that might otherwise go to the UN but often assume its role. It was NGOs, not the UN, that pushed the recent treaty to ban antipersonnel land mines.

Annan's staff talks about such things in whispered tones, when in fact the questions should be asked openly. Rather than fighting (unsuccessfully, as it turned out) to transfer the decolonization unit from the prestigious political department to services, reformers should have asked whether the UN still needs a decolonization unit. A bit like a struggling country, the UN often makes the mistake of measuring reforms by its own historical standards rather than against those of the world outside its walls. Over the past two decades, almost every large business organization—and, at least in the Anglo-Saxon world, almost every big government one, too—has been forced to answer the question "What can I do that other people cannot?" The result has been takeovers and layoffs in the corporate sector and privatization in the public. Despite several committees on reform, nothing structural has really changed at the UN since the war. It has simply added new committees and spread itself ever thinner.

UN-bearable

Almost all disinterested observers believe that the UN should become a narrower, deeper organization, focusing on the truly global problems that nobody else can tackle. The UN's core political activities pass this test fairly easily: Only the UN can reasonably take responsibility for refugees and peacekeeping. It is also a natural forum for debates on global problems, from collisions with asteroids to drug trafficking. In some social and economic fields, the UN plays an important role as a coordinator (as it did initially with the environment), but much of its development work is duplicating work that others do better.

A narrower, deeper UN would not necessarily be a weaker one: It might well include a small standing army, for example. Had the UN been able to deploy peacekeeping troops rapidly in Bosnia and the Congo, it might well have been able to nip disasters in the bud. Instead, it had to stand idly by while national governments deliberated. A tighter structure would also offer a way to tidy up the agencies, funds, and programs. Those organizations that wanted to stay within the UN would have to accept Annan's writ.

So why has this not been done already? The answer is interesting not just because it reveals a lot about the UN but because similar problems plague almost all multilateral organizations. Even if most national governments would gladly swap a revised UN for the existing one, potential reforms open four fault lines. The deepest is the one between the North and the South. Any sensible reconfiguration of the UN would shift its emphasis from economic and social projects to political ones, but it is the former that three quarters of its members hold most dear.

The three other fault lines all run off the major one. The first lies in the particular problem of the United States and its nonpayment of dues in the 1990s. In 1999, Congress announced arrogantly that it would pay one billion dollars—around two thirds of the money it owed—and the UN should be grateful. The deal came with various conditions, imposed unilaterally by the United States. It is difficult to overstate the disgust with the United States at the UN, even among its allies. "They have poisoned the well [of reform]," says one senior ambassador, citing not just the unpaid bills but the way that Washington used the UN's inspectors to spy on Iraq. Many doubt that George W. Bush really wants to see a more efficient UN—just a smaller one.

The next fault line concerns the anachronistic composition of the Security Council and the relentless politicking that this generates. There is a strong case for widening the permanent membership of the Security Council, but India's membership would infuriate Pakistan, Germany's would infuriate Italy, and Brazil's would infuriate Argentina.

The final fault line has to do with the UN's budget. Ten countries pay for more than three quarters of the current $1.3 billion budget. Although nobody begrudges the fact that the world's poorest nations contribute only thirteen thousand dollars each, many fairly prosperous countries escape lightly. China, which pays less than Belgium, is understandably no great proponent of reform.

If the UN does eventually bicker itself into oblivion, the blame will lie with its members rather than its secretary-general. Even those governments that support reform have no clear policy toward the UN, and so no one is taking the lead. Even so, the excuse that Annan is purely the club secretary does not wash. As Dag Hammarskjöld stressed repeatedly, the post is not just about fulfilling mandates but also about representing the world's broader interests, which surely include a healthy UN. Put another way, if he wants to change the UN, the diplomatic Annan will have to try to force his club members to accept changes that most of them do not want. There were hopes that some sort of "big bang" solution would emerge from the UN's special millennial assembly in 2000. Without leadership from Annan and cooperation from the United States, that prospect ebbed away.

I'M Fired

If the UN's main challenge over the past decade has been how to persuade people to take an interest in its problems, the International Monetary Fund has had no such problem: It is probably the most reviled international institution in the world. And hatred of the fund is not limited to the financial losers—in the United States, anti-IMF feeling is as wide as the political spectrum. In the eyes of the Republican right, it is an "economic arsonist" that uses taxpayers' money to bail out international speculators. The Democratic left accuses it of putting economic orthodoxy before the well-being of the poor.

More generally, people just do not think that the IMF works very well. In a 1999 poll of some thirteen thousand people around the world, only one in twenty said they had "a lot of confidence" that the IMF could solve the world's economic problems. (The figure crept over one in ten only in the Philippines and India.)[5] The fund has also attracted the opprobrium of all manner of panjandrums: George Shultz and Walter Wriston have called for its abolition; Jeffrey Sachs of Harvard accuses it of driving much of the developing world into recession; Rudi Dornbusch, another celebrated economist, once compared Michel Camdessus, the fund's boss during the Asian crisis, to "a croupier" in "the casino" of emerging markets.[6] Even the World Bank has distanced itself from its twin.

What kind of institution could produce this sort of response? The broad answer is, one full of people like Stanley Fischer. A Zambia-born economist, Fischer rejoined the fund in 1994 from the Massachusetts Institute of Technology, where he worked with Dornbusch and Paul Krugman. Technically, Fischer was second in command during the Asian crisis, but he was often the IMF's public face, though, one suspects, not entirely of his own choosing. Although he has the vigorous obstinacy of a professor who knows his subject so much better than his pupils do, the quiet Fischer does not look like a natural pugilist. Even when he had time to attend public gatherings, he often gave the distinct impression that he would rather be reading a book. Had his boss not been a Frenchman—or as Newt Gingrich liked to stress, "a French socialist"—Fischer might have been spared such ordeals.

Most conspiracy theories about globalization are balderdash, yet it is certainly true that many important decisions about the world economy in the late 1990s were made by a small cabal of technocrats at four institutions in

Washington, D.C.: the World Bank, the IMF, the U.S. Treasury, and the Federal Reserve Board. All the people involved—not just the technocrats but also their leading critics—had spent their lives pontificating in Boston and administrating in Washington. Larry Summers, the former treasury secretary, once worked as the World Bank's chief economist, a job he inherited from Fischer; the two men also shared a house on Martha's Vineyard and wrote a number of papers together. Summers's right-hand man during much of the Asian contagion, his former classmate David Lipton, worked at the IMF for eight years and spent some time advising eastern European governments with Jeffrey Sachs. Joseph Stiglitz, the World Bank's chief economist and a fierce critic of both the IMF and Fischer, earlier worked with Summers on a report on the Asian "miracle."[7]

Not all of these people are as reserved as Fischer. One European prime minister privately described the talkative Summers, who subsequently became president of Harvard University, as "the Richard Holbrooke of economics." James Wolfensohn, the World Bank's chairman, is sociable to a fault, hugging almost everybody he meets. But many of them still seemed uneasy about even the moderate amount of celebrity that came with their jobs. (One technocrat learned that he was famous from his dry cleaner, who had just seen him on a Korean-language channel.) There was also something rootless about their lives. Throughout the late 1990s, the likes of Summers and Fischer seemed to be almost permanently airborne. During South Korea's crisis, the IMF's economists shuttled from the luxury of the Seoul Hilton to a collection of cubicles at the Bank of Korea, where they meted out economic justice to local bankers pleading for dollars. The one thing they rarely saw was the country itself.

Both critics and admirers have pointed to similarities of such people to Robert McNamara's whiz kids, who did a decent job running Ford before going on to do a lousy one running the Vietnam War. They shared the presumption that all they needed to do was apply their brains, and the world's messes would be cleared up. On the other hand, there has also been something decidedly "unwhizzy," almost sluggish, about the IMF. For starters, it has never quite recovered from being put in a city, over Keynes's objections, where the finest art is that of the filibuster. In today's volatile world economy, long-winded overviews of economic data matter less than the ability to react to minute-by-minute changes in the real world. Worse, the IMF's doors are closed evenings and weekends, and its employees switch off at the end of the day rather than remain on call—a fatally irresponsible approach in a world in which the currency reserves of entire countries can be decimated in a matter of hours. IMF lore has it that one desperate Asian finance minister calling at a late hour found himself explaining his problems to the only person in the building: a security guard.

The fund's basic problem is that it tries to combine several incompatible roles: those of a bank, an insurance company, a regulator, and a public-sector charity. The principle behind the organization is simple enough: Its 184 member governments keep money on deposit with it in return for being able to draw on its collective resources if they ever need help supporting their currencies or paying their debts. But the practice is fraught with contradictions. The fund's general approach is a strange mixture of sternness and generosity. It insists that borrowers change their ways immediately, but it lends money at extremely generous rates.

The fund's culture is an equally strange mixture of arrogance and impotence. Unlike the Federal Reserve, it does not deign to release its minutes, and its internal audit system is something of a farce. On the other hand, it can barely write a check without calling the U.S. Treasury first. America, which has 18 percent of the votes at the fund, calls the shots, and finance ministers often bypass the fund to talk to American officials.[8] In 1999, when *Time* magazine rather strangely decided to hail on its cover the three men who had "saved the world economy" (*Time*'s definition of *the world* presumably excluded most of Asia, Latin America, and Russia), it picked Summers, his predecessor, Robert Rubin, and Alan Greenspan.

Beyond the Report Card

The *Time* cover also points to what is perhaps the most important question of all: Was the world really saved? Or did it just get lucky? There is already a temptation to forget just what a close call it was in August 1998 when both Russia and Long-Term Capital Management hit the rocks.[9] The late 1990s saw a vast number of national economies devastated by runs on first their currencies and then their banks.

Optimists tend to blame a good deal of what happened on the fund. Certainly, its report card was mediocre at best. Until shortly before many of the busts, the fund was lauding the economic management of the countries concerned. Many of the hardest-hit countries (notably Indonesia and Russia) were operating under IMF programs when their economies disintegrated—the equivalent of a suspiciously large number of patients dying in a hospital. And in the best tradition of the medical profession, the subsequent bill was enormous.

There are some excuses. Some of the IMF's patients had spent the past thirty years on diets of cigarettes and cholesterol. Others tried to commit suicide when they were told that they needed to mend their ways. And to make matters worse, the hospital's board spent half of its time ignoring the hospital itself and the other half squabbling about what should be done. Bill Clinton waited fourteen months after the crisis started before taking his first serious initiative: support for global cuts in interest rates.

On the other hand, the fund should bear a good deal of the blame for both causing and prolonging the crisis. In selling Anglo-Saxon capitalism to emerging countries, the fund was (to adopt another metaphor) rather like a hard-selling pet-shop owner who tells you what a wonderful companion a dog is but neglects to mention that it needs to be fed and walked every day. Anglo-Saxon capitalism is not a rule-free utopia; on the contrary, it relies on a mass of rules and institutions, such as bankruptcy laws, central banks, and trust-busting authorities. In Indonesia, the Suhartos presumed that they had the IMF's blessing to treat the country as their personal property. In Thailand, regulators saw nothing particularly unusual about lying about their reserve levels.

The IMF's bungling continued after the crisis had begun. Its policy of pushing interest rates to sky-high levels and forcing governments to slash budgets ushered in a wave of bank closures. In Indonesia, the IMF's decision to call for an end to food and fuel subsidies at a time when millions of people could no longer afford the necessities of life was blatant political interference that sparked riots. In a typically defensive report issued in January 1999 that analyzed its record in South Korea, Indonesia, and Thailand, the fund admitted that it had "badly misgauged the severity of the downturn" but then went on to claim that, since the affected countries eventually followed its medicine (which they did only once they had no choice), the signs of recovery were evidence that it had been right.[10] But the recovery also reflected external factors, such as the American consumer's enormous appetite for cheap goods, not to mention the resilience of the fund's patients.

A Better Way to Do Things?

Some of the causes of the black marks on the IMF's report card are now being fixed. The fund is already putting more stress on market regulation in the countries it oversees; it is also becoming a little more transparent and its senior officials a little more market savvy. A few of its technocrats now admit that it should not meddle in domestic politics. But many of its failings are plainly institutional. The IMF is an organization that was set up to do one thing (monitor a system of fixed exchange rates) but now does two others (supervise the global financial system and be the lender of last resort) for which it lacks both the resources and the formal independence. Symptomatically, even the IMF's best-known success, the bailout of Mexico, was not its own work; it was the United States that stepped in, prepaying for two billion dollars' worth of oil.

The fund's failures—and the unspoken fear that it could all happen again—has led to a fierce debate about the need for a new financial architecture. This debate has at least forced the IMF to come up with new ideas of its own, rather than just sulkily defend its actions. But this debate is a classic example of the "bright shining city" type of argument. Most reformers want to conjure up a system that will satisfy what Zanny Minton Beddoes has dubbed "the Impossible Trinity": It must respect national sovereignty (nobody wants the IMF to boss around the Fed), deliver firm regulation (to prevent global panics), and allow global capital markets to be as free as possible. In practice, we can nearly devise a system that can satisfy two of these three things, but never all three.[11]

Given the Impossible Trinity, consider two of the most straightforward remaining options: imposing capital controls and abolishing the IMF. While capital controls are usually restrictive and even counterproductive, many developing economies are, in the words of Barry Eichengreen of the University of California at Berkeley, "not ready for prime time." Precautionary taxes on short-term capital inflows, then, can help protect undeveloped financial systems, if used in moderation.[12] There is also something a little hypocritical about mutual funds—which usually impose penalties on savers who want to withdraw their money—screaming bloody murder when countries try to do the same thing. Yet for anybody who sees the enormous potential of globalization, capital controls remain a step backward.

Relative to the specific question of how to redesign the global financial system, capital controls obviously respect national sovereignty, since they are imposed by the countries concerned. But they equally clearly fail to allow free capital markets. And, unless they are applied with great subtlety, it is not clear that they help regulation much either. Capital has a way of finding its way around barriers, and even if it is caged, it then tends to become ever more prone to cronyism. Gangsters everywhere welcome the introduction of controls.

Getting rid of the IMF would satisfy two elements of the trinity: respecting national governments and allowing free capital markets. Many would add that it would also improve regulation of the world economy. By one calculation, in the fifteen years before 1998, there were one hundred banking crises in emerging markets.[13] Nor is there much evidence that the IMF has obviously improved the lot of the poor. A Heritage Foundation study of the eighty-nine poorest countries that received IMF money between 1965 and 1995 found that in forty-eight people were no better off than they were before they received the loans and in thirty-two they were poorer.[14]

The heart of the institutional case against the fund, however, is that it encourages "moral hazard": The very existence of the IMF prompts both lenders and borrowers to engage in ever riskier behavior. If the IMF had not bailed out Mexico, people would have thought twice about lending their money to Russia, and Russia might have been a little more disciplined about how it spent it. But the moral-hazard gambit can be used to undermine just about any sort of insurance scheme, and it willfully ignores the political (and perhaps moral) need for such schemes. The same Republican leaders who want to abolish the fund would not dream of depriving their voters of bank-deposit insurance, even though it clearly encourages moral hazard. The prospect of a systemic failure of the world's financial system is sufficiently horrifying that it is worth taking precautions against it, even if they encourage some risky lending.

The serious debate is, thus, about reforming the fund, not abolishing it. The participants fall into two groups: builders (who want to expand the fund's role as a financial supervisor and also turn it into a better-equipped lender of last resort) and trimmers (who want to cut back one or both of these roles). This squabble inevitably ties into the wider argument about exchange rates. To simplify, trimmers nearly all support freely floating exchange rates: If the IMF did not need to help countries defend their currencies, it would not need so much money. The IMF's addiction to fixed rates has, the trimmers point out, cost a fortune and also, through high interest rates, caused untold misery. Builders reply that pegged exchange rates have given plenty of countries the chance to develop their economies in relative security without the plague of inflation. Today, people tend to forget that in 1993 prices in Brazil were rising at an annual rate of 2,400 percent.

The builders naturally include the IMF itself. Fischer argues that there is a way for the IMF to become a credible crisis manager without being able to print its own money.[15] Under his scheme, the fund will judge countries by a variety of criteria, such as how they supervise their banking systems; "good" ones will "prequalify" for IMF money in times of crisis. Cash will also be available to countries that do not qualify, but they will have to pay higher interest rates. Another builder is George Soros. Under his much sketchier scheme, the IMF will become a global central bank that will somehow provide liquidity to all markets; meanwhile, a spin-off of the IMF, an international credit-insurance corporation, will calm jittery foreign investors by guaranteeing international loans (up to a limit) in return for a fee.

The problem with building up the IMF is that it runs straight into questions of national sovereignty: National politicians will never allow such an unaccountable body the power that it needs. If the fund were the same size relative to world trade that it was at its foundation, it would have $2.5 trillion at its disposal—roughly nine times what it has at the moment.[16] (Fischer argues that the fund could get by with a lot less.) But even when the IMF thinks it has enough money and even when it dispatches it well in advance, it still often cannot defend a currency. When the IMF dispatched the first $9 billion of its $41 billion package to Brazil in October 1998, it boosted the country's reserves to more than $50 billion; the markets, however, correctly sensed that the local currency was overvalued—and within three months the Brazilian authorities were defeated.

The builders also put a lot of faith in the IMF's technocrats, who would establish the criteria for "good" countries (in Fischer's scheme) or decide upon the country credit limits (in Soros's). For Fischer, this trust in his own kind is perhaps excusable; for Soros, a man who owes much of his fortune to the incompetence of bureaucrats, it beggars belief.

Above all, there is the underlying problem that, when push comes to shove, political expediency always triumphs over economic principles. Some countries—Russia is one, China almost certainly another—would fail the IMF's transparency tests. Yet they would also plainly be too important to fail.

The trimmers, who want to hand over bits of the IMF's job to other institutions, are on slightly firmer ground, but they also face questions of practicality. In a world of freely floating exchange rates envisaged by Jeffrey Sachs, the fund's main job in a crisis would be to prevent overreaction, reassuring investors that a country's finances are sound and mitigating the impact of devaluations on the poor. The actual rescue would be left to a new global bankruptcy court, similar to America's chapter 11, which would bail creditors "in," forcing foreign lenders to pay part of the price. In other schemes, the IMF would remain a lender of last resort but lose its regulatory role to a body that would specialize in international markets.

These schemes at least have the advantage of forcing governments to be specific. But they are fraught with practical difficulties. People in the United States cannot even agree on who should regulate its national financial markets, let alone on how a global market ought to be organized. And even if a bankruptcy court could be created, you cannot replace the government of a country in the same way that you can remove the management of a company.

A better trimming solution would be to concentrate the preventive side of the world financial system on banking regulators and the Bank for International Settlements in Basel. Since borrowed money is the gelignite of financial crises, the BIS could use its position as setter of capital standards to bully bankers into doing things most want to do anyway. Force banks to put aside more capital for loans to companies in countries with murky capital markets or poor accounting standards, and borrowers will push for changes in the countries concerned. It would also be wise to increase the amount of capital needed for both loans to hedge funds and proprietary trading. And as before, we favor the concept of narrow banking, in which regulators decouple the insured, deposit-taking parts of banks from the rest.

The BIS could also exert some pressure on bankers to change loan contracts to prevent single bankers from being able to opt out and start the sort of stampede that happened in Asia. Naturally, a super-BIS would suffer from some of the same disadvantages as the IMF. But the BIS is closer to the practitioners who matter—the bankers—and it puts the onus of enforcement on national regulators (thereby binding them into the system) and on commonly recognized standards rather than on clever young economists descending from on high.

Dollarizing the World

There is even—and here we begin to drift into the realms of hope rather than expectation—a chance of a similar bottom-up solution to the problem of exchange rates. As we have explained, there are good reasons why many emerging economies favor fixed exchange rates, as well as good reason why the chances of defending an arbitrary peg are small, however hard the IMF tries to help. Argentina had a currency board, where each unit of the local currency was backed by a similar amount of dollars at the central bank. That made it a much harder nut for the market to crack than Thailand. But it did crack in the end, the victim of the government's failure to reform other parts of the economy. Even while the fixed peso "worked," Argentina's interest rates were often five percentage points above those in the United States.

The idea of a global currency was discussed seriously prior to Bretton Woods. One letter written by Henry Morgenthau, the American treasury secretary, to his assistant, Harry Dexter White, just after Pearl Harbor specifically envisioned a postwar monetary system built upon a single international currency. In reply, White enthused about the importance of stable exchange rates not just for investors but also for governments that could avoid "the disrupting effects of flights of capital and inflation," competitive devaluations, and protectionism, "World Enemy Number One."[17] The same arguments apply today: A single global currency would make it much more difficult for governments to interfere in the lives of businesspeople.

The obvious rejoinder is that it is not practicable. It has taken Europe centuries to produce a single currency. Many emerging countries would regard dollarization as colonization, or at least their politicians would. But the tide may be shifting. In January 2000, Ecuador announced plans to adopt the dollar. Admittedly, the country was in a terrible state and the practicalities were murky, but other countries may follow. One poll taken in Mexico in 1998 found that nine out of ten people prefer the prospect of dollarization to floating exchange rates; Argentina looked at the option. It is not hard to imagine the Americas as a dollar bloc, or much of eastern Europe adopting the Euro, with much of Asia drifting toward the yen or the dollar. There would be holdouts, naturally: China and India are the two immediate examples. But regional currencies would hand power from unaccountable global institutions such as the IMF (which would probably still exist to look after the outsiders) to much richer and more transparent regional ones such as the Federal Reserve Board and the European Central Bank.

So close your eyes and imagine a world blessed with competing regional currency blocs, a set of common accounting standards, an international bankruptcy court, and an IMF that remains open on the weekends. Would that mean that financial crises were a thing of the past? Hardly. As Stanley Fischer himself has pointed out, "The vision that propels most proposals for reform of the international financial system is that international capital markets should operate at least as well as the better domestic capital markets." But that is a recipe only for a safer world, not a safe one. Banks still make plenty of idiotic decisions in their national markets, and there are still huge stock-market bubbles. As the first line of Charles Kindleberger's *Manias, Panics, and Crashes*, the best book to date on financial catastrophes, reminds us, "There is hardly a more conventional subject in economic literature than financial crises."[18]

The Parliament of Man

In other words, financial panics will continue, just as their political counterparts will. And the somewhat ramshackle army of multinational bureaucrats—both financial and political—will find themselves being pilloried for the mess. Perhaps even more frustrating for those who think that a magical structure exists, the chances are that in the end most of the decisions that matter will be not just national (and often American) but also personal. What would have happened to the world economy in 1998 if Alan

Greenspan had not loosened monetary policy? What would have happened (or not happened) in Kosovo if Bill Clinton had taken his eye off the polls and displayed a tougher face to Slobodan Milosevic much earlier?

This is one of the more worrying things about globalization: Despite its logic, its fate seems to rely on human decisions made by people who normally have national interests closest to their hearts. Yet knowing that you face a near-impossible task is no excuse for doing it badly. The political and economic branches of "world government" offer contrasting lessons in how not to structure things. The UN has become an ungovernable sprawl gathered under one roof. The IMF, by contrast, is only one of several semiautonomous financial bodies (many of them confusingly connected to the UN) that do not work well together. Neither seems to have learned two of the basic lessons of multilateralism that seemed obvious even a century ago: Commonly agreed-upon standards tend to be more useful than institutions; and specific small goals are much better than vague lofty ones.

What about the third lesson: All the great powers must be part of the endeavor? The multilaterals seem to have confused representation with accountability. On the one hand, they remain rich men's clubs. The composition of the Security Council reflects the status quo sixty years ago. The world's main economic organizations, such as the G8, provide no voices for the developing world. One of the ironies of the attacks on the WTO is that the organization, with its 144 members, usually looks like one of the fairest global institutions and certainly has a good record of helping poor countries take rich ones to court. Even so, twenty-nine of the poorest countries do not have missions at the WTO's headquarters in Geneva, and many more complain that bringing cases against rich countries is prohibitively expensive in all but surefire cases.[19]

On the other hand, the distribution of jobs among most multilateral organizations is done entirely on the basis of nationality rather than ability. It is difficult to imagine prospective successors to Kofi Annan sitting for public examinations. Yet the system by which countries "reserve" a certain number of places for "their own people" on international organizations seems increasingly dotty. International civil servants should be forced to reapply for their jobs every few years. Outsiders—particularly businesspeople—should be brought into the bureaucracy as a matter of course rather than as exceptions.

Earlier in this chapter, we referred to that brief moment of pragmatic utopianism in the 1940s. That moment has passed, and with it the chance to build a new shining city. But the 1940s had not just goodwill but some degree of direction. The institutions that were forged in the white heat of war were created with clear objectives in mind: They were to *do* something rather than just to *exist*, as most of them are today. Given the growth of economic interdependence and the necessity of building coalitions to battle global problems, such as terrorism, there are grounds for hoping that institutional globalism, albeit of a more limited sort, could muster support, providing that it retains a similar respect for precise objectives. The gradual lifting of tariffs over the past half century has shown that countries are willing to give up sovereignty if there is a clear goal in mind (in this case the greater prosperity that comes from freer trade). Both the IMF and the UN could learn from it.

In many ways, the case needs to be made over the heads of national politicians and to the people in the same ways that NGOs do. Unfortunately, when the IMF tries to justify itself, it does so in the etiolated language of economics. Asked in November 1998 whether he thought globalization was in trouble, Stanley Fischer pooh-poohed the idea, insisting that most of the people he met at international meetings—finance ministers, central bankers, and the like—thought that globalization would continue. But they, as even some central bankers realize, are not the problem. The real challenge—as Guillermo Ortíz Martínez, the governor of the Bank of Mexico, pointed out to Fischer's peers at a conference in Davos—is "to explain to a Mexican housewife why she has to pay higher interest rates on her housing loan because Russia has defaulted."[20] That has never been the IMF's way.

As for the United Nations, our comparison of it to the medieval papacy should both inspire and frighten Annan almost as much as the more obvious parallel to the League of Nations. On the one hand, by using their pulpits effectively, some strong popes did manage to lead Christendom, regardless of their lack of battalions. On the other, the failure of most popes to face up to the manifold abuses within the church opened the way first to irrelevance and then to a reformation that split Christendom down the middle.

10

The Closing of
the Global Mind

THE MINISTRY OF CULTURE in Paris does not look like the sort of institution in which pessimism ought to flourish. Everything about the place is designed to reflect the glory of the French mind. The ministry occupies a wing of Cardinal Richelieu's Royal Palace, a magnificent building that has been kept in pristine condition, its paint fresh and its gilding aglow. And yet this is clearly not just a museum to a glorious but dead past. The reception area is thoroughly modern. The chairs are black and angular, sacrificing comfort for elegance, in classic Le Corbusier style; an entire wall is taken up with a bank of televisions. On their way to lunch, the ministry's inhabitants have to pick their way through throngs of tourists that have come from all over the world to worship French culture. The Comédie Française is just around the corner, the Louvre and the Opera short walks away.

Yet pessimism flourishes here nonetheless. The ministry's inhabitants are convinced that a rising tide of American popular culture is swamping France. And they spend much of their lives administering a complex system of quotas and subsidies that are designed to protect French culture from being completely submerged. Here, protectionism is not just a ruling intellectual orthodoxy but a way of life. The ministry has almost uniform support among the French elite, from the professors at the Académie Française who are desperately trying to keep their language from being polluted by Franglais phrases, to television executives who insist (at least in public) that their loyalty to their mother country comes even before the need to turn a profit.

The elite is most worried about the threat that America poses to French film. This is partly because film—officially France's seventh art—plays such a prominent role in French culture. Two Frenchmen, the Lumière brothers, put on the first public film showing, in the basement of the Café Royal in Lyon in 1895. A French company, Pathé Frères, invented the modern studio system, helping the French capture 70 percent of the American domestic film market by 1908.[1] French directors such as François Truffaut and Jean Renoir produced some of cinema's finest products. The French, at least in their own eyes, have even been responsible for the canonization of the greatest Hollywood directors, from Alfred Hitchcock to Martin Scorsese. America may be a land of film fans, but France is a land of that infinitely more sophisticated creature, the film buff.

Despite all this, the French are seeing "their" art form being taken over by Americans, thanks, in their view, to unfair competition. Because of the high cost of making and distributing films, cinema is a highly unusual enterprise. Hollywood has the advantage of a gigantic domestic market that allows filmmakers to recoup the costs of their productions before dumping them on the rest of the world. A big film in America can open on three thousand screens, ten times the number in any European country.[2] This allows Hollywood to make not only more films (around seven hundred a year, twice as many as Britain and France combined) but more expensive ones. The average budget for a studio film is above thirty million dollars; very few non-American ones ever reach ten million. Hollywood has the further advantage of using a language that is rapidly becoming ubiquitous. And it has the enthusiastic support of the world's most powerful government. In 1946, the Truman administration made free trade in films a condition of Marshall Plan aid for Europe. In the 1980s, the White House was occupied by the star of such classics as *Bedtime for Bonzo;* in the 1990s, Hollywood and Bill Clinton were shamelessly infatuated with each other.

There is, however, more to the French obsession with American films than this. The French see Hollywood as a Trojan horse: It gives birth to theme parks; it popularizes fast-food restaurants; and it provides free advertising for a mass of Americana from jeans to baseball caps. "America is not just interested in exporting its films," says Gilles Jacob, the head of the Cannes Film Festival. "It is interested in exporting its way of life." One survey in 1999 by *Libération* found that two thirds of the French do not "feel close to the American people"; roughly the same proportion thought that America was "too influential culturally," and there were also solid majorities that disapproved of its economic, political, and military clout. The young and the educated were especially anti-American.[3]

This feeling has deep roots. In the 1950s, the French communists tried to turn their countrymen against Coca-Cola. (A cartoon at the time showed a sultry Coke bottle diverting a Frenchman away from his legitimate Beaujolais wife.) Earlier, Georges Clemenceau had complained that America was the "only nation in history which miraculously has gone directly from barbarism to degeneration without the usual interval of civilization." If the premier were to wander up the right-hand side of the Champs Élysée toward the Arc de Triomphe, he would encounter, among other bits of Americana, a Gap, a Disney Store, and, inevitably, a McDonald's. The fact that McDonald's was also the official food of the 1998 World Cup, held in France, would probably cause Clemenceau more pain.

Je Ne Voudrais Pas Mon MTV

Anxieties about Americanization are not peculiar to Paris. A willingness to denounce Hollywood for its formulaic plots, cartoonish characters, and unerring ability to pander to the worst in human nature is almost a requirement for admission into the intellectual elite in every country in the world, including America. Disney is despised wherever claret is drunk, not just for its greedy executives and corporate paranoia (though for anyone who has ever talked to the company, those are reasons enough) but also for its products. Euro Disney was famously denounced by one European intellectual as a "cultural Chernobyl." In his diatribe *Team Rodent*, Carl Hiaasen, a Miami-based novelist, warned that "Disney will devour the world in the same way that it devoured America, starting first with the youth."

Other elites argue that the enemy is a force even more pervasive than Hollywood: the English language. Some 343 million people speak it as a mother tongue; another 235 million speak it fluently as a second language; and somewhere between a hundred million and a billion people around the world are in the process of learning it.[4] English is the language of the global economy, the argot of the Internet and business meetings. This inevitably creates resentments among the speakers of the world's ten thousand other languages. The French ministry of culture tried to ban three thousand English words in 1994. (It was stopped on freedom-of-speech grounds.) The anti–English language movement in India has denounced the America-based Cartoon Network, a favorite with children across the country, for undermining local Indian languages and furthering the hegemony of the tongue used by the country's former colonizers. In Germany, the Institute for German Language recently protested Deutsche Telekom's decision to start billing people for "city calls" and "Germany calls" rather than their much longer German equivalents. Smaller languages seem particularly protective. The mayor of Barcelona has tried to push through a law that would force all popular films shown in the city to be dubbed into Catalan.

This resentment has allowed the French to assemble a global guerrilla army that is dedicated to limiting American cultural hegemony. In 1989, the French persuaded the European Community (as it then was) to decree that at least 40 percent of the programs shown on its members' television should be domestic products. (The quota policy was called, with a completely straight face, Television Without Frontiers.) In 1993, just as Steven Spielberg's blockbuster *Jurassic Park* was defeating Claude Berri's *Germinal* at the box office, Jack Lang, then France's culture minister, threatened to sabotage the GATT round in order to get audiovisual materials (which account for a tiny proportion of world trade) exempted from free-trade agreements. "Cinema used to be the side salad in world commerce," observed one French commentator, "now it's the beef."[5] Director Bertrand Tavernier—who is a sophisticated historian of the American cinema—proclaimed that America had the same attitude to the French cinema as it had toward the American Indians. "If we're very good, they will give us a reservation."

The French have found a particularly vocal ally in Canada, which has long been terrified of being swamped by its closest neighbor. Ninety-six percent of the films shown on Canadian screens are foreign ones, primarily American. Four of five magazines sold at newsstands and six of every ten books sold are foreign ones, again primarily American. The American influence is so pervasive that, in a poll taken in 1998, a quarter of Canadians identified "life, liberty and the pursuit of happiness" as a Canadian constitutional slogan. Canada has plenty of protectionist measures on its books. Television stations must offer 60 percent Canadian content, radio stations must devote at least 35 percent of their playlists to Canadian music (whatever that is), and the Heritage Ministry is pushing for a measure that would force cinemas to show a fixed share of Canadian films.

In 1998, Canada organized an international meeting in Ottawa to discuss the problem of American cultural dominance. Representatives from nineteen countries attended, including Britain, Mexico, and several other close allies of America; the United States was pointedly excluded from the meeting. The delegates discussed ways to exempt cultural goods from international treaties aimed at lowering trade barriers. They argued that things such as films, books, and magazines were too important to be governed by the same rules as the trade in turnips.

Less Than Total Recall

In a world in which *Titanic* has replaced *Les Enfants du Paradis* as the most successful film in French history and in which Saddam Hussein chose Frank Sinatra's "My Way" as the theme tune for his fifty-fourth birthday, it is not hard to worry about American cultural imperialism. But is it right to do so? Is Hollywood as powerful as its enemies imagine? Is there really such a thing as "American culture"? And does American dominance extend to every corner of popular culture?

The resistance is certainly right to think that America dominates world cinema. American films are the only ones that reach every market in the world (the highly successful film industries of India and Hong Kong barely travel outside their regions), and they dominate almost all of them. Around the world, lists of the top-grossing films are essentially lists of Hollywood blockbusters, written in slightly different orders and with one or two local products thrown in for the sake of variety. In the European Union, the United States has around three quarters of the film market; in Japan, more than half. Even in tiny Bhutan, a Himalayan nation that only five thousand people visit a year, street peddlers hawk illegal videos of Hollywood's latest blockbusters.[6]

Hollywood's empire also appears to be expanding by the year. Tinseltown now gets roughly half its revenues from overseas, up from just 30 percent in 1980; indeed, entertainment is now America's second largest export, after aerospace. At the same time, few foreign films make it big in the United States, controlling less than 3 percent of the market.

Symptomatically, dubbing American films into native languages is a huge industry worldwide. In Italy, there are more than eighty dubbing companies and one thousand professional dubbers, and the local equivalent of the Oscar has a category for the best dubber of the year.[7] In Hong Kong, the people who translate the titles of American films into phrases that will entice the locals are held in similar respect. The Cantonese version of *Nixon* was simply *The Big Liar*, *As Good As It Gets* became *Mr. Cat Poop*, *The Full Monty* became *Six Stripped Warriors*, and, even more memorably, *Boogie Nights* became *His Powerful Device Makes Him Famous*.[8]

But Hollywood's success is as much about attitude as structure. We will return to the subject of subsidies in Europe later, but it cannot be entirely coincidental that Britain's unsubsidized rock-music and book industries compete well with their American equivalents, while its film and television industries, founded on the BBC and generous tax breaks, have failed miserably. Hollywood is quite simply the most profit-driven film industry in the world. Many of the immigrants who built Tinseltown and who "stole" the film industry from France's intellectuals sprang from cut-throat businesses such as textiles and music halls; they may not have been to college (indeed, several were semiliterate), but they knew the importance of giving the public what it wanted, which was good stories and pretty faces. The French had some appreciation of the latter, too little of the former.

A focus on "butts on seats" has made Hollywood into one of the world's great business clusters, a center of excellence that is every bit as successful as Silicon Valley or Wall Street. This image may be a little difficult to square with the Academy Awards, at which Tinseltown struggles hard to give the impression that it is run by sentimental narcissists whose only concerns are designer clothes and the latest way to demonstrate political correctness. But it has all the attributes over which management gurus swoon: It is flexible, networked, virtual, innovative, and hypercompetitive.

Rather than controllers of the system, the studios are essentially the bankers and distribution arms of an entrepreneurial network of small firms. Only a handful of film companies have more than one thousand employees. The vast majority—an estimated 85 percent of firms connected with the industry—have fewer than ten workers, and these small firms do battle with astonishing ferocity. Their employees work grueling hours, take huge risks, and strike deals with anybody who is willing to make them, regardless of national origins. And they are constantly finding new places to apply their technology, from theme parks to video games.

Hollywood has another important quality that sets it apart from its rivals: It is a global operation, drawing capital, ideas, and talent from all around the world. Many of the key figures in Hollywood history, from Charlie Chaplin and Alfred Hitchcock to Arnold Schwarzenegger and (in his Paltrowized incarnation) William Shakespeare have been imports. Hollywood is so full of British actors, screenwriters, electricians, and costume designers that there are several cricket teams in the area. Three of the major studios, Columbia–Tri-Star, Fox, and Universal, are owned by foreign media conglomerates. Plenty of films and television shows are derived from ones made overseas.

It is at least arguable that it is not so much Hollywood that is corrupting the world as the world that is corrupting Hollywood. The more Hollywood becomes preoccupied by the global market, the more it produces generic blockbusters that are designed to play as well in Pisa as in Peoria. Such films are driven not by dialogue and plot but by special effects that can be appreciated by people with minimal grasps of English. Their characters are cartoonish, their appetite for fine-grained cultural analysis minimal; they focus instead on universal subjects that most can identify with, regardless of national origin. There is nothing particularly "American" about boats crashing into icebergs or asteroids that threaten to obliterate human life. From this perspective, the barbarian at the gate is not Walt Disney; it is the teenager in Shanghai.

Is This America?

In fact, many Americans question the easy identification of Hollywood with American culture. From the right, Michael Medved, a Hollywood screenwriter turned cultural commentator, argues that, far from popularizing traditional American values, Hollywood is bent on undermining them. "America's long-running romance with Hollywood is over," he argues. "Tens of millions of Americans now see the entertainment industry as an all-powerful enemy, an alien force that assaults our most cherished values and corrupts our children."[9] Terry Teachout, a music critic, points out that educated Americans might be just as quick as their Parisian counterparts to applaud if an earthquake were to reduce Hollywood's soundstages to a pile of smoking rubble. If a school massacre occurs in the United States, Tinseltown is the first suspect after the National Rifle Association.

Whenever French protectionists and American neoconservatives agree on anything, it is always worth taking a closer look. In fact, American culture is much more diverse and, dare we say it, interesting than they think. In September 1998, The Wall Street Journal produced an impressive list of facts that suggest that high culture was hardly declining in the United States More than 110 American symphonies—including the Louisiana Philharmonic Orchestra in New Orleans and the Northwest Symphony Orchestra near Seattle—have been founded since 1980. The number of nonprofit professional theater companies has grown from fewer than sixty in 1965 to more than eight hundred today. Opera attendance, spurred by the use of computerized supertitles that provide translations of lyrics above the stage, rose during the 1990s. There are now 110 professional opera companies in the United States, thirty-four of which have been founded since 1980.[10]

Book sales are at unprecedented levels. The biggest book market in the country is now greater Los Angeles, the very heart of the beast according to the French intelligentsia. The annual Los Angeles Times book fair attracts more than one hundred thousand visitors and draws speakers from all around the world. On television until recently, Oprah Winfrey recommended a serious book to her viewers once a month, increasing sales by hundreds of thousands of copies. In virtually any medium-sized town in America, you can walk into a store such as Barnes and Noble and browse through a book while sipping a latte.

Nor are books the only high point. Wherever you live in America, cable television offers ways around the diet of cop shows and sitcoms that the networks serve up. Americans can watch classic movies on The Movie Channel or American Movie Classics or recent independent releases on Bravo or the Sundance Channel; they can brush up on their education with The History Channel or the Discovery Channel or overdose on politics with CNN, CNBC, MSNBC, or Fox News.

The most important face of cultural diversity, however, is ethnic. The 1980s and 1990s saw the biggest surge of immigration into the United States since the turn of the century. On a typical Saturday night in New York City, you can visit dozens of different national celebrations, from Jamaican reggae parties to Chinese operas. But it is Los Angeles that seems like the Ellis Island of the late twentieth century, with more than fifty languages spoken at Hollywood High School and a population that is now 40 percent Latino.

Accordingly, rather than imposing cultural uniformity, the media is increasingly reinforcing diversity. At a time when people were announcing the death of networks, two Spanish-language networks managed to add plenty of viewers throughout the 1990s. In Los Angeles, one Univision station, KMEX, is the most popular channel in the region at some times of the day. Los Angeles also boasts channels that broadcast exclusively in Korean, Cantonese, and Japanese, and others that rent airtime to Yiddish and Russian broadcasts. The Internet has taken this even further. During NATO's bombing of their homeland, many Serbs in California evaded the "lies" of the American media and relied on their motherland's impartial coverage. Even in the shadow of the Hollywood sign, ancestral loyalties are proving more powerful than American popular culture.

Outside the Door

Culture ministers outside America might scoff at this analysis, pointing out that the inroads that Spanish and Korean television have made into the United States are as nothing compared with the progress of American television into their countries. Once again, this is true, but it shows only part of the picture.

Most countries in the world have now deregulated their television industries. Meanwhile, technology has made it possible to squeeze many more channels into the spectrum. From Budapest to Bombay, viewers have finally been given alternatives to dire state outfits such as India's Doordarshan and Hungary's Magyar Television (whose MTV call sign had proved misleading in the past). As channels have multiplied, so has demand for content. American television producers have not been the only people to profit from this desperation. Brazilian soap operas, for example, have proved so popular in Russia that trendy Muscovites have taken to calling their dachas *fazendas*.[11] But the Americans have profited more conspicuously than anybody else. Indeed, in many cases, people have imported not just individual American programs but whole American channels, such as CNN, Nickelodeon, and MTV.

It is this as much as anything else that seems to have got under the skin of the cultural elite. Yet the Americanization of commercial television looks increasingly like a short-term phenomenon. As the market matures, stations have to build their brands and appeal to audiences that still have marked preferences for the homegrown. That means making more of their own programs and leaving American pap for the times of day when few sane people are watching. For instance, Nova, the Czech Republic's first private channel, began in 1994 by showing mostly American shows because its only competition came from state-run stations of the sort that considered square dancing a hot program. But as the market grew, so did the appetite for local programming. Within three years, ratings for Nova's American shows had dropped by 45 percent and it was pouring money into the production of local soaps, sitcoms, and so on.

Nowadays, the most popular television program in each European country is nearly always a local production. In 1998, each of the main western European markets had no American series among the top ten programs.[12] Three quarters of all the programs launched are now local productions. The most successful of these owe their appeal precisely to the fact that they are rooted so clearly in their local cultures. *Julie Lescaut*, a French police drama, is no less quintessentially French than *Inspector Morse* is intrinsically English. Global giants are bowing to this preference for the local. There are now twenty-two different versions of CNN, including one in Turkish and two in German. The percentage of programming on the English-language version of CNN International that might be described as American has fallen from 70 percent in 1996 to 8 percent in 2002.

The strength of local ties is even more apparent in pop music, long supposed to provide the sound track to America's cultural hegemony. Ever since four mop-haired Liverpudlians appeared on *The Ed Sullivan Show*, the United States has been obliged to share the music market with Britain, which has a pop cluster that is nearly as vicious as the visual one in Hollywood. But now this Anglo-American hit machine has begun to sputter. In the past, it was relatively easy to launch a global pop star. But as the attention spans of audiences contract and markets fragment into tiny niches, from rap to techno, this is getting more difficult.

In Europe, few self-respecting teenagers would once be caught dead listening to local groups. Now French groups such as Air and Daft Punk and Swedish groups such as the Hives and Sahara Hotnights are decidedly cool. In Germany, France, and Spain, local groups account for around half the sales.[13] Challenged by local language channels, MTV has responded by producing different programs for different regions. In the United States, Spanish-speaking Latin American bands are commanding ever higher shares of the market. And Continental bands are battling their way into America (sometimes with unfortunate results: One of the favorite groups of the schoolboys who massacred their fellow students at Columbine High School was Germany's Rammstein). Even Iceland has a global star in Björk.

Turning to the theater, the British have made a growing impression on the most commercial end of that particular art—the popular musical—since the appearance of *Joseph and the Amazing Technicolor Dreamcoat* and *Jesus Christ Superstar* in the mid-1970s. Andrew Lloyd Webber and the producer Cameron Mackintosh revived what had become a geriatric art form with catchy tunes, occasionally clever lyrics, sumptuous sets, and relentless marketing. *The Phantom of the Opera* has been seen by more than fifty-two million people and done better box office than the movie *Titanic*. Basel built a theater specifically for *Phantom;* Bochum, Germany, has one for *Starlight Express.* Indeed, were it not for the success of Disney's *The Lion King*, one might argue that, with musicals at least, the British dominate the mass market and American shows cater to sophisticates.

The "American" book- and magazine-publishing industries that so worry the Canadians also seem something of a paper tiger. The most influential magazine editor in New York in the past decade has been an Englishwoman, Tina Brown, who, depending on whom you talk to, either revived or DiCaprioed both *Vanity Fair* and *The New Yorker* before founding the short-lived *Talk.* America's tabloids are run largely by Britons. Foreigners own half of America's top twenty book-publishing houses. America's biggest firm, Random House (the publisher of this book), is now owned by Germany's Bertelsmann. The pied piper of America's media industry for the past two decades has been the Australian-born Rupert Murdoch.

In fact, at a time when American teenagers seem almost as besotted by (Britain's) *American Idol* as their younger siblings are by (Japan's) Pokémon, you might wonder why Washington has not set up some protective ministry of its own. In fashion, the great houses of Milan and Paris still gaze down on middle-of-the-road Americans. Walk down Los Angeles's Rodeo Drive, with its outlets for Gucci, Valentino, and Armani, and it is America that looks like the cultural colony, not Europe. In kitchens across America, Asian and Latin American dishes are gradually supplanting national staples such as meatloaf and hamburger. Nor is it just a matter of human cuisine: Corina's Biscuits, a pet-food company based in Athens, Ohio, produces ethnically flavored dog treats, including Mongolian beef, Korean barbecue, and chicken taco.[14]

The most popular sports in America—football, basketball, and baseball—are hardly the most popular elsewhere. Attempts to export football have made little progress. By contrast, soccer, the only sport that deserves the adjective *global*, seems finally to be colonizing the United States. An advocate for the homeless in Los Angeles, Ted Hayes, has enjoyed so much success in importing cricket to South Central (his team, which features former gang members, was invited to play at Lords) that he has now begun to introduce the Gaelic sport of hurling.

Waiting for the Ratings

So the "Planetized Entertainment" envisaged by Michael Eisner of Disney is not as American as people think.[15] But is there "a global culture"?

The mere phrase has a quixotic feel, calling to mind such doomed projects as Esperanto. More than perhaps any other area of globalization, culture defeats categorization. The same technology that helps to make the world less parochial can also reinforce ethnic identities. The Internet allows students in Beijing to download a Janet Jackson concert at exactly the same times as their counterparts in Heidelberg, but it also allows Chinese Americans to download Cantonese pop.

In some cases, there is genuine intermingling. In the United States, Spanglish, a hybrid of English and Spanish, has become common in Latino communities and magazines such as *Latina*. Perhaps the dominant trend in haute cuisine at the moment is "fusion"—mixing elements from different culinary traditions to come up with unique mixtures. Kipling's old line that "East is East" is mocked by authors such as Arundhati Roy and Salman Rushdie.[16] Successful pop musicians have often looked for inspiration abroad. (The Rolling Stones hail from Dartford but their souls are from the Mississippi delta.) But nowadays anybody who does not include a sampling of a Zulu war song or a Tibetan prayer on their latest record looks decidedly passé; indeed, several musicians, including Paul Simon, have resuscitated their careers by mixing different ethnic flavors.

This intermingling is likely to increase, if only because people are getting more used to seeing different parts of the world. Americans now make more than fifty million international flights a year, up from 14.3 million in 1975. The number of American college and graduate students studying abroad for university credits has been doubling each decade (82,900 in the 1995–1996 school year). And an increasing number of students are looking beyond such predictable destinations as Britain, France, and Spain to eastern Europe, Latin America, Africa, and the Far East. In 1996, fourteen countries each attracted more than one thousand American students.[17] Such people return to, say, Michigan convinced that their first novel, though set in Ann Arbor, should be a meditation on a Hindu incantation.

However, the idea that culture is inevitably becoming a global goulash, with different flavors mixed into one intoxicating stew, does not stand up for two reasons. First, most people are fairly local in their cultural tastes. Even when different groups enjoy the same experience, they often do so for different reasons. The British warmed to *Titanic* because of its love story, but some critics complained that the movie's depiction of the upper classes was unfair and anti-British; some Japanese, on the other hand, were attracted to the film precisely because of the stiff upper lips displayed by the doomed aristocrats.

Second, many "mixed" products are fairly weak. In the literary world, Rushdies are very few. (Would you want to read that first novel based on the Hindu incantation?) The best novelists tend to draw on what they know, which still tends to be local. Culture is becoming not so much a stew as a smorgasbord from which people can choose whatever takes their fancy. An Englishwoman might think nothing of picking up an Australian novel, but she would still expect it to be Australian. Globalization makes it easier for her to get hold of that book and perhaps easier for her to understand bits of it, but she will recommend it to her friends only if she likes it.

This leads to a rather more optimistic definition of the effect of globalization on culture: It is really about leveling the playing field. Suddenly, it is possible for teenagers in Shanghai to have passports to two different worlds: the one of global blockbusters and their own. And suddenly it is also possible for quintessentially British films such as *The Full Monty* and *Bridget Jones's Diary* to top the charts around the world for no better reason than that they are funny. Nor is it just a matter of light entertainment. The level playing field also allows works that might otherwise be deemed uncommercial to be made. The audience for a new recording of a Michael Tippett symphony or for a nature documentary about the mating habits of flamingos may be minuscule in any one country, but round up all the Tippett and flamingo fanatics around the world, and you have attractive commercial propositions. The cheap distribution offered by the Internet will probably make these niches even more attractive financially.

There is still a hefty premium for any product that can sell to more than one niche. Everywhere you look, from books to techno, there are plenty of greedy people determined to promote the next big thing. Even the museum world seems to have succumbed to the idea of the blockbuster, with people talking about "mega-exhibitions," and museums around the world piecing together deals a little like film studios do. This may also increase pressure on those stuck between the blockbusters and the niche products. In an interesting essay in *The New Yorker*, John Seabrook worried about this "midspace." He foresaw "an apocalyptic heath, which the mid-list authors, the good but not brilliant authors, and the solid but not spectacular bands, who were once the de facto standard bearers of the culture, haunt like ghosts. It is like Las Vegas at night: a tantalizing, amoral world lit by the sparks of artists, actors and musicians who are in transit between success and failure."[18]

Yet the no-man's-land that Seabrook depicts has always existed, and there have always people who have found themselves stranded in it: "The second novel syndrome" and the "good character actor" are not new phenomena. Moreover, the presumption that only the truly awful will hit the global artistic jackpot seems wrong. *Saving Private Ryan* and *Cold Mountain* may not be *Citizen Kane* and *Humboldt's Gift*, but they probably count as art by most reasonable definitions of the term. Even in the world of evil lizards and sinking ships, quality still counts for something. Although they were both given the same amount of hype, *Titanic* succeeded, but *Godzilla* did not, partly because *Titanic*, for all its faults, was a better film.

One cannot go far down this particular road without tripping over the old argument about art and commerce. For many European intellectuals, financial success is so odious that it can only be proof of failure: true artists should die like van Gogh did, penniless and maimed. When confronted by a painting by Julian Schnabel, one is tempted to agree. But the underlying assumption that the audience cannot be trusted is surely wrong. Some rubbish inevitably does better than it should. Some young artists and writers will get praised too early. But, in general, the really good stuff will win out. As one French dramatist wrote, "If they go to see one of my plays, it is probably a good play. If they don't go, it is probably not a good play." But then Voltaire would probably not be welcome at the Ministry of Culture.

Wrong Diagnosis, Terrible Remedy

It is hard to know whether the culture bureaucrats in Europe really believe their own depiction of Hollywood as some sort of artistic Terminator, as soulless as it is irresistible. After all, those noble guardians of culture in Paris have seen fit to make Sylvester Stallone a Chevalier de l'Ordre des Arts et des Lettres (for his painting or his acting, one wonders) and bestowed a similar honor on Sharon Stone (don't ask). The men from the ministry seem to enjoy the glitter at Cannes as much as anybody from Hollywood does. As any American mogul will tell you, the same self-righteous young Britons who harp on the need for artistic integrity at the Groucho Club would be the first to jump at the chance to direct *Die Hard 23*. In fact, it is very tempting to write off the fight against America as just another fairly harmless example of sour grapes and bureaucratic job preservation. But the catch is the quotas and subsidies that emerge as solutions.

The obvious problem with quotas is that they are increasingly easy to avoid. Any European who wants to poison his mind by watching an American television program during prime time can flick through an ever-increasing number of channels or rent a video. (In Greece, you can even tune in to one of fifty unlicensed TV channels that broadcast nothing but American fare, much of it pirated.)[19] Quotas also have the perverse effect of encouraging the production of "quota quickies"—excruciatingly banal local productions that are designed to satisfy official mandates.

The case for subsidies is a little more robust but not much. In France, where a film is more likely to get made because the producer has good connections with the ministry rather than because it has anything so boring as a good script, the local industry has lost ground to American imports. In Germany, half the films are so awful that they never even get a commercial showing. Government handouts also tend to go to the people who have least need of them. France's Centre National de la Cinématographie deliberately hands the biggest subsidies to the country's most successful film producers, thus encouraging an inefficient, cosseted gerontocracy. (In 1995, one study found that 85 percent of the French film industry's directors were over fifty years old.) Britain's national lottery has duly given most of the money to people with good track records (i.e., the ones who could raise money anyway). Anecdotal evidence suggests that much of the "extra" money has gone not into more films but straight into the pockets of "the talent," whose agents simply upped their prices to reflect the lottery windfall.

The only clear winner from all this is Hollywood. It is not hard to find senior people in Hollywood who will admit privately that Tinseltown has "a Detroit problem": Its exorbitant costs make it vulnerable to competition. Given the importance of the English language and the vibrancy of its other culture industries, Britain would seem to be the obvious rival. But the government's fascination with subsidies and what one studio chief refers to as "that BBC thing" means that there is no chance that "they are going to do a Toyota on us" and make good, cheap commercial films.

In the meantime, the subsidies often end up supporting the sort of Hollywood fodder that they are designed to combat. Britain's tax breaks are of most use to films with budgets of ten million dollars or so and thus go to big action movies.[20] The past decade has seen a steady stream of Hollywood producers to Canada—particularly Toronto—in search of government subsidies as well as lower costs. Films and television shows made in Canada—even by foreigners—are eligible for government handouts; Canadian television channels also pay a premium for programs that help them meet government requirements for Canadian content.

Moreau's Way

Against this background, it is refreshing to discover that the doyenne of French film actresses has very little to do with all this. The real problem of the French film industry, Jeanne Moreau argues, breathing heavily on yet another cigarette in her tiny office, is that it lacks the savoir faire of the Americans. The star of *Jules et Jim* is now more than seventy years old, but she remains remarkably optimistic about the possibilities for her own country's film industry. French film producers, she insists, should stop relying on protectionism ("an attitude born from fear") and should start believing in themselves again. They should realize that the construction of new cinemas and the explosion of television channels provides them with a massive opportunity. ("The beast needs to be fed.") They should learn from Hollywood's storytelling skills. And they should form alliances with Hollywood studios in order to turn America's technical skills and marketing might to their own advantage.

Rather unfortunately, Moreau chooses to call her solution "the third way." But her answer is a practicable one because it incorporates both technological innovation and the latest thinking in Hollywood. For some time, the big studios have been creating and acquiring independent studios in order to reduce their dependence on extravagantly expensive blockbusters and to reach parts of the audience whose taste extends beyond the juvenile.

Now, their relentless quest for new ideas and talent—as well as new markets—has persuaded most of the big studios to set up shop in Europe and to convert their offices there from distribution hubs to production centers.

In the end, cultural protectionism simply misses the point. *The Full Monty* is no more a product of American culture because it was coproduced by Fox Searchlight than a John Grisham novel is a product of German culture because it is published by an imprint of Random House. Far from gaining from insulation, culture depends for its vitality on the ability of people to reach beyond their own societies to embrace different traditions and perspectives; in other words, culture and cosmopolitanism go hand in hand. The greatest cultural movements—most obviously the Renaissance and the Enlightenment—involved the promiscuous mixing of cultures. Elizabethan England was a cauldron of creativity because its artists were discovering the ideas of both their Continental counterparts and their forebears. From Sparta to Singapore, most cultural deserts have been produced by officials trying to preserve "their" cultures from corruption at the hands of aliens. Goethe made the point well in 1827 with respect to German nationalism and literature:

> We Germans are very likely to fall too easily into this pedantic conceit, when we do not look beyond the narrow circle that surrounds us. I therefore look about me in foreign nations, and advise everyone to do the same. National literature is now rather an unmeaning term; the epoch of world literature is at hand, and everyone must strive to hasten its approach.

Globalization is not just preparing the ground for the triumph of American culture and mass-produced trash. It is also opening people's minds to an unprecedented range of ideas and influences. It is encouraging creative artists to mix ideas from a dizzying variety of sources. And it is encouraging the rapid proliferation of new cultural forms.

The United States will always have a huge influence on the world's popular culture. America has the advantage of a huge domestic market, a language that is gaining market share, and a genius for selling itself. It is also the country that reached postmodernity first, inventing many trends, from blue jeans to rock and roll, that have since been adopted and adapted by most other cultures. But cultural protectionists err if they think that they can direct the taste of their citizens through subsidies and quotas. And they err even further if they think that, given a free choice, their citizens will automatically prefer poor global rather than good local products. The French Ministry of Culture has much less to fear than it thinks.

Part Five

Winners and Losers

11

Silicon Valley and the
Winner-Take-All Economy

THESE DAYS, even envy is interactive. At www.paywatch.org, a site established by American trade unionists, disgruntled employees can tap in their
own pay and benefits—they are asked sarcastically whether they receive free
country-club membership, a luxury company car, or the use of a penthouse
suite—and find out how many times more their boss's compensation is than
theirs. Recent figures from the site show that the average boss took home
531 times what the average factory worker received in 2000. In 1980, the
boss received only forty-two times as much.

Bosses are not the only people to be making out like bandits. Sports stars,
pop stars, film stars, even, goddamn them, literary stars sign contracts
worth tens of millions. These are only the most conspicuous of an enviable
group of winners. While median incomes in America are barely two thousand dollars higher in real terms than they were in 1972, managerial pay
packets have at least doubled. And this inequality extends to countries as
well, with the gap between rich and poor countries widening.

For many observers, these growing gaps have a lot to do with globalization. The global economy is also a winner-take-all economy, they argue, in
which the fortunate few amass an ever larger proportion of the world's rewards, the poor are left with ever fewer crumbs, and society is divided into
two ever more distant camps. "For unto every one that hath shall be given,
and he shall have abundance," argues the book of Matthew, "but from him
that hath not shall be taken away even that which he hath." The same argument can be heard, put rather less eloquently, in almost every contemporary
critique of globalization.

Capitalism has always been good at distinguishing between winners and losers: That is one of the secrets of its dynamism. But by hugely increasing both the size of the market and the potential rewards for success, globalization puts this process into overdrive. Robert Frank and Philip Cook, two economists who have made their names studying winner-take-all markets, illustrate how this happens in the world of opera. Before the invention of the gramophone, the most talented singers could perform before only a few hundred thousand people in their lifetimes. This had the effect of not only putting a ceiling on their earnings but also ensuring that there was plenty of work left over for their less talented contemporaries. Now that sound can be reproduced so easily, there is no reason to listen to the second-best singer in the world, let alone the local warbler.[1]

Globalization has helped a growing number of labor markets become celebrity markets. The more international markets become, the more desperate the competition for the star salesman or chief executive. The most renowned lawyers or accountants or even academics can now sell their talents across several continents. Meanwhile, globalization also increases what economists call networking effects. If everybody else uses one computer operating system, then it makes sense for you to do so, too: That, they argue, is why Bill Gates is so rich. The same thing in broad terms applies to movies or books: One reason why people see the latest film is to be able to participate in the buzz of social and office life. By increasing the size of the world's networks, whether cultural or electronic, globalization again increases the rewards of winning.

A different sort of networking also works for individuals. Doing well at school increases your chances of going to an Ivy League university rather than a state college, which in turn increases your chances of being accepted by McKinsey or Goldman Sachs rather than a second-division consultancy or bank, and so on. This law of accumulated privileges works for places as well as people. Places that develop a comparative advantage over their competitors—such as Hollywood in films or Seoul in wig making—tend to pull farther ahead of their rivals as the years go on. They attract more star players and shape the surrounding culture. In Hollywood, the dry cleaners call themselves "celebrity cleaners."

But is the winner-take-all argument really convincing? And is it really as powerful a critique of globalization as some people imagine? What makes a particular place or group of people into winners? Are the winners a permanent class, or is it possible for other people and places to join in? How imitable or fragile is their success? And does it really come at the cost of others? We will examine these questions in some detail with reference to a narrow strip of land between San Francisco and San Jose that used to be known as the Valley of Heart's Delights and now might be more appropriately rechristened the Valley of Money's Delights.

Do You Know the Way to San Jose?

We have chosen Silicon Valley for a simple reason: Despite the bursting of the dot-com bubble, it has invented the world's most successful and influential formula for manufacturing wealth. It interests us here not for its technology but its way of doing business and organizing (or not organizing) society. Indeed, Silicon Valley is in many ways an exaggerated version of the sort of society that globalization is helping to create everywhere else. Whether as a showpiece for the virtues of immigration and meritocracy, or as the home of the world's most borderless industry, or even perhaps as the ugliest industrial center in history, Silicon Valley is something of a test tube for globalization. In the same way that California is famously "like America, only more so," Silicon Valley is like the global world, only more so.

That success has been tarnished by the dot-com bubble. But it still stands. One testament to it is the number of imitations Silicon Valley has spawned. America alone is home to Silicon Desert (Utah and Arizona), Silicon Alley (New York), Silicon Hills (Austin), and Silicon Forest (Seattle and Portland). The following pack includes such unlikely locations as the Côte d'Azur ("Europe's California") and Egypt's Pyramid Technology Park. Mahathir bin Mohamad of Malaysia has set aside twenty billion dollars and a space roughly the size of Chicago for a new Multimedia Super Corridor that will include an information-technology city of one hundred thousand people, called Cyberjaya.

And even this understates the Valley's influence. Look around the developed world, and you will see the gradual Siliconization of many sorts of commerce, not just high-tech industries. By some counts, gazelle firms— ones that have grown by at least 20 percent in each of the past four years, a species particularly prevalent in Silicon Valley—have accounted for over three quarters of America's new jobs in the past five years (and probably the same proportion in Europe and Japan). Everywhere, product cycles are speeding up: Even fairly humdrum companies are learning how to live with the same economics as Intel, where each new chip becomes obsolete within a matter of months. Everywhere, big firms are becoming looser organizations, breaking themselves into smaller units or devolving more power to their frontline workers. And an increasing number of these workers are having to learn how to be portfolio workers—to juggle different careers—just as workers in Silicon Valley have.

Interestingly, many of these fundamental changes in society are more often blamed on globalization than credited to Siliconization. Yet many of them reflect the Valley's influence and the success of its six thousand high-tech firms. The Valley's 2.2 million inhabitants control an economy about the size of Chile's. Even after the bubble had burst in 2001, Silicon Valley still provided jobs for 1.35 million people, and its productivity and income levels were double the national averages.[2] For many workers, it remains a mecca, a place where jobs still pay well, where promotion can still be swift, where receptionists still tell you about their share options, and where the office canteen serves spring ginger–seared *ahi* tuna for less than five dollars.

This would immediately seem to indicate that even if Silicon Valley is a winner-take-all society, there are an enormous number of winners. But before getting into that argument, it is worth trying to define exactly what Silicon Valley is and why it is so successful. To do this, imagine that you are one of the many foreign bureaucrats now charged with trying to build Silicon Valleys of their own—a courtier in one of Dr. Mahathir's periodic delegations, say, or one of the scores of visitors from the Japan External Trade Organization. As you battle the traffic from the venture capitalists' offices on Sand Hill Road to Stanford University, you are haunted by the great question, Why did it happen here?

What a Long, Strange Trip It's Been

The first depressing thing to note for our foreign bureaucrat is that the Valley has taken a long time to become what it is today. Fred Terman, a professor of electrical engineering at Stanford University, laid its foundations in 1938 when, irritated by the fact that his star students had to go east to further their careers, he persuaded two of them, Bill Hewlett and David Packard, to set up, in a garage, a company that would make electronic measurement equipment. The resulting company, Hewlett-Packard, took almost forty years to reach revenues of one billion dollars.

Next, the Valley is the product of an unpredictable combination of circumstances rather than the result of official fiat. As Ed Zschau at the Harvard Business School puts it, the Valley is an "existential creation: nobody said 'let's build an entrepreneurial, technological center.' " This is not to say that the government played no role at all. By one count, the Pentagon paid for one billion dollars' worth of semiconductor research in the formative period between 1958 and 1974. The Internet, too, began as a government project; several companies, including Netscape, have arisen, directly or indirectly, from state-funded research projects. But the government was nearly always a customer rather than an organizer. Certainly, unlike the governments of Europe, which relentlessly mollycoddled their technology industries, which are now nearly a decade behind America's, Washington's main contribution has been to stay clear.

So what ingredients does such a place need? Until recently, economists and politicians tended to explain the Valley's success in terms of some fairly tangible assets: the size of its labor pool, the breadth of its network of suppliers, its access to venture capital, and the excellence of its educational and research institutions—notably the universities at Stanford and Berkeley and the Xerox Palo Alto Research Center (PARC). All these things have indeed helped to put the Valley on the commercial map. One way or another, around one thousand companies have arisen out of Stanford University. But it is now clear that such physical factors tell only part of the story.

AnnaLee Saxenian, a professor at Berkeley, has pointed out that Massachussetts Route 128 corridor was more than a match for Silicon Valley in terms of both venture capital and access to research.[3] Yet by the late 1970s, Silicon Valley had created more high-tech jobs than Route 128 had, and when both clusters slumped in the mid-1980s, the Valley proved far more resilient. This, according to Saxenian, had to do with the structure and culture of the organizations involved. Big East Coast firms such as Digital Equipment Corporation and Data General were self-contained empires that focused on one product: minicomputers. Silicon Valley was also overreliant on one product (semiconductors), but its companies were more decentralized and more likely to spawn other companies. This networked economy was able to adapt much more quickly.

To an unusual degree, the resilience of Silicon Valley's economy comes from that old cliché "creative destruction."[4] This principle is as simple to spell out as it is difficult to imitate: Old companies die, and new ones emerge, allowing capital, ideas, and people to be reallocated. Essential to this process is the presence of entrepreneurs, as well as a culture that attracts them. Those seeking the secret of economic success have concentrated increasingly on clusters—places (such as Hollywood or Silicon Valley) or communities (such as Jews or overseas Chinese) where there is "something in the air" that encourages risk taking. This suggests that culture is more important to Silicon Valley's success than economics or technology are.

The Ten Habits of Highly Successful Clusters

Attributing success to culture can be a convenient way of avoiding saying anything specific. However, we can enumerate ten cultural attributes—call them the ten habits of highly successful clusters—that have proved vital to the Valley's success. It is interesting that, in terms of the "winner-take-all" debate, nearly all of them involve ways of spreading wealth rather than concentrating it.

The first quality is a firm belief in meritocracy. Rather than ossifying into an oligarchy, Silicon Valley endlessly renews itself with new brains. Age and experience, which elsewhere get people promoted, are no help in the Valley; on the contrary, there is a distinct bias toward youth. Nowadays, the average software-engineering qualification becomes obsolete in around five years, so a student fresh out of college may be more valuable to a company than a forty-year-old dinosaur.

Similarly, the Valley is one of the most immigrant-friendly places on earth. Cupertino's fifteen thousand elementary-school students speak fifty-two languages among them. Around one in five of the Valley's workers, including Andy Grove of Intel and Jerry Yang of Yahoo!, come from abroad. According to AnnaLee Saxenian, 27 percent of the four thousand companies started between 1990 and 1996 were run by Chinese or Indians (double the proportion in the previous decade). There are around seventy thousand Chinese-speaking engineers in the Valley. Down in Los Angeles, the Hollywood Cricket Club, once a lonely oasis of Anglocentric civilization, is now routinely trounced by visiting Indian teams from Santa Clara.

The second habit is an extremely high tolerance for failure. In Europe, bankruptcy is seen as a stigma; in several countries, someone who has run a company into bankruptcy cannot start another one. The United States, which has never had a debtors' prison, has always been more tolerant, but in the Valley bankruptcy is treated rather like a dueling scar was in a Prussian officers' mess. If your pen-computing company crashed, that is no disadvantage in starting one that specializes in video streaming. It is hardly surprising that the Internet—the industry in which, as *Doonesbury* put it, "profitability is for wimps"—gravitated toward Silicon Valley.

The third habit is tolerance of treachery. Secrets and staff are both damnably hard to keep in Silicon Valley. In 1957, the so-called traitorous eight walked out of one company, Shockley Laboratories, to found Fairchild

Semiconductor. One of them was Gordon Moore, subsequently of Intel fame. Fairchild Semiconductor itself eventually spawned thirty-seven different firms, including Intel. Just as tolerance of failure has a structural underpinning in America's relatively kind bankruptcy law, tolerance of treachery is linked to the fact that in California, unlike in Massachussetts, the law regards postemployment noncompetition clauses as unenforceable: That means that it is much harder to tie down staff. But it is plainly more than just law. "I left a company myself," says Scott McNealy, the boss of Sun Microsystems. "I don't want to lose people, but I don't want to employ people who don't want to work here, when I have twenty thousand excellent people who do." Far from feeling aggrieved by employees leaving to set up companies, he boasts about the number of CEOs that Sun has produced.

One of those CEOs is Kim Polese. Until February 1995, she was in charge of marketing Sun's Java project. Then, together with a couple of colleagues, she left Sun to set up Marimba, a company devoted to "push" software. That technology, which allows firms to reach consumers directly, rather than waiting for them to come to their websites, has not lived up to the enormous hype conferred on it in the mid-1990s. And Polese, a willowy blonde in an industry in which most executives are not noted for their appearances, has been accused of hogging the limelight (often by the same magazines that once rushed to take pictures of her). But Marimba went public successfully in 1999. Its success is partly because Polese (who is now the company's chairman) found some practical uses for push technology; but she has also been helped by a fourth Silicon Valley habit: collaboration.

Polese has been part of a large *keiretsu* of contacts. Marimba's main backer was a hundred-million-dollar Java fund set up by Kleiner Perkins Caulfield & Byers, the Valley's most powerful venture-capital firm. Amazon.com's boss, Jeff Bezos, chose Kleiner Perkins to launch his company, even though it offered a worse price. Jeff Hawkins, the inventor of the Palm Pilot, also sought out John Doerr of Kleiner Perkins when he set up his new venture, Handspring, at the beginning of 1999, "even though we did not need any money." In Silicon Valley, venture capitalists do not just give money, they also help find customers and employees.

Nor is this collaboration just a case of different *keiretsu* looking after their own. Companies and individuals endlessly form short-term alliances, both formal and informal, with foes whom they would normally try to kill. Log on to any Silicon Valley chat site, and you will find a virtual version of the conversations in Silicon Valley bars, in which self-interested altruism sets the tone. Staff are borrowed, ideas shared, favors exchanged. Often, the motivation is time: It is not worth trying to develop something yourself (whether it is a Java applet or a public-relations department) if somebody else can make it happen faster.

The fifth habit is a penchant for risk: There are no problems, it seems, only opportunities. Ask Hawkins how he will make Handspring's Visor even smaller or faster, and he replies, "We'll do it—or somebody else will." Elsewhere in Europe and America, investors are obsessed by the minutiae of business plans, however nebulous their end products. By contrast, Arthur Rock, a veteran Silicon Valley venture capitalist, says simply, "I have always backed people and opportunities." Indeed, the whole idea behind the venture-capital industry that Rock helped to pioneer is to follow a winner-take-all approach: One winner pays for scores of losers.

Once again, this entrepreneurial attitude runs deep. In Europe, large companies are famous for bullying small ones into paying bills early. Californian giants such as Hewlett-Packard, however, have always viewed young firms as potential investments rather than potential bad debts. "Most of the firms here were start-ups themselves fairly recently, and they know how to help," argues Michael Skok. A slightly stocky Englishman, who in his pinstriped suit might be confused for a merchant banker, Skok is an example of that rare breed: a European who can't stop starting companies. When he came to Silicon Valley for three days in 1996, he had already run one successful software company in the Thames valley and was on the point of signing a lease for another one, to be called AlphaBlox, in Boston. His three days in Palo Alto were a revelation. Not only did he run into most of his potential customers and employees at his hotel or in restaurants, but he also found a small squadron of people prepared to take a bet on him. Silicon Valley Bank arranged a line of credit for him to lease equipment within a week. Specialized accountants, lawyers, and headhunters all offered to work at reduced rates; real-estate agents accepted equity in Skok's company instead of a fee. Within a month, an old warehouse was converted into a suitably with-it office, covered in pink and yellow dots, and he was off.

One reason why it is fairly easy for people such as Skok and Polese to get off the ground is that Silicon Valley's sixth habit, reinvestment back into the cluster, seems to come naturally to successful technologists. Howard Stevenson, a professor at Harvard Business School, points out that many clusters die because their founders or their founders' children invest their fortunes elsewhere. Sometimes this is because they despise the muck that made their brass: Victorian coal barons from Barnsley ploughed their money into estates in Shropshire. More often, it is because it makes financial sense for a family business to diversify. So far in Silicon Valley, most of the money made in the technology industry has gone straight back in, either via people starting their own companies or via "business angel" investors.

The seventh habit is enthusiasm for change. Even venerable Hewlett-Packard has metamorphosed countless times, producing, among other things, oscillators, medical equipment, calculators, and laser-jet printers. The new generation of small Internet companies changes its spots even more frequently, with "strategic" decisions sometimes being made on a monthly basis. This nimbleness is born of fear. Any company that gets stuck in a rut ends up dead.

The eighth habit is obsession with the product. Silicon Valley was founded by engineers who were fascinated by technology, not just by making money. It remains a place where somebody at Sun can tell you in all seriousness: "If you don't understand the modestly parallel scalable multiprocessing environment, then you might as well leave." It is full of consumers known as "digital upscale believers" who will buy new products just because they look interesting. John Seely Brown, a former director of Xerox PARC, points out that much of Silicon Valley's value lies in what he calls "the conversations on the periphery": the chat in restaurants, the buzz in the bars. Just as every waiter in Hollywood has a script hidden behind his menu, plumbers in Silicon Valley will entertain their customers with disquisitions on the relative merits of Microsoft's Internet Explorer and Netscape's Navigator.

This obsession with product helps explain why the best one wins. This might seem an obvious point, but in both economics and Silicon Valley it is something of a controversial one. Winning products do tend to get enormous market shares: There is a network effect, as people tend to move toward a common standard, but there is precious little hard evidence to support the fashionable assertion that a bad product can thus triumph over a good one. It now seems pretty clear that neither the Dvorak keyboard nor the Sony Betamax videocassette were superior to their alternatives.[5] In 1999, the two economists responsible for demolishing those myths, Stan Liebowitz and Stephen Margolis, turned their attention to Microsoft's products, charting their market shares against independent product reviews.[6] From word processing to spreadsheets to browsers, Microsoft products moved into winner categories only after they outperformed the market leaders; in areas such as personal-finance software and Internet service, where Microsoft lagged behind Quicken and AOL, it failed to make headway. Prices tended to fall faster after Microsoft took the lead as well.

This points toward the ninth habit, which might be described as one of generous opportunity. For all the howls of fury about Microsoft, there are plenty of people making money on software and a seemingly endless supply of people prepared to take a commercial slug at Bill Gates. Once again, this has much to do with attitude. In Britain you hear talk about ambitious young people being too big for their boots and being brought down to earth. In Silicon Valley, where in 1999 several hundred millionaires were being created each week, jealousy is rare because most people believe that they, too, have a chance of becoming rich.[7] As many do in Hollywood, anyone who lives in Silicon Valley for any length of time will have at least one friend "who makes it big." There are not only a lot of winners but an enormous number of people who think that they can become one.

The tenth habit is a strong inclination toward sharing wealth, at least within companies. When Kingston Technology was sold to Softbank for $1.5 billion in 1996, its founders set aside $100 million to be shared among the firm's workers.[8] A surprising number of other software companies still offer complete health care, free lunches, and generous pensions. With AlphaBlox having grown to one hundred people by 1999 and bankers encouraging him to go public, Michael Skok still says that he spends much of his day "working out how to reward people." Once again, this altruism has a selfish ingredient: In a knowledge industry, companies need to keep good staff. But it seems to go a little deeper than that. None of Intel's founders has a private office; one of them, Gordon Moore, complains about spending twenty minutes every morning looking for a parking space. It would not occur to him to demand one.

Put these things together, and the idea that Silicon Valley is a winner-take-all place seems true only if you include hundreds of thousands of people as winners. People do not keep coming to Silicon Valley just because it is the only place where you can steal your billionaire boss's parking space, or even because the median wage is relatively high. They keep coming because there are lots of chances to make it really big and because the penalty for failing is relatively light. In other words, if you want to find the classic, pyramid-shaped, winner-take-all societies, you are much more likely to find them in those places trying to imitate Silicon Valley than in the real thing.

Make Me Anywhere

Listening to many of its inhabitants, you can soon jump to the conclusion that Silicon Valley is the only place to be. As Michael Skok puts it, "You are either one of the people at the middle spinning the wheel or one of those on the outside being spun." But that leads to another worry: Even if the Valley is reasonably good at sharing the technological spoils among its inhabitants, you still have to live there to be a winner, so it is fulfilling the winner-take-all formula by being the winner itself. You can hear similar triumphant noises coming out of Hollywood and Wall Street.

This is wrong, too. Geography may not be dead (see chapter 6), but it is not everything either. Consider, just to begin with, the awkward fact that the three richest individuals in each of America's three main clusters live and work far away from them. Bill Gates is based in Washington State, not Silicon Valley. America's most successful investor, Warren Buffett, lives in Omaha, Nebraska, not on Wall Street. And George Lucas lives near San Francisco, not in Hollywood. In each case, the winner has certainly lost a little by putting a distance between himself and the gossip factory. (Gates's relative lateness to spot the importance of the Internet is one example.) But that distance has also given them perspective. Buffett has made his billions by making long-term bets that Wall Streeters would have found difficult to leave alone. Unlike his more frenetic peers, Lucas makes films only when he wants to. Gates has been through several revolutions in the software industry without losing his head in any. He may have been late on the Internet, but he was not *too* late.

Besides, Gates has been busy creating a cluster of his own. Washington State has more than two thousand other software and Internet companies, including Amazon.com. The pool of talent may not be as deep as it is in Silicon Valley, but it is still fairly wide. The same can be said for an increasing number of other places in the United States—notably Boston, New York City, Utah, and Austin. Austin is particularly interesting because, despite being barely a quarter of Silicon Valley's size, it still feels distinctly Siliconesque. The University of Texas acts as its Stanford, pumping out technology-trained students. (Dell Computer was founded in a UT dorm room in 1984.) Austin is just as rich, liberal, and hip as northern California, but it is a lot easier to live in, with cheaper houses and better schools. Despite complaints about Austin's infrastructure ("the traffic lights aren't even synchronized," moans one Motorola man), it is far easier to get around than Silicon Valley, and the air is noticeably cleaner. "Every time I go to Silicon Valley," says Michael Dell, "I thank God that we are based in Texas."

Around the world, plenty of young engineers are making similar decisions, comparing Silicon Valley to their local imitation and often choosing the latter, in the process ensuring that the largesse of the computer revolution is being scattered far and wide. American companies may control two thirds of the world's software market, but the United States is home to only a third of the world's estimated six million software programmers.[9] Gates himself calculates that there are more than twenty countries with what he calls "concentrated programmer populations"—including the Holy See, Finland, and New Zealand—where "cool work is being done."

Many people in Silicon Valley argue that southern England and Israel are the closest international competitors. But the Silicon Valley model is also being exported to much more distant cultures. One example is Hsinchu Science Park in Taiwan. On the face of it, Hsinchu's main bond with Silicon Valley is that they are both irredeemably ugly. But once you get past the somewhat militarist outlook of some Taiwanese entrepreneurs, you discover more than a hint of Santa Clara. Around half the firms in Hsinchu were started by expatriates, mainly from Silicon Valley. In terms of profits and market capitalization, Hsinchu is about a fifth of the size of the Valley, and much of its work is in making high-tech widgets that Silicon Valley no longer does. The Taiwanese make nearly all the world's handheld scanners, two thirds of the world's computer mice, and around half of its monitors and modems.

To be sure, Hsinchu owes the Taiwanese government a lot: It provides cheap land and even some start-up capital. But unlike its peers in Japan and South Korea, the Taiwanese government has concentrated on attracting small firms and left decisions about products to the entrepreneurs. Perhaps most important of all, it has not rescued them when they go bust. As a result, it has fulfilled its main aim of providing an alternative destination for its young and technologically gifted. Rather than going to the Gold Mountain, as some Chinese speakers call San Francisco, engineers can go to the New Gold Mountain, as Hsinchu is known. At Taiwan Semiconductor, engineers have been known to earn $500,000 a year and janitors $50,000 a year.[10]

Hsinchu's strongest competitor in Asia is Bangalore, in the southern Indian state of Karnataka. Visiting a software firm in Bangalore can be a little like uncovering Q's workshop in a James Bond film. On one side of a wall you are in a busy street battling with hawkers and farm animals; on the other, you are in an air-conditioned room, watching rows of young Indian programmers rewrite software for large American companies. (Much of the work is transmitted across the Internet to customers.) Bangalore is arguably the only technological hub in the world with worse traffic than Silicon Valley. It also suffers from many of India's vices—notably venal local politicians. But Indian universities are mass-producing software programmers in much the same way that they once mass-produced bureaucrats, and many of them end up in Bangalore. Three of India's five wealthiest men are software bosses, and software engineers have now achieved unprecedented eligibility in newspaper matrimonial columns.[11]

Already, people in Bangalore are muttering about another place full of cheap programmers, Russia's Silicon Taiga. Nikita Khrushchev had begun sending mathematically gifted children to Akademgorodok, a specially built Siberian scientific city some two thousand miles from Moscow, rewarding them with good food, relatively comfortable houses, and dachas by the Ob Sea (where he even built a beach for them, too). Most of the work at Akademgorodok (literally "academics town") was military, but it was also the site of Mikhail Gorbachev's expensive attempt to build a Soviet Intel. At the end of the cold war, the city's thirty-five institutes held forty thousand scientists; now many of them are unemployed, and the town is something of a hotbed of nasty conservative Russian movements. But the same harsh economics that has left some mathematicians living off homegrown potatoes also means that there is a supply of cheap software programmers, who can be hired for between $1,000 and $1,500 a month. Firms such as Sun, Nortel Networks, and Microsoft are keen hirers. But, just like Bangalore, Akademgorodok is also building its own software industry, with forty firms nestling in the empty university buildings and selling their products over the Internet, out of reach of Russia's kleptocracy.[12]

We could continue traversing the globe, finding other Silicon Valleys, but the underlying point is clear: You can now live a fairly passable imitation of the Silicon lifestyle just about anywhere. On the island of Orkney, John Ruscoe begins each day by looking after his flock of seven hundred Shetland sheep; then he begins his other job as a software developer for ICL. He visits the computer firm once every eighteen months; the rest of the time they talk by e-mail.[13]

The Not-So-Visible Threat

Does the existence of rival clusters actually threaten Silicon Valley? People in Silicon Valley like to boast that the Valley of Heart's Delight is still "the mother lode." Austin's most important piece of infrastructure is arguably the "Nerd Bird," a twice-daily flight to San Jose. (In one poll by *Fast Company* magazine, 35 percent of the passengers admitted to being nerds, and another 37 percent said that they were in denial about it; one replied, "I carry a differential-equations problem solver and a periodic table in my wallet. What do you think?") Hsinchu also has a similar lifeline—a China Airlines red-eye to the Valley, the regulars on which are known as "astronauts."

On the other hand, the growing significance of places such as Austin and

Akademgorok is changing the balance of power. It is no longer safe to assume that you can keep up with the high-tech world just by dropping into Il Fornaio in Palo Alto. You also need to know what is happening at watering holes in Austin and in New York. Linux, the upstart operating system that so unsettled Bill Gates, was invented by a student at the University of Helsinki in 1991.

Nobody has yet been able to explain why some dominant clusters, such as Sheffield for steelmaking, lose their way, while others, such as the City of London, have so far been able to renew themselves. A cluster can become too dominated by big companies (like Detroit before Toyota and Honda set to work on it), but it can also be too fragmented (like the Lancashire textile mills). All the same, as Richard Tedlow, a historian at the Harvard Business School, points out, three things clearly play important roles: self-absorption (two Chicago stores, Sears Roebuck and Montgomery Ward, competed so fiercely that they failed to spot the rise of Wal-Mart); forgetting what your customers want (Detroit offered buyers cars with tail fins instead of inexpensive, reliable ones); and major outside shocks, such as a political upheaval or a technological discontinuity.

Silicon Valley is not immune to these pressures. Even its most ardent defenders would have a hard time claiming that a place where people in the late 1990s boasted about having got their "two commas" (meaning that they had cashed in their options for more than $1,000,000) was not self-absorbed. It is also open to charges that it ignores customers, tending to opt instead for "field of dreams" business plans: If technologists come up with a cool new idea, customers will come. Yet many computer owners (like American car buyers thirty years ago) seem to want fewer frills, not more. They use only a fraction of the programs that come with their machines; all the rest is "bloatware" that merely slows everything down.

Technological discontinuities could be more brutal. Silicon Valley has survived one such discontinuity in the leap from the mainframe to the personal computer, and it seems to be doing pretty well so far out of the much larger discontinuity that the Internet presents. But it is still early days. Out of the three most prominent Internet firms, only Yahoo! is in Silicon Valley; Amazon.com and America Online are both outsiders. And technological changes are by their nature devilishly difficult to predict.

In fact, Silicon Valley's inhabitants have been remarkably successful at dealing with the commercial implications of rapid technological change. The bigger, long-term problems for Silicon Valley in our view are not commercial but political and social. One final observation about previous clusters that failed is that they simply stopped being nice places. Lancashire's "dark Satanic mills" were places that you left as soon as you could. Detroit in the 1970s was a city that most people avoided going near in the first place. Silicon Valley will only stay ahead if it keeps attracting the best people. That is not just a question of promising them money. Again fulfilling its role of being like globalization only more so, Silicon Valley is often guilty of being an economic success but a social and political failure.

The Digital Divide

Many of the things that make the Valley such a successful commercial unit do also tend to make it a fairly admirable society. Meritocracy, for instance, is a civic virtue as well as an economic one. Even the Valley's obsession with product arguably helps make it a nicer place. Certainly, its engineers' tendency to celebrate function over form has at least partly restricted the winners' propensity to be obnoxious. Of course, there are billionaires such as Larry Ellison who will happily buzz rivals in their MiG fighter planes. And as the 1990s wore on, the number of Ferraris increased exponentially. But the typical cybermillionaire still likes to drive an engineer's car, such as a Lexus or a BMW, and the most ostentatious items in many houses tend to be things such as expensive stereos and high-tech stoves.

In a society where people worth half a billion dollars still sleep under their desks, it is relatively hard to have airs and graces.[14] Down south, Hollywood executives may engage in Machiavellian maneuvering to get the right table at Spago. But in Silicon Valley, the ideal food is like the ideal computer: fast and cheap. At Netscape, Marc Andreesen was so enamored of junk food that he gave meeting rooms names like Curly Fries, Jelly Donut, Pringles, Jolt, and Pork Rinds. In fact, there is something endearingly gauche about many of the new millionaires. Up in San Francisco, socialites snigger about a madam alleged to have made her fortune entirely by catering to rich young engineers. *Accidental Empires*, an amusing chronicle of Silicon Valley's rise, is subtitled *How the Boys of Silicon Valley Make Their Millions, Battle Foreign Competition, and Still Can't Get a Date.*

So what is wrong with Silicon Valley as a society? Two things: The first is the flip side of meritocracy. The test may be eminently fair, but those who cannot keep up get left behind. Silicon Valley is certainly not a pyramid-shaped winner-take-all society—rather, its shape is more like that of an egg timer, with fairly big groups of people at both ends—but that structure creates its own problems. The second problem is the flip side of the absorption in the product: The winners have become disengaged from politics. That partly means that they do too little to help the losers, but it also means that they are ill equipped to defend the system from which they profit.

Silicon Valley is a hard place to live if you are either poor or uneducated. According to Joint Venture: Silicon Valley, the poorest fifth of the Valley's households saw their real income fall by 8 percent in the boom years between 1991 and 1997. (By contrast, income for the richest fifth rose by 19 percent.) In a world where the average house price is half a million dollars, the people who clean those houses are being forced to live farther and farther away or in more and more desperate circumstances. When a storm ripped the roof off two apartment buildings in East San Jose in 1996, it revealed three hundred people living in just forty-two apartments.

Meanwhile, jobs seem to require ever more qualifications. Until the early 1990s, manual dexterity was often enough to secure a job; now, one in three of Santa Clara's adults has a degree (compared with one in five nationally). High-tech giants such as Hewlett-Packard once prided themselves on their ability to promote talented shop-floor workers. Now they have contracted out much of their manufacturing to specialists, many of them abroad. The tone of the Valley is being set by smaller companies that value speed and flexibility above all else: a marvelous development for educated job hoppers but a dismal one for people who start at the bottom.

The school system is hardly constructing a ladder of opportunity for its poorest citizens. Elite institutions such as Stanford and Berkeley continue to produce fine students, but below that level the system is cracking audibly. The high-school graduation rate for students in Santa Clara and San Mateo counties has declined from 80 percent in 1993 to 70 percent in 1998. Only about a quarter of teenagers study any math more demanding than elementary algebra. Despite the Internet's importance to the local economy, by the end of 1998 nearly a third of the schools in Santa Clara and San Mateo still lacked high-speed connections, and roughly the same proportion of households with incomes of less than forty thousand dollars lacked any connection. In addition, the technology industry's admirably global mind-set also works against the poor locals.

This growing inequality has a potentially explosive ethnic component. Latinos make up 23 percent of the region's population and more than 30 percent of the children under fifteen. But when the *San Francisco Chronicle* investigated thirty-three high-tech firms in 1998, it found that only 7 percent of the workforce were Latinos, and hardly any of these held managerial jobs. That is not wholly disastrous: A large number of the Latinos are poorly educated immigrants who are better off with the crumbs of Silicon Valley than the fruits of rural Mexico. So long as there is a ladder of opportunity from Taco Bell to Intel, there would be really no need to worry. Unfortunately, Latinos are finding it ever harder to make it out of poverty. Only around a fifth complete the basic high-school courses you need to get into college. The barrios of East Palo Alto and East San Jose are as rough and tough as the rest of the region is soft and cerebral. East Palo Alto even earned the dubious distinction of being dubbed homicide capital of the United States by the FBI in 1992.

Ruben Barrales, the former president of Joint Venture: Silicon Valley, which collects many of the above statistics, points out that his father, who immigrated from Mexico in the late 1950s, began as a laborer but eventually started a roofing business and bought his own house, along with several other bits of property. His investments have set him up well for retirement. Such upward mobility is a lot harder to achieve now. A survey of the area's fastest-growing companies found that 84 percent of their jobs required education beyond high school. And given the average house price, even the middle classes, let alone the poor, cannot get into the housing market.

Do They Care?

One might imagine that this degree of poverty on their doorstep would have sparked off a reaction among Silicon Valley's rich. After all, these are educated, liberal people who endlessly tell you that they want to improve the world, not the cruel blood-and-thunder businessmen of yesteryear. In fact, most of Silicon Valley's winners seem oddly detached from their surroundings.

One or two locals—notably the founders of Hewlett-Packard—have tried to instill a charitable sense in their peers. But there is not much sign of it. As a whole, workers in Silicon Valley give away around 2 percent of their income to charity—about the same as the rest of the nation. According to a 1998 report by Community Foundation Silicon Valley (CFSV), around one third of households there earning more than $100,000 give $1,000 or less to charity. The Santa Clara county branch of the United Way collapsed in May 1999 after donations fell short of expectations.

Indeed, you only have to visit Silicon Valley to see how much its winners care about the place. The Valley is one of the ugliest commercial meccas the world has ever produced: a boundaryless sprawl of freeways, low-lying factories, shopping malls, and unremarkable (but remarkably expensive) suburban bungalows. In their heyday, Venetian merchants created a city so stunning that people have not ceased to marvel at it. Silicon Valley appears to have been built by people who think that *Aliens versus Predator* (the computer-game version) passes for high culture.

In many cases, the problem does not seem to be miserliness so much as ignorance. As the CFSV report notes, one third of the "high net worth" individuals in the Valley were paid with shares, but only 7 percent gave away shares, even though there are tax advantages in doing so. There is no shortage of venture angels prepared to reinvest in the cluster as a business; why don't they think about their social community in the same way? One explanation is that they are all simply too young: It will come in time. Another factor seems to be a complete absence of guilt. Many of England's finest museums, hospitals, and schools were built by slavers. But who can feel guilty about Yahoo!? Another problem is that obsession with the product: Not only does there seem to be very little time to do anything else, but the product itself, at least in the eyes of its creators, is a great social good. Very few people in Silicon Valley have come to understand the dark side of technology, that most of their wonderful programs are increasing inequality just around the corner from them.

This lack of interest ties into a wider aversion to politics. The deeply held prejudice that "government is the ultimate big company" began to change in the late 1990s. John Heilemann, a San Francisco–based author, argues that the Valley's exceptionalism—the idea "that the industry expected nothing from the government except to be left alone"—has given way to a pragmatic understanding that lobbying works. Politicians are tripping over each other to be identified with technologists. There is also, according to Eric Schmidt, head of Novell, a gradual acceptance by some technologists that if they really are "defining the economic structure of the world," then that brings responsibilities. One of Washington's newest think tanks, the New America Foundation, is funded largely by Silicon Valley money and devoted to exploring the sort of political topics that will be at the heart of the digital age: digital democracy, the future of privacy, and the digital divide.

Even so, the Valley has clearly failed to redefine politics in anything like the bold way that it has redefined commerce. Silicon Valley may have the potential to reinvent individualism, re-creating Thomas Jefferson's yeoman farmer with a PC rather than a plowshare, yet so far it has done far less to reshape politics than did the business barons and trade unionists of the late nineteenth century. And it remains in general much less trustful of the political process. Even the bitterest opponents of Bill Gates regretted having to involve Washington's antitrust authorities in their squabble.

The best place to look for signs that the cyberelite is taking politics seriously is in its own backyard. Joint Venture: Silicon Valley tries to bring the Valley's social networks together so that the cyberelite rub shoulders with minorities. Some local firms such as Intel and Cisco Systems are bringing both computers and computer education to schools. At Wilcox High School, which is about 30 percent Latino, students "recycle" old computers, revamping them with the latest chips and then handing them down to local elementary schools; they also help to create and maintain computer networks for the school district.

The question is how much this matters. Getting involved in society is still seen as a necessary evil rather than a positive good. In terms of Heilemann's exceptionalism, Silicon Valley may no longer expect to be left alone, but it has plainly not made the jump to thinking that it should put something back. Indeed, there is a strong feeling in many Silicon Valley offices that the virtual world matters more than the real one. Its ruling class would rather remain in that pure sphere where only intelligence matters than try to fix problems, such as awful freeways.

All this makes Silicon Valley look like a grander version of one of California's less attractive features, the gated community: rich, elitist, and insular. It is hard to see why Silicon Valley should give up being rich and elitist; those are just the flip sides of being successful and meritocratic. But it may regret its insularity.

Indeed, one could argue that the new economy is colliding with the new demographics. Latinos are becoming a powerful political force in the Valley: In 1998, San Jose became the first major California city to elect a Latino mayor, Ron Gonzales. The trade unions have been notably more successful in recruiting Latinos than high-tech bosses, scoring big hits with their "justice for janitors" and "living wage" campaigns. The area's deeply rooted black population also feels left out. In 1998, local blacks demonstrated outside Intel, singing, "Intel, Intel, You're No Good: Bring Computers in the Hood."[15] Blacks make up only 4 percent of the Valley's workforce, though they account for a tenth of its population.

Future Not Quite Perfect

However, one can only take this nitpicking so far. Most other societies would kill to have the Valley's problems. Silicon Valley may be imperfect, but, as even a quick look at the jobs pages in any other area's local newspaper can tell you, it certainly tends to beat any of the alternatives.

We would not pretend that Silicon Valley answers all the questions about globalization and the winner-take-all economy. But in broad terms, we still think that the Valley, which is closer to realizing the future economy than anywhere else is, gives the lie to the idea that globalization favors only a few. Silicon Valley, like globalization, certainly provides its winners with breathtaking rewards. But then, there are a lot of them; they tend to win for good reasons; and the whole system seems to be built around trying to create more of them.

Two other similarities with globalization also stand out immediately. The first is that many of the Valley's weaknesses are the fault of local people— usually politicians—rather than the system itself. There is nothing Siliconesque or indeed global about the bad schools that turn out poorly educated Latinos. The second thing is that critics seldom consider the alternatives. If, for instance, America tightened its immigration rules or imposed a wealth tax, Valley firms might have to employ more locals, and the gap between its wealthiest and its poorest might narrow, but what then?

"If you sit on the lid of progress, you will be blown to pieces." Henry Kaiser's aphorism, nailed to the wall just above a "virtual snowboard" in one of Palo Alto's shops, is a reminder that Silicon Valley has avoided that fate better than most. For all its faults, there is nowhere else in the world that begins the twenty-first century with as many advantages as the Valley of Heart's Delight.

12

The Cosmocrats:
An Anxious Elite

GREG POWER, a thirty-seven-year-old Irishman who works as a banker in New York, has a poor record when it comes to making speeches at weddings. His first performance, as a best man in Las Vegas, was, he admits, mildly disappointing. His next outing, again as a best man but this time in Gloucestershire, flopped so terribly that the next day a stranger walked up to him in the pub and declared to all and sundry, "Son, we will all live for thirty years before we hear another speech as terrible as the one we witnessed yesterday." Yet when Greg began his speech at the party for his own engagement to Victoria Lam, a consultant from Hong Kong, by announcing "I feel like I am addressing the United Nations," everybody laughed.

The reason lay in the speeches before. As the microphone had been passed from table to table, a babel of accents—Irish ("We know where all the bodies are buried"), English ("I'd just like to say how poor we are, so we'll go anywhere for a meal"), American ("I met Greg at remedial math at business school"), Chinese ("Victoria and I went to school in England, and we had to speak to each other because we couldn't understand anybody else"), even a few mutterings from what Greg referred to as "the Iranian contingent"—had risen to toast the happy couple. The three people jocularly competing to be the couple's best friend were a Brazilian, a Spaniard who grew up in Argentina, and an American who grew up in Greece. Friends flew in from Beirut and Baku.

Perhaps the most remarkable thing about Greg and Victoria's engagement party was that nobody seemed to find it remarkable: an Irishman marrying a Chinese girl in New York. Every other facet of the couple's characters was teased, lauded, or forgiven, but nobody thought the couple was doing anything strange. For the sizable number of guests who had been with them at Columbia, it was just another business-school match. For the thirty some-things who had flown from London for a long weekend, it was certainly a treat, but not a special one. ("I left the children with my sister; it's really not that much more difficult than going to Yorkshire.") Despite having been born into just about every conceivable level of every conceivable society, everybody seemed to know their way around New York, just as they would Los Angeles, London, or Hong Kong. Everybody seemed to have been to a lot of universities, and everybody seemed to work extremely hard.

If you were looking for an indication of just how hard the sort of people who attended Greg and Victoria's party work, you might try dropping in on Ellen Knapp's office in New York. The chances are that you wouldn't find her there. Her staff still talk about the last time the fifty-one-year-old spent a whole week in her office. Normally, one day every two weeks is all that she can manage.

One reason for this is that the company she works for, Pricewaterhouse Coopers (PwC), is the product of a big merger, as its rather clumsy name suggests, and Knapp, who is its chief knowledge officer and chief information officer, is one of the people trying to knit together the two giant accountan-cies-cum-consultancies. Yet even before the merger in 1997, Knapp spent barely a day a week in the office. Nor is she alone in her peregrinations. At one point in her travels, she congratulated herself on having taken three red-eye flights in six days; then, at a meeting near Heathrow Airport, she met a colleague who was undergoing such ordeals on successive nights. At an-other point, en route from her home in Florida to Frankfurt and London, she bumped into her equivalent at McKinsey, who was on her way to New Delhi. Five nights later, the two knowledge officers met again, picking up their lug-gage at Kennedy Airport in New York.

A few tycoons have always been famous for keeping their bodies (if not their heads) perpetually in the clouds. Rupert Murdoch maintains offices on three continents. When he was head of Asea Brown Boveri, Percy Barnevik used to claim that his office at the company's headquarters in Zurich was simply the place "where my mail arrives before the important letters are faxed to wherever I happen to be."[1] One airline boss even designed his draw-ing room to resemble the front of a 747, to make himself feel at home.[2]

Yet globalization has given a less glamorous cast to the international jet-set. In 1998, *The Wall Street Journal* followed Michael Bonsignore, the chair-man of Honeywell, on a typically grueling nine-cities-in-eleven-days trip around China and Europe: Deprived at different times of sleep, showers, and the correct backup, Bonsignore, who "did" a mere two hundred thousand miles a year, kept going on Unisom, a mild muscle relaxant.[3] For every boss in a corporate jet, there are plenty of road warriors like Knapp filling business-class seats. And for every Knapp, there are plenty of humbler creatures crammed into cattle class. Knapp points out that her regional knowledge and technology officers move people around "their" continents (or "theaters" as Knapp likes to call them) just as busily. Most big multinationals now expect much of their growth to come from emerging markets, whose cultures they do not understand well. Bringing places such as New Delhi and São Paulo into the system will require yet more meetings and yet more frequent-flyer miles for people like Knapp.

You might think that advances in technology would reduce the amount of necessary travel. But Knapp spends a small fortune of her firm's money in that pursuit, since e-mail and video conferencing can go only so far—particularly for the officers of PwC. Technology, Knapp says, depends on trust, and trust depends on personal communication. PwC employs nearly 150,000 people in 152 countries; a bossy e-mail from somebody you have never met might well solicit a less than positive response, particularly if that somebody was on "the other side" before the merger. Knapp thinks that you have to meet people first: "It is important to gesticulate." A bubbly lady with an endearing manner, Knapp and her powers of persuasion would indeed be diminished by e-mail.

This sort of life requires dedication and organization. The resolutely cheerful Knapp says that her blessings include a constitution that is immune to jet lag, the fact that her two children have grown up, and two extremely efficient assistants, whom she compares to Mission Control at NASA. She sticks to airlines and hotels that she knows well—hotels that have been "rewired," notably the London Ritz, are particular favorites—and exercises whenever she can. Like many other big firms, PwC tries to make life easier for her, scheduling meetings at hubs (all the partners from the western United States come to Los Angeles to meet, for example); it also has started a "hoteling policy" at its offices, providing itinerants with a desk and a phone connection whenever they turn up. "My place of work," she says, "is simply where I am."

This sounds endearingly contemporary. But it is hard to listen to Knapp describe a typical week without feeling exhausted oneself. The perpetual peregrinations of today's managers provide much of the explanation for the rising figures for executive stress. They also provide much of the explanation for why so many people are earning more but feeling less fulfilled. The over-worked manager is usually an overtraveled one.

Today Belongs to Us

The idea of "a global ruling class" has been one of the great canards of modern history—a trigger for resentment, persecution, and paranoia. Before the rise of democracy, European politics were indeed the preserve of a fairly coherent elite. Most monarchs—and many leading politicians—were related to one another. Everybody who mattered had read the same classical texts. French had established itself so firmly as an international language that both Frederick the Great of Prussia and Metternich wrote their memoirs in it. National leaders were so pally that they even held honorary positions in each other's armies. In 1910, for example, Kaiser Wilhelm II of Germany turned up at Edward VII's funeral dressed in the scarlet uniform of a British field marshal. Some fragments of this life survive even today. (It is still possible to meet elderly French aristocrats who insist that Prince Charles should have married Princess Astrid of Belgium.) But in general this dandified class has been swept away by revolutions, nationalism, the "discovery" of the Americas, Africa, and the East, and let's face it, progress.

Since then, the idea of an elite has become both more global and more soiled by trade. By the time that Marx came to consider the enemy in the mid-nineteenth century, he was thinking about not the aristocracy but an inter-locking network of all-seeing capitalists and financiers. More positively, Cecil Rhodes dreamed of creating a clique of clean-cut men who could knit the English-speaking world together, while H. G. Wells and his fellow Fabians argued that the only way to save the world from self-destruction was to create an international class of Platonic guardians. At the end of the Second World War, some people imagined that the United Nations might represent some new seat of power. With the exception of the odd Republican congressman scanning the skies for black helicopters and of the Montana Militia, nobody seems to take that very seriously today.

Indeed, the idea of a global elite seems to have ebbed away into a fringe fascination of extremists and conspiracy theorists, the oxymoronic nature of whose views was illustrated neatly by two demonstrators standing outside a recent meeting of Bilderberg, a secretive transatlantic conference of business and political leaders. One man's sign denounced "the liberal Jewish conspiracy"; his neighbor's lamented that the world was being run by "a right wing cabal." Like the old joke about two men claiming to be Jesus, at least one of them must be wrong.

But is the global ruling class destined to remain a figment of the imagination? Globalization is not only tightening the world's economic links. It is also throwing up an increasingly conspicuous class of people who possess the ideas, connections, and sheer chutzpah to master the international economy. Cosmopolitan in taste and usually Anglo-American in outlook, these are the people who attend business-school weddings around the world, fill up the business-class lounges at international airports, provide the officer ranks of most of the world's companies and international institutions, and, through their collective efforts, probably do more than anyone else to make the world seem smaller. These cosmocrats are members of a new ruling class—a much more meritocratic ruling class than we have ever seen before, a much broader one, numbering some twenty million people (we will come to the numbers later), and a much more uneasy one, but a ruling class nevertheless.

There has always been a delay between the economic changes that usher in a new way of life and the formation of a new economic elite. It took decades for the factory owners who wrought the first industrial revolution in Britain to transform themselves from an economic interest group into a self-conscious class, sending their children to the same schools and making sure they married each other's sisters. The businesspeople who dominated the great American cities took even longer to lift their gazes above purely local affairs: It was not until after the First World War that the ivy leaf and the Porcellian pig became national symbols of upper-class membership, recognized even in Pasadena and Palo Alto. The past two decades of pell-mell globalization is finally beginning to produce a group of people who have the classic characteristics of a class.

Such a loaded sobriquet requires a little more definition. When most people talk about the winners from globalization, they tend to focus on the superrich: the global tycoons who spend half their lives on private jets. To be sure, such figures are cosmocrats. Yet for every Larry Ellison there are thousands of people like Knapp, Charlie Woo, Marcus de Ferranti, Patrick Wang, or any of the other characters we have met in this book. Many readers of this book probably live equally global lives without the benefits of a private jet.

Samuel Huntington was close to the mark when he dubbed this "Davos man," but that definition—limited as it is to chief executives and people who prick up their ears at the letters *IMF*—seems far too narrow. You can get a much better idea of rank-and-file cosmocrats by skipping the bigwigs at Davos and scanning the enormous MIPCOM film market in Los Angeles—where thousands of entertainment hustlers from all around the world gather to sell their products with remarkably homogeneous insincerity—or dropping in on Comdex, a similar high-tech trade show in Las Vegas.

On the other hand, the definition of a cosmocrat is much tighter than just "somebody who has prospered from globalization." Cosmocrats are defined by their attitudes and lifestyles rather than just their bank accounts. That separates them from the widest class of winners from globalization, who are simply local people who have plugged into global networks—everybody from small businesspeople such as the Madini brothers in Tangiers to the hapless consumers in New Delhi finally tasting proper Coca-Cola. In fact, there is a class of emerging-market tycoons—one could call them local-crats—who have prospered precisely because globalization has not been as complete as the cosmocrats would like. Li Ka-shing, for instance, has rented out plenty of buildings in Hong Kong to cosmocrats; he has competed against them; he has hired them to run parts of his empire; and he has even fathered a couple of them. But unlike for his mobile phone–obsessed, business school–trained sons, his commercial (and, one suspects, psychological) heartland remains the Hong Kong property market.

So who are the cosmocrats? The backbone of the group is still provided by people such as Knapp: the loyal retainers of sprawling multinationals. But many of its members work for companies that have few resources other than a bright idea and a modem connection (at the end of the 1990s, nearly one in six M.B.A.s in America were joining start-ups of one sort or another); and many cosmocrats work for themselves. Some of the stereotypes are obvious: the young overworked lawyer whose social life consists of watching *Sex and the City*; the connected people whom *Wired* has dubbed "Digital Citizens" and "MTV man"—those leathery figures who fill the upper-class section of Virgin Atlantic flights between Los Angeles and London; the young Taiwanese "astronauts" who take the China Airlines red-eye that links Silicon Valley with Hsinchu Science Park. In London, *Eurotrash* has passed into the popular diction. In France, a comic strip features Largo Winch—an irritatingly young and good-looking boss with an M.B.A. from Insead. In Japan, one television show is about an American company taking over a Japanese one; the antiheroine is an aggressive, profit-maximizing American, Sara Stanton, who is given to telling the hapless, consensus-loving salarymen that "performance is everything."

The cosmocrats are found not only in commerce. There is "sabbatical man," those high-flying academics who are forever neglecting their students in favor of another semester in Florence. (One joke about a well-known theology professor—let us call him Professor Smith and say he is officially attached to Birmingham University—asks what the difference is between Smith and God. The answer: God is everywhere; Smith is everywhere except Birmingham.) There is agency man: the international bureaucrats who cluster together in Washington and Geneva in order to alleviate the woes of the inhabitants of Lagos and Nairobi. There is even Carville man, the traveling circus of political operatives who bring their spin doctoring to elections the world over.

Lest you pigeonhole them too easily, the assorted cosmocrats are forever trying on each others' clothes. Company man abandons ship to become an entrepreneur. Sabbatical man supplements his salary by consulting, writing, or forming a hedge fund. Agency man forsakes a job at the World Bank for the emerging-markets division of Goldman Sachs.

Not all cosmocrats are Westerners. McKinsey, the Vatican of the cosmocracy, is now run by an Indian. So is Ispat, the most global company in the steel industry. When consumer-electronics firms want to test high-tech gadgets, they ignore America's digital citizens and try their peers in Hong Kong, who have adopted the world's first widely used interactive television service, the first cybercash cards, and the first mobile-phone network that works in a subway. Many of Ikea's busiest shops are in eastern Europe, where the nouveaux riches line up to buy the same allegedly "easy to assemble" furniture that frustrates young couples the world over. Half the teachers at the London Business School do not have English as their mother tongue. Flick through the magazine of the Stanford Business School, and you not only discover a rainbow coalition (more than half the students are either from minorities or from abroad) but also plenty of evidence of the gospel spreading around the world. "More than 30 years ago, American warriors came to Vietnam and found it a quagmire," writes one Vietnamese-American graduate who has been working in his homeland for Procter & Gamble. "In the 1990s, a different type of American warrior, the corporate warrior, came to Vietnam."[4]

Even if the people concerned are not Western, their values usually are. In some places, cosmocrat icons have become bywords for Americanness. Marc Lassus, the boss of Gemplus, a French smart-card company, insists that even temporary employees must be able to speak English and derides things he does not like as being "Too Frenchie."[5] The autobiography of Stan Shih, the similarly evangelical boss of Taiwan's Acer, has the decidedly un-Confucian title *Me-Too Is Not My Style*. In Argentina, Juan Navarro, a former Citibanker who introduced buyouts to the country, has been compared rudely to Gordon Gekko, and Alejandro and Eduardo Elsztain, who have become Argentina's largest farmers, are usually bracketed with George Soros.

In fact, cosmocrat values are only American to the extent that they are the values of men and women on the move and on the make rather than of a society comfortable with its traditions. They are the sort of people who embrace both Jack Welch's definition of the "universal values" that he thinks define General Electric (meritocracy, dignity, simplicity, speed, a hatred of bureaucracy) and his intolerance for "any pompous horse's ass" who does not share them. Cosmocrats are forever eliminating barriers, overcoming limits, removing "rigidities." "I go to Davos and can talk to Newt Gingrich," Richard Yan, a bumptious young Shanghai entrepreneur who was one of the first mainland Chinese to go to Harvard Business School, told *Time* in April 1998. "I call him Newt. And I realize we are all the same: the trousers go on one leg at a time. Most people in China don't realize that."[6]

This attitude to life—whether admirable or arrogant—is built into the way the cosmocrats make their living. Older elites owed their position in life to property, which inevitably bound them to particular places; the cosmocrats, by contrast, owe their positions to information and expertise, which flows easily across borders. Their loyalties—if such a feudal term can be applied to such a quintessentially modern crowd—are international rather than local and calculating rather than emotional: They are far more concerned with the smooth operation of the system as a whole than with the health of any particular part of it.

William Whyte pointed out that organization man used the word *brilliant* only when it preceded the word *but* ("We are all for brilliance, but . . .") or when it was "coupled with such words as erratic, eccentric, introvert and screwball." The cosmocrats, on the other hand, value intelligence far more than loyalty. This meritocratic approach means that many cosmocrats are no great respecters of age, race, or gender. Indeed, they may be the first elite in which women play a nearly equal role with men. American women own one third of the country's businesses. Even in fusty old Europe, the omens are good. In 1996, for the first time, more women entered German universities than men.

Common "global" aspirations have led to common global habits. E. Digby Baltzell, the man who invented the term *WASP*, once noted that, at some point between the two world wars, privileged Americans began wearing college ties and hatbands in order to advertise their membership in a national, as opposed to a merely local, elite. Most cosmocrats would not be so crude as to wear business-school ties, but they have developed more subtle ways to signal their membership in the global elite.

A worrying number of cosmocrats dress alike. A consultant in Bangkok doesn't look any different from her peer in São Paulo; an advertising director trying to secure a table at the Ivy in London wears no less Armani than his counterpart outside the Ivy in Los Angeles; many technologists share the same somewhat minimal hygiene the world over. The cosmocrats' common fetish for overworking means that exercise is popular: Cosmocrats can often be spotted working out at midnight in the gyms of international hotels or jogging through the early-morning mist of this or that major city. Books on tape—sadly, of the *Seven Ways to Mental Health and Financial Success* variety— are popular. For all their access to expense accounts, they tend to ignore alcohol with meals. Worst of all, they have an unhealthy weakness not just for *Harvard Business Review* English but also for global conferences. For a cosmocrat, an invitation to spend a weekend in Ankara discussing supply-chain management is not necessarily a burden to be avoided.

Two things in particular are proving endemic. The first is an emphasis on cosmopolitan consumerism. Set beside their 1980s ancestor, the yuppie, cosmocrats usually seem relatively restrained and often a little scruffy: The Gap usually matters more than Gucci. But they do want choice. Few things annoy them more than a "buy local" campaign—unless, of course, they are visiting Shanghai Tang's in Hong Kong. Cosmocrats believe in buying the best on the market, regardless of national origins, and, thanks to globalization, they are increasingly able to indulge this dream.

Fresh sea bass from Chile is now old hat for Manhattan cosmocrats; the fish displays in restaurants groan with *loups de mer* from the Mediterranean, *hamachi* from New Zealand, and various other clunky-looking specimens that have been plucked out of the depths that once used to be Jacques Cousteau's preserve and flown to Kennedy Airport. At Matsuhisha, a Los Angeles restaurant, one signature dish, anticucho, includes salmon from Alaska, spices from Peru, sake and bamboo leaf from Japan, and chives from California. Magazines such as *Wallpaper, Condé Nast Traveler,* and *Cigar Aficionado* all act as informal cosmocrat search engines, scouring the world to explain where the best cushions, holidays, and smokes can be found.

The second thing is their desire to stay in touch. Cosmocrats have friends not just in high places but in faraway places—hence their almost pathological need to remain in touch through voice mail, e-mail, and relentless travel. It is not enough for cosmocrats to keep mobile phones with them at all times; they equip themselves with tri-bands, which can be used in both Europe and America, or even with satellite phones, which can be used anywhere in the world. When Rupert Murdoch's then wife, Anna, forced him to take up sailing in a desperate attempt to stop him from working all the time, the tycoon secretly loaded the yacht with high-tech communication gear.[7] For lesser figures, networking has a passionate, even demented side. One member of the class talks about marriage as a way of doubling your Rolodex; another, resorting to the language of the Palm Pilot (the cosmocratic gadget par excellence), refers to it as the "ultimate hotsynch."

Meanwhile, sometimes their inability to understand life beyond their Rolodexes leads to embarrassing mistakes. John Browning, a London-based consultant and writer, tells the story of gradually getting to know Frances D'Souza, an international campaigner for freedom of expression, at various conferences and forums around the world. Eventually, they traded numbers and addresses. They discovered that they lived next door to each other in London.

A Different Sort of Elite

Counting cosmocrats is something of a mug's game in which the available statistics offer only vague clues: CNN International is delivered to 140 million homes and CNBC to 100 million; on the other hand, only around ten million Europeans, five million Americans, and one million Southeast Asians take an international air flight each year; the combined circulation of *Time, Newsweek, Fortune, Forbes, BusinessWeek,* the *Herald Tribune,* the *Financial Times, The Wall Street Journal,* and *The Economist* is under 20 million.

Trying to analyze the elite by nation is not easy. In the United States, around 1.5 million people report income of more than two hundred thousand dollars. Although that figure certainly includes a fair number of Texan car dealers who have never even owned a passport, it surely misses many more young cosmocrats. *Wired*'s survey of digital citizenry in 1997 found that "connected" Americans (who used e-mail three times a week) accounted for 8.5 percent of the total population (about twenty-three million people). Outside the Anglo-Saxon world, estimations get bogged down by debates about language and culture. Many Europeans—particularly those from small countries—are multinational by nature. And once you hit emerging markets, the guesswork becomes even more hazardous. Huntington, for instance, calculates that, outside the West, fewer than fifty million people shared the sort of cosmopolitan culture he associates with Davos man.[8]

Mix these various statistics, add in a few similar findings, and we will stick to our estimate that there are around twenty million cosmocrats, of whom around 40 percent live in the United States. And, guessing a little more boldly, we estimate that that figure should double by 2010. Even if the true figure is barely half that size, it certainly represents a much broader elite than any previous one. But it remains a very small proportion of the world's six billion people. Most people still live in the villages where they were born rather than in pressurized cabins hurtling across the skies between one great city and another. Only about 1.5 percent of the world's labor force worked outside their home country in 1993, and half of them were concentrated in sub-Saharan Africa and the Middle East, which import workers for reasons that have more to do with feudalism than globalization. Even in the European Union, with its much-vaunted free movement of labor, only 2 percent of its nationals worked in another member state in the same year.[9] Two thirds of the world's labor force is still employed in agriculture. Half the world's population has never made a single phone call, let alone trolled through dozens of voice mails a day.

This gulf between the cosmocrats and the rest of the world is one reason why the localcrats' lives are often cushier. All the same, there is no question which class has momentum on its side: Visit any prominent localcrat fiefdom, and you will find a gaggle of sons eager to discuss their time at Stanford or Wharton. Richard Li, one of Li Ka-shing's sons and now a force in his own right in the Internet business in Asia, started his business training in time-honored fashion, listening to his father discuss his deals and strategies at dinner every night; but when he was thirteen, he was carted off to high school in Menlo Park, California (where he earned spending money working at McDonald's and caddying at the local golf club), before studying computer science at Stanford and then working in a Western investment bank.

Three institutions are playing vital roles in binding together this new elite. The first are the business schools. Where the old elite studied history at Oxbridge or in the Ivy League, the new elite acquires an M.B.A. "The people at the business school actually looked like the people in ads for Caribbean vacations or for expensive liquor," wrote one star-struck M.B.A. student at Harvard Business School. "They looked like *winners*."[10] Business schools are turning themselves into the boot camps of globalization. They recruit both their students and staff from as far afield as possible. (Europe's leading business school, Insead, was born global; American business schools are having to make more of an effort.) They also expect a good many of their alumni to spend some time working abroad. And you are never too old or far away to start—or to come back for a refresher course. Cosmocrats can join virtual programs such as Duke University's Global Executive M.B.A. Program, in which much of the teaching is done by CD-ROM and students work together using electronic bulletin boards and e-mail. The students spend a couple of weeks at Duke, but they are also supposed to take two-week trips to eastern Europe, Asia, and Latin America. The cost is $82,500, excluding airfares.[11]

The second kind of institution in this transformation encompasses the big professional-service firms: law firms, accountancy firms, and, especially, investment banks and management consultancies. For much of the 1990s, from Johannesburg to Taipei, it was impossible to interview the chairman of any decent-sized company without finding some young person from Goldman Sachs or Merrill Lynch hanging around the door. "They're young; they're focused on global markets and they're not afraid of new technology," cooed BusinessWeek in 1997, as it hailed "the JP Morgans and Walter Wristons of the new era of global finance."[12]

For a time, investment banks took the cream of the cosmocrat crop. Now, they have to fight it out with management consultancies and Silicon Valley start-ups. Every year, McKinsey screens fifty thousand résumés and undertakes tens of thousands of interviews, many of them involving senior partners, in order to hire five hundred new associates. The consultancies then devote an equally impressive amount of time to drilling their tyros in the language and techniques of management theory: Accenture subjects its new recruits to almost a thousand hours of training during their first five years, much of it in their in-house university in Saint Charles, Illinois. Consultancies allow their members to amass a far broader range of experience than regular business executives have by setting them to work in a wide variety of countries and industries. They also keep their people constantly on the move, switching them from posting to posting, lending them to other offices for short-term stays, and obliging them to fly hither and thither for specialized meetings.

The result is that former consultants are beginning to form a quasi-Masonic elite at the summit of modern business—and this elite regards the global life as a precondition for success. The frenetic pace of the business is such that junior consultants seldom see anybody outside work and thus form bonds that last long after they have moved on. But just in case these informal bonds are not enough, McKinsey has produced an alumni directory, complete with contact numbers, which means that products of the firm can be sure of finding others of their kind in whatever city they happen to touch down. McKinsey's five thousand alumni form an "arboreal slum" at the top of most walks of life in much the same way that Balliol men were once supposed to in the heyday of the empire, running institutions as diverse as IBM, American Express, and the British Conservative Party.

The final key institution in this process is the Internet. The Net is an impeccably cosmocratic gadget: global, unrestrained by national rules, stuffed full of knowledge, and "gender irrelevant." For a tribe as focused on staying connected yet as geographically dispersed as the cosmocrats, the Internet is much more than just an information center. "Dushan," who would rather not be identified, is a successful Serbian businessman who has lived in Boston for nearly a decade. His wife is a Croat. They married, as he puts it, "at a time when Yugoslavia used to mean something." Thanks to Slobodan Milosevic, they no longer have the option of living in either of their native homelands. But Dushan would not want to go back anyway. He has spent most of the twenty years since getting his engineering degree outside the country working in satellites and consulting. He likes his adopted home, but he would not think twice about moving somewhere else if he had to. His job often means that he is away most of the week anyway.

When Dushan thinks of his friends or where he "belongs," he does not think of either Belgrade or Boston but about the network of friends he has built up through his travels around the world. In the past, keeping up with them was a drag, particularly for somebody who puts in long hours. "There is," as he puts it, "no correct time to ring New Zealand." Now, the Internet has given a sort of geographic center to the "community" of people about whom he most cares. He can send his friend in New Zealand a photograph of a pint of Guinness, which they used to drink together when they lived in Britain. He can check the scores of soccer teams in Yugoslavia and argue about them with other cosmocratic émigrés. "It is a series of small things that add up to one big thing."

The Anxious Elite

The way in which they have embraced the Internet points to perhaps the most interesting thing about the cosmocrats: their insecurity. Cosmocrats are often fabulously rewarded for their understanding of globalization. But they pay a high price for their material success, both psychic and social. They are an anxious elite.

How does this sit with the sort of arrogant can-do Americanism that we described earlier? They seem to be two sides of the same coin. By any standard, America's cosmocrats, for instance, are better rewarded than any of their predecessors. People talk about a growing group of "gold-collar workers"—young, fickle knowledge workers who resent having to pay their dues at consultancies, law firms, or banks. Kirshenbaum Bond and Partners, an up-and-coming New York ad agency, used to get desperate pleas for work (one desperate applicant sent in a toilet-paper roll with the words "I'm will-ing to start at the bottom" written on every square); now, the firm gets notes from people who have chosen to go elsewhere just saying, "You lose."[13]

Yet there is also plenty of evidence that all this money and power is not making America's managers particularly happy. Consultants talk about companies producing burned out "human cinders" and about the rich-but-unhappy syndrome known as "affluenza." Overworked young lawyers have their own "greedy associates" website that is "a place for the over-privileged to complain." Some successful companies, including Intel, have engendered rebel websites on which current and past employees warn people against joining them; Jeffrey Pfeffer, a professor at Stanford Business School, says that some companies are "toxic workplaces." Many American companies, including the big car companies, have been embarrassed by the speed with which senior managers have accepted early-retirement packages. The wealth of Scott Adams, the creator of *Dilbert*, has increased in direct propor-tion to the ghastliness of American managerial life.

And, of course, there is the age-old horror of losing your job, something that has increased since the slump, though many of the extra profits of the 1990s came from thinning managerial ranks. A survey by Challenger, Gray and Christmas in 1998 showed that 41 percent of discharged managers had worked for four or more firms.

One immediate response to all this is to say that the managers who are suffering are usually not the cosmocrats but their parents, the trusting orga-nization men. In terms of overall job losses, that is probably true. It is hard to imagine that many of the elderly white-collar workers at General Motors who took early retirement had global values or saw themselves as knowl-edge workers. In *Wired*'s poll of digital citizens, almost seven in ten of them felt they could "control change," compared with an average of five in ten. But that does not mean that cosmocrats avoid such savagery altogether. They tend to work either in industries that have hire-and-fire habits (e.g., fi-nance, the media, and technology) or in ones in which a career path is really no more than a succession of gambles with big prizes but long odds. The grottier duplexes in the San Fernando Valley and Palo Alto are full of tal-ented film producers and software engineers who have toiled away lovingly on dozens of projects that have failed to catch fire. The phrase *portfolio career* sounds quite romantic until you have children and realize that you have no company pension plan or medical insurance.

Even when they are established more firmly, America's cosmocrats still suffer from several symptoms of affluenza. The first is overwork. According to Laura Lofaro, a Wall Street headhunter at Sterling Resources, these days an investment bank will typically ask three managers to do the work that it would have once had five do, and pay them more. This behavior is goaded by analysts who often judge firms according to their profits per employee. In Silicon Valley, people talk about "sleep camels"—people who can work throughout the week and then get their rest on weekends.

Numerous studies have shown that American managers would willingly give up some pay for shorter hours. Sleep, *The Wall Street Journal* has decided, has become "the new status symbol," with entrepreneurs such as Jeff Bezos of Amazon.com boasting about the "regular eight hours" he gets.[14] Indeed, the ability to set your own hours is one reason many cosmocrats in large firms gaze enviously not only at Bezos but at their peers who have become independent consultants. The contraction of corporate America, as it deals with both the deflation of the bubble and the aftermath of Enron, has forced people to work harder than before to keep their jobs.

A particular bone of contention for many cosmocrats is expatriate life. Study after study shows that companies of all sizes want to send more people to work abroad, yet the same studies show that persuading them to go is getting increasingly difficult—particularly now that the destination is as likely Shenzhen as San Francisco. For married cosmocrats, moving abroad is often a two-career decision. Both the proportion of married expatriates and the number of expatriates taking children with them are declining.[15] And family concerns are still the most common reasons why people want to return home early. Things have gotten so bad that companies such as Whirlpool and Quaker Oats have taken to sending retirees to overseas posts for six-month stints.

The number of hours worked or the number of people sacked are fairly easy to measure; status and peace of mind are not. Cosmocrats often smirk at the official perks that organization men enjoyed, but the democratization of the American workforce has not always helped the managerial classes. Vice presidents have been forced to give away power to semiautonomous teams in order to make their organizations more flexible. Firms have outsourced operations that managers used to regard as part of their fiefs. Status-enhancing perks, such as executive dining rooms, have long since disappeared; now some companies expect their managers to be out on the road so often that they are forced to "hotdesk" and share offices. Perhaps the most important perk that has disappeared is the reliable career ladder. Careers now tend to proceed in great jumps. Those who are left out tend to feel as if they are going nowhere. Some cosmocrats who are promoted quickly flourish; others arrive at their new positions unprepared and, because of the flatter structures, there are far fewer consiglieri to help them.

What is missing often is a sense of belonging. Most cosmocrats revel in the freedom they have to change jobs, but they do not enjoy the same freedom being shown to them. One day you go to work as one of Du Pont's 2,600 information-system employees; the next day, after an outsourcing deal, you are all working for Computer Sciences Corporation. Many cosmocrats are haunted by the memory of "the day that Dad got sacked"; determined not to suffer the same fate, they jump from place to place. A McKinsey survey in 1998 found that the average number of companies an executive would work for during his career had increased to 5.2, from 2.9 ten years earlier, and was likely to increase to 6.9 in another ten years.[16]

Some business-school professors such as Jeffrey Pfeffer point to the growing number of American companies that are trying to build cultures that can retain the young and the talented; they also argue that pay is not the best way to engender loyalty. On the other hand, the cosmocrats' insecurity seems an inevitable part of their meritocracy. Meritocrats in a fluid society are never quite as sure of their position as are aristocrats who have inherited their positions in a much more stable world.

The Perils of Placelessness

Are cosmocrats a good thing? Their anxiety may not be terribly good for them as individuals, but it is arguably good for their class as a whole. In his castigation of Davos man, Samuel Huntington argued that the species was doomed to disaster because of its own complacency. In fact, it is hard to see how this new elite will degenerate into a self-satisfied establishment in the manner of older national elites. Bill Gates may be arrogant, and he may be wrong, but there are not many grounds for calling him complacent. Globalization hugely increases people's power to bypass established players in order to get what they want: to use FedEx if the national mail system is too slow, cable TV if the networks serve up too much pap, and Amazon.com if the local bookshops charge too much for too little. That means that everybody has to stay on their toes.

Indeed, the great virtue of life under the cosmocrats is that the elite is relatively open and meritocratic: Anyone who can get a good degree at a respectable university or who can invent a clever new product can enter it. The cosmocrats believe that people should be judged on the basis of what they achieve rather than on who their parents were. To be sure, the cosmocrats are a decidedly Western class, but within the elite this is seen as a problem to be overcome rather than anything to be proud of. The elite is going out of its way to recruit people from the rest of the world.

Yet even as one admires their openness, there are several things that give pause. The first is superficiality. A young example of the breed is often far better traveled than even the most wizened sailor that Joseph Conrad could invent. But the very ease of modern travel imposes limitations. The cosmocrats have no Conradian depth. Just as it is all too easy to confuse motion with thought, it is all too easy to confuse a business trip with an in-depth study of another culture. Cosmocrats tend to think they know a country because they have shuttled between the airport and a hotel. But they seldom meet ordinary people, let alone study their lives in any depth. This faux familiarity leads to mistakes. Rupert Murdoch's television empire in Asia would have done better if his lieutenants had realized earlier that Indians, Chinese, and Indonesians (just to name the populations of the three biggest countries in Asia) are profoundly different people. Had the IMF's bright young economists ventured outside their hotel rooms in Seoul and Jakarta, they might have understood the relationship between business, politics, and society in the economies they were trying to guide.

Similarly, the cosmocrats' reverence for brainpower is usually one of their redeeming features. Yet as William Fulbright pointed out, "the best and the brightest" can still succumb to the arrogance of power. Indeed, in some ways this elite is more likely to than previous ones: Even the stupidest monarch must have harbored the occasional private doubt about the divine right of kings, but nobody is allowed to argue with a top SAT score. A host of cosmocratic institutions, including both the IMF and Long-Term Capital Management, have been prey to the idea that all they needed to do was apply their formidable brainpower to any problem and it would disappear in a puff of smoke. In Russia, what was obvious to mere taxi drivers—the country was degenerating into a kleptocracy—somehow escaped many of the "new Morgans" that *BusinessWeek* profiled. In Asia, the localcrat billionaires were certainly mauled, but they tended to survive, unlike cosmocrat know-it-all institutions, such as Peregrine, a Hong Kong investment bank.

The biggest set of worries concerning the cosmocrats have to do with what Robert Reich dubbed the "secession of the successful."[17] The cosmocrats are increasingly cut off from the rest of society: Its members study in foreign universities, spend a period of time working abroad, and work for organizations that have a global reach. They constitute a world within a world, linked to each other by myriad global networks but insulated from the more hidebound members of their own societies. They usually secrete themselves in isolated suburbs, send their children to private schools, and in general avoid city centers. Although they tend to cluster in certain areas, such as Bangalore or London, they have little in common with their working-class neighbors. They are more likely to spend their time chatting with their peers around the world—via phone or e-mail—than talking to their neighbors in the projects around the corner. Manuel Castells, a professor at Berkeley and Silicon Valley's favorite social theorist, has summed up the problem neatly: "Elites are cosmopolitan, people are local."[18]

True, the offices of global companies in emerging markets are increasingly run by locals, yet these are locals with a difference, the modern equivalents of Macaulay's Musalmans, "Indian in blood and color, but English in taste, in opinions, in morals, and in intellect." Wherever they triumph, the cosmocrats seem to eliminate whatever is distinctive about the local. International hotel chains often have the same design the world over, even down to the texture of the towels and the make of the toiletries. All these features help to persuade the cosmocrats that they are lords of humankind; they can also instill a dangerous sense of abstraction from the host society.

In the United States, a large number of cosmocrats seem to live in the sorts of places where signs promise immediate armed responses. In the emerging world, the isolation is even more complete. In Johannesburg, razor wire glints behind the swimming pools. In Moscow, heavily built "chauffeurs" take the children to school. At a beachside brunch in Brazil, behind yet more gates and guards, two foreign bankers' wives whisper about a friend who had to go home after she was carjacked. One gated community in China, Shanghai Links, boasts a country club, an eighteen-hole golf course, an American international school, a baseball diamond, a strip mall, a hospital, a five-star hotel, and eight hundred ranch-style houses, each equipped with built-in air purifiers. Everything about the community, including the grass, has been imported; the power, sewage, and water-treatment plants are private, freeing the inhabitants from dependence on China's unpredictable public sector.

Earlier ruling classes often felt responsible for the less fortunate because they all lived in the same town for generations. English dukes might not care for the working class in general, but they were often good to "their people." The cosmocrats have little idea what *their people* means. They usually think that they have nobody to thank for their success but themselves. And they seldom have the time to put down deep local roots. Few of them work in the town where they grew up. (It is significant, as Rosabeth Moss Kanter notes, that the most footloose of all professionals, management consultants, are among the least involved in their wider community.)[19] Even when these wandering souls do become attached to a place, they spend most of their time doing business and socializing with people very much like themselves; they have little time left over from their busy schedules to engage in good works. And there is also perhaps something of an attitude problem. Dushan, the good-natured Serbian from Boston, talks about the people working in a town dominated by an old, dying International Paper factory: "Why don't they leave?" he kept on asking himself.

. The companies that the cosmocrats work for are increasingly careless of ancestral loyalties. They regard themselves as world players, locked in life-and-death struggles with others of their kind, rather than as corporate citizens, bound by unwritten ties to the cities that provide them with homes. Around the world, corporate headquarters are detaching themselves from the old city centers and moving to edge cities, where land is cheap, parking spaces plentiful, and the pathologies of urban life nothing more than entertainment on the television. In 1968, New York City was home to 131 Fortune 500 companies; by 1997, the number had declined to just 46.[20] Many newer companies have chosen even greater isolation, building campuses in the countryside. Nike developed an estatelike "university" around a man-made lake ten miles outside Portland, Oregon; Microsoft commissioned a new campus outside Seattle in the style of a monastery. The furious pace of mergers is further detaching companies from the old urban centers and destroying the old civic elites who used to look after their city's welfare from inside smoke-filled rooms. Kanter quotes Stanley Marcus, the former head of Neiman Marcus, as complaining that it is impossible to get philanthropic projects off the ground in Dallas these days. You used to be able to call a handful of local business leaders and raise a quick half million; "now the decisions are made in Tokyo or Hartford or in Kalamazoo."[21]

But Will You Love Me Tomorrow?

Therein may lie one of the key weaknesses of the cosmocrats: In giving back less than they take out, they forfeit the support and undermine the health of their host societies. Their very rootlessness makes the cosmocrats infuriatingly hard to regulate. But they are already arousing hostility. Pat Buchanan rages against "Goldman and Sachs." Mahathir bin Mohamad and Lee Kwan Yew have railed with equal impotence against cosmocrats of all races for undermining Asian values. European leaders such as Jacques Delors have denounced cosmocrats as "golden boys" and "Anglo-Saxon speculators." Such criticisms are not just confined to tub-thumping politicians. Christopher

Lasch condemned these cosmopolitan elites for their "indecently lavish way of life," their contempt for ordinary Americans, and their hubristic revolt "against the constraints of time and place."[22]

In fact, one could argue that there is no "clash of civilizations," just the growing pains of one ascendant civilization—that of the cosmocrats— rising against the dozens of civilizations that seek to constrain it. In this battle, the cosmocrats would at first sight seem to have the upper hand. They possess the brains and a good deal of the money. Many of the Western world's rising politicians are cosmocrats in one way or another. Bill Clinton has perfect cosmocratic credentials, from his background as a Rhodes Scholar to his use of obtuse language in any difficult situation. Al Gore is even more of a globalist than Bill Clinton; George W. Bush is a Harvard M.B.A. who has spoken publicly in Spanish. In Britain, the last election saw the McKinsey-trained William Hague face Tony Blair, who rejuvenated the Labor Party by importing plenty of Bill Clinton's ideas from Washington and surrounding himself with British cosmocrats, such as Jonathan Powell, Ed Balls, and Philip Gould. The Blairite Demos think tank in London and the Democratic Leadership Council in Washington are full of interchangeable young men who have been educated on both sides of the Atlantic. The European Union is now headed by the multilingual Romano Prodi. Most sensible political discourse is carried on in more-or-less cosmocratic terms.

You can even make the argument that the cosmocrats also have the future on their side. As the transition from an agrarian to an industrial society in the nineteenth century gave rise to giant political machines with umbilical ties to labor and capital, the rise of knowledge-intensive industries in the late twentieth century may yet produce a political system that is much more in tune with the cosmocrats' individualist and meritocratic values. Loyalty to political parties is falling to an all-time low in places such as California, as well as among young voters, while membership of other civil associations is rising, suggesting that people want pragmatic solutions rather than ideological posturings.

Yet the cosmocrats' hold on modern politics still strikes us as fragile. Political parties still represent the main source of power, and the cosmocrats have been less successful in remodeling those parties than were either the industrialists or the trade unionists of the late nineteenth and early twentieth centuries. In America, the Democratic Party remains wedded to vested interests that have little enthusiasm for meritocracy, particularly the teachers' unions, while the Republican Party is lumbered with what Eric Schmidt, the boss of Novell, calls Neanderthal social views. Across Europe, social-democratic parties are largely still rooted in the world of mass production, and conservative parties tend to have unpleasant nationalist streaks. (For British cosmocrats, the Channel Tunnel is simply a convenient way to visit their friends at Insead rather than a dangerous breach in Albion's defenses that will be totally secure only when Eurostar trains are equipped, like Boadicea's chariots, with scythes on their wheels to cut down any Continental types trying to sneak into the green and pleasant land.)

The business community has proved a fairly fickle ally of globalization: Individual companies will happily turn against globalization if it serves their interests. And the trade unions have been a much more doughty opponent than most people realize. Most fundamental of all, the cosmocrats simply do not seem to be involved enough.

America's venal political system should offer the cosmocrats a chance to control things: They, after all, have the money. Yet politics' very tawdriness seems to put them off. They are much more confident about the private sector's capacity to fix things than about the public sector's. They do not have the time to organize initiatives; they are away on business trips during elections. If there is ever to be a great battle about globalization, then the people one might have expected to form the heart of the defense will probably be on a plane somewhere, sitting next to Ellen Knapp.

13

Outside the Red Lacquered Gates: The Losers from Globalization

> In the central halls there are fair goddesses who clothe their guests with warm furs of sable, entertain them with the finest music, feed them with the broth of camel's pad, with pungent tangerines and oranges ripened in frost. Behind the red lacquered gates, wine is left to sour, meat to rot. Outside these gates lie the bones of the frozen and the starved. The flourishing and the withered are just a foot apart.

THIS COMES FROM a description of the eighth-century Chinese imperial court by the poet Tu Fu. But for many it might as well be a description of the sort of society that is being created by globalization. On one side of the red lacquered gates sit the cosmocrats, pampered but boringly similar from one part of the world to another. (The competition for business-class passengers is so intense these days that it would hardly come as a surprise if an airline started offering broth of camel's pad.) On the other side sit the losers, in all their infinite and depressing variety.

Variety is one of the qualities that make the losers so hard to analyze. What does a schoolteacher in Buenos Aires who thinks that *capitalismo salvaje* ("savage capitalism") has deprived her kind of their civilized life while enriching "bandits" have in common with the wretchedly poor farmers in the northern province of Jujuy where the problem is not that everything has changed but that nothing has? Or with an environmental activist in Córdoba protesting smoggy industrialization? Or a policeman worrying that the Mercosur free-trade pact will make life easier for the international drug trade? And these people are all from the same country! No wonder so many books on the downside of globalization read like long-winded travelogues.

Another reason why the subject is so frustrating is that every statement cries out for qualification, even in a country as battered as Argentina. Yes, Jujuy is still locked in wretched poverty, but the region's real problem is a generation of chronically inefficient local government, not the workings of the global economy. Yes, Córdoba is a bit of a dump, but surely that stems from the Peronist dream of Argentina building every sort of industry imaginable? Yes, the peso crisis caused havoc, but the government failed to curtail spending. And so on.

But the biggest reason why the subject is so frustrating is that supporters and opponents of globalization rarely listen to each other. There is so much evidence available that each side can go on ad infinitum without ever bothering to acknowledge the other. Occasionally, specialists tangle over a statistic—the exact size of America's underclass, the number of degrees the globe has warmed (or not)—but rarely do they see the picture as a whole.

In fact, that picture is a fairly easy one to describe. The same competitive, enriching, liberating process that we laud in most of this book does indeed exact costs, occasionally terrible ones. The doctrine of competitive advantage is a wonderful one if you have advantages with which to be competitive. But what if you have a history of oppression, poor education, and malign government? Like many human things globalization can often be just downright unfair or carelessly vicious. That does not mean that some people have to lose for others to win. But globalization has unquestionably worsened some people's lives. Rather than trying to deny these failings, it seems better to confront them, set them in some sort of context, and try to work out what governments and people on the comfortable site of the red lacquered gates can do to solve them.

Given their numbers and diversity, cataloging the victims is a rough-and-ready process. You can dice them by income, slice them by geography, or even just divide them by the way that globalization has affected them (some bowled over by market forces, others gradually pushed aside). We will try to get around some of these problems by focusing on just three countries: the United States, Russia, and Brazil. We begin by looking at three people who represent three of the main groups of losers: "the has-beens"; "the storm damage"; and "the nonstarters."

The Deer Hunter

We visit the first on a brisk June morning in 1998. The union hall of United Auto Workers Local 659, which represents the workers of the General Motors metal-stamping factory in Flint, Michigan, seems an unlikely hotbed of radicalism. Outside stands a well-kept monument to veterans from the local union; the grass and picnic tables are neat and tidy. Inside, it feels like the final preparations for an over-fifties bus trip, perhaps one going off on the golfing vacation advertised on the notice board. A gray-haired striker brings his granddaughter into the kitchen to get some doughnuts. Dwight Bobo, a mild-mannered fifty-four-year-old electrician, helps her choose one, then goes back to his task of making coffee. It is a nice day: He would prefer to be out on the picket line, but it was his turn in the kitchen.

His slightly odd name notwithstanding ("Apparently we were called Le Beaux Le Beaux once"), Bobo is a typical Flint man. In 1998, GM still employed thirty-three thousand workers at eighteen different factories and offices in the Michigan town. Like many of his peers, Bobo has worked for General Motors since high school, his only break a two-year stint in Vietnam. His father worked for GM; his brother still does. Bobo's wife, Jo Ann, also comes from a GM family. He would never dream of driving a Ford, let alone a Toyota. Normally at this time of year, he coaches Little League softball in the evening then heads off to the night shift at the stamping factory; he comes home at 7:00 A.M., watches *Good Morning America,* and then falls asleep. The only break in his routine is when he heads off to the mountains to hunt deer (with a bow and arrow, like his father).

Yet this summer, Bobo and his compatriots are costing GM about fifty million dollars every day and helping shave off 0.1 percent of America's GDP for the second quarter of 1998. The strike that he and his 3,400 colleagues at the stamping factory began has now rippled around Flint and the rest of the car company. Most of GM's 250,000 workers in North America stand idle. Officially, the local is striking about health and safety grievances, but the underlying issues are job security, productivity, and globalization. GM makes nearly one thousand dollars less profit per vehicle than Ford, largely because it has too many small factories with too many workers; the Flint stamping plant, where the average worker costs forty dollars an hour, is particularly inefficient. The UAW replies that stamping is a machine-intensive business, and GM has reneged on a promise to invest three hundred million dollars in modernizing the plant. The actual casus belli came when GM "sneaked" into the factory over Memorial Day weekend and removed several dies needed to produce hoods and other parts for a new line of pickup trucks.

Bobo, who earns twenty-three dollars an hour plus benefits, seems exhausted by all this bickering, which he compares to a marriage in which even the smallest row leads to divorce: "We are all only on this earth for seventy years; we should get along." He still drinks regularly with friends who are in management (and thus still work in the factory that he pickets). He does not exempt the UAW from blame. For him, the strike is a matter of principle: "GM said it would invest the money; it hasn't. When I sign a contract with GMAC [the car firm's finance arm] to buy a car, I can't renege on it."

Globalization has made this only "more of a crapshoot" because it takes what Bobo calls the American dream out of it. "You can't just work hard and get ahead; your job could just be shipped overseas." The strike is following hard on the heels of Daimler-Benz's takeover of Chrysler, a merger that would have been unthinkable when Bobo started working. Back then, Detroit was all that mattered. Now when old-timers at Flint want to criticize younger workers for doing shoddy work, they say things like, "What are you trying to do, move your job to Mexico?" Since 1978, GM has built fifty car-parts factories in Mexico. Now, most fears are centered on Brazil, where GM is growing quickly and working on a new factory code-named "Blue Macaw." As Bobo wearily admits, it seems a battle that the unions cannot win: Each strike only increases the likelihood that GM will push more jobs overseas. Meanwhile, other car companies are entering the American market. Bobo says he does not mind fair competition, and he admits that, on the whole, cars have got better and cheaper; but he still worries about the foreign firms cheating and not paying people properly. Bobo himself may take early retirement.

That is pretty much what General Motors wants him to do. For the car firm, he is a has-been, an expensive liability. It is an open secret that GM wants to force the older workers (the average age is forty-eight) to leave early, so it can lose the thirty thousand workers it needs to in order to be able to match Ford's productivity. GM is not being unusually hard-hearted; Ford and Chrysler are both pouring money into overseas plants.

You can hear different versions of Bobo's story from Wolfsburg, Germany, to Hitachi City, Japan: Decent, hardworking people—to use the cliché—no longer feel wanted. Throughout much of the developed world, the middle class is splintering between those who benefit from globalization and those who are being left out. However, even when they are not being elbowed out of the way, blue-collar workers have been losing their perks. At the same time that Bobo was brewing coffee for the picketers, some five hundred thousand Danes were on strike because their employers, citing the pressure from foreign competition, had refused to grant six weeks' vacation. A month and a half is a pretty long holiday, but, as with the UAW's often absurdly cozy perks at Flint, it still hurts when you lose it.

It hurts that much more when you think you are being left behind. The

Bobos have been cushioned by Dwight's UAW-protected wages, but like most blue-collar families they think that they did not get the full benefits of the 1990s boom. Although median wages in America finally crept to new highs in real terms at the end of the 1990s, those gains came only because women were being paid more. The median wage for American men was 3.6 percent lower in 1998 than in 1989 and 12.4 percent lower than in 1979. And, even when you include women, the gains per household were paltry. By 1997, the median American household earned only $1,260 more than it did in 1973.[1] In the 1960s, when Bobo started his career, those sorts of increases often happened in a single year, and people did not work as hard. The average wife now works fifteen hours a week more than she did at the beginning of the 1970s.

This failure to advance hurts even more when you see others steaming ahead. The gains from the 1990s bull market went disproportionately to the rich, with as much as 90 percent of the paper profits going to the top 10 percent of households.[2] Talk about inequality being wrong per se angers many Americans. Envy is supposed to be un-American: A European seeing a Ferrari might think about puncturing its tires; an American might dream only of owning one, too. A Chicago-trained economist might argue that when people like the Bobos discover that the number of Americans reporting annual income of one million dollars rose from 14,348 to 111,728 between 1990 and 1997 or that yacht sales doubled in that time, they should warmly celebrate the workings of the hidden hand.[3] But critics such as Edward Luttwak argue that inequality, particularly in a culture in which the accumulation of wealth is promoted so assiduously, has costs as well as benefits. People are more likely to go into debt to try to keep up with the Joneses. Some people feel that they have not done well enough; many more feel that they have been cheated. The American dream is hard to sustain if people think that the driver of the Ferrari stole it.

And in fact, the only subject that seems to make Bobo's blood boil is executive pay. The last time the men at Flint had made concessions, GM's then boss had picked up a multimillion-dollar paycheck. Bobo has no problem with managers being paid well or with workers being replaced, when necessary, by machines. He does, however, think a lot of the struggle between labor and management comes down to a difference of attitudes as fundamental as the one separating him from the people who protested Vietnam thirty years ago. "I think about how things will be when I'm dead; the guys in the boardroom don't. I'm not worried about my job; I'm worried about my children's, and the towns around here. They just care about bonuses."

Perhaps the saddest thing about Dwight Bobo is the fact that he is a decent man who must surrender to the inevitable. A bit like the deer that he hunts so selectively, he is simply being culled. The wonder years for the people of Flint are long gone, brought to an end by forces beyond Bobo's control, forces that he does not always understand but whose result is as final as an arrow through the neck.

Storm Damage

In many ways, Sergei Orelsky is Bobo's opposite. The jaunty young Russian is still at the beginning of his career and remains, at least on the surface, an optimist—or as much of one as you could be in Saint Petersburg at the end of the twentieth century. A typical product of the ambitious Russian middle classes, the twenty-eight-year-old marketing executive boasts about the things that he has learned, the countries he has been to, and the things he plans to do. All the same, one does not have to dig far to find pockets of bitterness. The differences between Orelsky and Bobo arise not just from character or age or even from the gap between advertising chutzpah and blue-collar phlegm. Rather, their attitudes are defined by what has been done to them by the outside world—by capitalism. Bobo at least has some good years to look back on. In Saint Petersburg, however, there were no real wonder years, just the brief promise in the mid-1990s of a much better life, a promise that was blown away in a matter of weeks.

Until the storm hit in August 1998, Orelsky would have called himself a winner from globalization. At that time, he was the manager of the Saint Petersburg office of a Swedish supplier of ceramic roof tiles, in the center of the city on Vasily Island. Orelsky had a big office in a newly renovated building where many foreign firms were represented. For Orelsky, getting to the ceramic-tiles firm had been a simple matter of hard work and application. A Saint Petersburg native, Orelsky graduated from the Dnepropetrovsk Engineering and Construction Institute in Ukraine. He specialized as a construction engineer, but he also completed courses in management and marketing. He joined the ceramic-tiles company in 1996. Like many young Russians, he was always looking for ways to travel, so he cheerfully took part in numerous training courses in Latvia, Norway, Sweden, and Finland. Of course, there were problems, but Russia, he sensed, was gradually if unevenly joining the market economy. The mid-1990s were a good time to be a young, clever man in Saint Petersburg. Orelsky settled down with his wife, Xenia, in a comfortable apartment.

That same August, however, Russia's financial crisis broke and the ruble plunged. The assets that Orelsky had carefully amassed for just such a rainy day disappeared. Unfortunately for Orelsky, his firm's license to do business in Russia expired at almost the same time, and the Swedes decided not to extend it. Orelsky does not quarrel with that decision and even praises the Swedes for giving the workers three months' notice. Instead, he counts his blessings ("Thank God our company never played any games with the state: It never bought government bonds or shares.") The fact that so many of Orelsky's friends were in more or less identical positions seems to have softened the blow. They all argued that it was a form of release, a chance to start again. Orelsky and a few friends immediately set up an advertising company in his office.

Orelsky's young firm is still going, and he talks about expanding it. All the same, looking at Orelsky, surrounded by ceramic roof tiles that were left behind by his previous employer, it is plain that his path upward has met a considerable obstacle. As he readily admits, starting the company was a real struggle. To begin with, he and his partners fantasized about renting a new office and buying some new computers. The crisis soon put paid to that idea. Nearly all the smaller foreign companies that might have been clients have either left or, as he puts it, frozen their activities.

The crisis has also changed Orelsky's lifestyle. Like most of his upwardly mobile friends, Orelsky had been taking home between seven hundred and one thousand dollars a month at Braas. In 1999, even after a year and a half of hard work, he makes less than half that amount. "I had planned to completely renovate my flat during the winter, but now it will have to wait until the summer. Before the crisis, we spent more time going out and had free time. Now I have no free time at all." He points gloomily to the number of lights burning in his offices late on Saturdays and Sundays.

Orelsky is living evidence that financial domino theory—according to which Thailand knocked over Korea, which knocked over Wall Street, which knocked over Russia—actually worked in a way that political domino theory, the creed of the cold war, never did. The storm that blew away Orelsky's first stab at capitalism threw many emerging markets into their worst recession since the war. In the countries hit by the Asian contagion, the jobless rate, having been practically nonexistent, tripled to around 10 percent. Roads soon clogged with the migrants who had been summoned to do the "three d" work (dangerous, difficult, or dirty) now returning to their homelands. Children, particularly girls, dropped out of Indonesian schools by the thousands. In some cases, the contagion seemed to have all the discrimination of a machine gunner at the Somme. In July 1998, in a decision that was barely reported in the Western press, Chinese officials said that the state-owned textile factories were to lay off six hundred thousand of their 4.3 million employees during the next year because of competition from Asian countries whose costs had dropped.

At times, Orelsky can almost force himself to argue that the crisis has been good for Russia: It has taught people that capitalism is not easy. The mass exodus of foreigners has also made it easier for domestic firms such as his own. Yet the way that money flowed in and then abruptly retreated has left some scars. "As the Japanese say, life is always most difficult in times of change. These constant changes reflect badly on people's psyche and result in bitterness and negative changes in behavior." Russians, he thinks, have become more like their stereotypes and do not trust their government or foreigners. "Practically every day, in the papers or on television, we see reports about murders. If we stopped and thought about it even for a moment we would be angry." But he repeats, with a note of professionalism, that "showing feelings is unacceptable when working with Russian clients."

This odd mixture—a determination to get on with life mixed with sporadic bouts of recrimination and pessimism—is typical of the Russian middle class. After the collapse of the ruble, Western newspapers filled with pictures of impoverished old peasant women hawking vegetables. There was talk of famine. Yet driving through the Russian countryside that winter, a visitor was left with a more callous conclusion: Russia's poor and hungry had got a little hungrier and poorer, but they were not starving. The subsistence barter economy, which had never gone away, expanded.

Meanwhile, at the other end of the scale, Russia's rich—the localcrats—also picked themselves up off the floor. In August there had been plenty of stories of fallen billionaires, of houses sold in Saint John's Wood and perilous meetings with Western bankers demanding their money back. All these things happened, too, as many investment bankers will tell you with ill-disguised glee. Yet despite these humiliations, well-connected entrepreneurs tended to survive, just as their peers did in Asia.

The real losers from Russia's disastrous initial flirtation with global capitalism were its middle classes. Not quite rich enough nor quite dishonest enough to squirrel their money away in, say, Cyprus, their hard work was destroyed by devaluation. By one estimate, within a month of the crash, sixty thousand professionals in Moscow were either laid off, sent home on "temporary unpaid leave," or forced to take salary cuts of one third.[4] And such figures take no account of the entrepreneurs—people like the professor's wife who made some money from buying and renovating one apartment and then borrowed money to do another, bigger one. She had suddenly found that her bank, run by one of Russia's more unpleasant kleptocrats, was trying to foreclose on her, while prospective tenants scuttled back overseas; meanwhile, her savings disappeared at another bank. Unsurprisingly, she wants to leave.

But most Russians are like Orelsky and either want to stay or have nowhere else to go. In many ways, the biggest hit has been to their pride. Many of them believed that they were helping to build a better country. They knew, as everyone did, that their capitalism was of a rough-and-ready sort, but America, they reminded themselves, had also had a Wild West and robber barons. Now, Russia's entrepreneurs have woken up to discover that the real comparison for Russia is often Africa rather than the United States. Russia has become a banana republic, except that it grows energy instead of fruit. Oil and gas account for nearly all its exports, and the revenues they earn are looted with Nigerian finesse by a group of kleptocrats who, unlike America's robber barons, have built only connections, not businesses. All the values associated with an emerging middle class—hard work, respect for the law, education—count for little. That is not a country to which one should sell ceramic tiles—or, indeed, anything else.

Hope Is the Last Thing That Dies

For Reginaldo and Rose Marie Gobetti and their two-month-old son, Filipe, the sort of calculations by which Orelsky and Bobo measure globalization are fantastic things: salaries, benefits, travel. They live in the Villa Prudente, one of São Paulo's 2,500 favelas, the most beautifully named slums in the world. Though Brazil overall is a middle-income country, nearly two thirds of its total household income goes to the richest fifth of the population, with a mere 2.5 percent for the poorest fifth. Some fifty-three million people— around a third of the population—are poor. Many of them live in favelas— shantytowns that take shape under roads, on hillsides, and near dumps.[5]

It should be said immediately that Villa Prudente is one of the nicer favelas. The first squatters arrived nearly half a century ago. Most of its houses include some sort of brick. It is reasonably near the center of town and built on flat land, not perched on the edge of a hillside. Unlike in many favelas, there is a water supply and electricity. And although nobody officially owns anything, there is an informal system of property rights that usually allows people to inherit and buy and buy and sell places. But it is still recognizably a slum, with twenty thousand people crammed into a space about half a mile long, partly divided by a freeway. It appears that most of the inhabitants are women and children. Unemployment is the norm. Gang-related violence and drug abuse are both on the rise. AIDS is spreading.

Reginaldo, who is twenty-two, was born here and has done his level best to get out of it. A scrawny young man with a gap between his front teeth, he exudes an almost childish good nature. It is easy to imagine him as a circus clown—which in fact was one of his early jobs. Rose Marie, however, is warier.

Like two out of three Brazilian workers, Reginaldo did not finish secondary school; as the oldest of seven, he had to leave at fourteen. He briefly landed a good job as an assistant in an electrical store, getting paid five hundred reals (then about four hundred dollars) a month, but when the economy began to turn down in 1998, he was laid off. He now works in what is loosely known as the informal sector. From Monday to Thursday (there is no point trying on Fridays), he takes a bus to one of the industrial areas and then begins a long, meandering walk back to the favela, asking for work as he goes. It is a lonely, dispiriting business. (He would go with a friend, but that would only frighten potential employers.) If he is lucky, he will get hired lifting, pushing, or washing something for a few hours.

Between this and the household jobs that Rose Marie sometimes picks up, the Gobettis hope to bring in one hundred reals a month—about sixty dollars at the new devalued exchange rate. But it does not always work out, and sometimes they have to buy bread on credit. Thus, Reginaldo's main search is for permanent work. One of his friends has a telephone and lets Reginaldo use the number. The biggest problem, Reginaldo admits shyly, bitterness finally working into his voice, is his address. When he fills out the form, the excuses come out: Jobs suddenly require him to have a driver's license or three years' experience.

The favela in Brazil has its counterparts worldwide—a barrio in Venezuela or a *jhuggie* settlement in India. In places such as Dar es Salaam and Caracas, roughly half the housing stock is squatter level. Every continent has its nonstarters: woefully underequipped people living miserable lives that, it seems, globalization has done little to improve. By any measure, an unacceptably large group of people is poor, indebted, malnourished, and without aid. Around one in four of us—1.3 billion people—lives on less than a dollar a day; one in five is illiterate.

There are more extremely poor people in rich countries than many people would like to admit. In 1998, the World Bank offered one million dollars' worth of support to the capital of the new world order, Washington, D.C. Although it was dressed up as a piece of good citizenship by the Beltway-based bank, critics such as *The Wall Street Journal* pointed out that the city, where 39 percent of the children live in families below the poverty line, had more in common with the bank's regular customers than it would like to admit: Washington's infant mortality rate of 16.2 per 1,000 births (more than double the American average) is about the same as Sri Lanka's; the number of babies born underweight is a little higher than the figure for Zambia.[6]

All the same, most nonstarters live in developing countries. Almost all of Africa's 750 million people qualify. Most of the forty-five countries at the bottom of the United Nations' Human Development Program are African. The average African home consumes 20 percent less than it did a quarter century ago, and it is the only place where the proportion of children not attending school is rising. It is difficult to see how things are likely to change, given the continent's neglect of education and penchant for incompetent governments. What can we offer, say, Niger, where more than 90 percent of the population live on less than two dollars a day, life expectancy is forty-seven years, and thousands of children die every year of curable diseases?[7]

The easiest way to illustrate the backwardness of some countries is simply to look at the people. A modern Bangladeshi weighs about the same as a Western great-great-great-great-great-grandfather did for the simple reason that he eats just as badly. The French *citoyens* who stormed the Bastille consumed about 2,700 calories a day and averaged about five feet two inches in height. Now that French people get 4,000 calories a day, they have grown to about five foot ten.[8]

Wade through the literature about the nonstarters, and four gruesome things stand out.[9] The first is the pathetic vulnerability of children such as Filipe Gobetti. More than eight million die each year because of polluted water or dirty air; six million die from malnutrition; two million die from diarrhea-related diseases. In Africa, 174 out of every 1,000 children fail to reach age five, against an average of 89 for the world.

Second, it is the very poor who tend to suffer most from human violence. Most of the seven hundred murders that happen each month in São Paulo are committed in places like Villa Prudente. Reginaldo Gobetti says that the police come into the favela rarely, and when they do, they then leave in a blink of an eye. He would willingly go through a few stop-and-frisk ordeals if it meant that the police were around more. More generally, the nonstarters tend to be gathered in places where the forces of law and order are often themselves great threats to safety. Poor countries account for almost all the

116 countries that Amnesty International accuses of practicing torture. In 1998, for example, Laurent Kabila's radio station broadcast the following public-service announcement: "People must bring a machete, a spear, an arrow, a hoe, spades, rakes, nails, truncheons, electric irons, barbed wire, stones and the like, in order, dear listeners, to kill Rwandan Tutsis."

Third, the same sort of inequality that irks Dwight Bobo reaches epidemic proportions when you consider the nonstarters. Brazil, as its former president, Fernando Henrique Cardoso, once remarked, is not so much an underdeveloped country as an unjust one. Half its farmland is occupied by just 1 percent of its landowners. When you begin to examine inequality on a global scale, it becomes still more unfathomable. In 1999, the UNDP estimated that the assets of the world's three leading billionaires were greater than the combined GNPs of all the least developed countries, which contain six hundred million people. In the 1960s, the richest fifth of the world enjoyed an income only thirty times that of the poorest fifth; in 1998, the ratio had risen to 74:1. Even that figure is open to interpretation since it tends to sort whole countries by category (for instance, there are no Chinese people in the bottom quintile). Adjust the figure for inequality within countries, and the disparity jumps to 135:1. And as Raymond Baker and Jennifer Nordin, two academics who have pored through the World Bank's figures, point out, even that figure is probably too low since it relies on the rich reporting their income accurately. They estimate the figure for 2000 to be around 150:1.[10]

The figures for consumption are even more depressing. In 1998, the top 20 percent of us consumed roughly 86 percent of the world's $24 trillion in goods and services, according to the UNDP—sixteen times more than the poorest 20 percent did. The richest fifth consumes eleven times more meat, seventeen times more energy, and 145 times more cars than the poorest fifth. In some countries, there are fewer goods and services available today than there were twenty years ago.

Fourth, most nonstarters live in places that get relatively little help from the outside world. Foreign aid to poor countries from OECD countries was $77 billion in 1997, about 20 percent less in real terms than what it was in 1992. Only four Western countries—Denmark, Norway, the Netherlands, and Sweden—reach the UN's target of giving away 0.7 percent of GNP. America gives less than 0.1 percent. In the stronger emerging economies, such as Brazil, this shortfall has been more than compensated for by private investment (even though very little has reached the Gobettis). But poorer emerging countries get almost nothing. The forty-eight least developed countries receive just 1.5 percent of the foreign direct investment (FDI) going to emerging markets and only 0.5 percent of the total FDI. Their one source of money has been loans. In 1998, the debt mountain for sub-Saharan Africa stood at $222 billion, or $370 for every inhabitant.[11]

Only the most idiotic critic would try to lay all these failings directly at the feet of globalization. In the favela, only a few people specifically link their misfortunes to the process—and then often for slightly bizarre reasons. Silvio Pereira da Silva worked as a magician in the circus where Reginaldo briefly clowned. Globalization, he says (bringing it up unprompted) ruined his trade. Thanks to rising prices caused by the Asian crisis, people don't want to spend money at the big top; they just sit and watch their television. And now, to cap it all, some American from Las Vegas has appeared on a TV program, explaining how all the tricks are performed, ruining Pereira da Silva's act.

But if specific victims of globalization are hard to find in the favela, so too are beneficiaries. Despite a decade of opening its economy to the outside world, Brazil (just like Argentina) still had a higher unemployment rate at the end of the 1990s than at the beginning. Most of the new jobs it created were in the informal sector. Globalization, Reginaldo says, has made no real difference to his life. "The people who know people have done well out of it," he scoffs. It is fine for people like President Cardoso, traveling around the world. But the process has merely made Reginaldo's disadvantages, particularly his lack of education, more acute. His head tells him that he will still be in the favela in two years' time, but he keeps on trying, motivated above all by his desire "to make sure that Filipe does not end up in the same situation." His latest hopes are with a new shopping center that will be built over a neighboring favela. Asked why he still seems so chirpy, he replies without irony, "Hope is the last thing that dies."

The Wrong Man in the Dock

We must be careful not to take the hand-wringing too far. Miserable though the situations of Bobo, Orelsky, and Gobetti are, they are not the whole story. To begin with, the human race is, in general, advancing rather than going backward. Even the richest of those tiny Frenchmen at the time of the storming of the Bastille would, in many ways, consider himself a pauper today. Back then, infant mortality and childhood diseases meant about a 50 percent chance of reaching adulthood; life expectancy was just thirty-four years. The same researchers at the UNDP who unearthed the figures about inequality also have the honesty to admit that the sixteenfold increase in consumption in the twentieth century was an "unprecedented improvement in humanity."

This sort of improvement is most obvious in rich countries. Three out of every four families living below the poverty line in America today own a washing machine and at least one car. Ninety-seven percent own a television; three out of four have a VCR. Thanks to all that terrible competition, many gadgets are much more affordable, particularly in terms of the number of work hours needed to acquire them. A cell phone now takes only a fiftieth of the time to earn that it took in 1984. A bottle of Coca-Cola is roughly half the price it was in 1970, and a Big Mac 20 percent less. Meanwhile, the dynamism of the economy also means that the poor are not "always with us." They can climb out. Only one in twenty of those in America's poorest fifth are still stuck there sixteen years later.[12]

In most poor parts of the world outside Africa, there have also been enormous improvements in standards of living. Most of the world's poor live in India and China. It is not difficult to find examples of gut-wrenching poverty in either country, but it is also clear which way the momentum is going. Deng Xiaoping's decision to open China's economy in 1978 helped some eight hundred million peasants more than double their real incomes in just six years, arguably the single greatest leap out of acute poverty of all time.[13] The past five years have been tough for poor Asians, but the long-term trend is upward: By 2020 some two billion poor rural people should be lifted out of poverty. Half of India's ninety million poor households own watches, and a third have radios. The Gobettis may be poor, but they still have a television and a VCR. In Saint Petersburg today you see a visibly better-clothed population than you did in, say, 1985.

Critics who ignore these general advances are perhaps merely forgetful. They become more dishonest when they focus on specific victims of globalization and fail to mention the specific winners created by the same process. Nowadays, Flint is always depicted as a victim of capitalism. A century ago, it was the aggressor itself, as the car industry lured in sharecroppers, coal miners, poor farm boys, and large numbers of immigrants. Far from being on the defensive, General Motors was eating up other car companies. The creative destruction continues. Jo Ann Bobo works at Manpower; her and Dwight's daughter is also looking for a job in services, possibly tourism. In other parts of the United States, particularly ones where the UAW's writ does not hold, car factories are symbols of hope and prosperity. In Evansville, Indiana, Toyota's new factory has greatly increased local pay levels for blue-collar workers.

Venture down to Brazil, and you will find that the "crapshoot" that Bobo resents is helping to change the life of Marcos Andrade for the better. A tall, thin young man, almost exactly the same age as Reginaldo Gobetti, Andrade got a job as a machine operator at GM's stamping plant at São Caetano do Sul in 1997. The plant, which we visited briefly in chapter 4, is an old one; but it feels completely unlike Flint. There are a few old-timers at São Caetano, and, just as in Michigan, there are even a few GM families, with fathers and sons working together. But the average age of the four hundred workers is only thirty-five. The talk is of soccer, not golf trips. Andrade earns one thousand reals a month (six hundred dollars), enough for him to start thinking about getting a house with his girlfriend, Marie Jose, rather than worry about making ends meet, as most of his friends do. Nor is it just a matter of money: GM also provides him with training (around fifty hours a year) and even picks up half the tab for his English lessons. The factory is safe and clean, and lunch is free.

Andrade might hail the process that has brought him this new life—he admits that it has been good for him—but he does not like the way that a crisis in Asia can spark problems in Brazil. Like everybody else in São Paulo, he is worried about his job. In 1998, the Brazilian market shrank by nearly a fifth. On the assembly line, people sometimes talk about China in the same way that people in Flint talk about Brazil and Mexico. Like most of the other workers, he feels some sympathy for the workers in Flint, but when he hears how much they are paid, he whistles. He has not bothered to join a union himself: He thinks they are too much trouble. But now he has a new goal: a position in the Blue Macaw project in southern Brazil. The money will be better. Other people in the plant are thinking about it, too. In many ways, he is no different from the sharecroppers turning up in Flint one hundred years ago.

Swings and Roundabouts

Knowing that winners outnumber losers—or that both are part of a fundamentally beneficial process—is scant consolation to people such as Gobetti, Orelsky, and Bobo. We will return to the question of what governments and the more successful members of society can do to help the losers in chapter 15, but prevention would be far preferable to a cure. One of the most persistent myths about globalization—and one that politicians love to hide behind—is that its excesses are unavoidable, just like the hangover that comes after a heavy drinking session.

Globalization can clearly be a savage process, but it is frequently not the underlying cause of the harm that it spreads. The rich world's unemployed are better off blaming technology for their fate than foreign competition. Even if GM had never set foot in Latin America, more efficient technology would probably nonetheless have left them with too many stamping plants in the United States. (It has fourteen such plants in North America; it probably needs only ten.)

Africa's problems have their roots in decades' worth of corrupt and incompetent governments, which singularly failed to prepare that continent for a competitive world. It is notable that Botswana, one of the few places in Africa to have a two-party democracy, has been growing almost as fast as the Asian tigers. Some of the world's biggest tragedies have been caused by governments trying to obstruct globalization. It is hard to think of a single thing that would help the poor more than getting rid of protectionist laws that restrict imports of basic foodstuffs, textiles, and so on in the rich world. Scrapping Europe's Common Agricultural Policy, as egregious a system of protectionism as any, could do wonders for Africa's agriculture. The only places where the losers massively outnumber the winners are in countries, such as Cuba, that have shut the door on globalization completely.

All three of the losers that we have selected have been cruelly let down by their leaders. Russia's deplorable economic state is overwhelmingly a legacy of communism, and the failure of reform is largely the result of not liberalizing enough. Russia has too little business competition, too little foreign input into the economy, and far too much power in the hands of ex-communists who were simply handed huge monopolies during the country's botched privatization.

In the favela, the Brazilian flag hanging in the Gobettis' home carries a sadly ironic motto: Ordem e Progresso. Every aspect of government in Brazil has let down the favelas, from the corrupt leaders at the top, through its sluggish education system, to the local politicians, who, as Reginaldo notes, come through the favela just before election and then forget about it. The favela elects its own president; the last one took all the residents' money and now lives in a house that has a Jacuzzi.

It is harder to find evidence of misgovernment in Flint. Instead, the blame lies with the UAW and GM. It was noticeable how few unions flocked to the UAW's cause during the great strike of 1998. (By contrast, part-time workers at UPS, who seemed to be getting a rawer deal, received widespread support.) But it is also clear that in an age when industrial clusters are much in demand, General Motors wasted an enormous opportunity in Flint.

Bobo, who often works six-day weeks by choice, patently loves his job. He talks nostalgically about his early days at GM when it seemed more like a family business. He remembers the excitement when new models were announced. He admits that change is necessary, but he has never heard managers set an honest vision for the car firm's future—just a succession of unrealistic promises that have since been broken and ugly rumors about closures that have since come true.

A few years ago, Bobo and a friend put in a successful suggestion for a new welding-wire system. Savings from such suggestions were supposed to be split with the employee up to a limit of twenty thousand dollars, but GM did not measure the savings and fobbed them off with eight hundred dollars each. "It wasn't so much the money as the principle. . . . It's like we are the peasants and they are kings." Since then, things have not improved. Bobo has never met the current head of his factory; and, despite being a relatively well-read man, he can't even remember the name of GM's boss, Jack Smith. "I kind of gave up being interested in those things," he admits good-naturedly. "What's the point?" Had GM been better at answering that question, then Flint would have a more secure future, and nobody would have to blame globalization for anything.

Smoke Gets in Your Eyes

Our point is not to deny that globalization causes damage but to argue that it usually does so only because of bad decisions or weaknesses that nobody has ever sought to fix. Look behind any "global" disaster story, and you tend to find a trail of woeful mistakes or willful crimes by governments, companies, and individuals. As a final example of this, consider a victim that some critics of globalization hold up before all others as an example of capitalism run amok: the environment.

Here is an early critic of unrestrained commerce:

> The centralization of population in great cities exercises of itself an unfavorable influence. Putrefying vegetable and animal substances give off gases decidedly injurious to health and if these gases have no way to escape they inevitably poison the atmosphere. . . . The poor are obliged to throw all offal and garbage, all dirty water, often all disgusting drainage and excrement into the streets, being without any other means of disposing of them; they are thus compelled to infect the region of their dwelling.

Friedrich Engels's description of the condition of the working classes in nineteenth-century Manchester, England, could apply easily to slums all around the developing world and certainly to the favelas. The changes that globalization spurs on, from industrialization to urbanization to the spread of the internal-combustion engine, have produced not only human tragedies but environmental ones.

In Green circles, Brazil will always be associated with the rain forest (about which more below), but arguably its biggest environmental problems nowadays are brown. This is even true in the Amazon region, where cities such as Manaus and Belém have been growing rapidly. The gradual drift of tree harvesters into these cities is one reason why the depletion of the forest has slowed. But just like São Paulo—and cities throughout the developing world—the Amazonian cities are spitting out their own sort of muck: dirty water, foul air, and polluted soil. Urbanization has always been a dirty business, but now it is done with the added help of motor cars. In rich countries, there are forty cars per hundred people; in Latin America there are eight, and in China only two. The full horror of what is to come can be appreciated only from the back of an un–air-conditioned taxi on one of São Paulo's or Shanghai's already clogged freeways.

From a brown perspective, Brazil's biggest eyesore is Cubatao. For most visitors to Brazil, the capital of its petrochemical industry is only a ghastly aberration on the way from São Paulo to the beach—a brief smoggy valley of chimneys stuck between two long tunnels. (At night, the fires of the refinery can give the area a *Blade Runner*ish feel.) Until the 1950s, Cubatao was a marshy valley of Atlantic forest stuck halfway between São Paulo and the harbor at Santos. This convenient location proved its undoing. Chemical and oil companies from around the world filled in the marshes, ruining ecosystems and clogging waterways. As with Los Angeles, the surrounding hills made Cubatao into a natural smog trap. Workers poured into predictably horrible squatter camps. By the 1980s, the town's factories belched out 236.6 metric tons a year of what scientists like to call particulate matter. In 1982, one out of three Cubatao newborns failed to reach its first birthday, and there were particularly high instances of genetic diseases. Cubatao was known as "the valley of death" or "the most polluted city on earth" and inspired an ironic pop song, "Honeymoon in Cubatao."

Until 1983, the industrialists successfully managed to resist regulation. Then the cleanup began. Under pressure not just from Western Greens but also from groups such as the Association of Victims of Pollution and Bad Living Conditions, the companies introduced controls, and factories were forced to switch from oil to gas. Close to one billion dollars has been spent by the companies concerned. Nowadays, by whatever measures you use, air, water, and soil pollution are all a tiny proportion of what they once were.

Visit any company, and you will be shown a proud series of charts showing the reduction in emissions.

Nobody has more charts or tables than Ademar Salgosa does. This is partly because he is chairman of the local manufacturers association. But he also runs the best-known monument to the new Cubatao, a big chemical factory owned by Carbocloro, a joint venture between America's Occidental Petroleum and UNIPAR, a local firm. Carbocloro, by all accounts, was as dirty as any other Cubatao plant in the 1980s. Yet in the past decade it has twice won Occidental's competition for most environmentally friendly plant. In 1984, it used to consume ninety grams of mercury to make one ton of chlorine; in 1998, it consumed just 0.7 grams, and its emissions of mercury are now less than those from a dentist's office. The hillside behind the factory, which only a decade ago looked as if it had been napalmed, has regrown its Atlantic forest and become a wildlife sanctuary. And, in Salgosa's pièce de résistance, the effluent from the factory is pumped through an aquarium stocked full of carp and goldfish: There has been only one "accident" in thirteen years, and the worker responsible for the piscine slaughter was sacked.

One might imagine that Salgosa's efforts would have made him a pinup for the environmental movement—an example to other manufacturers in developing countries. Roberto Kishinami, Greenpeace's executive director in Brazil, gives Salgosa some good marks for transparency. But he is still adamant: The plant should be closed sooner rather than later. The problem is not how Carbocloro makes things but what it makes. Chlorine compounds are dirty and unnecessary, responsible for, among other things, ruining the ozone layer and lowering sperm counts. PVC, a chlorine product, is also hard to recycle.

The debate about whether chlorine is really that bad tends to set rich-world Greens against poor-world workers. Industrialists point out that chlorinated water saves millions of lives a year. Greenpeace prefers to concentrate on chlorine's often disastrous use as bleach in paper mills. But the question mark it poses over Carbocloro leaves the firm as an apt symbol both of how far Cubatao has come and how far it still has to go. "The town has recovered, but it still has the disease," says Aluizio Gomes de Souza, the leader of Cubatao's main environmental movement. None of the dozen or so industrialists and regulators we interviewed lived in the city and most smiled politely when it was suggested.

Moreover, as more companies come to the city, pollution is gradually rising again. The somewhat harassed local regulator, Sergio Pompeia, insists that it will be brought down, but many others are doubtful. To put it simply, the people of Cubatao need the companies to stay. As one recent academic study of the town puts it, the main argument against closing the plants is "the belief that industries have gone as far as they will in carrying out pollution control before closing their plants."[14]

For many environmentalists, this situation is symptomatic of globalization, as is the Hobson's choice it seems to give poor countries: pollute or be poor. "Though the market is a wonderful tool for economic progress," one relatively moderate guide to the subject concludes, "where its edges meet the planet it is mainly as a saw, shovel or smokestack—as an instrument of destruction rather than protection."[15] Globalization, as both the regulators and the Greens in Cubatao concede, sometimes helps restrict this damage: Multinational companies tend to be cleaner than their Brazilian counterparts and keener to abide by international standards. On the other hand, both the Greens and the regulators think that the relentless pressure from global competition forces firms to cut costs, and they suspect that corporate greenery is often one of the first things to be trimmed.

The root of the problem is nearly always that the cost of the environment is rarely accounted for correctly. Air pollution, in the dry language of economics, is a negative externality—something that companies price cheaply because they do not have to pay the cost. Meanwhile, clean air is a positive externality—something in which few people invest because the rewards are so dispersed. In China, according to the World Bank, air and water pollution incur costs of fifty-four billion dollars a year, 8 percent of the country's GDP; the health costs of air pollution in Bangkok are proportionately just as big. But it is not the polluter that pays the cost. Occasionally, you can nail a particular company (lead pollution fell dramatically in Mexico City after Pemex was ordered to make cleaner petrol), but normally it is hard to find the offending parties.

Easily the worst example is the oceans. The high seas of the world provide a textbook case of the "tragedy of the commons." Because nobody owns them, nobody feels responsibility for them. If a Norwegian fisherman does not pillage them, then his British rival will. In 1965, the world caught around fifty million tons of fish. Now the figure is 110 million. According to the Food and Agriculture Organization, around 60 percent of available fish stocks are now being harvested at unsustainable levels. The rain forest, too, appears to confound the market. To put it crudely, Brazil provides an environmental service to the world—its rain forest helps keep the planet cool—but it never receives any payment for it.

All this makes the environment a very difficult challenge. But it is equally obvious that many of the problems have nothing to do with unfettered capitalism. In fact, they can arise from exactly the opposite. One reason why fishing fleets continue to ravage the oceans is because governments pay them to do it: They spend twenty-one billion dollars a year supporting fish industries.

Far from preventing the destruction of the rain forest, Brazil's government initially spurred it on. In the 1960s and 1970s, under the slogan *integrar para nao entregar* (loosely translated as "Grab the Amazon before the foreigners do"), various military governments encouraged people to move into the Amazon. Much of the worst spoliation occurred during this period. Even today, the main reason why an area the size of Belgium is still felled each year is largely because there are no adequate rules concerning land tenure. Like the fishermen in the North Atlantic, people harvest their crop because they are worried somebody else will claim it.

These sorts of mistakes are repeated around the world. The most prominent source of pollution in Cubatao is an old steel foundry owned by Cosipa, a privatized steel company. The government has repeatedly come up with excuses for why the factory needs to stay open. Germany spends $7.3 billion a year to keep open coal mines—about ninety dollars per German or eighty-six thousand dollars per miner. In Australia, the state of Victoria spends $170 million more per year building roads for loggers than it gets back from the wood hauled out of the forest. The Worldwatch Institute reckons that there are $650 billion worth of subsidies going to environmentally destructive activities. Merely halting them would knock two thousand dollars off the average tax bill in the United States alone. Another way to accommodate the imbalance between the market and Green priorities would be to introduce tradable pollution permits, so that clean factories could profit from their cleanliness. These have been introduced with some success in America, but they remain much easier to talk about at economics conferences than to put into practice; in Cubatao, the idea remains literally a pipe dream. The regulatory agency that could address it does not have the resources to install permanent monitoring equipment on each of the chimneys.

The Buck Is Passed

Listen intently to people talking about how globalization is destroying the environment, and you can hear the sound of a buck being passed. Nobody would deny that Cubatao—just like Bobo, Orelsky, and the inhabitants of the Villa Prudente—has gotten something of a raw deal from globalization. Yet the town's recent history is living testament to the fact that local actions matter. Cubatao's cleanup happened because local politicians and business-people eventually took responsibility into their own hands. Salgosa's fish are a daily reminder to his workers to watch the environment.

Pollution is always somebody else's fault, and when there is nobody clear to blame it is just put at the feet of globalization (just as unemployment is in Flint). In fact, having some vague force on which all these things can be blamed suits everybody: the factories who would rather not have to spend more money making themselves cleaner; Greens who would rather not have to make precise cost estimates for the measures they favor; and even the people of Cubatao, who would rather not have to make a choice between the options.

This exemption from responsibility is worrying. It means that a process that should be associated with freedom often seems at odds with the concept of accountability. The losers end up hating the system rather than the people whose mistakes have left them in their predicament. In short, it prepares the way for a backlash.

Part Six

A Call to Arms

14

The Enemies Gather:
The Backlash Against Globalization

CONSIDER THE following warning, delivered at the beginning of 1999:

> If globalization is ruled merely by the laws of the market applied to suit
> the powerful, the consequences cannot but be negative. These are, for ex-
> ample, the absolutizing of the economy, unemployment, the reduction
> and deterioration of public services, the destruction of the environment
> and natural resources, the growing distance between rich and poor, un-
> fair competition which puts poor nations in a situation of ever increasing
> inferiority. . . . More and more in many countries in America a system
> known as neo-liberalism prevails; based on a purely economic concept of
> man, this system considers profit and the laws of the market as its only
> parameters, to the detriment of the dignity of and the respect due to indi-
> viduals and people.

You might imagine that these words sprang from the lips of Fidel Castro
or a particularly eloquent European trade unionist. In fact, the speaker was
one of the men who has done most to turbocharge the pace of globalization.
As archbishop of Kraków, Karol Wojtyla acted as the unofficial leader of the
Polish resistance to communist rule; on becoming Pope John Paul II in
1978, he took the cause global, throwing the weight of the Universal
Church behind his crusade. The businessmen and bankers who subsequently flooded into the former Soviet bloc in the 1990s did not carry portraits of the pope, as striking Polish workers had done during some of the
most heroic moments of the 1980s, but they had him to thank for helping to
remove the greatest barrier to the universal rule of market capitalism.

And yet, as the 1990s wore on, the pope became increasingly uneasy about what he had wrought. As he contemplated the spread of sin, selfishness, and inequality, he worried that "unbridled capitalism" was little improvement on "savage Marxism." In his Apostolic Exhortation to the Catholic Church in the Americas in January 1999, from which the above extract was taken, he urged priests not just to administer to the poor but to persuade the rich to forsake the false idols of globalism for the one true God. Globalization began to assume the same role in his life that communism once had.

The pope is hardly alone in his worries. George Soros, a man who has benefited financially as much as anyone from globalization, likely agreed with every word of the pope's exhortation. So did another beneficiary of tumbling international barriers, Nelson Mandela. "Is globalization only to benefit the powerful and the financiers, speculators, investors, and traders?" the South African leader demanded angrily of the gathered bigwigs at the World Economic Forum in Davos in 1999. "Does it offer nothing to women and children who are ravaged by the violence of poverty?"[1]

"Our global village has caught fire, from where we do not know," President Hosni Mubarak of Egypt agreed, in a speech at the same meeting. "In the emerging world there is a bitter sentiment of injustice, a sense that there must be something wrong with a system that wipes out years of hard-won development because of changes in market sentiment."[2] Even Kofi Annan warned that the spread of markets seemed to be outpacing the ability of many societies to adjust to them, leaving the world remarkably vulnerable to all the "isms" of the post–cold war world: populism, nationalism, chauvinism, fanaticism, terrorism, and protectionism.

There are still plenty of more visible scapegoats on which the great army of the disappointed can mistakenly pin its misfortunes: the Chinese in Asia, Turks and Algerians in Europe, the Jews almost everywhere. But for a remarkable number of people and a remarkable number of reasons, globalization itself is now the bogeyman of choice. In the United States, it is summoned up to explain every job lost in the Carolinas. Britain's Prince Charles blames it for the spread of genetically modified tomatoes. In Russia, it is held up to explain the brutality of NATO. To the Académie Française, and until recently to the Taliban, it has been synonymous with American degeneracy, albeit in slightly different ways. In 1999, the World Health Organization and the International Labor Organization even decided that globalization was officially bad for your health, blaming it for the 1.1 million deaths a year caused by work-related injuries.[3]

One convenient way to dismiss this backlash is to point out that it is as old as globalization itself. In 1774, two years before Adam Smith published *The Wealth of Nations*, Johann Herder worried that "all nations and all continents are under our shadow, and when a storm shakes two twigs in Europe, how the entire world trembles and bleeds!"[4] Early critics even anticipated today's worries about the environment: "Society expands and intensifies," lamented Adam Muller, a German economist, in 1809. "By a letter, by a bill of exchange, by a bar of silver, the London merchant reaches out his hand across the oceans to his correspondent in Madras, and helps him to wage the great war against the earth."

Globalization and antiglobalization seem to be dialectically related: The more globalization advances, challenging established ways of doing things, the more some retreat into the certainties of their ancient cultures. The overflowing airport leads inexorably to the overflowing mosque, but the former, crucially, is more powerful. For every tribal elder who warns against the corruption of the outside world, there are usually dozens of youngsters who cannot wait to get their hands on Coca-Cola and Pamela Anderson; and so the process continues.

This argument has been put perhaps most starkly by Thomas Friedman in his recent appraisal of globalization, *The Lexus and the Olive Tree*. Globalization for Friedman is as inevitable as the dawn. ("Generally speaking, I think it is a good thing that the sun come up every morning. It does more good than harm. But even if I didn't much care for the dawn, there isn't much I could do about it.") This view, understandable though it might have been with the Dow at record levels and the Asian contagion apparently tamed, seems naively similar to the outlook of Keynes's "inhabitant of London" on the eve of the First World War.[5] The world economy rapidly unraveled in the years after 1914, and the past twenty-five years of global integration have been anything but smooth. The great scare in the autumn of 1998—particularly the moment when Russia went bankrupt—now seems like a momentary blip. But at the time it was a damned close-run thing.

The current supremacy of what Friedman calls the electronic herd was not just a product of technology and financial cunning. It required liberalizing politicians to step out of the way and laws to change. Those laws, however, could be changed back again. Given the carnage that globalization has caused (or is said to have caused) in much of the third world, not to mention the loathing that America often inspires, it is not inevitable that Pamela Anderson and Coca-Cola will always trump the mullahs. Meanwhile, throughout much of the developed world, the constituency for globalization seems distinctly fainthearted.

In fact globalization's own status is not unlike that of Catholicism. The real problem often has less to do with staunch opponents than tepid believers and the abuses of its leaders. The world did not simply lurch into protectionism after the First World War; the seeds were sown long before by people who claimed to be free traders: politicians making compromises and industrialists claiming exceptions. We will return to these faint hearts, but we will begin at the fringes with the outright heretics: the people who hate globalization and encourage others to do the same.

Rage Against the Machine

As good a place to start as any is the protest against the World Trade Organization in Seattle in November 1999. The Seattle riots, which attracted fifty thousand protestors, were a bizarre event, balancing the comical and the terrifying, the organized and the anarchic. Most of the organizing was done by the growing group of nongovernmental organizations dedicated to halting, or at least emasculating, globalization. Long before the WTO met, pamphlets had been posted, meetings organized, alliances formed, and, most important, e-mails sent. Around 1,500 NGOs signed an anti-WTO declaration set up by Public Citizen. The WTO was arguably stung to death by a new on-line phenomenon that researchers at the RAND Corporation have dubbed an "NGO swarm—a movement with no central leadership or command structure; it is multiheaded, impossible to decapitate."

The comedy came from many of the protestors. Some dressed as turtles; self-described Vegan Dykes went topless; banners declared that "the WTO is a hazardous waste" and advocated the need to "make love not profits"; for a while at least, everybody seemed to enjoy the street theater. But other banners suggested a more sinister agenda on behalf of some of the protestors— "Clinton, Blair, they're no good, hit them on the head with a piece of wood," said one; "Fuck the civil, let's get disobedient," screamed another. The protests eventually degenerated into violence (in much the same way that an initially cheerful Carnival against Capitalism had in London earlier that year). Eventually, the whole of the center of Seattle became a war zone.

Many Americans seemed perplexed by this display. Seattle—an export-oriented port city—was an odd place to protest against trade; previous urban protests in the country had touched most people in an immediate visceral way. Everybody knew somebody in Vietnam. The Los Angeles riots sprang from feelings of injustice that anybody who saw the Rodney King video could understand. But why riot over the level of tariffs on textiles from India or the need to reconsider trade-related intellectual-property rights? For many, the issues seem quaint and arcane, even if the National Guard had to be called out. In fact, the revolt against globalization in Seattle could have been an early insight into the official politics of the next century: a continuing battle between a technocratic commercial elite with a minimal grasp of politics and a disenfranchised, angry minority with a minimal grasp of economics.

The opposition is not only from the left and its army of trade unionists, environmentalists, and students. Some of the most terrifying assaults have come from the right. In the same year as the WTO meeting, some two hundred federal agents were combing the woods of western North Carolina for somebody who had allegedly taken a much more brutal response to globalization: Eric Rudolph. An alleged member of a group called Christian Identity, Rudolph stands accused not only of shooting abortionists but also of planting a bomb at the Atlanta Olympics. Letters that the police believe Rudolph wrote promise "Death to the New World Order." As Mark Potok, an academic who specializes in hate groups, told *The New Yorker*, it was not surprising that Rudolph chose the Olympics: "The Olympics is the apotheosis of race mixing, of one worldism, of everything that Christian Identity despises."[6]

For people like Rudolph and Timothy McVeigh, the main perpetrator of the Oklahoma City bombing that killed 169 people, the United States is the victim of a conspiracy that is being masterminded by sinister international organizations—the United Nations is a particular favorite—and assisted by internal traitors such as the federal government, Wall Street, the media elite, and, most loathed of all, the Bureau of Alcohol, Tobacco, and Firearms. Groups such as the Patriots and Christian Identity generally consist of Americans who have been left behind: blue-collar workers whose wives now must work; unemployed people who imagine that immigrants are taking their jobs; and ranchers in Montana who have seen urban billionaires buying up huge chunks of the state. Every day, God-fearing Americans are being turned into slaves in a worldwide plantation economy, they argue, and the only way to avoid enslavement is to take up guns and fight.

Outside the United States, antiglobal groups tap into the same emotions of despair and incomprehension, but they reach exactly the opposite conclusion: The United States is not the slave but the enslaver. In an uncanny repetition of the way that Continental reactionaries regarded liberal, globalist, "Jewish" Great Britain a century ago, nearly all antiglobalists focus on "the Great Satan." In some cases, these are merely childish repetitions of old fables. Mahathir's thundering against America's Jewish speculators could be based on the kaiser's suspicions about England or on the tract by a nineteenth-century Frenchman entitled "Is the Englishman a Jew?" that cleverly decided that "Anglo-Saxon" is actually just a misheard version of "Isaac's son."[7] But there are also plenty of other people prepared to pick up their guns and bombs to fight this menace.

Two groups whose antiglobalist messages often go underappreciated are Japan's Aum Shinrikyo and Mexico's Zapatistas. The former is a paramilitary religious cult that draws its inspiration from a combination of Buddhism, yoga, and paranoia. Its members believe that Japan will respond to intensified competition from other Asian nations by subjecting its citizens to military rule; this in turn will provoke the United States to launch an all-out war on Japan before trying to establish a puppet world government. The organization's decision to release sarin gas into the Tokyo subway in March 1995, killing twelve people and injuring five thousand, was part of a bizarre preparation for this conflict.

The Zapatista movement—a coalition of Indian peasants and urban intellectuals that has fought a long-running guerrilla war against Mexico— also fears globalization. It equates the current drive to open up the Mexican economy with the invasion of the country by the Spanish in the sixteenth century. The movement chose the first day that NAFTA was in force, January 1, 1994, to seize control of several cities in the southern Mexican state of Chiapas. Meanwhile, the Zapatistas' local opponents in Chiapas also blame foreigners for the area's misfortunes, with local mayors accusing outsiders of "twisting the minds of the Indian people," local columnists snarling about the satanic intervention of foreigners, and one local union calling for them all to be rounded up and expelled.[8]

However, the most powerful antiglobalist group is militant Islam. This is partly a matter of size (it touches the lives of a billion people, from Indonesia to the former Soviet Union to inner cities across Europe) and partly a matter of stridency: Witness not just September 11, but also the way that the mullahs passed a death sentence on Salman Rushdie, a citizen of another country who wrote an allegedly heretical book. Militant Islam may be an exercise in globalization in its own right (it is indifferent to national and ethnic boundaries and determined to unite the entire world in the worship of Muhammad), but it appeals powerfully to people who have seen their lives disrupted by urbanization. In Iran, the Ayatollah Khomeini rose on a wave of popular opposition to the reigning shah's wide-ranging attempt to modernize the country. An article in the subsequent Iranian constitution even prohibits "extravagance and wastefulness in all matters related to the economy, including consumption, investment, production, distribution, and services."

Naturally, there are hundreds of millions of Muslims who take the antiglobalist part of their creed as seriously as many Western Catholics take the ban on contraception. You can find weird signs of globalization even in the hotbeds of Islamic extremism: In 1995, in a particularly beleaguered corner of Beirut, an advertisement for a total-quality-management seminar sat surrounded by the familiar yellow flags of Hezbollah. Nevertheless, there is a wing of Islam that is dedicated to the overthrow of everything globalization stands for.

Osama bin Laden, who declared a jihad against the United States in 1997, is part of that wing. As early as 1982, bin Laden was preaching in Saudi mosques on the necessity of boycotting American-made goods, even though the United States was supporting his own movement in Afghanistan. Bin Laden's fury at the modern world, particularly its American component, was explicit in 1997. "In our religion it is our duty to make jihad," he explained to CNN, "so that God's word is the one exalted to the heights and so that we drive the Americans away from all Muslim countries." The new world order, according to bin Laden, was simply an American ploy:

> The collapse of the Soviet Union made the U.S. more haughty, and it has started to look at itself as a master of this world and established what it calls the new world order. . . . The U.S. today has set a double standard, calling whoever goes against its injustice a terrorist. It wants to occupy our countries, steal our resources, impose on us agents to rule us . . . and wants us to agree to all these.[9]

Sympathy for the Devil

Osama bin Laden neatly illustrates two ironic but disturbing things about the way in which globalization and its opponents interact. The first, which might be described as terrorist specific, is that the same forces that have helped speed globalization—the end of the cold war, the spread of technology, the lowering of borders—have made life easier for maverick bombers. Rather than being worried about missiles from Moscow raining down on New York, security people now fret about rogue states and individuals. Globalization has made it easier for a single person to acquire a nuclear device, take it across relatively undefended borders, and leave it in New York. Indeed, one horrifying way in which globalization might come sharply to a halt would be the terrorist detonation of a nuclear or biological bomb, something that, since September 11, no longer seems so remote.

The second point is more general: Globalization's opponents, both violent and peaceful, have been among the cleverest exploiters of its process. The sadly untrue rumor put around that bin Laden was a member of White's, a smart London gentlemen's club, did have an element of believability: In his youth, bin Laden had shown every sign of being a regular young Saudi cosmocrat. In his interviews, he talks articulately about things such as oil prices and the effects of supply and demand (before blaming any problems on "America's agent," Saudi Arabia). Even while bin Laden lived in a part of Afghanistan that could be described as medieval, he transferred money undetected around the world, keeping in touch with his followers by satellite phone—an appropriate form of communication for a man whose brother was on the board of Iridium. His various *fatwas* were faxed from Afghanistan to sympathizers in other countries, especially England; many of them were reprinted in Arabic newspapers based in London that were themselves transmitted to the Middle East. Even his 1997 interview with CNN was a masterful piece of global dissemination. The alleged mastermind of the bombing of the American embassy in Nairobi, Haroun Fazil, said that he found out about the jihad from CNN rather than from bin Laden's organization.[10]

Similarly, the Zapatistas have cleverly used the Internet to organize a worldwide network of supporters—a public-relations coup that has proved to be a powerful restraint on the Mexican government. The anarchic coalition that is the American Patriot movement is held together, above all, by the Internet. Any Montana-dwelling gun nut with a computer and a modem can easily become a member of a worldwide network of fellow travelers. The Internet is chockablock with militia bulletin boards. (There are several websites devoted to Rudolph.) Log on to the World Wide Web, and you can learn everything from who belongs to the Trilateral Commission to where to buy the most powerful semiautomatic weapons.

There is even a new group of activists, nicknamed "hacktivists," who engage in "digital rebellion" against the information-industrial complex. Where their radical ancestors trespassed and poached, they unleash viruses or write graffiti on corporate websites. More legally, activists set up derogatory websites. A page established by the NikeWatch Campaign, which is devoted to the shoe firm's labor practices, comes under the heading "Just stop it." Following the success of websites such as walmartsucks.com, various big firms have registered domains with their own name followed by *sucks* or preceded by *I hate*.

Indeed, as the swarm of NGOs that descended on Seattle demonstrated so emphatically, the best pressure groups are often better at playing the globalization game than the multinational companies that they demonize. The world's largest environmental pressure group, Greenpeace, is everything that today's multinationals dream of being: networked, flexible, project driven, and value led. The organization is both tightly centralized and wonderfully decentralized; it can draw on a membership of two million people and annual revenues of one hundred million dollars, yet it usually reflects the immediate concerns of its local members. Greenpeace's humiliation of Shell over the Brent Spar rig was a master class in global media management: The oil firm was universally condemned for trying to sink the rig, even though it was by no means clear that sinking it would be the environmentally damaging option.

As Seattle showed, again, radical activists are increasingly turning their attention from particular companies to free trade itself. A decade ago, none of the main American environmental groups had anybody permanently working on the subject.[11] Now they seem to focus on little else. The Sierra Club took out advertisements against "fast track"; the head of the National Wildlife Federation also testified against expanding NAFTA. Trade unions helped scuttle not just fast track but also the Multilateral Agreement on Investment. Articulate spokespeople have learned how to blend protectionism with more emotional calls for human rights. Listening to Thea Lee of the AFL-CIO explain gently how in the United States "lives were lost to limit the working day and for the right to bargain collectively," it is hard to understand why the United States should allow its companies to seek out cheap workers abroad. And, as with the environment, some of the points raised are fair ones: Why, for instance, do multinationals insist that the developing world accept Western patent law but not its labor or environmental ones? Under NAFTA, claims Lee, a Mexican factory can be closed down if it is suspected of counterfeiting but not if it employs children.[12]

Fundamentally, globalization is quite a hard-hearted process. By increasing transparency, it unearths harsh facts that can be used against it. As Nadine Gordimer recently pointed out, the old saying "The poor are always with us" has now been joined by "We are always with them." She then went on to explain: "We come face-to-face with the victims of pandemic ethnic conflicts and multinational manipulative greed on television and on the Internet."[13] Here as elsewhere, globalization is never praised for bringing this evidence to the court, just immediately put in the dock. Multinational greed may be the force that has done the most to rid the world of poverty, but it will seldom get the credit.

All the antiglobal movement needs for success in most countries is some clever person to give antiglobalism a respectable, intellectual face and political leadership. There is a long line of people trying to fill both roles.

Gray's Elegy

The London School of Economics has globalization written all over it. The school was founded by Sidney and Beatrice Webb to provide professional administrators for Britain's expanding empire. Today, more than half the school's students are from outside the United Kingdom, and the faculty is stuffed full of sabbatical men, forever on the move from one international freebie to another.

Yet it is here, in a poky room in the school's European Institute, that one of the most uncompromising critics of globalization has his lair. In the 1980s, John Gray was a leading member of a tiny and embattled band of academic Thatcherites. He wrote a fine book on F. A. von Hayek, hung around in Liberty Fund circles, and became a member of Margaret Thatcher's informal brain trust. As the Conservative Party collapsed in the 1990s, however, so did Gray's faith in free markets, and he embraced a succession of alternatives, ranging from communitarianism to environmentalism and culminating in antiglobalism.

Gray is no Luddite. He celebrates the fact that trade and technology have been bringing people together for centuries. His taste in ideas is as cosmopolitan and eclectic as anybody's. (The only decorations in his austere office are two pictures of his mentor, Isaiah Berlin.) But Gray is convinced that the "Washington consensus," which insists that global free markets will spread prosperity and democracy across the planet, is spreading misery and alienation instead. The globalists are guilty of cultural illiteracy, he argues, in that they fail to realize that different societies produce different sorts of capitalism and that the sort of free-market relationships that seem natural in the United States often seem perverse in other societies. Worse still, they are guilty of intellectual utopianism, justifying the misery with talk about the long run. For Gray, Marxism and globalization are peas from the same Enlightenment pod.

Gray argues that "imperial laissez-faire" is responsible for a storm that is destroying social bonds across the planet and preparing the way for a bloody fundamentalist backlash. In the United States, where the storm has blown most ferociously, it has already broken the family, proletarianized the middle classes, and swollen the prison population to gulag proportions. In the rest of the world, its consequences will be even more devastating.

Free-trade fundamentalism confronts the world with a choice between two equally unappealing futures. The first would see the application of a "new Gresham's law," in which bad capitalists would drive good ones out of business, and decent wages and career ladders would become things that you read about in history books. The second prospect would feature the rise of prosperity-destroying protectionism, as more and more mixed-economy moderates are forced to choose between bowing down to pure capitalism or protecting their traditional ways of life. "Americans don't realize how peculiar they are," Gray sighs, casting a wistful glance at his twin portraits of Isaiah Berlin.

All along the Watchtower

This is not the place to go into why Gray is wrong but simply to consider how many other intelligent people think generally the same as he does. Gray is no longer a lone wolf in the groves of academia in the way that he was as a Thatcherite. The reigning orthodoxy in most of the world's humanities departments is antiglobalism. In many parts of Europe it is hard to think of any intellectual who might be described as "proglobalization." An antiglobalist screed called L'Horreur Économique by a French novelist, Viviane Forrester, is set to be the continent's biggest economics best-seller since Karl Marx's Das Kapital, having sold six hundred thousand copies in France and Germany alone. Anointed gurus such as Michel Foucault taught that Western history is a history of repression. Ethnic study courses teach that what used to be called the triumph of the West involved the oppression and impoverishment of the third world. The bookstores of most university towns are groaning with books like The Silent Takeover; No Logo; One World, Ready or Not; and When Corporations Rule the World. One of the better academic summaries of the sociological effects of the process is titled simply Globalization and Its Discontents.

Already some respected leftish critics of globalization have started to warn that the current system might lead to fascism. "If a new political economy cannot emerge to tame the new force of turbo-capitalism, the wave of the future could be populism," warns Edward Luttwak, "a revolt of the less educated against elite rule, elite opinions, elite values and the elite's consensus on how the economy should be run."[14] In one rather frightening article, Richard Rorty, a leading philosopher, forecast that globalization will produce a world economy owned by a cosmopolitan upper class "in which an attempt by any one country to prevent the immiseration of its workers may result in depriving them of employment." As workers gradually realize that they are getting a raw deal, the ordinary people will decide the system has failed and start looking around for a strongman, "someone willing to assure them that, once he is elected, the smug bureaucrats, tricky lawyers, over-paid bond salesmen, and post-modernist professors will no longer call the shots."[15]

There are also plenty of businesspeople committed to taming globaliza-tion. The list of people who have written books warning about the evils of unregulated markets includes both George Soros, the greatest speculator of the age, and Jimmy Goldsmith, perhaps its greatest corporate raider. Inter-estingly, both men are cosmopolitans par excellence and have made a virtue of their rootlessness. Goldsmith spent most of the last years of his life, not to mention a considerable sum of his own money, warning against "the trap" of free trade. His brother Teddy continues the fight to this day.

In mainstream politics, antiglobalism has managed to unite people from both ends of the political spectrum. Patrick Buchanan sounds like an old-school socialist when he rails against American companies that export American jobs. Wages rise while profits soar, he laments; wealth becomes more concentrated while the middle class is decimated; and society begins to fall apart at the seams. "Broken homes, uprooted families, vanished dreams, delinquency, vandalism, crime," he writes in *The Great Betrayal*, "these are the hidden costs of free trade." Protectionism, claims Buchanan, is not "some alien dogma" but an all-American policy supported by Lincoln, Washington, and Teddy Roosevelt.[16] Appropriately enough, the support for his "pitchfork rebellion" comes from the sort of blue-collar patriots who used to provide the hard core of the Democratic Party.

From the other side of the political spectrum, Jerry Brown, a frequent lib-eral candidate for the presidency, has reached much the same conclusion. The former governor of California is now mayor of Oakland, a port city that would seem to have much to gain from globalization. Yet Brown will have none of it. He was a fierce opponent of both NAFTA and the Clinton admin-istration's decision to bail out Mexico during the peso crisis. Before he be-came mayor, Brown hosted a radio program on which antiglobalization was a well-worn theme and multinational companies were often treated as little more than tools of the devil. Sitting in his gloomy office, Brown worries that the port of Oakland brings few jobs and plenty of "particulate matter." Wouldn't it be better to turn it into a waterfront playground, just as his hometown, San Francisco, has done? He complains that Oakland is being forced "to serve up the good life for people who live elsewhere." He loathes

Bill Clinton's drive to put "a human face on globalization." This is "gibberish masquerading as deep concern," he says. It is also "mendacious," "Orwellian," and "contemptuous of the common sensibilities of the people."

In one way, the idea that "Governor Moonbeam" (as he has been known) is against globalization is something of a relief. On the other hand, Brown's record of being ahead of the curve on a whole range of issues—from the environment to flat taxes to campaign-finance reform—is an extremely impressive one. And, as history shows, men like Buchanan and Brown do not have to win for their ideas to triumph. In 1896, a political hurricane named William Jennings Bryan hailed from the farm states and proclaimed that mankind was being "crucified on a cross of gold." The agricultural recession and price deflation that had raged since the end of the Civil War meant that a farmer who could have paid off his debts with one thousand bushels of wheat in 1865 needed three times as many in 1896. Bryan's solution was a fairly mad one: increase the money supply by moving America off the gold standard, replacing it with free silver. But his rebellion picked up the support of the silver owners. Bryan was defeated at the polls by William McKinley in both 1896 and 1900, but he undoubtedly helped pave the way for Teddy Roosevelt's crackdown on the robber barons.

From this perspective, it is worrying that opposition to globalization seems to be spreading inward from the political extremes. Moderate conservatives who blanch at Buchanan's nativism still worry that bad culture is driving out good. Liberals wonder if the global economy is being transformed into a giant casino. A particular worry is the rise of third-way politics. So far, this wonderfully vague and thus eminently expandable creed has been largely a rubric under which pragmatic social democrats such as Gerhard Schroeder and Tony Blair can show that they have accepted the domestic market-driven reforms of their conservative opponents. Yet the urge to intervene is strong, and their suspicions of the workings of the free-market economy are palpable.

Having been forced to shield these impulses in the national arena, the urge to intervene in the international one is often strong. The European Union may be unable to nationalize industries, but it is an obsessive regulator. Third-wayers jumped on the Asian crisis as evidence that "intelligent regulation" is preferable to the creative destruction of unfettered capitalism. "A very important debate has begun, sparked by the general realization that you cannot leave people unprotected before the global market," argued Anthony Giddens, the director of the London School of Economics and Tony Blair's globalization guru. "There is a will to recognize the need for some new

governance of the world economy." "A way must be found to bring the
Frankenstein of deregulated global markets under control," chimed in Jean-
Paul Fitoussi, an adviser to French prime minister Lionel Jospin.[17] *Le Monde*
hailed the protests in Seattle as a victory for "a new idea"—that "the world is
not for sale."

Intervention is far from politically foolhardy. Public opinion is about
evenly split on the merits of free trade. A *BusinessWeek* survey in December
1999 found that 52 percent of those questioned felt sympathetic to the protestors in Seattle. A late 1998 survey by the Angus Reid Group (on behalf of
The Economist) of twelve thousand people in twenty-two countries found
that 48 percent of them favored protection. In the same year, *L'Humanité*
commissioned a poll of French attitudes toward capitalism: Fifty-three percent associated it with fear or rebellion, against just 22 percent with hope or
enthusiasm.[18] In America, another poll carried out at about the same time
(when unemployment was close to a thirty-year low) found that 58 percent
of Americans agreed that foreign trade was "bad for the American economy
because cheap imports hurt wages."[19] Most Americans' opinions of the merits of unrestrained capitalism dived further after the Enron saga in 2002.

On specific issues, the protectionists can often outmaneuver the free-
traders. The losers from open markets are usually concentrated and visible,
popping up on television whenever a steel mill is closed or a factory moved
abroad; the winners are dispersed and invisible. As Robert Reich has put it:

> Buried in the economic theory of comparative advantage is one stark po-
> litical reality: trade benefits an economy only to the extent that it restruc-
> tures the economy, making it more efficient. Trade reduces the demand
> for people and capital where they are less productive and increases the de-
> mand for them where they can be more productive. The bigger the gains
> from trade, the bigger the dislocation. . . . The number of Americans
> who feel they are among the losers—or, more importantly, sense that
> they could be—is a large portion of the electorate.[20]

Globalization is such a broad and brutal process that it often seems hard
to defend. You do not have to be particularly left-wing to shudder at the
Guardian headline that read WHAT IS THE DIFFERENCE BETWEEN TANZANIA AND
GOLDMAN SACHS? ONE IS AN AFRICAN COUNTRY THAT MAKES $2.2 BILLION A YEAR
AND SHARES IT AMONG 25 MILLION PEOPLE. THE OTHER IS AN INVESTMENT BANK
THAT MAKES $2.6 BILLION AND SHARES IT BETWEEN 161 PEOPLE. Is Peter Drucker—
arguably the most reliable prophet of our times—wrong to warn American

bosses that their capacity for rewarding themselves while sacking others cannot continue? Few modern bosses, he says, "can even imagine the hatred, contempt and fury that has been created." Who has not worried that a global financial virus will have the same effect on their savings that it has already had on the savings of millions of middle-class people across Asia? And who has not wondered if Hollywood's love affair with violence is barbarizing the world's youth?

The Enemy Within

It is precisely these sorts of doubts that represent globalization's greatest weakness. In the end, all the militant Muslims and pitchfork rebellions probably matter less than the much more powerful people who claim to be in favor of globalization in theory but find endless excuses to oppose it in practice. The political ineptness of the cosmocrats aside, globalization's main problem is not the ideologues who hate it but that familiar old villain, the pragmatic politician.

The most obvious problem is the naked opportunism that drives the typical politician. Far too many of them want to reap the benefits of a smaller world without bearing any of the costs. Thus, they approve of exports and the jobs they generate but disapprove of imports. Or approve of money flowing into their countries but disapprove of it flowing out. Or approve of economic liberalization but disapprove of political rights. Lee Kwan Yew denounces "the boys in red suspenders" with one breath and invites international companies to make Singapore their regional hub with another. Lee and other Asian leaders are engaged in a delicate experiment to see whether you can combine Western economics with "Oriental politics." The Chinese leadership is trying to create "capitalism with Chinese characteristics"— namely, authoritarianism and xenophobia.

Two phenomena make it particularly easy for pragmatic politicians to find problems with globalization. The first is nationalism. Refusing to accept a country's cars or cheese is a politically inexpensive way of showing patriotism. In some emerging countries, this has a more violent undercurrent. India's decision to explode its nuclear bomb was as much an obscene salute to the new world order as its discrimination against Kentucky Fried Chicken restaurants. ("The air is thick with ugliness," Arundhati Roy wrote about India in 1998, "and there's the unmistakable stench of fascism in the breeze.") In places such as Quebec and Scotland that are not countries but want to be, politicians claim that their only chance to defend local identities in a world of footloose capital and Hollywood trash is to keep as much power as close to home as possible.

The other thing that predisposes many pragmatic politicians against globalization is the threat that it poses to their bailiwick: the state. Free trade challenges modern governments' habits of taking on mind-boggling ranges of responsibilities, from steering the economy to guaranteeing collective welfare. As soon as the government starts to regulate (or run) an industry, it becomes the prey of lobbyists and pressure groups. And as soon as it claims to look after the welfare of its citizens, it becomes the protector of workers who claim that free trade is damaging their livelihood. Granted, the past two decades have seen governments try desperately to reduce their responsibilities. But the expansion of the state has merely been slowed, not reversed.

In such circumstances, drift is often the main enemy. There may be no new Smoot-Hawley Tariff on the horizon, but free trade is constantly in danger of being eroded by a thousand small cuts: All those "trifling" concessions to lobbyists and "compassionate" exceptions for the vulnerable few eventually add up. Few of the American congresspeople who lined up to condemn the "flood of cheap steel" into their country in 2002 viewed themselves as protectionists; they were just less interested in the principle of free trade than they were in the fact that American steel towns looked as if they were being devastated. Few of the Republicans who voted against giving Bill Clinton fast-track authority in trade negotiations wanted to gum up the world trading system. They just gave more mind to their hatred of Bill Clinton than they did to a little thing like the international economy. By the same token, Bill Clinton seemed to be thinking principally of the election hopes of Al Gore (and the need to cuddle up to American trade unions) when, in Seattle, he tried to impose strict labor-standards provisions on poor countries and talked about his sympathies with the demonstrators. And these examples were during the good times. Ever since the American economy turned, more attention has been paid to the trade deficit, which is caused by evil foreigners unfairly selling cheap goods to Americans.

The WTO's disaster in Seattle may have grabbed the headlines, but the almost unnoticed collapse of the Multilateral Agreement on Investment (MAI) in 1998 may prove a longer-lasting case study in the politics of drift, opportunism, and complacency. The basic idea of the MAI was a good one: to do for cross-border investment what the Uruguay round of the GATT had done for trade in goods and services. Cross-border foreign direct investment had grown to $350 billion in 1996; the MAI was supposed to be a rule book that would give people building factories in foreign countries some security. But the execution was seriously flawed. To begin with, the project was given to the OECD, the rich country club, rather than the broader WTO. This predictably enraged the very developing countries the MAI was designed to help. A massive antiglobal protest began, typified by a full-page advertisement, sponsored by the International Forum on Globalization, asking whether corporations should govern the world and warning readers that "the same wonderful people that brought you NAFTA, the WTO, Fast Track and the Asian financial mess" now had a new product that would lead to all sorts of horrors, including the "McBig Ben," "The Mitsubishi Taj Mahal," and "Disney presents the Canadian Broadcasting Corporation."[21] Angry at the roles granted to businesses in the discussions, labor movements and environmental groups demanded specific protection for workers and trees, and the project was rapidly shelved.

However, the interesting point is that even without this fusillade support among the developed countries was weak. Politicians of all sorts seemed unconcerned about a project that seemed boring and arcane. When Jack Straw, a senior minister in Tony Blair's government, was asked to give his opinion about the MAI on *Question Time*, a BBC talk show, he said he would be happy to do so, but he did not know what it was. The only politicians who were interested in the MAI were those trying to stop it. The European Union and the United States, the two bodies you might expect to support the package, both demanded concessions that would have made nonsense of the whole project: The EU wanted to be able to discriminate in favor of local investors, while the Americans thought that states should be allowed to stop foreigners from buying farmland. Politics, clearly, is still a local affair.

You Say "Tomato"

At the end of his polemic against globalization, Edward Luttwak reassures his readers that what he calls turbo-capitalism is just a phase: It, too, will pass. Even leaving aside another huge terrorist attack, it is possible to imagine any number of events that might mark that passing: a war in the Middle East, the complete collapse of the next round of the WTO, a savage post-Enron recession, the rise of a populist politician committed to reining in the modern "malefactors of great wealth," as Teddy Roosevelt called them. The chances remain, however, that the globalization caravan will not career off the road so much as just run out of gas: The passengers will realize that they are gradually slipping back down the hill only when they are already halfway down.

How will this happen? If we knew the answer, we would be shorting the necessary stock markets and hoarding supplies rather than writing a book.

However, consider the way that two disturbing trends—the drift toward regionalism and the repeated trade battles over food—might encourage each other.

Nobody has ever managed to find out whether there is such a thing as a guilt-free General Motors executive. Yet for anybody from GM who is even slightly insecure about his or her position, a trip to London recently has likely been a distinctly Kafkaesque experience. Pick up a tabloid newspaper, flip on a television talk show, study the graffiti on walls, and you are greeted by a constant refrain: "GM is evil." At Notting Hill dinner parties, people plot how to drive GM back to America; in Soho pubs, people mutter that GM is dangerous and disgusting. Just about every titled person in London from the marchioness of Worcester to Prince Charles wants to get you.

In fact, the *GM* that has so enraged Britons stands for *genetically modified*, as in GM food (though opponents now seem to have stopped adding the word *food*, presumably out of fear that it will be contaminated by the deadly initials). The furor in Britain dates back to February 1999 and a bit of routine political tit for tat. Britain's Conservative Party, which took a drubbing over the mad cow–disease fiasco, accused Tony Blair's Labor government of ignoring health risks about GM food. Labor replied (correctly) that there was no credible scientific evidence that it was dangerous. But somehow the phrase *Frankenstein food* got out, and soon Monsanto, the American multinational that some public-relations genius had rather creepily decided to rebrand as a "life sciences" company, was on trial.

One MP labeled Monsanto "public enemy number one" in a debate in the House of Commons. "Frankenstein," a costumed environmentalist, started appearing outside supermarkets, warning that they sold GM foods, from which, inevitably, the supermarkets soon refrained. According to one piece of research for the British government in 1999, only one in a hundred Britons (a pollster's way of saying nobody) thought that GM products such as herbicide-resistant soybeans and late-ripening tomatoes were good for society. An organic farmer from Gloucestershire named Charles Windsor gave the anti-GM crusade a royal seal of approval, warning about "an Orwellian future" in the *Daily Mail*.

Nor is this just a British phenomenon. Despite an expensive advertising campaign by Monsanto, antagonism runs deep across most of Europe. A number of powerful Japanese food-buying cooperatives—which claim nearly two million members—are trying to screen out or label GM foods. In India, people working under the name Operation Cremation Monsanto have burned fields of GM seeds.

To many Americans, these odd noises coming from overseas may seem like a slightly dottier, more global replay of Britain's mad-cow farce. After all, there are GM foods in most American supermarkets. In the United States, biotechnology has generally been something that you buy shares in, not something you boycott. Most of the arguments against GM are more sentimental than logical. Genetic modification, albeit of a more gradual sort, has taken place in fields for centuries without any harm to humans. The charge that efficient farming per se despoils the countryside seems a little Luddite, not to say selfish. In many inhospitable corners of the world, GM's efficiency might be the difference between a harvest and starvation. The area in which there seems to be the most genuine scientific uncertainty has to do with GM seeds' effect on local ecosystems; potentially, they could spread with the winds and contaminate neighboring plants and insects.

With clearer labeling (something that the multinationals insanely resisted at first) and a degree of goodwill on both sides, some sort of consensus should have been achievable. Yet it has not emerged. Some of the reasons for this failure have nothing to do with globalization. In particular, the concern about GM foods reflects a much more general (and arguably overdue) questioning about what agribusiness has been thrusting down our throats. The fuss about GM food in 1999 coincided, first, with a scare about Belgian chickens and pigs being fed a carcinogenic substance, which led to a huge culling, and then with a widely publicized incident in which people became ill after drinking poorly made Coca-Cola. Many would argue that the only reason why a similar backlash has not happened in America is that politically well connected agribusinesses have done better jobs of hiding their disasters.

On the other hand, a second, nastier trend is also at work. Ever since a certain tea party in Massachusetts, the need for nourishment has been a potent force for transatlantic disharmony. Food safety now looks like one of the easiest places for ugly nationalist emotions to hide. Europe's Common Agricultural Policy is the single most harmful piece of protectionism in the world; its American equivalent is not much better. OECD countries spent $362 billion on farm subsidies in 1998—around 1.4 percent of GDP. Politicians, whether they are presidential candidates in Iowa or prospective deputies in Normandy, conspicuously avoid talk of reform. The vilification of Monsanto (not to mention the fuss about Coke) was just one example of a growing anti-American slant to the debate about food in Europe. The GM controversy comes in the middle of other battles over beef, cheese, and bananas. Most trade wars do not start with a resounding declaration that trade is evil; they start over rather silly issues that produce retaliation and then counterretaliation. In 1999, the world's two biggest economies, the United

States and Europe, almost started a full-scale trade war over bananas, a fruit that they grow few of, that provides them with next to no jobs, that matter to only a handful of companies in each region, and that, by common admission, have no strategic importance to either side.

Unlike steel and microchips, food is personal. To a Frenchman, the idea that Camembert and Brie will be replaced by Cheez Whiz strikes at his very essence. In July 1999, France's farm minister pointed out that America has the "worst food in the world." Some forty thousand people around the world are members of Slow Food, a movement founded by an Italian food critic in 1986 as a protest against the opening of the first McDonald's in Rome.[22]

Certainly, many of those who long for a backlash against globalization regard food as one of the main opportunities. John Gray thinks that America's sinister enthusiasm for Frankenstein foods could just be the thing to destroy the world trading system that he detests. In Japan, where subsidies for rice are regarded as nonnegotiable trade issues, radicals such as Mika Iba believe they finally have an issue that will make people see the light about globalization. Iba at first sight has very little in common with rice farmers. An obvious member of a distinctively global caste—the herbal left—right down to her hair band and granny glasses, she is nevertheless a passionate opponent of globalization: She thinks that the fragile earth is being sacrificed on the altar of corporate greed, along with a gigantic bundle of "human and social rights." Her cluttered office in Tokyo is covered with posters and books that all proclaim—in English, naturally—her interest in a series of issues that the average Japanese salaryman would dismiss as disturbingly Western. "Assert Women's Rights: Resist Globalization" is not a slogan one hears much in Japanese offices, let alone its paddies.

Iba, like many other radicals around the world, has discovered that food is a touchstone for discontent. Her message—that America's agribusiness, with its factory farms, fiendish laboratories, and foul pesticides, is driving small farmers out of business and leaving consumers with no choice but to eat its tasteless products—resonates widely. Ten years ago, you could go into a Japanese supermarket and choose from a wide variety of foodstuffs, many of them Japanese, she says; now you can get anything you want, so long as it is agribusiness generated. She has also managed to weave globalization and food into her wider preoccupation with women's rights. Food used to be controlled by women, she says. Now they are lucky if they are allowed to function as the handmaidens of foreign scientists and capitalists. Iba urges Japan to rid itself of its dependence on foreign food. A particularly effective recruiting tool of hers is to take supporters to see giant American farms in places such as Iowa. "People just hate it," she says. "It's so big, so unnatural. There is no community, no children, no humanity, just endless fields."

Block Against Block

The fuss about food could fizzle out, though it is extremely hard to see how. But it certainly gives yet another helping hand to those in Europe and Asia who think that regionalism is a more civilized alternative to globalization. Most economists may view regional trading areas such as the EU and ASEAN simply as building blocks of global free trade. But there are plenty of pragmatic politicians who see regional blocs as fortresses against the forces of global anarchy and barbarism. Isolated nation-states are too feeble to resist such powerful enemies as hot money or junk culture, so the only hope for like-minded countries is to pool their resources.

This view is almost official doctrine among the French elite, which has predictably taken the strongest line against GM food; but it has many surreptitious allies around Europe. The EU has repeatedly put regional comfort above its global calling: Witness its unwillingness to absorb the former communist states of eastern Europe and its inability to solve the problems of the former Yugoslavia. The end of the cold war has already dissolved some of the glue that bonded Europe to the United States; repeated conflicts with the United States over trade and foreign policy are dissolving it further still. Despite the trade liberalization of the 1990s, Europe's economy was only slightly less protected by the end of the decade than at the beginning: In 1999, the citizens of Fortress Europe were forced to spend about 7 percent of the EU's GDP—or $600 billion—for the privilege of keeping cheaper products out.[23]

Some Asians calculate that a pan-Asian empire is their best chance of preserving their way of life against the toxic influence of the West. During the 1980s, the same Japanese bureaucrats that Iba frowns upon urged a "flying-geese strategy," pushing their country to invest trillions of yen in ports, dams, and other megaprojects across Asia. Asians need to band together to protect their traditions from the Western cultural onslaught, the argument goes, and the best way to do this is to strengthen Asian economic ties and be self-sufficient.

Regionalism is particularly alluring because it seems to gather up most of the benefits of economic integration without the unpleasantness of having your car industry be run by somebody several thousand miles away. Indeed, at first sight, the division of the world into three giant regional trading blocs does not look too cataclysmic. The two biggest blocs are already fairly self-contained. In the eleven European countries that have introduced the Euro trade with the rest of the world accounts for only 11 percent of GDP, and in the United States it accounts for 14 percent. Regional fortresses would still leave plenty of room for companies to compete and for countries to exploit comparative advantages: France can continue to trade its wines for Germany's cars.

In fact, the loss under such a system would be immense. The EU and the United States do four hundred billion dollars a year worth of trade with each other. And the long-term cost would be even bigger: Europe would lose its access to America's expertise in high technology (to take just one example); America would lose its access to Europe's luxury industry (to take another). Asia would lose its access to the world's markets. Everyone would lose some of their incentive to innovate and specialize. The creation of regional fortresses would also exacerbate all that is worst in each region. The European political class would get more self-important, and the European welfare state more unwieldy. The United States would become isolationist. The poorer parts of the world—particularly Africa—would lose massively, as barriers to the world's markets would condemn them to stagnation. And the sight of the rich world patrolling those barriers would exacerbate political antagonisms.

The biggest loser from regionalism, however, would not be this or that region but liberty itself. The freedom for Americans to drive German cars or the freedom for Germans to use American software might seem a little prosaic, but it rankles when you lose them. What rankles even more is that the loss of these liberties leads to the loss of others. Travel becomes more difficult. Exchange students find obstacles in their way. And as continents turn in on themselves, the exchange of ideas and arguments that drives intellectual enlightenment dries up. A Frankenstein world could yet evolve out of the squabbles about Frankenstein foods.

15

Membership Has Its Responsibilities

There is only one cure for the evils which newly acquired freedom produces; and that cure is freedom. When a prisoner first leaves his cell he cannot bear the light of day: He is unable to discriminate colors, or recognize faces. But the remedy is, not to remand him into his dungeon, but to accustom him to the rays of the sun. The blaze of truth and liberty may at first dazzle and bewilder nations which have become half-blind in the house of bondage. But let them gaze on, and they will soon be able to bear it. In a few years men learn to reason. The extreme violence of opinion subsides. Hostile theories correct each other. The scattered elements of truth cease to contend, and begin to coalesce. And at length a system of justice and order is educed out of the chaos.[1]

IF ONLY MACAULAY were completely rather than just mostly right. It is tempting to argue that the responsibility for making globalization work—for protecting it from its enemies, smoothing out its imperfections, and spreading its rewards—lies with the process itself. The best way to improve the living standards of the poor is, indeed, to give them access to the best bargains and the brightest ideas that the world has to offer. The best way to prevent the sort of turmoil that has engulfed Asia, Russia, and Latin America is to subject their crony-dominated economies to outside inspection and international competition. Give globalization time, and it will prove itself.

The problem is that the world is not quite as simple as that. Globalization, no less than the nineteenth-century liberalism that so attracted Macaulay, needs to be fought, politicked, and argued for. Things rarely change of their own accord; somebody has to change them. Schools do not build themselves, tariffs do not disappear. Lousy policy in the wake of the First World War ushered in an era of dog-eat-dog protectionism that crippled the economy and nurtured Nazism. A more enlightened series of decisions in the wake of the Second World War laid the foundations for decades of expanding trade and roaring prosperity. Are today's leaders worthy of comparison with the giants who remade the world in the 1940s? Or are they more like the homunculi who ushered in the drift and disaster of the 1920s? And, above all, what should they do?

A Place in History

The responsibility for making sure that globalization works lies principally with two groups of people: politicians and businesspeople. Neither group seems an ideal steward. Politicians make a profession of appeasing vested interests; businesspeople would rather think about making money than improving schools. If Macaulay were right, it would be a simple matter of reminding these reluctant guardians of the common good. But the common good can sound like a pretty vague goal when it means sacrificing immediate self-interest.

And yet there are a few glorious examples of people from each of these professions who have made exactly that sacrifice and who have been rewarded amply by posterity. Consider as role models Sir Robert Peel and John D. Rockefeller. Each man could easily have been remembered as just another examplar of human folly. Peel received a seat in the British Parliament as a twenty-first birthday present from his father, a parvenu cotton spinner who worked his child laborers fifteen hours a day and expected the day workers to slip into the beds vacated by the night workers. The young Peel spent most of his leisure time on the great landed estates of Tory England and was emotionally drawn to Lord Eldon's curmudgeonly "thin end of the wedge" version of Toryism, under which you should defend all traditions, however vile, in order to prevent everything from collapsing together.

For his part, Rockefeller was the architect of one of the most ruthless business monopolies of the nineteenth century: Standard Oil.[2] Rockefeller's business methods were so unscrupulous that he became the most vilified of all the robber barons—a hard contest to win. For some time, his most famous contribution to society came from the fact that he had managed to create such a threat to competition that the American government was forced to invent antitrust policy.

But both men illustrate the virtue of the long view. In 1846, Peel split the Conservative Party—and earned the passionate hatred of his landowning cronies—by opposing the corn laws and championing free trade. The split kept his party out of office for a generation, but in the long term it benefited both conservatism and Britain. It prevented the Tories from degenerating into a die-hard party of the landed elite, a fate that befell similar parties on the Continent, and instead turned it into the greatest vote-gathering machine of the twentieth century. Further, ditching the corn laws advanced industrialization by reducing the price of food.

For his part, Rockefeller remade his image by rethinking philanthropy. As with the other robber barons, there were selfish reasons: self-promotion, a desire to protect his property from expropriation, even a sense of wanting to protect his children from ruination. ("You must give it away," one of Rockefeller's advisers urged him in 1905. "It is rolling up like an avalanche that will crush you and your children and your children's children.") But philanthropy was also plainly part of his character: He started giving away his money as a clerk in Cleveland, never handing over less than 6 percent of his annual income. By the end of his life he had given away five hundred million dollars, creating one of the most powerful universities in the country, the University of Chicago, and founding several medical institutions.

Such leadership on either the political or the commercial front is in scarce supply these days. For businesspeople, there are some good excuses for inaction—not least the prevailing wisdom that they should stick to business rather than worry their rich little heads about anything so meaningless as society. In politics, we are caught in a downward spiral of expectations: Public-opinion surveys show that faith in government is sinking relentlessly lower; and the lower it sinks, the less room politicians have for heroic actions. It is hard to think of any substantive issue on which Bill Clinton really risked his credibility—and he was a man of iron resolve compared with most politicians in, say, Japan. The times call for Brobdingnagian leaders; we are led by Lilliputians instead.

For a modern Peel or Rockefeller, the potential list of things that might spread the benefits of globalization is a long one, and one rife with clichés. Chapters—nay, books—stretch before us on the need to reform education, construct a new world order, retrain older workers, finance global public goods, and reach out to the socially excluded. The danger of composing such lists is that they tend to be as disingenuous as they are unreadable. We have tried to point to opportunities for profound change, but we remain skeptical about the likelihood of such change happening, other than in the direst emergencies. Of course, a full-blown trade war between NAFTA and the European Union would prompt a few clever souls to reconsider protectionism, but by then what would be worth saving? It would be easy to suggest that the people of Nigeria merely embrace the economic policy of New Zealand, borrow the FBI for a year to clean house, and recruit the staff of the Bundesbank to oversee monetary policy. But it is not going to happen.

Instead, the accent has to be on what Sidney and Beatrice Webb christened "the inevitability of gradualism": intelligent and relentless pressure in the direction of reform. If the odd glorious revolution happens along the way, so much the better, but we cannot count on it. We will consequently confine our discussion to a limited number of examples that most people of all political persuasions would support: the case for reinventing government; the importance of comparing education performance across borders; the power of partnerships between government and business; and, for the budding Rockefellers, the awesome potential of American philanthropy.

The Three Great Leaps

The idea that politicians need to "rethink the nation-state"[3] has attracted a lot of fire from two sorts of people: hard-line globalists who argue that, since the nation-state is doomed to wither away, there is little point in reforming it; and old-fashioned leftists who argue that the state is being reduced to a puppet of international capitalism. These arguments underestimate both the power and the flexibility of the modern state.

The nation-state, as we saw, is not going to disappear any day soon; indeed, in most of the world, government has continued to expand. Globalization undoubtedly punishes arbitrary state actions and brings closer scrutiny of economic policies. But it does not force states into a common mold or force them to follow a fixed agenda. What works in New Zealand might be inconceivable in New York or New Delhi. Globalization is the enemy of incompetence, not idiosyncrasy.

This undermines the great excuse of all the Lilliputians who govern us: They have been rendered powerless. If they could be forced to read one contemporary book (once, naturally, they have been tested and retested on the intricacies of this one), it should be David Landes's *The Wealth and Poverty of Nations*. Prosperity, Landes shows, has always followed policy. In discussing why Britain pulled away from its rivals in the eighteenth century, Landes explains that this was "itself an achievement—not God-given, not happenstance, but the result of work, ingenuity, imagination and enterprise."

Britain, as he puts it, "had the makings, but it also made itself," through the sort of institutions it created, its system of property rights, its meritocratic traditions, and so on.[4] Time and again, leaders cripple their countries. Islam rejected clocks because they might undermine a mullah's skill in bringing people to prayer. It has also effectively eliminated the half of its talent pool that happens to be women and is mollycoddling the other half. "One cannot call the male children 'Pasha' or, as in Iran, tell them that they have a golden penis without reducing their need to work," notes Landes.

In essence, globalization has raised the cost of bad government. Mismanagement, pure and simple, has halved the per-capita income in Nigeria—a country where energy is plentiful but the local electricity utility, NEPA, is known as Never Expect Power Again. In 1998, *Forbes* magazine tried to calculate "the cost of Castro." During his reign, the average GDP per capita in Cuba had fallen in real terms by about $500 to $1,300. If the generalissimo had merely managed to keep his country's per-capita income at the same percentage of Florida's as it was in 1959, it would have been $4,169; if he had made the same sort of progress as a moderately well run country like Mexico, it would have been closer to $10,000. The citizens of Cuba could pay Castro five billion dollars to go away—and make a profit fairly quickly.[5]

This suggests, however, that open markets generally strengthen rather than weaken the case for a fairly elaborate state, provided that it is reasonably efficient and honest. Globalization's benefits are much harder to deliver when the state has all but collapsed (as in Liberia or Somalia) or degenerated into a branch of organized crime (as in pre-Putin Russia). Globalization has tended to wreak its worst havoc where state structures are weak. It is no accident that the cleanest and most efficient parts of Asia—such as Singapore, Taiwan, and Hong Kong—have coped best with open markets. As Nicholas Van Praag of the World Bank puts it: "Increasingly, we see that states need markets, but markets also need states. It's not enough to say that markets can do it all. You need security, you need an education system that works."[6] Remember Hobbes's dictum that man needs Leviathan in order to save him from anarchy.

By the same token, many parts of the welfare state are not defensible only on moral grounds; they may well turn out to be competitive advantages, too. When thinking about where to build factories, multinational companies usually look beyond wages to things like skills, environment, and culture. By reducing crime, New York City has probably done more to tempt back multinationals than any number of tax breaks would have. European countries' anxieties about bloated government tend to obscure the fact that universal health care and good public education may yet stand them in good stead. Sweden has one of the most global economies in the world (far more reliant on trade than the United States), but it also has one of the largest welfare states.

The key, then, is not necessarily to make the state smaller but to make it more efficient. This is easier said than done, of course. The public sector has traditionally been immune to the productivity improvements that have swept through private business. A popular idea for closing the productivity gap is to force the public sector to learn management methods from the private sector—in effect, to send bureaucrats to business school. But the results of this have often been disappointing, largely because bureaucrats have usually just grafted their new skills onto their existing structures, rather than ask whether those structures should exist in the first place. It does not matter how many times you reengineer your department of agriculture if you should not have one.

The most important lesson to be learned from management theory is shamefully simple: Stop doing many things badly, and start doing a few things well. The state needs to focus its energies on one thing above all: the creation of human capital. Investing in human capital is the best way not only of making nations competitive but of helping the people who are currently not benefiting from globalization.

Regulation or Research?

Most third-way politicians maintain that they are trying to make their governments more selective. Tony Blair has declared that "the presumption should be that economic activity is best left to the private sector." Bill Clinton repeatedly called for higher educational standards to prepare workers for global competition. Even European socialists can be heard echoing Thomas Paine's warning that "the greedy hand of government . . . watches prosperity as its prey, and permits none to escape without a tribute."

But the hand of government remains greedy nonetheless. One shudders to imagine what future commentators will make of the team of French civil servants that is trying to track down people who work too hard and thus break its thirty-five-hour workweek. Things have reached such a state in France that entrepreneurs have been fleeing to perfidious Albion, but Britain is hardly a model. The London School of Economics calculated that regulation under the last Tory government was costing taxpayers up to 1.5 billion pounds a year—not counting the much greater compliance costs for those being regulated—and things have got much worse with Blair's proliferating inspectorates.[7]

These national regulations, which the European Union has usually merely duplicated, form a set of nontariff barriers to foreign competition and also stifle entrepreneurs and job growth. Martin Wolf, a columnist for the *Financial Times*, likes to remind people that, over the past thirty years, real labor costs have risen by 70 percent in Europe, and employment has grown by around a tenth. By contrast, American labor costs have risen by about a quarter and jobs have grown by 70 percent. Thanks to rigidities in its labor market, the level of unemployment has risen in each successive business cycle in Europe. The ongoing pressure of having to raise ever more taxes to support pensioners and the unemployed will make Europe still less competitive and entrepreneurial. In America, nineteen of the twenty-five most valuable companies did not exist thirty years ago. In Europe, it is hard to think of one newcomer. In Sweden, all the large companies apart from Tetra-Pak seem to be close to their hundredth birthdays.

America's approach to regulation shines only when set beside Europe's. The red tape involved in hiring a nanny legally in either California or New York has driven almost everyone who does not want to run for public office to the gray market. (The gray economy now amounts to around 15 percent of the GDP of the developed world.) The American tax code is an abomination, not just at the federal level (Citigroup's 1998 return was thirty thousand pages long) but also at a local level. For instance, under the rules of New York State's deranged sales-tax system, M&M's are taxable, but mini-M&M's are not. A single Twix candy bar is taxable; a box full of them is not. A hot knish is taxable, a frozen knish is not. Buy regular cotton balls, and you are taxed; buy sterile ones, and you are not. The result is not just unfair but, like all regulation, costly. Retailers waste ages trying to find which items to tax and which not.[8]

As in Europe, such taxation does not even achieve its aim of disciplining companies. By using the same complicated rules, more than half America's 2.3 million corporations paid no tax at all between 1989 and 1995. Four out of every ten firms with more than $250 million in assets or $50 million in sales paid less than $100,000. Transfer-pricing abuses alone cost the government $2.8 billion a year; others put the figure ten times higher.[9] Indeed, you can argue that a good measure of a global company's success is how easily it (legally) avoids the thicket of taxes. News Corporation's tax rate rarely reaches 20 percent of its pretax profits.

The time and money that governments waste on regulation only seems more harmful when set alongside the dwindling amounts going into basic research, a category that is declining in government budgets just about everywhere. Most people accept that basic science is one of those areas in which the market can fail. Companies concentrate on the development part of R and D, and they typically ignore wider benefits to society. Lester Thurow points out that American companies have typically derived a return of about 24 percent on their R and D spending. But the total "social" return, adding in all the benefits for society as a whole, averages about 66 percent.[10] That, argues Thurow, indicates that this is one area where public spending really can deliver returns. It is possible to debate Thurow's figures (a lot depends on how the money is spent), but the fact is that most governments only claim to support basic research.

In one particular area—drug research—this failure is more than just inefficient. At the moment, there is a grotesque mismatch between the diseases that kill people and the diseases that drug companies are trying to cure. Billions are being spent on trying to find pills to fight rich-country ailments, such as heart disease, baldness, and impotence, while a mere eighty million dollars a year is spent on research into malaria, which kills 2.5 million people annually. No big firm, argues Jeffrey Sachs of Harvard, is prepared to invest in finding a vaccine for malaria (even though the genome of the malaria parasite has been mapped) because they do not think they will get a return: The poor cannot pay. Sachs suggests that rich-world governments should therefore create a market, perhaps by guaranteeing to pay ten dollars per dose for a vaccine for the twenty-five million children who are born each year in Africa; no money would be disbursed until a vaccine was produced.[11]

This also ties into a wider argument about the rich world's obligation to the very poor. We have already pointed out that rich countries give shamefully little to poor ones and also criminally discriminate against the industries—notably agriculture—that offer the best chance of the poor world earning its keep. It is common in the soppier books on globalization to include several chapters on the need to forgive the debts of poor countries, currently $270 billion (about three quarters the size of one year's worth of agriculture subsidies in OECD countries). Supporters of debt relief from Pope John Paul II to Bono are guilty of all sorts of woolly thinking, whether blaming international banks rather than incompetent governments or trying to construct an economic case when there is no clear one. But the moral case for debt forgiveness is already unanswerable: The amount is relatively small, there is no point in saddling the very poor with yet another handicap just to punish their rulers, and it will remove a festering sore between the South and the North that might cost us all much more.

Cynics might argue that relieving debts or providing medicine for African children has little to do with sorting out Citigroup's tax return. And we can already hear the screams of agrocrats at our daring to compare third-world debt with agricultural subsidies. But this is to miss the key point about resources. At the moment, governments devote too much effort to holding back the entrepreneurial forces that represent the good side of globalization and not enough concentrating on the areas where the public sector can really help. Until politicians reverse this, all the talk about reinventing government is nothing more than hot air.

Brains in the Balance

There are very few things New Yorkers can agree upon. One exception is that their city's huge public school system has been an embarrassment. Its history has been shaped by repetitive political rows among the schools chancellor, the mayor, and the once-autonomous Board of Education, all of whom have assumed that they run the system. But even when they are working together, the system, which serves more than one million schoolchildren, has often been close to anarchy. At the ground level, there are thirty-two school districts, each of which has its own elected board—a hint of direct accountability sadly limited by the fact that turnout for its elections rarely reaches even 10 percent of the potential voters. Until recently, school principals had tenure after five years in the job, making it difficult to remove even the worst ones. Thanks to the bizarre concept of social promotion, now belatedly being phased out, several hundred thousand students who flunk their studies each year have been automatically promoted to the next grade. Oh, and the money to keep this system going comes from all three levels of government: federal, state, and local.

According to the mayor's office, only about half of the ten billion dollars spent on education in New York actually reaches the classroom; the rest disappears into the bureaucracy. You might imagine that fixing such a mess would be at the top of the political agenda. Instead, for at least a generation, New York politicians have regarded education as a hornets' nest. Democrats have been too frightened of the teachers' unions to contemplate reform. The previous mayor, Rudy Giuliani, did not really get around to the subject until 1999, when he suddenly announced his enthusiasm for a series of reforms, including shifting responsibility for the schools to himself and introducing a pilot voucher scheme. This might have been expected to win some support. In Chicago, for example, the schools have gotten visibly better since they were put under the firm control of the mayor. Voucher schemes in places such as Milwaukee have been reasonably successful. But Giuliani failed on both counts. Eventually, in 2002, Mike Bloomberg stitched up a deal with the teachers that gave him control over the infamous "Board of Ed," but even this was technically only a temporary measure.

New York is perhaps an extreme example of an educational establishment with its head in the sand. But similar stories can be told just about everywhere. The reasons vary from country to country, but there is usually one overarching one: Education is still a surprisingly parochial affair, in which politicians routinely refuse to learn from each other. It is as if they have gotten as far as admitting that the education race is now more important than the arms race without going on to ask the next question: Who is winning? And why?

For the most part, the educational establishment treats the idea of comparing schools across borders as only slightly more ridiculous than comparing them within them. In the United States, national standards remain a mirage. As any recruiter can tell you, a mathematics qualification earned in Michigan can mean something completely different from one earned in California. In Britain, teachers are still complaining about comparing Solihull's results with Southampton's; the idea of comparing them with Seoul's seems outlandish. This is a pity, because when you begin to make these comparisons some interesting results emerge.

The world's three great educational systems—those of Europe, the United States, and Asia—all have conspicuous strengths and weaknesses. The United States boasts a system of higher education that is second to none. The elites of developing countries used to dream of sending their children to Oxford and Cambridge; now they choose Harvard and Stanford. Lower down in the educational system, however, the picture is a lot darker. The United States spends more per pupil than most other advanced countries do. But in a March 1997 international test of thirteen-year-olds in forty-one countries—significantly enough, one of the few global studies ever done—American children were twenty-eighth in mathematics, well below their peers in much poorer countries such as Hungary and South Korea.[12] America's overall high-school dropout rate is at least 14 percent, compared with 9 percent in Germany and 6 percent in Japan, and the figures are much worse in poor neighborhoods. In many parts of New York, literacy and numeracy rates resemble those of a third-world country.

The reason has less to do with money than with structure. The American school year is 180 days—sixty days fewer than in some other countries. Japanese children do five times as much homework a week as their American counterparts. Even when they are working, American children are seldom stretched. The lack of a core curriculum encourages a shopping-mall approach to education: Pile up the soft options and leave the hard stuff on the shelves. Ironically, the society most devoted to the ideal of equality of opportunity now has an educational system that is more corrupted by class than its rivals in Europe and Asia. At Beverly Hills High School—the school that gave the world Monica Lewinsky—the most urgent question is how to provide enough parking spaces for pupils' cars; in South Central, a few miles away, the schools are factories of failure, where more than half the pupils drop out before graduation. Giving the poor such a dismal start in life was a risky enough policy in the days when there were plenty of blue-collar jobs to go around. But now that these jobs are being exported or mechanized out of existence, it guarantees the creation of a permanent and combustible underclass.

The European system is in many ways the mirror of America's. Europe's state high schools are generally much more rigorous; in particular, the German tripartite system remains the envy of the world, with grammar schools that stretch the academic elite and vocational schools that supply German industry with technically trained workers. Yet the Europeans let their pupils down after high school.

The French university system is an overcrowded shambles. The German apprenticeship system—which depends crucially on the participation of the trade unions—is fine for churning out machinists but hopeless when it comes to computer programmers. The German university system, which was the envy of nineteenth-century Europe, is degenerating into an expensive joke, with about sixty students for every professor, compared with fifteen in the United States. Undergraduates can dawdle for a decade: The average age at graduation is twenty-eight, justifying former chancellor Helmut Kohl's famous complaint that Germany has the oldest graduates and the youngest retirees in the world.

Perhaps the most impressive continent in terms of education is Asia. To be sure, it lacks America's wonderful universities and Germany's magnificent grammar schools. It also lacks the West's enthusiasm for innovation. But Asians tend to possess a relentless will to succeed. Classes across the continent may contain forty or more children, and schools may be crumbling slums that lack air-conditioning, but many Asians make up in enthusiasm what they lack in resources. In Japan, neatly uniformed children stride to school at 8:00 A.M. on Sunday morning. In South Korea, every other side street houses a cramming school. In Hong Kong, a newspaper contains a letter from a pediatrician blaming an epidemic of spinal curvature on the fact that children carry such huge piles of books home with them.

Parents make big sacrifices to help their children succeed. Families pack their children off to cramming schools. (The best of these are so popular that there is a secondary industry in cramming people to get into cramming schools.) Mothers help their children with their homework. The latest fashion in Singapore is computer clubs for toddlers. All this effort has paid off in spades (not to mention grades). In the 1997 international test, the top four slots went to Asian sites: Singapore came first, followed by South Korea, Japan, and Hong Kong. All this investment in human capital should be enough to continue to power economic growth in Asia as the Asian crisis recedes into memory. It will also pose severe problems for both Europe and the United States.

There are three big lessons to be drawn from this tour of the educational horizon. The first is that we should be skeptical of people who blame educational problems on lack of money. The Czech Republic, for instance, produces better mathematics scores than the United States, while spending only a third as much. Canada devotes a higher proportion of its GDP to education than any other rich country does without being conspicuously successful, and Japan devotes a lower portion without being particularly unsuccessful. It is the way that you teach children, not how much you spend on doing it, that really matters. Many of the countries that scored well on the global math test, including Singapore and Switzerland, were ones where considerable effort was put into teaching basic math; in America, children are often given a calculator before they can add.

The second is that high-stakes national examinations do make a difference. French and Asian schoolchildren keep their noses to the grindstone because they face a tough test—the *baccalaureate* in France—at the end of their school years. But many American children look like stars of sequels to *Dumb and Dumber* because they are allowed to drift from year to year, being promoted regardless of performance and ending up with a school certificate that they cannot even read.

The third lesson is that public and private sectors can thrive side by side. One of the reasons why the United States has the world's best university system is that it has a healthy mixture of public and private institutions. This ensures not only that more people have a chance of going to college than anywhere else in the world but also that the United States is the world's center of academic research. Much of Asia has two parallel educational systems: a public system for the day and a private cramming system for the evening. This has allowed the continent to make a rapid and dramatic improvement in the quality of its human capital.

There are a few heartening signs that better practices are beginning to spread. One of the reasons why the British toughened up their educational system in the 1980s with a national curriculum and a renewed emphasis on core academic subjects is that they were worried by competition from Asia. Several American states are introducing statewide examinations and abolishing social promotion because they are embarrassed by their dismal performances. And at the top end of the market, competition to get into the best high schools is so tough in places like Manhattan that parents have started resorting to such "Asian" devices as hiring personal tutors and sending their children to cramming schools. Some Asian schools, meanwhile, are trying to put a little more emphasis on creativity and a little less on rote learning. *The Straits Times* has taken to running desperate editorials titled BE INNOVATIVE, SINGAPOREANS—HERE'S HOW.

But learning is slow. This is partly because the teaching unions form such a powerful and ferociously reactionary lobby throughout the world. (They are huge contributors to America's Democratic Party, for example.) But even more important is the fact that there is a worrying disconnection at the heart of educational policy: The right has most of the better ideas but lacks the necessary trust; the left has the necessary trust but is tied too closely to the educational establishment to make any progress. Vouchers, for instance, represent a real chance for poor people to determine their children's future. (A remarkable 168,000 poor New Yorkers applied for just 2,500 places in a privately financed voucher scheme offered by the Children's Scholarship Fund.) But so far no major figure on the left has had the courage to "betray" the educational establishment in the way that Peel "betrayed" the protectionists. When Peel died, he was mourned from one end of the country to the other. Bill Clinton and Tony Blair could well be remembered as the people who had the chance to reform education and did nothing about it.

The absence of political leadership is forcing private philanthropists to step into the breach. The Children's Scholarship Fund was the work of Ted Forstmann, an LBO honcho. The revitalization of New York University over the past two decades has been led by Lawrence Tisch—a billionaire previously known only for greedily ripping the core out of CBS, the onetime Tiffany Network. Nothing should excuse New York's politicians for the shambles in the school system. But if we wait for politicians to tackle our most pressing social problems, we might wait forever. Increasingly, the burden of reform must lie with the winners themselves, the successors of Rockefeller.

The Gospel of Wealth

It would be hard to find a more dramatic example of the vitality of American philanthropy than the Getty Center. Jean Paul Getty was, by all accounts, a fairly obnoxious man, yet thanks to the magic of philanthropy he has now been transformed into one of America's greatest patrons of the arts. The Getty Center, which sits on top of a Los Angeles hillside like a modernist parody of a Greek city-state, did not raise a penny of the billion dollars it cost to build from the public purse. And yet it serves public purposes galore and is a spectacle for tourists, who come in such numbers that parking spaces are booked up months in advance.

Alexis de Tocqueville noted that Americans were much more inclined to rely on voluntary associations to solve their social problems than were Europeans, who tended to regard the state "as the sole reliever of all kinds of misery." America's voluntary sector not only employs more people (around 7 percent of the population) than that in any other developed society but also receives more money. In 1998, Americans donated $175 billion to nonprofit organizations.

You might think that a conference on the future of philanthropy held at the center would be a triumphant affair—particularly if the delegates collectively controlled more than eighty billion dollars in assets. After all, far from being an isolated folly, the center is more like a turret on a particularly grand country estate. And yet the hundred people who gathered at the Getty in August 1998, courtesy of the American Assembly, were in no mood to celebrate. American philanthropy is "a tradition in jeopardy," they argued, and the only way to save it from disaster is to strike "a new covenant" with the American people. There are many reasons why philanthropy feels so besieged, and some of the wounds are self-inflicted. The amateurishness of much of the sector has led to a deluge of scandals. And public criticisms of the sector mount as the right accuses it of showering grants on a predictable list of modish causes—physically challenged Latino dance troupes and the like—and the left berates it for wasting money on things that already have too much of it, like Harvard Business School.

Another problem is globalization, which is weakening the connections that bind companies to their communities. The Bank of America, for example, has been the backbone of philanthropic life in San Francisco since 1904; now it has merged with Nations Bank and moved its headquarters to Charlotte, North Carolina. As the new behemoth attempts to go global, there is no reason why it should treat one city on the Pacific Rim more favorably than any other. Twenty years ago, the new giant Citigroup could have been looked upon to give money to New York City; now it might prefer to be seen as a corporate citizen of the world.

Yet the main reason for unease is simple: So far, philanthropy has drawn too little on the money and ideas of the new generation of entrepreneurs that is reshaping global business. The most frequently invoked names in philanthropic circles are still those of people like Rockefeller. And the most successful institutions in the philanthropic world are those designed to deal with national problems rather than those that can deal with the emerging problems of a globalized world.

We have already looked at the lack of generosity in Silicon Valley. These figures are reflected nationally. By one count, eight out of every ten Americans who earn more than one million dollars a year leave nothing to charity in their wills. And although America's richest people do give more than their share by income (one analysis of 1995 tax returns showed that people who earned one million dollars that year accounted for just under 0.1 percent of the tax returns but 8 percent of the charitable giving), many charities argue that the real test should be not income but net worth.

The most damning data comes from the Newtithing Group, a San Francisco–based nonprofit organization that has constructed an economic model showing how much rich Americans could "afford" to give away, taking into account their assets and spending as well as their income. The model works on a sliding scale, assuming that poorer Americans need to increase their net worth while the richest merely want to keep it stable, after allowing for inflation and personal spending. Altogether, it reckons that individuals could afford to give away some $242 billion more a year than they do. More than half of that amount comes from the 111,000 people who Newtithing reckons earn more than one million dollars a year and whose total net worth is around twenty-one million dollars.

You can argue with some of these numbers: Some new money is fairly illiquid and hard to get hold of, for example. But even more important than money are ideas. Andrew Carnegie put philanthropy at the heart of his gospel of wealth: "Anybody who dies rich dies disgraced," he declared, and went on to give away more than $4.5 billion dollars (in 1996 terms) during his lifetime. Like Rockefeller, he used his fortune to help decide what sort of country America was going to be. As a profoundly local society struggled to come to terms with the creation of a national market, Carnegie provided poor areas with schools and libraries so that everybody had "ladders within reach upon which the aspiring can rise." Other families founded art galleries so that America was a cultivated as well as a commercial society.

Today's new rich have the opportunity to shape the world just as pro-

foundly as Carnegie and Rockefeller shaped the United States. Yet little philanthropic giving seizes the imagination. Some of it is plain quirky. (Family
planning in Mexico enjoyed a brief vogue with software millionaires.) Much
of it—such as donations to hospitals and old universities—is utterly predictable. Software companies are excessively fond of providing local schools
with free computers—the moral equivalent of Rockefeller showering the
Midwest with kerosene lamps. Warren Buffett's commitment to give away
his money when he dies should be applauded, but in a knowledge economy,
Buffett's money is less valuable than his brain.

Understandably, the voluntary sector feels annoyed, even with the few
moguls who have been generous. People at the UN whine that Ted Turner's
attempt to give away one billion dollars has already been "wiped out" by the
much greater gain on his Time Warner shares. When Tim Wirth, a former
U.S. senator who now runs Turner's United Nations Foundation, explained
Turner's plans to the UN in April 1998, one of the loudest cheers greeted another speaker who begged the "other robber barons" to do their bit, too.

Reasons to Hope

The refusal of the rich to give more seems shortsighted. A century ago, the
robber barons were all too aware of the gap that had opened up between
their images in the business pages—where J. P. Morgan, for instance, was
hailed as "a Financial Moses"—and their reputations on the streets, where
Morgan was known as the "great Financial Gorgon." The United States can
already boast more than 200 billionaires and 3.3 million millionaires. In
1998, the combined income of the 13,000 richest families in America was
almost as big as that of the 20 million poorest families. And many of the rich
have done nothing to earn their wealth other than sit on booming assets. An
American who owned five hundred thousand dollars' worth of shares and a
five-hundred-thousand-dollar New York apartment in 1988 and has done
nothing since other than hang on to them is now around five million dollars
richer.

But the biggest reason why the rich should reach into their pockets is
more positive than mere moral obligation: Philanthropy offers them a
chance to shape the world just as dramatically as their predecessors shaped
the United States. Today's global institutions are hopelessly undeveloped,
just as national institutions were at the turn of the century. The United Nations and the Bretton Woods twins are rigid and inflexible, run by global
bureaucrats, squabbled over by national governments, and hamstrung by

prejudices about everything from family planning to profit making. The new rich have a unique opportunity to create institutions that are both flexible and imaginative enough to solve some of the problems that have flummoxed the public sector.

There are even some signs that the new rich are beginning to bring their methods as well as their money to philanthropy. Rosabeth Moss Kanter characterizes the attitude of the new givers as: "We fixed American business; now we need to fix charity." These budding "social entrepreneurs," as some of them like to call themselves, are keen to give away their money themselves, rather than creating foundations to do it. They want to solve specific problems in a specific way, rather than just earmark money for some vaguely benevolent purpose. They focus on performance. And they try to make projects self-sustaining, so the recipients do not keep coming back for more. The past twenty years have seen a proliferation of courses in American business schools designed specifically to train people for the voluntary sector.

Typical of this group is Social Venture Partners, a Seattle-based fund that is trying to apply the principles of venture capital to charity. SVP wants to give the charities it selects (mostly focused on children and education) the benefit of its expertise as much as of its money; it also wants to train future philanthropists. City Year, a charity set up by two Harvard Law School graduates in Boston that has since spread to other cities, helps young people to come up with "business plans," which local firms then back. The Robin Hood Foundation—which was set up in 1988 by three Wall Street dealers to help the poor and which was prominently supported by the late John F. Kennedy, Jr.—makes use of management consultants and puts an unusual emphasis on helping its clients to look after each other.

There are also growing signs of changes of heart among the richest of the rich. Consider George Soros and Bill Gates. We have given Soros's theoretical musings on globalization short shrift, yet he is arguably the most imaginative philanthropist since Carnegie. He devotes some of his money to American causes, much of it to countering what he regards as the cowardice of politicians on prisons, immigration, and drugs. But the bulk of his donations go to global causes.

Soros operates in more than thirty countries, displaying astonishing ambition. A particular favorite is his grand project for converting communists into capitalists—a natural passion for a native Hungarian. He has tried to do foreign-policy jobs that governments used to regard as theirs. Between 1989 and 1994, he spent $123 million promoting democracy in eastern Europe, five times as much as the American government's National Endowment for

Democracy did. In 1996, he outspent the American government in providing aid to Hungary, Yugoslavia, and Belarus, earning him a reputation in the former communist world as a one-man Marshall Plan.

Soros has made mistakes. His operation took a hit when some of his employees in Russia were found to be siphoning money into Swiss bank accounts and spending it on fast cars. But his philanthropy is animated by a grand purpose. Soros's passion is not for marble memorials but for creating what Karl Popper, his tutor at the London School of Economics, called the "open society." Soros's skepticism about free markets grows ever deeper, but his philanthropic giving proves quite the opposite case: The private fortunes that the free market generates with ever greater abundance can often solve social problems much more effectively than government action can.

Bill Gates also deserves more credit than he is usually given for philanthropy. Gates's numerous critics point out that, as was said of Rockefeller, his interest in giving away money coincided with a government antitrust action and the collapse in his own personal popularity. But even so, his ambition to give away 95 percent of his money is staggering. Gates's foundation—worth twenty-three billion dollars in 2002—focuses on two things: health in poor countries and education. His enthusiasm for giving computers to libraries is perhaps a little predictable, though Gates deserves some marks for being one of the earliest to spot that technology can cause inequality. His global health program—in which the first money has gone into speeding the delivery of new vaccines to children in the developing world—is much more interesting, for two reasons.

The first is that vaccines are the quickest way to save lives. Many countries still have rotten distribution systems for drugs (a fatal flaw if more than one shot is required), and some governments in Asia even fail to admit that they have some diseases in the first place. But the biggest problem is pricing. Thanks to the high prices of new vaccines, there is a fifteen-year gap between a vaccine arriving in the first world and its introduction in poorer countries. Drug firms, particularly American ones, remain nervous about selling new medicines of any sort at lower prices in poorer countries. They could still make money under a tiered price system in which some countries paid less, but the American drug barons are worried about a political backlash in Washington (the government is their main domestic customer). They also have not always hit it off with the more idealistic UN types who are the main buyers for the third world.

Any solution—which could probably be applied to drugs other than vaccines as well—will come only by banging together a lot of heads, not just those of the companies and the agencies but of various governments and institutions such as the World Bank. This is the sort of thorny problem that requires brains as well as money, which is the second reason why Gates's role is so interesting. The economics of the vaccine industry, he points out, are much like those of software, in that the marginal cost of each copy of a new product is very small. He, too, thinks that tiered pricing looks like "the best solution," and he seems to want to get involved in some of the discussions between the private and public sectors. Reports are filtering back of meetings of scientists and fund-raisers at his house, where he peppers his guests with detailed questions about the business and the technology involved.

This is interesting because it raises the hope that the new rich, who are comparatively young, are only just getting around to giving away their money. Gates argues that anybody can give away money; the point is to give it away intelligently. At present, philanthropy occupies only around five hours of his time each week. All the same, he ranks medicine as his second biggest interest after information technology, and his relentlessly curious and competitive brain is plainly beginning to whir.

The hope remains that Gates's involvement with vaccines may have the same galvanizing effect on his peers as Rockefeller's foundation of the University of Chicago in 1892 had on the robber barons. "I worked my way almost to a nervous breakdown in groping my way through the ever widening field of philanthropic behavior," the oil man recalled later; but that struggle also forced him to rethink his giving in ways that others then copied. One result was that he appointed a man to look after all his philanthropic activities. His name, funnily enough, was Gates.

16

The Ant and the Silversword: Working and Investing in the Twenty-first Century

TO APPRECIATE the plight of the individual in the global economy, consider the tale of the ant and the silversword. The latter is a magnificent though rare plant that grows on slopes of volcanic craters in Hawaii. When people first saw a white fringe on the mountains, they imagined it was snow—and in some ways the silverswords seem only slightly more durable. The silverswords pollinate rarely—only once every fifty years in one case—and sometimes die afterward. They have survived so long because they live in a place that, in ecological terms, is among the least global in the world. With 2,500 miles of ocean to protect them from the mainland, the islands of Hawaii evolved in splendid isolation for roughly seventy million years. They were thus able to develop all sorts of peculiar, unhardy species—not just the silversword but also birds that could not fly and thistles without thorns.

Ever since humans came to Hawaii roughly 1,500 years ago, this ecology has been under attack. Now that several million people come every year, every shoe, every shopping basket, and every shipping container is a potential carrier of "alien species" that eat, harass, or harm the locals. Hawaii's twenty species of flightless bird are all extinct: They were unable to fly away from rats and other invaders. Perhaps a sixth of the islands' native plant species are already gone, and another third are set to follow them. The islands have roughly one third of America's endangered plants and even more of its endangered birds.

One problem for the silverswords has been feral goats, which like gnawing the plant. But the silversword's biggest problem is one of the tiniest creatures to get into Hawaii: the Argentine ant. The ant, which is famed for its organizational abilities (it does not waste time in internecine struggles, as many other sorts of ant do), eats the larvae of the native yellow-faced bees and other insects that are the silversword's main pollinators. In short, the ant destroys the silversword's already fairly fragile reproductive system.

The Law of Unintended Consequences

It might seem a little insulting to compare one's readers to a plant that has sex only once every fifty years. But the tale of the silversword and the ant is, first, an exaggerated warning of what happens when the outside world arrives and people fail to adapt; second, a reiteration of the idea that globalization is about not just financial logic and political ideas but physical happenstance; and third, and most important, an example of the importance of unintended consequences. Globalization can shape all sorts of people's lives in all sorts of unpredictable ways. It is a process that may well bring you a wife, a father-in-law, an adopted child, a new job, a pink slip, better coffee, cheaper marijuana, a dishwasher, a working telephone, or even a fatal disease.

Or it may not. Just as a plant as pathetically vulnerable as the silversword has managed to survive 1,500 years of human invasion, some of us will be able to continue in much the same way as we do at present—doing the same jobs, living in the same places, and the rest of it. Globalization will simply be a process that happens in the foothills of your particular volcano. Yet even if an Argentine ant does not manage to find you, it seems silly to plan your life on the assumption that it won't come up the mountain.

Trying to tell people how they should cope with globalization is awkward territory. As we shall see, it is easy to look at things like careers and exaggerate the degree to which they have actually changed; statistically, the evidence is at best patchy. And, even if they are changing, it is not clear how much of the blame (or credit) lies with globalization.

The biggest difficulty of all, however, lies in the fact that individuals are exactly that: unique and various. The frustrating answer to people who ask how they should react to globalization is that it all depends on where they live and what they do. The sort of job insecurity that has become so frightening to a salaryman in Tokyo has long been normal for a construction worker in Dallas (and not that odd for a construction worker in Tokyo either). The effect of globalization on industries in America (where there is already plenty of competition) is inevitably muted compared with the way that it has shattered the "iron rice bowl" of lifetime employment in China (which relied on keeping foreigners out). Indeed, in some cases, offering any kind of advice seems either condescending or inappropriate. Reginaldo Gobetti is a portfolio worker of sorts, though his portfolio is very small.

Yet such warnings should not get in the way of one of the basic messages of this book: Globalization hands power to individuals. The idea that each of us is sovereign (or at least more of a monarch than most of us have been before) is something we applaud; indeed, it represents a triumph for the sort of liberal ideas that we celebrate in our conclusion. But it also presents choices that many of us have not really thought through and may not be altogether thrilled about having to make.

Nowadays, if there is any certainty in our lives, it comes increasingly from within rather than from without: You have to manage yourself rather than waiting for other people to do the managing. But how do you manage yourself? And how do you chart a course that leads to reasonable prosperity rather than dumps you in some prefabricated shack in Nowheresville?

This chapter will focus on the two things that keep you out of that prefabricated shack: your career and your investments. It will also confine its advice on those two things to people in the more advanced countries—in part because what is true of the rich world today will be true of the poorer world tomorrow. However much we try to plan our lives, we cannot be entirely sure that we will not be undermined by some human equivalent of the Argentine ant. But plan we must, and the things that we must plan most carefully, in an age of both individual sovereignty and growing uncertainty, are our investments and our careers.

The Global Wallet

Before anybody listens to a word that we say about investing, they should know that the first investment one of us made was in shares in Eurotunnel, while the other chose to spend the golden years of the 1980s writing an academic book that thanks, he still insists, to the myopia of Cambridge University Press, netted less than one thousand dollars. Financial gurus we are not. But there does seem to be a curious disconnection between the global way that most businesspeople think about their own industries and the still largely national way that most people think about investment. That does not mean that people should rush to invest a set proportion of their money overseas, but it increasingly implies two things: first, they should pick winners regardless of where they are based—at least when they deal with well-known large-cap stocks in developed countries; and, second, that they should look for trends that cross borders.

The heart of the problem is the fixation on country indexes. The typical investor still measures his or her shares against a local index; and if he or she considers globalization at all, it is by diversifying and buying foreign-country funds, which measure their performances against other national indexes. Fund-management companies work in a similar way, splitting their asset-allocation models by country. If a New York–based consumer-goods analyst decides that Unilever looks like a better bet than Procter & Gamble, the decision to switch still has to go through the bank's country-allocation committee and may even have to be made through London or Amsterdam, even though you can buy Unilever American Depository Receipts in New York. The reason is that Unilever, despite being pretty similar to P&G, happens to be headquartered in London and Rotterdam. The only industry where a large number of investors treat the nationality of shares as irrelevant is oil.

The first problem with this is that national stock-market indexes in developed countries are lousy guides to just about anything. In many countries, the stock market bears as much relation to the local economy as an international hotel does to its host city. Rio Tinto, for instance, is considered a rock-solid British share. Yet the world's biggest mining company has no assets in the country other than its headquarters. Five of the FTSE 100 companies are South African; three are Asian; and more than half of the aggregate earnings of the one hundred companies come from outside the country.

Any American investor who buys a British country fund in the hope of providing himself with diversification is thus buying a dud. But if the same investor eschews, say, Swiss stocks because the local economy looks as if it is a mess, he is probably making an equally big mistake. In 1998, Switzerland's stock market soared while the rest of the country languished. Drug stocks were hot, and Roche and Novartis, two drug giants that make less than a tenth of their sales in Switzerland, drive the local index.

You might argue that this is merely a statistical quirk. But as industries become more global, these quirks become much more costly, particularly if you happen to live outside the United States. Guy Monson, the chief investment officer at Bank Sarasin, a Swiss private bank, in the City of London, points out that one of the most dramatic explosions of wealth in history took place in computers and software in the 1990s.[1] Any European who restricted investments to domestic companies would have missed out, since the boom happened almost exclusively in the United States. Given the size of the American stock market and the current preeminence of its companies, investors there have been much better served. But there are still some industries—luxury goods, mobile telephones, and consumer electronics, for instance—where the better companies are probably in Europe or Japan.

A typical American investor puts about a seventh of his money abroad; in Britain, the proportion is about a third. In the past, there have been good reasons for investing most of your money at home. If you are investing to pay for your retirement, then you want to have your assets in the same economy as your liabilities (so if inflation pushes up the cost of keeping you in a nursing home, it pushes up the dividends from your shares, too). Next, there is the problem of currency risk: A New Yorker who invested in a good Italian company might have seen his money double in lire and then euros but barely budge in dollars. Above all, there is the problem of ignorance and trust: Why invest in a firm whose management you know too little about and whose accounting practices may be dodgy?

All these arguments have become progressively weaker—at least if you invest in big companies from big countries. As they become more global, large companies the world over are getting a lot more familiar: For a Briton, GE is almost as well known as GEC once was. Also, shareholder rights and even accounting practices have become more uniform. Currencies still matter, but most studies show that, at least for long-term investors, the currency effects tend to cancel each other out in three to five years. The Euro not only knocks currency considerations out of a swath of investment decisions (the German can now invest in Italy with impunity) but also provides a heftier counterweight to the American dollar. As for inflation, the risks of a surge in prices destroying the purchasing power of your foreign nest egg have lessened as inflation and interest rates have tended to elide one another.

Indeed, the correlation of stock-market returns in most countries has increased. Put a chart of Germany's DAX over the S&P 500, and they look increasingly alike. The one big exception is Japan. But, as Monson points out, if you concentrate on what might be called Global Japan—exporters such as Toyota and Sony and software firms such as Softbank—you find a clear correlation with their counterparts in other markets.

Once again, this does not mean that shareholders should immediately double the proportion of international shares in their portfolios; but it does mean that if, for instance, you think that DaimlerChrysler makes better cars than Ford, then you should put money in it. Of course you should take into account geography when deciding how good a particular firm is: A key source of Daimler's competitiveness (or lack of it) is its Germanness. But the question of where it is listed looks increasingly secondary.

There is nothing strange in thinking like this: Most of the world's leading businesspeople have been running their businesses that way for decades. Microsoft is as American as apple pie, but it is run as a global software firm. The move toward a more international view of company performance ought to be strongest in Europe. Fund managers within the Euro zone are already starting to measure themselves against regional indexes. For a French investor, sticking to the CAC-40 index will soon seem as bizarre as an inhabitant of Portland limiting himself to companies based in Oregon.

A Heretical Idea about America and Europe

The next thing to do after deciding to judge companies globally is to take advantage of the fact that most people have not caught up with you. As we have shown, globalization is a process rather than a fact: It pushes ideas and best practices around the world at different speeds. For instance, the consolidation in the American banking sector in the early 1990s generally lifted share prices as coldhearted managers trimmed branch systems and replaced people with machines. Exactly the same inefficiencies existed in the British banking sector, but it was valued at far lower multiples. In due course, the revolution arrived, and share prices of groups such as Lloyds TSB soared. In 1998 and 1999, the same pattern was repeated on the Continent.

More generally, the diffusion of management ideas means that the chances of any one company or country remaining top dog for long are slim. In 1989, a Japanese member of parliament, Shintaro Ishihara, bragged, "There is no hope for the United States." At the same time, assorted American academics lauded Japan's tradition of industrial planning. The *Harvard Business Review* hailed the country's "unsurpassed" financial regulators. And a rash of books implied that most of California would end up as a subsidiary of Matsushita. In the following decade, Japan's share of the world's stock market shrank from around 40 percent to around a tenth.

At the beginning of the twenty-first century, much the same air of invincibility surrounded American companies. "Dot-com" books, adorned with pictures of hairy men in T-shirts, took the place of all those worthy tributes to *kaizen*. Flexibility, speed, inventiveness, ruthlessness were just a few of the virtues that were deemed innately American. In *Fortune*'s annual list of the world's most admired companies, the top ten firms in 1999 all came from the United States; there were only three non-Americans—Sony, Toyota, and DaimlerChrysler—in the top twenty-five. The American stock market accounted for roughly twice as big a proportion of the world stock market as the United States' underlying economy did of the world economy.

Despite Enron and WorldCom, the success of American companies is surely built on much firmer foundations than that of the Japanese. Regardless of what you think about the new economy or accounting standards, American firms such as Wal-Mart and Oracle are still, by most measures of competitiveness, beating the bejesus out of their peers. America also has a substantial lead in most of the sunrise industries of the future. So a premium is certainly justified. But investors may still have underestimated the idea that non-American firms might recover some ground.

Start with the presumption that in business, even more than politics, the only constant thing is change. One way that American firms caught up with their Japanese peers (assuming that they were ever behind in the first place, which is another debate) was by copying them. All those books about total quality management and lean production had an effect. If you buy an American car, you no longer offer up a prayer as you drive it off the lot.

Can the Europeans and Japanese catch up, too? Buoyed by fads such as reengineering, American firms spent much of the early 1990s slimming not just their number of blue-collar workers but their managerial ranks, too; and they have kept on slimming and outsourcing jobs to other places. By contrast, in Europe and Japan companies have, depending on your point of view, been kinder, lazier, browbeaten by their governments, or simply true to their stakeholders' principles. Although sales growth in Europe has broadly kept pace with that in America, Continental profit margins are roughly half those in America. There are four times as many start-ups per capita in the United States than in Europe.[2]

There are signs of change, however. In Europe, the hostile takeover of Telecom Italia by the far smaller Olivetti in 1999 might prove to have been a watershed. European giants such as Daimler and Fiat, which once considered themselves invulnerable, have begun to lop off "noncore" operations. Shareholder activism is on the rise in Europe; so is performance-related pay. And there is also the pressure from the single market and the single currency. Europe has twice as many carmakers as the United States, eight times as many rail-engine manufacturers, and ten times as many tractor and battery makers, to name just a few of the industries that are ripe for consolidation.

Japan is several years farther behind. But takeovers are also on the rise in Tokyo. Witness the way that Cable & Wireless was able to wrest International Digital Communications from NTT in 1999. Meanwhile, fairly conservative groups such as Mitsubishi and NEC have announced restructuring drives. And as in Europe, there is a group of younger companies that are far less tradition bound.

On technology, much the same seems true. American firms have a substantial lead, but Europe in particular is not without hope. In pharmaceuticals, the Continent is America's equal. There are a few countries—Finland, for instance—that are actually more wired than America. And in one increasingly crucial technology—wireless telephony—Europe (and to a lesser extent Japan) enjoys a sizable lead.

There are plenty of things that could slow Europe down—most notably its politicians. Even if France produced a business leader who combined all the verve of Bill Gates, Jack Welch, and Warren Buffett, he or she would still have to find a way around the country's ludicrous thirty-five-hour workweek. But investors have good reason to expect the Continent to catch up a little—and some of the premium currently being paid for American shares to be reduced.

Another pessimistic message that applies to investors of all sorts, not just American ones, concerns globalization itself. Put crudely, companies never seem to make quite as much money out of globalization as they think they will. In some cases, this is simply because they exaggerate particular opportunities. (In the mid-1990s, companies calculated the size of the Chinese market by working out how many tubes of toothpaste, or whatever, the average Westerner used per year and then multiplied by a billion.) But it also reflects a more fundamental hunch that despite all the articles portraying modern capitalism as a battle between capital and labor, the winner will actually be a third party: the consumer.

That is not to deny the fact that capital has often used globalization to bully labor. European companies have used new, more flexible factories in America to blackmail their domestic European unions into being slightly more cooperative. In the 1990s, average wages in America rose by 27 percent, but corporate profits rose by more than 107 percent (and the S&P 500 by more than 200 percent).[3] But in industries in which there is intense global competition, even more value tends to end up with the consumer in the form of lower prices. Globalization has spurred deflation in industry after industry: If you don't sell your widget cheaply, then your rival from the other side of the world will (and, look, your rival has just outsourced his processing unit to India, so you had better cut prices to keep up). Making money in such cases is not impossible, but it is probably much more difficult than competing against a handful of neighbors.

Deflation seems particularly rampant in the industry that has often traded on the highest multiples in America, high technology. Almost everything you need to join the wired universe—computers, operating software, applications software, browsers, Internet access—is being given away by somebody somewhere, and consumers have gotten used to it. Even at their postbubble levels, stock-market valuations seem to assume, first, that virtually every company will become the global leader (a logical impossibility) and, second, that they will be able to turn that market share into profits. So far only a handful of companies have managed to do that, and even the most successful, notably Microsoft, have had to cut prices.

Once again, from the perspective of the global economy this is a good thing. Consumers get better, cheaper products, and the wheels of global commerce pick up speed. But investors counting on rising profit margins in global industries could be in for a nasty surprise.

How Flexible Is Flexible?

In *The Hungry Spirit* (1997), Charles Handy has a nice story about visiting the Soviet Union in the 1950s. His official guide—in those days you could not visit the country without one—asked him whether it was true that in the West "you have to find your own job and place to live." "Of course," the young Irishman answered; and when his guide demurred that this seemed frightening, he announced, by his own admission rather smugly, "We call it freedom." It was "only later on the plane leaving Russia *en route* to my oil company that I realized that my benevolent employers also told me what job to do and where to live, and would do so for the rest of my working life."[4] Shell even insisted on the right to approve Handy's choice of wife and to write appraisals on her.

Such an attitude was not that uncommon. Organization man, that quintessential fifties figure, was firmly told by his creator, William Whyte, that he "must smile when he is transferred to a place or a job that isn't the place or job that he happens to want."[5]

Perhaps the only thing that the oddly assorted group of people who gathered together in a slightly shabby classroom in Manhattan in October 1999 had in common was that they would never dream of smiling while somebody else organized their lives for them. A young man in a neat blue suit introduces himself to the group as Walter before describing the lessons that he has learned from his job search. "Be prepared, know your story, and network, network, network." That was the way that Walter hopped from a job in the construction industry in Canada to one in human resources in New York; and if the current job does not work out, that will be the way that he will jump to his next job. His network will be ready, his "brand" established. Afterward, the teacher repeats the message to the middle-aged managers who fill the room: Start preparing for the job after the one that you are looking for at the moment.

The Five O'Clock Club is an "employee advocacy organization" with twenty branches around America. Most members have jobs, and around a third earn more than one hundred thousand dollars a year. The club offers plenty of regular career advice ("the first one to mention a figure for salary loses"), but it is based on two things that organization man never entertained: disloyalty (even if about a fifth of the members end up staying at their companies, they are constantly looking around for better deals) and, worse, feelings.

Rather than allowing jobs to define their lives, as organization man did, the club's members are encouraged to decide their own goals—to imagine what sort of person they want to be in forty years, for example—and then design their careers toward that goal. It also caters to people whose needs are more psychological than financial—like the Internet manager who in 1999 had made three million dollars in the past eighteen months "but still [felt] left behind."

This sounds like a bull-market phenomenon. But the club's founder, Kate Wendleton, argues that it has thrived because it is catering to fundamental changes in working life. And she is not alone. McKinsey has warned its clients that the biggest challenge for companies is "the war for talent." Business magazines are still full of advice columns on how people should take control of their jobs, how you should be hotdesking with colleagues, telecommuting from home, and generally reconsidering your whole future. In *The Brand You 50* (1999), America's best-known management guru, Tom Peters, delivers the following rant.

> It's over! It's over! **Praise God . . . its over.** (That's my view, anyway.) What's over? The world in which "we"—the best and the brightest, the college kids—depended on "them," the Big Corps., to "guide" (micromanage! dictate! control!) "our" careers.
>
> Alas, my Dad was no more than an indentured servant to BG&E . . . the Baltimore Gas & Electric Co. . . . for 41 years. . . . Same door. West Lexington Street. Day after day. Month after month. Year after year. Decade after decade.
>
> It was no way to live . . . if living it was.
>
> But . . . "it" is finished. Kaput.[6]

Most people on the left—particularly in Europe—share Peters's fundamental analysis while drawing the opposite conclusions. They believe that the very forces that Peters celebrates—technology, globalization, the shift toward services—are breaking down the old social contract, leaving workers at the mercy of a new and ruthless variety of capitalism. In another recent book, *Sharing the Wealth*, Ethan B. Kapstein of the University of Minnesota, one of globalization's more thoughtful critics, argues that modern capitalism forces governments into a game of "beggar-thy-labor," which will stir up a social backlash.[7]

There is no shortage of impressionistic evidence to support this case. In Continental Europe, with unemployment stuck at over 10 percent, university graduates are being forced into part-time jobs. In Japan, according to the *Asahi Shimbun*, the number of businessmen diagnosed as psychotic depressives has risen rapidly. Salarymen check into their shrinks on Saturdays and Sundays because the more frightening meetings happen on Mondays. There is even a special shop in Tokyo where you can go and plunge needles into models of your boss.

However, even in Japan, debates about the future of work keep being drawn back to the United States, the most flexible and forward-looking labor market. Throughout the booming 1990s, new records were set for the number of layoffs. As Alan Greenspan has pointed out repeatedly, wage inflation remains relatively low partly because so many Americans are terrified of losing their jobs. Just around the corner from the New York City branch of the Five O'Clock Club, you could hear muffled sobs from audiences during a much-praised revival of Arthur Miller's *Death of a Salesman*. Even though the most modern figure in the play should have been Willy Loman's brother, Ben—an early version of an Internet entrepreneur who keeps on boasting how he "walked into the jungle" at seventeen, walked out at twenty-one, and "by God I was rich"—it is Willy himself who seems to remind everybody of somebody. The broken salesman's lament—"You can't eat the orange and throw the peel away—a man is not a piece of fruit!"—still resonated, even with investment bankers.

Has It Really Changed?

Yet this sense of déjà vu also raises the question of whether globalization and technology are really doing anything radically new to careers, even in the United States. The statistics suggest a rather more complicated picture. The basic measure of job stability—how long the median American has been in his or her current job—was 3.6 years in 1998, a shade higher than in 1983. As David Neumark, one economist who has poured statistical cold water over the whole debate, points out, there are plenty of professions—teachers, doctors, even labor economists—where job hopping remains rare, and plenty of others—such as construction workers—where job hopping has been the norm for generations.[8]

And yet all the figures are distorted by two phenomena: the aging of the huge baby-boom generation, comprising people born between 1946 and 1964, which accounts for roughly half the workforce (many of whom no longer want to move); and the increase in mothers coming back to the workforce to permanent jobs. Look at particular types of workers, on the other hand, and you soon see signs of change. The number of workers who have stayed with an employer for more than eight years has come down. Job tenure for men aged thirty-five and over has also decreased sharply since 1983. At the other end, the average thirty-two-year-old in America has already worked for nine different companies.

These figures are much more consistent with two bits of anecdotal evidence that careers are changing: parents being surprised by the flightiness of their children (a generational change that will take some time to show up in the figures); and people being rather shocked by the news that Bernie in Accounts, who was always considered part of the furniture, was recently handed a pink slip. Job stability is a very different thing from job security. With sackings accounting for a much higher proportion of job turnover, polls show Americans—particularly older male workers of long tenure—are much more scared about losing their jobs than ever before. Asked about the relevance of *Death of a Salesman* in 1999, Arthur Miller replied, "Any Monday morning you can be told you are no longer needed. The company is moving to Guatemala."

Globalization may be culling far fewer older workers than technology is (Bernie probably lost his job to a computer, not a Guatemalan), but it is also helping drive other structural changes that affect our careers. In most developed countries, the workforce is inexorably moving to small service companies from large manufacturing ones—and even the large manufacturers that survive adopt the psychology of small companies, reorganizing themselves into collections of autonomous units. The old model for a career, in which you gradually climbed your way up a single company, is much harder to sustain if you work for a public-relations agency that has only three layers in the hierarchy.

The all-pervasive cult of flexibility helps some workers: If a firm has no idea what is coming around the corner, one of the few sensible strategies is to amass good people to deal with it. But globalization also increases the pressure on companies to contract out their noncore activities to specialized companies or to use more temporary workers (as four in five American firms now do). About one in ten American workers is a "contingent" worker, such as temporary-agency employees and independent contractors. Many more Americans work at least some time at home, and almost all of them work longer hours.[9]

Telescope your lens onto the most forward-looking part of the American economy—California—and you find more reasons to suspect that careers will change faster in the future. California has led the rest of the country not only in job creation but in job volatility. The fastest-growing part of the Californian economy is the temp industry, which has added as many jobs as the software and electronic equipment–manufacturing industries combined. Now the Internet seems to be having much the same effect on "job trading" in the state as it has already had on share trading. Career sites such as Monster.com offer an easy chance to indulge that whim to "see how much you are really worth."

In chapter 11, we talked about Silicon Valley producing an egg timer–shaped society. Much the same seems to be true of job volatility, with people at the top and bottom of companies job hopping much more rapidly than everybody else. During the 1990s, employee turnover in Silicon Valley was close to 20 percent a year. This created a market for companies such as Icarian, a firm that tries to apply "just in time" manufacturing principles to employment. In a matter of hours, its boss, Doug Merritt, can summon up not just secretaries and assistants but freelance engineers (for between $90 and $200 an hour), technical writers ($75–$150), marketing directors ($200–$500) and chief executives ($300–$800), and, lest you think these rates a bargain, there are still negotiations about how much equity the freelancers get. Merritt says that businesspeople are becoming more like film stars, equipped with talent agents who offer package deals for their clients.

Not everybody in Silicon Valley likes this sort of just-in-time lifestyle. Many people still like having normal careers (just as Clint Eastwood has stuck with Warner Bros., there are plenty of engineers at Hewlett-Packard who could earn more elsewhere). And a sizable minority of "no brand" workers at the other end of the egg timer see flexibility as a threat rather than an opportunity. The Valley is full of "software gypsies" who lack such basic things as health insurance, not to mention secretaries who have put up with low pay and few benefits, only to end up with a fistful of worthless options.

Whistle While You Work

Silicon Valley's experience will probably be replicated elsewhere, at least in the long term. Most new-economy industries are treading the same path toward flexibility. Icarian also sells its just-in-time jobs to the drug and finance businesses. Even in Japan, the home of lifetime employment, you can see glimmers of Siliconization in, for instance, the rising numbers of temporary workers.

Is a more flexible approach toward work a good thing? Optimists claim that a flexible workforce is a happier workforce. A survey of work trends in 1999 by Rutgers University and the University of Connecticut, for example, found that 91 percent of Americans said that they liked their jobs. Some people even claim to detect a "happiness effect" in the country's productivity numbers: People are working harder. Many of the jobs that globalization and technology have helped phase out have been fairly brutal, tedious ones (unless you think coal mining a noble art). And, for anybody with youth and talent, barriers have been removed. Organization man's children can do away with time serving and brownnosing and pursue several different careers.

Another reason to be optimistic is that good companies desperately want to keep people. In the early 1990s, bosses such as "Chainsaw" Al Dunlap were much admired; now they are reviled not only for creating "toxic workplaces" but also for making far less money than bosses who concentrated on growing their businesses.[10] Focusing on core competencies might mean outsourcing peripheral employees, but it also means creating a core group of long-term loyalists who are committed enough to the firm to transmit its ethos to new employees. Firms may not be able to offer people jobs for life, but most companies go out of their way to offer people "employability."

Yet there are still plenty of worries, starting with overwork. Cell phones and beepers function as electronic leashes, tethering people perpetually to their jobs. A study by the Families and Work Institute showed that around three quarters of college-educated people between twenty-five and thirty-two years old in Manhattan work more than forty hours a week; in 1977, only 55 percent did. According to the Department of Labor, American workers get only seven hours of sleep per night (365 hours a year less than recommended), and American parents now spend twenty-two hours less per week with their children than in 1969.

The demands of flexibility frequently come into conflict with the human predisposition for structure. Despite the brave talk at the Five O'Clock Club about individuals taking control of their lives, there is a palpable sense that people want to belong to something. Many of the club's members would, strangely enough, fit nicely into the books that Charles Handy now writes, which simultaneously celebrate the advent of "portfolio careers" and worry about the moral and social consequences of giving people so much freedom. The fashion for flattening hierarchies makes it harder for people to plan their careers. A few lucky ones make spectacular leaps (for which they are often not prepared), while the rest get stuck at the same level for years, insecure and frustrated.

Meanwhile, the downside for the educated is as nothing compared with the downside for the uneducated. Even a full-time contingent worker in America is paid typically only 80 percent of what a regular, full-time employee earns—and the benefits are often minimal. Manufacturing jobs may be getting more interesting, but the same can seldom be said of basic service jobs, such as delivering pizza. New technology often brings bad tidings for the poor, sometimes literally so. In 1999, an Oklahoma firm, Commercial Financial Services, set a first of sorts by using e-mail to tell its 1,450 workers that they had lost their jobs because it was declaring bankruptcy.

What should be done about this? In an article for the *Harvard Business Review* in 1999, Peter Drucker complained that "every existing society, even the most individualistic one, takes two things for granted, if only subconsciously: that organizations outlive workers, and that most people stay put. But today the opposite is true. The need to manage oneself is therefore creating a revolution in human affairs."[11] Even allowing for a little bit of exaggeration, this seems a fair point, and one that poses challenges both for society as a whole and for individuals.

Government's habitual inflexibility is often at its most damaging when it comes to employment policy. Most countries devised their job rules at a time when the main aim was to tide their citizens over from one stable if fairly undemanding job to another. That old social contract has plainly broken down, partly for political reasons (it left politicians at the mercy of militant interest groups) and partly for business ones (firms increasingly need to shed workers even when they are doing well). Now, institutions need to be redesigned with a view to keeping workers employable rather than employed.

In most countries outside America, transferring your pension from one employer to another is difficult. In most Continental countries, getting rid of full-time employees is both expensive and immensely time-consuming; employers predictably choose to expand by hiring part-time workers, putting the entire burden of economic adjustments on the shoulders of the young. By contrast, Japan has equally absurd rules mostly designed to prevent the young from getting temporary work. In 1998, only about a third of Japan's college graduates were able to find full-time jobs, and yet temporary agencies were still forbidden to offer work to anyone within a year of graduation. Many categories of jobs are off-limits to temporary agencies. There are even rules to stop temporary workers from sneakily evolving into full-time ones.

Although America has the advantage of fairly flexible labor laws, its problems come in other disguises. One is the ever-growing number of fraudulent employment and discrimination lawsuits: Nobody wants to hire a potential litigant. Another problem is health care. The difficulty that many portfolio workers find in getting coverage is one reason why so many people stay with their employers until the bitter end. Perhaps the biggest problem in America, however, is education. This land of second chances realized much earlier than other countries that education is a never-ending process, rather than a stage of life that ends when you leave college. Yet such prescience does not make up for the fact that basic education is so lousy. Too many people go to community colleges to learn to read and write rather than to acquire a new skill.

These are well-worn themes. But in the end, most of the responsibility for "managing yourself" falls on, well, yourself. From the individual's point of view, the main lesson is fairly stark: Educate yourself, and then reeducate yourself—particularly if you work in a fast-changing business. In Silicon Valley, people will tell you that a twenty-year-old degree in software engineering is less valuable than the ability to play the latest version of Tomb Raider. Even fairly routine industries, such as agriculture, now demand more sophisticated knowledge of things like chemicals and computers. Sensible workers will take jobs only in those organizations that promise not just decent pay but decent chances of giving them the skills they need to jump to a new job.

But how do you achieve this wonderful thing called employability? Is it just a matter of relying on your own initiative? Or do you need to bond with other people? And if so, who should organize the bonding? One way to frame the argument is to listen to two women who have thought about globalization a great deal: Hang Tran, a student at Stanford Business School, and Amy Dean, a trade unionist.

A Tale of Two Women

Hang Tran's argument that people should pull themselves up by their bootstraps is rooted in her experience. A young Vietnamese American in her final year at Stanford Business School, Hang is one of those people who have the gift of electricity. Despite her slight build, she fills the room with her personality, rattling off a relentless series of pointed observations of the sort that might give Margaret Thatcher's cabinet ministers an uncomfortable sense of déjà vu. She even seems tough on herself: "I think I have the ability to become a CIO or COO but not a CEO." But she makes up for it with an infectious sense of optimism, a fixed belief that the angels will smile on her.

Hang's parents came to Texas in 1975, frightened and destitute, refugees from a disintegrating Vietnam. The family avoided the "little Saigons" that were springing up around America at the time because they wanted their children to say *rice* rather than *wice*. They ended up living in the suburbs of San Antonio and put every penny they earned into sending their children to private school. Hang went to a local university, Saint Mary's ("I was too much of a mommy's girl to leave home for a fancy eastern school," she says, a little defensive of her Ivy-free c.v.), where she captained the running team and excelled in her studies. She then got the safest niche she could find: a job as a chartered accountant at Arthur Andersen.

Hang thrived at Andersen, twice earning accelerated promotions and ending up, by her mid-twenties, with a six-figure salary, a couple of secretaries, an expense account, and a gold-plated future. But her work seemed empty. She transferred to the firm's consulting side. Yet she was still frustrated by the idea of having to "wave good-bye" to a problem that she would rather have solved herself. When her boss told her that "this was as good as it gets"—that if she was not happy now she never would be—she screwed up her courage and left for a job at Enron, then a much admired employer.

Hang's decision to quit Andersen scandalized her parents. How could their dutiful daughter swap a dream job for an uncertain future? Hang understands why refugees who make their livings in the uncertain world of small businesses put such a premium on security. But she had developed a radically different view of her future: She wanted something that interested her rather than just something that paid her a safe salary; and she was not convinced that big companies provided any security. That came only from increasing your own marketability.

For her, Stanford, which she joined from Enron, is a way to get her "international business driving license," an M.B.A. Her time at Enron had taught her the importance of being at the center of a business cluster—"the person next to you on the treadmill might be a great contact"—and there is nowhere closer to the heart of modern business than the Valley. Her time at business school is providing her with a chance to "hang around and learn something" from people such as Scott McNealy and her particular hero, Steve Jobs. Every conversation in Starbucks eventually turns to the question of making a buck out of the new technology. Hang thinks that most of her classmates will end up as millionaires.

Already, Hang has a job at L'Oréal to go to, but she will stay with the

French cosmetics company only as long as it continues to upgrade her skills and provide her with challenges. (One of her dearest wishes is to get a foreign posting—particularly in her native Vietnam.) She expects that L'Oréal will be only the first of a succession of employers. But in the long run she shares the dream of most of her classmates of starting her own company. Wealth would give her time to indulge her hobbies (she is an aspiring pastry chef and antiques collector) and her taste for philanthropy. But the main incentive to go it alone is that it would allow her to be the architect of her own destiny.

If you had to teach a course in global career planning for young cosmocrats, Hang would be one of the first exhibits. But what about people with less ambition and less talent? Or people who lament rather than scorn some of the certainties of the old career structure? Two of Hang's passions are philanthropy and the introduction of more competition into America's public-school system—to set more people free so they can make themselves employable. By contrast, another woman just a few miles away from the Stanford Business School, in a nondescript low-rise building on the outskirts of San Jose, thinks that employability has to be a more communal aim.

For Amy Dean, the leader of the local branch of the AFL-CIO, the same forces that are setting Hang free will eventually send other people scurrying back to trade unions. In Silicon Valley, trade unionists are about as thick on the ground as manual typewriters. But as Donna Quixotes go, Dean has an impressive record. She is part of the new labor movement: young (in her late thirties); well educated (a degree in sociology and economics would have led to postgraduate work had she not been seduced into the International Ladies Garment Workers Union); and plugged into the new economy (her husband works for a software start-up).

When she took over the South Bay branch of the AFL-CIO, it was little more than a blue-collar rest home. Now it is humming, housed in what looks like a high-tech hatchery, staffed by bright young things, and elaborately "networked," along the best Silicon Valley lines. A sister group, Working Partnerships USA, which Dean set up in 1995, does research, trains local activists, and cultivates relations with universities. Dean's organization not only trounced the bosses' candidate in a brutal battle for a seat on the San Jose City Council ("I was up against the single most powerful political machine in the Valley," grumbled the loser) but also won its campaign to force San Jose to adopt a "living wage" for all municipal contractors. San Jose now has the highest minimum wage in the country, almost twice the mandatory level of the State of California.

Dean points out that temporary workers are often miserable workers. The worst-paid live hand-to-mouth existences without medical or other benefits. Even many of the best paid are fearful of the future and envious of those on the permanent payroll, as Microsoft discovered when some "permatemps" won a class-action suit against it. Dean has set up a temping agency of her own, Together@Work. The agency not only pays its workers better than its rivals pay theirs but also gives them medical benefits, pensions, and, above all, training.

The main problem with the idea that trade unions might become points of stability in the new labor market is the unions themselves. Even Dean's modernized trade unions seem much happier with reintroducing old rigidities than with responding to new flexibilities. (It is notable that Dean's power base is in the public sector and that her biggest success has been fixing a minimum wage for city-hall employees in San Jose.) If you go to countries where unions still have power, they tend to use it in inflexible ways. For instance, German unions have used their influence over training programs to defend old jobs rather than prepare people for new ones.

On the other hand, as firms become more nimble, many workers will want to look somewhere for things that make life secure and increase their employability. Pulling yourself up by the bootstraps is all very well, but sometimes you need a little help putting the boots on your feet. In the nineteenth century, unions grew out of the need for security and training: When people wanted a carpenter, they went to the union. In some areas of the new economy, notably Hollywood, unions still play that role. If you are a screenwriter, the screenwriters' guild provides you with various benefits and also negotiates some minimum standards with the studios. The organizers of the Five O'Clock Club are looking at the notion of providing health-care plans to the club's members. There are too many Willy Lomans out there for some organizations not to emerge.

Back to the Future

Many people outside California probably regard this sort of futuristic debate between aggressive individualism and what might be termed flexible collectivism as at best eccentric, at worst irrelevant. Most non-Americans shudder when they hear people talking about "adding to their portfolio of skills." And most European trade unionists think that the best way to deal with the new, flexible economy is to fight it tooth and nail. As we have seen, figures about jobs can be interpreted to show how little is really changing as well as how much.

But anyone who wants to bet on a static view of the future ought to remember two things. The first is Charles Handy's conversation with his official guide in Soviet Russia, which now seems to belong not just to a different decade but to a different world. The second is the story of the Argentine ant and the Hawaiian silversword. The silversword's future has not been planned by anybody, least of all the ant. But a string of unintended consequences may end up robbing the plant of its one chance to reproduce.

Hang Tran is right that each person needs to take his or her fate firmly in hand. But Amy Dean is equally right that they may need help in doing so, even if she puts far too much faith in trade unions. The point is that all sorts of institutions, from colleges to companies, will have to put more emphasis on making people employable; and all sorts of people, even the most comfortable and conservative, need to realize that in an interconnected economy even the tiniest new arrivals can end up changing their world for good. If you doubt that, consider the silversword.

Conclusion

The Hidden Promise:
Liberty Renewed

SOMETIMES AN IMAGE seems so contrived that you hesitate to mention it, for fear of arousing the suspicion that you are the one who has done the contriving.[1] Beneath a daunting plinth with the carved, solemn words "Workers of all lands unite" stands not just a freshly cut bouquet of red roses but also an empty bottle of Johnnie Walker Scotch and a crumpled packet of Silk Cut cigarettes. It is tempting to imagine that these endearing symbols of global commerce are regularly left there as part of some rite of passage for the young traders in the distant towers of the City of London, but the lady at the gate seems surprised ("We do get couples here sometimes"), and a subsequent visit reveals only another bunch of flowers.

Karl Marx's tomb in Highgate Cemetery is a sorry place. The sculpture of his great bearded head is sometimes soiled with pigeon droppings; the army of celebrated intellectuals and communist dignitaries that used to come to pay its respects to the master has dwindled into a tiny band of eccentrics. In one way, this is a pity. As a prophet of socialism, Marx may be kaput; but as a prophet of "the universal interdependence of nations," as he called globalization, he can still seem startlingly relevant.

For all his hatred of the Victorian bourgeoisie, Marx could not conceal his admiration for its ability to turn the world into a single marketplace. Some of this admiration was mere schadenfreude, to be sure, born of his belief that in creating a global working class the bourgeoisie was also creating its very own grave diggers; but a surprising amount of this respect was genuine, like a prizefighter's respect for his muscle-bound opponent. In less than a hundred years, Marx argued, the bourgeoisie had "accomplished wonders far surpassing Egyptian pyramids, Roman aqueducts and Gothic cathedrals"; had conducted "expeditions that put in the shade all former exoduses of nations and crusades"; and had "created more massive and more colossal productive forces" than all preceding generations put together. In achieving all this, it had begun to transform an agglomeration of warring nations and petty principalities into a global marketplace.[2]

Marx was at his most expansive on globalization in *The Communist Manifesto*, which he cowrote with Friedrich Engels, a factory owner turned revolutionary, and published in 1848, a year in which ancien régimes were tottering throughout Europe.

> The need of a constantly expanding market for its products chases the bourgeoisie over the entire surface of the globe. It must nestle everywhere, settle everywhere, establish connections everywhere.
>
> The bourgeoisie has through its exploitation of the world market given a cosmopolitan character to production and consumption in every country. . . . In place of the old wants, satisfied by the production of the country, we find new wants, requiring for their satisfaction the products of distant land and climes. In place of the old local and national seclusion and self-sufficiency, we have intercourse in every direction, universal interdependence of nations.[3]

Even Marx's final resting place is, to some extent, a vindication of this great insight. Opposite him in Highgate lies William Nassar Kennedy, a colonel of the Winnipeg Rifles who was "called home" in 1885 while returning to Canada from Egypt, where he was in command of the Nile Voyageurs. A little further down there is John MacKinlay and his wife, Caroline Louisa, "late of Bombay." Highgate Cemetery is strewn with the graves of Victorian soldiers, bureaucrats, and merchants who devoted their lives to turning the world into a single market.

What would Marx make of the world today? Imagine for a moment that the prayers of the faithful were answered and the great man awoke from his slumber. Having climbed out of his mausoleum, dusted himself off, and taken a frustrated sniff at the bottle of scotch, what would Marx find? There would, of course, be the shock of discovering that, on all the big issues, he had been proved hopelessly wrong. It was communism that succumbed to its own internal contradictions and capitalism that swept all before it. But he might at least console himself with the thought that his description of globalization remains as sharp today as it was 150 years ago.

Wandering down Highgate Hill, Marx would discover the Bank of Cyprus (which services the three hundred thousand Cypriots that live in London), several curry houses (now England's most popular sort of eatery), and a Restaurante do Brazil. He might be less surprised to find a large Irish community. But the sign inviting him to watch "Irish Sports Live," thanks to a pub's satellite-television linkup, might intrigue him. On the skyline, he would soon spot the twin towers of Canary Wharf, built by Canadian developers with money borrowed from Japanese banks and now occupied mostly by American investment banks.

Marx would hear Asian voices and see white schoolchildren proudly wearing T-shirts with pictures of black English soccer stars. Multicultural London (which is now home to thirty-three ethnic communities, each with a population of more than ten thousand) might well exhilarate a man who was called "the Moor" by his own children because of his dark complexion. He could stop at almost any newsstand and pick up a copy of the *Frankfurter Allgemeine Zeitung* that would be no more than a day old. Nearly swept off his feet by a passing Rolls-Royce, he might be more surprised to discover that the vehicle, like the rest of Britain's car industry, is now owned by a German company.

If Marx were to venture back to his old haunts in Soho, he would find a cluster of video-production companies and advertising agencies that sells its services to the world. If he climbed up to Hampstead Heath, the Marx family's favorite picnic spot, he might be surprised to discover that the neighborhood's most expensive house is now owned by an Indian, Lakshmi Mittal, who has built up one of the world's biggest steel companies. London is home to around a quarter of Europe's five hundred biggest companies. Its financial-services industry alone employs directly or indirectly 850,000 people, more than the population of the city of Frankfurt.[4]

Yet even as Marx marveled at these new creations of the bourgeoisie and perhaps applauded its meritocratic dynamism, it is hard to believe that some of the old revolutionary fires would not burn anew. Poverty of the grinding sort that inspired Engels to write *The Condition of the Working Class in England* (1845) might have disappeared; the rigid class system of the Victorians might have evaporated; Marx might even be slightly shocked by the absence of domestic servants. But the founder of communism would have no trouble tracking down inequality and sensing that it was on the increase.

Barely ten miles separate elegant Chelsea (where, ironically enough, the Marx family lived when they first came to London, before being evicted for not paying the rent) from the crumbling wasteland of Newham, but they seem like two different countries. In one, you might be forgiven for thinking that the biggest problem is the availability of residential parking permits; in the other, two thirds of the sixteen-year-olds fail their basic high-school exams, and the mortality rate for people under twenty-five is 50 percent above the national average.[5] As he studied the newspaper and looked at the pictures on the flashing television screens of, say, Somalia or even parts of Los Angeles, Marx might well see globalization as a process that is only just beginning—a job half done. Once again, he might consider, the world is hurtling toward a "crisis of capitalism"—not unlike the last one that his own theories did so much to make ruinous.

The Priority of Liberty

This, then, is the beginning of the future, perfect or not, that we have tried to describe in this book. The fact that it has much in common with the world of yesterday (and especially the world of a century ago) is not surprising. History condemns us to repeat ourselves, though not necessarily to repeat all our mistakes.

Throughout this book, we have tried to build a measured defense of globalization. Yes, it does increase inequality, but it does not create a winner-take-all society, and the winners hugely outnumber the losers. Yes, it leaves some people behind, but it helps millions more to leap ahead. Yes, it can make bad government worse, but the onus should be on crafting better government, not blaming globalization. Yes, it curtails some of the power of nation-states, but they remain the fundamental unit of modern politics. Globalization is not destroying geography, merely enhancing it.

In most cases, the bulwarks of our defense have been economic. The simple fact is that globalization makes us richer—or makes enough of us richer to make the whole process worthwhile. Globalization clearly benefits producers by giving them greater choice over their raw materials, production techniques, and human talent, not to mention over the markets where they sell their goods. Equally clearly, globalization benefits consumers by providing them with better goods at better prices. Globalization increases efficiency and thus prosperity.

These economic arguments need to be made, and with far more eloquence, by our leaders. Too many politicians take the Clintonesque tack of defending the easy bits of globalization—typically, the successes of their own country's exports—and shying away from talking about the benefits that flow, say, from imports or foreign takeovers of "their" companies. This is not only economically illiterate but dangerous, because it allows myths to emerge, such as the idea that globalization is a zero-sum game. But there is also a broader need to wrench globalization from all the dry talk of markets penetrated, currencies depreciated, and GDPs accelerated and to place the process in its proper political context: as an extension of the idea of liberty and as a chance to renew the fundamental rights of the individual.

Nowadays, "liberalism" has become just another political slogan. In the United States, Ronald Reagan made it into something of a swearword for Republicans, and Democrats still use it gingerly. Around the world, liberal parties stand for everything from conservatism (Canada), fascism (Russia), and people with beards who want to legalize cannabis (Britain). Yet most of the tenets of modern democracy actually stem from the classical liberalism of a group of writers and thinkers who, from the seventeenth century onward, argued that society should be based on the rights of individuals rather than on the hierarchy of a "great chain of being," stretching from God downward, with everyone assigned a fixed place.

This belief in individualism, which was at the heart of both the Enlightenment and the American Revolution, was actually a fairly global movement itself. Its foundations were laid in Britain by groups such as the Levelers (whose belief that "the poorest he in England has a life to live as much as the richest he" so unsettled their rulers) and thinkers such as John Locke, who argued that individuals had a right to break their contracts with their sovereigns if he or she trampled on their rights. Later British theorists such as Adam Smith and John Stuart Mill refined and expanded the creed, turning it into the foundation of a new academic discipline (economics) and a new branch of philosophy (utilitarianism). But by then it had been carried around the world—and adapted to local conditions—by everybody from Thomas Paine (who announced the birth of the "rights of man") to Thomas Jefferson, Voltaire, and Alexis de Tocqueville. As we have already seen, both John Maynard Keynes and Friedrich von Hayek claimed allegiance to it (though Marx, of course, despised it).

In the process, liberalism has become something of a broad church, yet it always returns to two fundamental principles and one fundamental prejudice. The first principle is that rights belong to individuals rather than to governments or to social groups. The second is that the essence of freedom lies in individual choice. The ideal society allows individuals to make as many decisions as possible without reference to some external authority. The fundamental prejudice is skepticism and an abhorrence of certainty. One reason why liberals are drawn to free markets is because they distrust the power of bureaucrats. Absolutist creeds, whether those of the seventeenth-century papacy or of Marxism, are to be distrusted. And, crucially, liberalism—unlike its bastard child, libertarianism—is also distrustful of itself: It may be predisposed against governments interfering in people's lives, but it is quick to admit that there are times when this makes sense—for instance, in order to tax them so that it can provide education and health care.

The twentieth century was an awkward century for liberalism. The creed managed to see off the horrors of totalitarianism, yet by the end of the century the state was enormously more powerful than it had been at the beginning. The Fabian presumption that "the gentleman in Whitehall" or Washington knows "better what is good for people than the people know themselves" lingers not only in the nannyish environmentalism of Al Gore but in the preachy moralism of many Republicans. (In Britain, Blairism has even managed to combine both.) As for technology, for much of the twentieth century it only strengthened John Stuart Mill's lament that "the tendency of all the changes taking place in the world is to strengthen society and diminish the power of the individual." Mass production reduced workers to cogs in an infernal machine. Computers gathered information on us all.

The Open Society

Globalization redresses this balance in two ways. The most obvious is that it puts limits on the power of government. This advantage is most obvious in commerce. Free trade makes it easier for businesspeople to escape from interfering officials by moving their money and operations abroad. As we have pointed out, companies seldom want to flee, but the very fact that they might acts as a brake on those officials. The sullen fury of a Bangalore bureaucrat staring at the satellite dishes that allow "his" software companies to export their products without his grasping fingers interfering would delight Mill (even though he worked for the often more extortionate East India Company). More important still, free trade allows ordinary people to buy products from companies who make the best of their kind rather than from those that enjoy cozy relationships with governments. Similarly, they can put their retirement money in pension funds that are not tied to schemes of national aggrandizement.

Governments are not retreating from this easily. They can still slap controls on the flow of capital (as Malaysia did in the wake of the Asian crisis) or even on the flow of information. (Singapore employs a staff of censors whose job is to surf the Internet ceaselessly looking for objectionable information to block.) But the world is nevertheless a lot freer today than it was just a few decades ago, before globalization got into high gear. In 1966, for example, the British Labor government imposed a travel allowance that virtually confined Britons to their own country except for two weeks' worth of penny-pinching foreign vacation. Today, any politician who suggested such a restriction, even to fight terrorism, would be carted off to an asylum.

Indeed, the recent history of globalization can be written as a story, albeit an uneven story, of spreading a political culture that is based on individual liberty to areas that have been longing to embrace it for years. The last dozen years of the twentieth century saw not only the spectacular death of the biggest alternative to liberal democracy, totalitarian communism, but also the slow death of other collectivist models. Around the world, countries have abandoned attempts to plan their way to prosperity. Even the Asian crisis, in its own awful way, has made it more difficult for the continent's authoritarians to boast that they had discovered a nondemocratic way to generate growth.

Many on the left would argue that globalization has merely involved a change of master. Globalization may have liberated us from the onus of having to get our television programs—or our health care and pensions—from our governments, but it has forced us to get the same things from giant companies that are just as remote and even less accountable. The gentleman in Whitehall has been replaced by the knucklehead in the boardroom or, if you work in the Académie Française, by the illiterate in Hollywood.

This suspicion is healthy and should be encouraged. But so far the evidence is that it is misplaced. Of course, businesses will try to control markets, but that does not mean that they will be able to. As we have seen, one of the wonders of global capitalism is its capacity to hurl challenges at incumbent champions. Most of the forces of globalization—particularly the availability of capital and technology—favor small companies. In parts of Europe and Asia, commercial oligarchies are clinging to power, but only because governments collude with them. There is nothing global about, say, the importance of *guanxi* in Asia—quite the opposite. By the same token, the Department of Justice campaign to restrain Microsoft's power, no matter how misguided, has a legitimately global aim of trying to open up a market.

In fact, many of the most vengeful howls directed at globalization come from self-interested business elites who are being forced to surrender to consumer choice. Globalization does not mean homogenization. People want to consume books, movies, even potato chips, that reflect their own identities, and those identities remain primarily national. When politicians complain that globalization is changing society, they are correct, but they seldom bother to ask whose society it is. When society is defined by a fairly compact national economy, an elite has a chance of co-opting it. But when society is an open-ended international system, it becomes increasingly difficult for any elite to identify their values with the common good.

The Individual's Prayer

Restricting overmighty states and elites is all very well, but globalization increases the basic freedom of individuals as well. We have already talked about the tyranny of place: Most people's lots in life are determined by where they were born, something illiberal regimes everywhere have done their best to reinforce. As Leszek Kolakawski, a Polish intellectual, points out, one of the defining features of communist regimes is their refusal to allow people to move from city to city without official permission; they even made short journeys difficult, providing few road signs or decent street maps. Even today, the lives of half the world's population are bounded by local villages, and local markets.

Travel and migration have long provided a fraction of the world's population with freedom from the tyranny of place. The printing press and the television have allowed others a more imaginary form of escape. Globalization is now making these freedoms more pervasive. The impact of the Internet, particularly as it goes wireless, will also be dramatic. The World Wide Web allows people to gain access to information anywhere at any time. And it allows them to do so in a way that undermines local elites and expensive middlemen. People will never escape the pull of geography entirely, as the tendency of business to cluster in particular places shows. But those clusters only survive if they work with the grain of globalization. And the penalty for being born a long way from those clusters is diminishing. Remember the Bangladeshi farmers using their cell phones to check the proper prices for their produce rather than having to accept the diktats of local grain merchants.

The more these ties weaken, the more people can exercise what used to be called God-given talents. Again, businesspeople are the most obvious beneficiaries: If you have a good idea and the entrepreneurial vim to pursue it, you can take it anywhere you want. If, like Michael Skok of AlphaBlox, you think that your business belongs in Silicon Valley, not the Thames valley, you can take it there. But there are also more spiritual, artistic reasons to believe that globalization is a good thing. The thousands of Miltons who remain "mute and inglorious" in their villages often begin to sing only after they move to the "mansion houses of liberty" that are the world's great cities. Bustling centers of trade from fifteenth-century Venice to twentieth-century New York have usually been centers of creativity, too. Even if your God-given talents are more prosaic, it is becoming ever easier to study abroad, and, thanks again to the Internet, you will soon be able to do so (more or less) without leaving home.

Somewhere behind the freedom to exercise our talents lies the most fundamental freedom of all: the freedom to define our own identities. This can sound like the moan of a petulant teenager, but it is at the heart of what is becoming one of the main debates of our time, between liberals and the growing band of communitarians. (To the extent that "the third way" means anything at all, its adherents are probably on the side of the communitarians.) Communitarians, as their name suggests, worry about the effect of things like globalization on communities. John Gray, one of globalization's most searching critics, has argued that human beings' "deepest need is a home, a network of common practices and inherited traditions that confers on them the blessings of a settled identity."

There can be no doubt that people need a home and a network. But does this home have to be the one they were born in? And does this network have to be the one provided by their ancestors? People also have a drive to better themselves, to extend their identities, to cross traditional boundaries, and to try out new experiences. John Gray himself happily abandoned the Newcastle working class into which he was born for the metropolitan intelligentsia. One of the many benefits of globalization is that it increases the number of people who can exercise Gray's privilege of fashioning his own identity.

This is not to say that conservative and communitarian worries about individualism run wild are empty. In the same breath that he praised America's faith in individualism, Tocqueville warned of the danger that each man may be "shut up in the solitude of his own heart."[6] One of the great risks of globalization is that it fosters anomie—the normlessness that comes from having your ties with the rest of society weakened. Anybody who spends long periods of time on business trips knows the loneliness of the long-distance traveler. Ex-pats complain that their children grow up not knowing their grandparents. The most common complaint among Internet addicts is that they end up feeling (rather like the compulsive masturbators of Victorian medical treatises) isolated, lonely, and depressed.

All too true. Yet the issue that separates liberals from communitarians is not the desirability of human ties but the question of coercion. For liberals, the best communities are the spontaneous creations of free individuals rather than the products of bossy politicians, and one of the many cases for globalization is that it lets a million of these spontaneous communities bloom. The smaller the world becomes, the more communities are defined by common interests and outlooks rather than by the mere accident of physical proximity.

The idea of spontaneous communities will hardly placate globalization's harshest critics. For some people, the idea that individuals take precedence over society is nothing more than Western cultural imperialism. Wee Kim Wee, the former president of Singapore, argues that "placing society above the self" is one of his country's "core values." It is all very well for the ego-maniacs of Manhattan and Los Angeles to abandon their gods in pursuit of self-fulfillment. But everybody else knows that such selfishness leads inexorably to the wasteland.

Yet the yearning for freedom is no more peculiar to the West than the yearning for prosperity. Other parts of the world have been quieter on the subject not because their peoples are wedded to collectivism but because their rulers have been less fussy about the methods they have used to hold on to power. Singaporeans bitterly resent the fact that their government gives them a superb education but then proceeds to treat them like children. The students who were brutally crushed at Tiananmen Square constructed replicas of the Statue of Liberty.

An Empire without End

Look around the world, and it is not hard to find examples of people for whom this message may seem a little empty. What does Reginaldo Gobetti care about the freedom to create his own identity; he just wants a job. Our argument is not that globalization is delivering the liberal dream, with billions of people gradually becoming the wired (or wireless) equivalent of Jefferson's yeoman farmers. Our argument is merely that globalization is delivering enough of that dream to make it worth pressing forward and to make it worth defending on more than just narrow economic grounds.

In fact, the two arguments should run in tandem. Globalization is helping to give birth to an economy that is closer to the classic theoretical model of capitalism, under which rational individuals pursue their interests in the light of perfect information, relatively free from government and geographical obstacles. It is also helping to create a society that is closer to the model that liberal political theorists once imagined, in which power lies increasingly in the hands of individuals rather than governments, and in which people are free, within reasonable bounds, to pursue the good life wherever they find it.

It would be nice if we could end on that optimistic, perhaps even slightly utopian, note. Yet we have also stressed the importance of vigilance and the need for not just politicians but also those who have prospered from globalization—particularly the cosmocrats—to help those who have done less well.

The trouble is that the devil has all the best tunes. One reason why globalization's enemies are so much more persuasive than its friends is that they are more visible: The victims are usually concentrated in particular places, whereas its beneficiaries are spread out all over the place. But supporters have also done a lousy job of making their case. We have already lamented the shortage of Peels and Rockefellers. But consider once again whether any modern leader would stand up and argue that "by encouraging freedom of intercourse between the nations of the world we are promoting the separate welfare of each and are fulfilling the beneficent designs of an all-seeing Creator" or invite his audience to celebrate "commerce, the happy instrument of promoting civilization, of abating national jealousies and prejudices and of encouraging the maintenance of general peace by every consideration as well as every obligation of Christian duty."

It is not just the passion that sets Sir Robert Peel apart from his modern peers. It is the fact that he bothered to make the case in what then amounted to the language of the streets—and made it, moreover, to the people rather than just to a group of bigwigs. When Peel died, tens of thousands of people contributed their pennies to construct memorials to the man who had masterminded the repeal of the corn laws. Naturally, it would be nice if, say, the IMF made more of an effort to explain its ways; but you need only spend half an hour with any of its denizens to realize that you are more likely to get Ciceronian oratory from your typewriter. Kofi Annan has tried to make his voice heard, but his need to please all the UN's members has simultaneously blunted his message. The proper place for the trumpets of globalization to sound is from national political figures. George Bush the elder ushered in his new world order. Bill Clinton, a far more agile communicator, failed to come up with one memorable phrase on the subject.

The time when such leadership will be needed could be close at hand. As we said at the beginning of this book, Osama bin Laden exploited globalization. So far George W. Bush's response has been brave on the military front, but too often he has taken a unilateral course, exaggerating the transatlantic rift. He has also needlessly stirred up the fires of protectionism. A serious downturn in the economy could be disastrous. Meanwhile, despite the terrible evidence of the Asian contagion, there are still plenty of countries around the world that are continuing to try to have it both ways, sucking in Western capital while refusing to open their economies. Given its penchant for funneling money into favored firms and concealing corporate and government activities from the prying eyes of outsiders, China could yet produce a disaster that would make the Asian crisis look like a tea party.

Highgate Man

Which brings us back to Highgate. It might seem perverse to end a book on globalization by returning to a hypothetically reincarnated German—particularly given that Karl Marx was a sworn enemy of the liberalism that we admire. Yet one of the things that Marx would recognize immediately about this particular global era is a paradox that he spotted in the last one: The more successful globalization becomes, the more it seems to whip up its own backlash. The process is not unlike waves sweeping up on a shore: Each one that rushes forward also creates its undertow.

The undoing of globalization, in Marx's view, would come not just from losers resenting the success of the winners but also from the winners themselves losing their appetite for the battle. Globalization's power, and much of its efficiency, is founded on its ability to keep on exposing weaknesses and imperfections. This is good for us all in the long run, but it makes it difficult for even the winners to enjoy the quiet life. The more relentless economic integration seems, the greater the short-term appeal of politicians who seek to resist it.

There is even a suspicion that globalization's psychic energy—the uncertainty it creates that forces companies, governments, and people to perform better—may have a natural stall point, a moment when people can take no more. As Marx put it in *The Communist Manifesto*:

> Uninterrupted disturbance of all social conditions, everlasting uncertainty and agitation distinguish the bourgeois epoch from all earlier ones. . . . All that is solid melts into air, all that is holy is profaned, and man is at last compelled to face with sober senses his real conditions of life and his relations with his kind.[7]

Overcoming this paradox—the seeming invincibility of globalization and its underlying fragility—is the central challenge of the new century.

Acknowledgments

In our authors' note we mentioned our gratitude both to our immediate families and to the editor of *The Economist*, Bill Emmott. In truth, both represent the tips of large icebergs on which we have floated for some time. Our families—not just our wives and children but our parents, siblings, aunts, uncles, and in-laws—have been bullied, harassed, bored, used, and generally let down in such a way that the words *your book*, even when not punctuated by expletives, have become bywords for inadequate behavior.

At *The Economist*, we have also leaned on the kindness and expertise of others. Ann Wroe, Barbara Smith, Barbara Beck, John Peet, Edward Carr, David Manasian, Oliver Morton, and Johnny Grimond either commissioned or edited some of the work that has found its way into this book. Other colleagues, including Iain Carson, Matthew Symonds, Carol Howard, and Nick Valery, pulled us up on particular points, while Gideon Rachman always provided us with a powerful reason to keep going whenever we thought of giving up. However, perhaps our biggest debt goes to those luckless souls who have had the misfortune of sharing offices with us: Zanny Minton Beddoes, John Parker, Matthew Bishop, Sameena Ahmad, Louise Katsiaouni, Tina Davis, Fiona Haynes, and especially Rachel Horwood and Rosemarie Ward.

We would like to thank the wide variety of people who let us into their homes while we were researching this book, from Marcus de Ferranti in London to John Rhodes and the Bruderhof at Rifton and the Gobettis in São Paulo. There is also a long list of people who helped us research the book: Michael Reid and Thiery Ogier in Brazil; Elizabeth Pisani and Robert Guest in Africa; Joel Kotkin, Kevin Starr, Gregory Rodriguez, and Allison Silver in Los

Angeles; Ali and William Mackesy in Hong Kong; Tessa Wheeler in Morocco; Jane Millington and Vladimir Kovalyov in Saint Petersburg; and Peter Bergen in Washington, D.C., who gave us a peek at his researches on Osama bin Laden. Similarly, there can be few more unpleasant things than a phone call from a writer announcing that he would like to come and stay with you: Lionel and Lidija Wigram in Los Angeles, Nick and Kim Hurd in Brazil, Percy and Clara Weatherall in Hong Kong, Andrew and Arianne Cowley in Moscow, Robert and Grania Read in London, and Charlotte and John Duthie, also in London, all somehow managed to sound pleased when that call came—even when it was for the second time.

A wide number of people took the time to read all or parts of this book when they surely had better things to do: Edward Carr, Anthony Gottlieb, Chris Anderson, Zanny Minton-Beddoes, John Parker, Matthew Bishop, Rosemarie Ward, Peter David, and John Heilemann. Mark Doyle and Rachel Horwood have patiently helped us update this version of the book. We would like to thank Aldon James and the National Arts Club in Manhattan for lending us a room in which to write; and Amanda Fellows for designing our website.

We have been extremely lucky in having Jon Karp as our editor. He has proved an excellent critic, in the better sense of that word. Even when we have been convinced that he was wrong about a particular phrase or point, we have, sooner or later, had to admit he was right. We would also like to thank Carie Freimuth, Timothy Mennel, and Will Weisser at Random House. Finally, we owe an immense debt to the Wylie Agency—to Sarah Chalfant, Liza Walworth, Georgia Garrett, and particularly Andrew Wylie. Right from the start, Andrew grasped what this book should be about and kept us from wandering too far from that vision. If we have let him—and, indeed, you—down, then the fault is entirely our own.

Notes

Introduction

1. John Maynard Keynes, *The Economic Consequences of the Peace* (London: Macmillan, 1919), p. xx

2. Peter Bergen subsequently published *Holy War, Inc.* (New York: Free Press, 2001).

3. John Helliwell, *How Much Do National Borders Matter?* (Washington, D.C.: Brookings Institution Press, 1997).

4. Joe Sharkey, "On the Road," *The New York Times*, June 11, 2002.

5. John Gray, "The Era of Globalisation Is Over," *The New Statesman*, September 24, 2002.

6. Adam Smith, *The Theory of Moral Sentiments* (1759), part III, chapter III. This is available online at www.adamsmith.org.

7. "Globalization, Growth and Poverty," World Bank policy research report, December 2001.

8. "The Prosperity League," *The Economist*, June 22, 2002.

9. Ibid.

10. Clive Crook, "A Survey of Globalization," *The Economist*, September 27, 2001.

11. Ibid.

12. These statistics all come from "How Big Are Multinational Companies?," a paper released in January 2002 by Paul de Grauwe of the University of Leuven and Filip Camerman of the Belgian Senate.

13. Crook, "A Survey of Globalization."

14. Hernando de Soto, *The Mystery of Capital: Why Capitalism Triumphs in the West and Fails Everywhere Else* (New York: Basic Books, 2000).

Chapter 1

1. Robert Skidelsky, *John Maynard Keynes: Hopes Betrayed, 1883–1920* (London: Macmillan, 1983), p. 170.

2. Quoted in Douglas Irwin, *Against the Tide: An Intellectual History of Free Trade* (Princeton: Princeton University Press, 1996), p. 188.

3. These examples are from the excellent "Schools Brief on Trade," *The Economist*, November 8, 1997.

4. In August 1843, James Wilson published the preliminary number and prospectus of *The Economist: or, The Political, Commercial, Agricultural, and Free-Trade Journal*.

5. Michael Bordo, Barry Eichengreen, and Douglas Irwin, "Is Globalization Really Different Than Globalization a Hundred Years Ago?" National Bureau of Economic Research, Working Paper 7195, June 1999.

6. United Nations, *World Investment Report 1994: Transnational Corporations, Employment and the Workplace* (New York and Geneva, 1994), p. 121.

7. Ibid., p. 120.

8. Skidelsky, *John Maynard Keynes: Hopes Betrayed*, pp. 121–22.

9. John Maynard Keynes, *The Economic Consequences of the Peace* (London: Macmillan, 1919), p. xx.

10. For an account and summary of the lecture, see Robert Skidelsky, *John Maynard Keynes: The Economist as Savior, 1920–1937* (London: Macmillan, 1992), pp. 476–80.

11. Skidelsky, *John Maynard Keynes: Hopes Betrayed*, p. 227.

12. Charles Kindleberger, *The World in Depression, 1929–1939*, rev. ed. (Berkeley and Los Angeles: University of California Press, 1986), pp. 63–64.

13. Quoted in Irwin, *Against the Tide*, p. 195.

14. Skidelsky, *John Maynard Keynes: The Economist as Savior*, p. 490.

15. E. J. Hobsbawm, *The Age of Extremes: A History of the World, 1914–1991* (New York: Vintage, 1994), p. 88.

16. Kindleberger, *World in Depression*, p. 278.

17. For more information, see www.wto.org.

18. The best history of the relationship between governments and markets is Daniel Yergin and Joseph Stanislaw, *The Commanding Heights: The Battle Between Government and the Marketplace That Is Remaking the Modern World* (New York: Simon and Schuster, 1998). This book has been most useful in the preparation of this chapter.

19. Bertrand Russell, *Autobiography, 1872–1914*, vol. 1 (London, 1967), p. 107.

20. Norman MacKenzie and Jeanne MacKenzie, eds., *The Diary of Beatrice Webb*, vol. 2, *1895–1905* (London: Virago, 1983), p. 63.

21. David Landes, *The Wealth and Poverty of Nations: Why Some Are So Rich and Others Are So Poor* (New York: W. W. Norton, 1998).

22. Yari Aharoni, *The Evolution and Management of State-Owned Enterprises* (Cambridge, Mass.: Ballinger Publishing, 1986), p. 2.
23. Ibid., p. 46.
24. Yergin and Stanislaw, *Commanding Heights*, p. 107.
25. Skidelsky, *John Maynard Keynes: The Economist as Savior,* pp. 457, 459.
26. "Delivering the Goods," *The Economist*, November 15, 1997.
27. United Nations, *World Investment Report 1999* (New York and Geneva, 1999), p. 131.

Chapter 2

1. Quoted in Richard Oliver, *The Shape of Things to Come* (New York: Business Week Books, 1998), p. 24.
2. Quoted in "How We Live: Air Conditioning," in "2000: The Power of Invention," *Newsweek*, special issue, winter 1997–1998.
3. "The Most Influential Innovations of the Millennium," *The Wall Street Journal*, January 11, 1999.
4. "Delivering the Goods," *The Economist*, November 15, 1997.
5. David Kirkpatrick, "Grove in China," *Fortune*, August 17, 1998.
6. Thomas Friedman, "The Internet Wars," *The New York Times*, April 11, 1998.
7. The European Information Technology Observatory Report, 1998.
8. Keynote address by William Kennard, chairman of the Federal Communications Commission, All-Africa Telecoms Conference, September 9, 1998.
9. Frances Cairncross, *The Death of Distance: How the Communications Revolution Will Change Our Lives* (Boston: Harvard Business School Press, 1997), p. 233.
10. Bob Davis and David Wessel, *Prosperity: The Coming Twenty-Year Boom and What It Means to You* (New York: Times Books, 1998), pp. 34–38.
11. "All Lines Engaged," *Financial Times*, August 7, 1998.
12. Quoted in Paul Taylor, "The Revolutionary Shape of Things to Come: Survey of Information Technology," *Financial Times*, January 13, 1999.

Chapter 3

1. Richard Barnet and John Cavanagh, *Global Dreams: Imperial Corporations and the New World Order* (New York: Simon and Schuster, 1994), p. 362.
2. "Time to Turn Off the Tap?" *The Economist*, September 22, 1998.
3. See work by Alan Taylor of Northwestern University, cited in "Capital Goes Global," *The Economist*, October 25, 1997.
4. Interview with author, September 16, 1998.
5. John Taglibue, "Selling Europe on the Stock Market," *The New York Times*, March 1, 1998.

6. Hearing of the House Banking and Financial Services Committee, September 15, 1998.

7. Glenn Yago and David Goldman, Milken Institute, "Capital Access Index: Emerging and Submerging Markets."

8. One summary of their positions can be found in "Capital Controversies," *The Economist*, May 23, 1998.

9. Gregory Millman, *The Vandal's Crown: How Rebel Currency Traders Overthrew the World's Central Banks* (New York: Free Press, 1995).

10. Examples taken from John Plender, "Revisiting a Deadly Disease," *Financial Times*, September 21, 1998.

11. Paul Krugman, "A Letter to Malaysia's Prime Minister," *Fortune*, September 28, 1998.

12. Patrick Lyons, "A Global Vote for U.S. Style of Corporate Openness," *The New York Times*, May 9, 1999.

Chapter 4

1. Wellford Wilms, *Restoring Prosperity: How Workers and Managers Are Forging a New Culture of Cooperation* (New York: Times Books, 1996), p. 203.

2. Keith Bradsher, "GM's Efficient Brazil Plant Raises Fears Closer to Home," *The New York Times*, June 15, 1998.

3. "American-Style Pay Moves Abroad," *The New York Times*, September 3, 1998.

4. "Gates' Law," *Context* 1:1 (winter 1998).

5. John Micklethwait and Adrian Wooldridge, *The Witch Doctors: Making Sense of the Management Gurus* (New York: Times Books, 1996).

Chapter 5

1. Richard Morais, "Porn Goes Public," *Forbes*, June 14, 1999.

2. Jeffrey Gettleman, "LA Economy's Dirty Secret," *Los Angeles Times*, September 1, 1999.

3. "Giving the Customer What He Wants," *The Economist*, February 14, 1998.

4. Jessica Mitford, *The American Way of Death Revisited* (New York: Alfred A. Knopf, 1998), p. 233.

5. Ibid., p. 191.

6. Ibid., p. 229.

7. Matthew Bishop, "Privatising Peace of Mind: A Survey of Social Insurance," *The Economist*, October 24, 1998, is the source for many of the statistics in the following paragraphs.

8. Peter Peterson, "Grey Dawn: The Global Aging Crisis," *Foreign Affairs*, January/February 1999, p. 46.

9. "Reading, Writing and Enrichment," *The Economist*, January 16, 1999.

Chapter 6

1. John Kay and Leslie Hannah, "Myth of Critical Mass," *Financial Times*, March 25, 1998.

2. Robert Samuelson, "Corporate Power? It's Actually Waning," *International Herald Tribune*, May 28, 1998.

3. Theodore Levitt, "The Globalization of Markets," *Harvard Business Review*, May–June 1983.

4. Quoted in Evelyn Iritani and Stuart Silverstein, "The World Makes Business Go Round," *Los Angeles Times*, May 10, 1998.

5. Nikhil Deogun and Jonathan Karp, "For Coke in India, Thums Up Is the Real Thing," *The Wall Street Journal*, April 29, 1998.

6. Paulette Thomas, "Minority Businesses Increase Cross-Ethnic Marketing," *The Wall Street Journal*, April 21, 1998.

7. Peter Schwartz and Peter Leyden, "The Long Boom: A History of the Future, 1980–2020," *Wired*, July 1997.

8. Nathan Myhrvold, "The Dawn of Technomania," *The New Yorker*, October 20, 1997.

9. Stephen Roach, "Where the Boom Busts," *Wired*, July 1998.

10. In November 1997, the editor of *BusinessWeek*, Stephen Shepard, wrote a long essay in which he accused "old economists" (including *The Economist*) of inventing a straw man by implying that new economists, such as his own magazine, had said that economics needed to be rewritten and that the new economy was a recipe for permanent bliss. Of course, he did not think that inflation was dead, or the business cycle extinct; merely that the speed limit for the U.S. economy should be raised. This argument only prompted a withering statistical attack from Paul Krugman in *Slate* (www.slate.com/dismal/97-12-18/dismal.asp). But Shepard was right to say that both sides have been prone to exaggeration.

11. James Glassman and Kevin Hassett, *Dow 36,000: The New Strategy for Profiting from the Coming Rise in the Stock Market* (New York: Times Books, 1999).

12. One of the best debunkings of antiglobalist thinking is Gary Burtless et al., *Globaphobia: Confronting Fears about Open Trade* (Washington, D.C.: Brookings Institution Press, 1998), which has been very useful in this chapter.

13. "White Man's Shame," *The Economist*, September 25, 1999.

14. See charts in "The Strange Life of Low Tech America," *The Economist*, October 17, 1998.

15. Julio Laboy, "Clothiers in the Barrio to Japanese Teen Rebels," *The Wall Street Journal*, April 8, 1998.

Chapter 7

1. Lowell Bryan et al., *Race for the World: Strategies to Build a Great Global Firm* (Boston: Harvard Business School Press, 1999).
2. General Electric finished first in *Fortune*'s list of the world's most admired companies in 1998 and 1999.
3. Leon Wynter, "Business and Race," *The Wall Street Journal*, April 1, 1998.
4. John Stopford, "Multinational Corporations Think Again: Organizational Reinvention Confounds Widespread Perception," *Foreign Policy*, no. 113 (winter 1998–1999).
5. Peter Drucker, "Management's New Paradigms," *Forbes*, September 5, 1998.
6. John Lawler and Johngseok Bae, "Overt Discrimination by Multinational Firms," *Industrial Relations Journal*, April 1998.
7. One survey by McKinsey, taking in seventy-seven companies and six thousand managers, found fairly unanimous agreement. The most important resource is not capital, strategy, or R and D; it is talent.
8. C. K. Prahalad and Kenneth Lieberthal, "The End of Corporate Imperialism," *Harvard Business Review*, July–August 1998.
9. Niraj Dawar and Tony Frost, "Competing with Giants," *Harvard Business Review*, March–April 1999.
10. "Out of the Shadows," *The Economist*, August 28, 1999.
11. Dawar and Frost, "Competing with Giants."
12. Adrian Wooldridge, "The World in Your Pocket: A Survey of Telecommunications," *The Economist*, October 9, 1999, esp. pp. 23–27.
13. Ibid., p. 24.
14. The best description of GE's culture is in Noel Tichy and Stratford Sherman, *Control Your Destiny or Somebody Else Will* (New York: Doubleday, 1993).
15. Paul Doremus et al., *The Myth of the Global Corporation* (Princeton: Princeton University Press, 1998).

Chapter 8

1. "The frontier is the basic political institution," argues Malcolm Anderson in his comprehensive guide to borders, *Frontiers: Territory and State Formation in the Modern World* (London: Polity Press, 1996). "No rule-bound economic, social or political life could be organized without them."
2. E. J. Hobsbawm, *Nations and Nationalism since 1780: Programme, Myth, Reality* (Cambridge: Cambridge University Press, 1990).
3. Benedict Anderson, *Imagined Communities: Reflections on the Origin and Spread of Nationalism* (London: Verso, 1983).
4. "The capitalism that exists there is like a Marxist's dream come true. What you have is absolutely raw theft, I wouldn't even want to call it capitalism."

Marshall Goldman, a Russian scholar, quoted in Steve Liesman, "Surprise: The Economy in Russia Is Clawing out of Deep Recession," *The Wall Street Journal*, January 28, 1998.

5. "Private Propulsion," *The Economist*, February 14, 1998.

6. Warren Hoge, "Ah, Britain! The Light at the End of the Tunnel," *The New York Times*, March 9, 1998.

7. Manuel Castells, *The Power of Identity* (Malden, Mass.: Blackwell, 1997), p. 258.

8. Paul Light, "Big Government Is Bigger Than You Think," *The Wall Street Journal*, January 13, 1999.

9. Ann-Marie Slaughter, "The Real New World Order," *Foreign Affairs*, September/October 1997.

10. Robert Cooper, *The Post-Modern State and the World Order* (London: Demos, 1996).

11. Helene Cooper, "Holland Is Doing Its Best to Disappear into the New Europe," *The Wall Street Journal*, March 6, 1998.

12. "An Era for Mice to Roar," *The Wall Street Journal*, February 25, 1999.

13. Raphael Samuel, *Island Stories: Unravelling Britain* (London: Verso, 1998).

14. Helliwell, *How Much Do National Borders Matter?*

15. Brian Beedham, "The New Geopolitics," *The Economist*, July 31, 1999.

16. Peter Drucker, "The Global Economy and the Nation State," *Foreign Affairs*, September/October 1997.

Chapter 9

1. See Adam Roberts, "Towards a World Community," in Michael Howard and William Roger Louis, eds., *The Oxford History of the Twentieth Century* (Oxford: Oxford University Press, 1998).

2. From the United Nations Charter.

3. Poll by the University of Maryland Program on International Policy, quoted in "Idealism, Past and Present," *The New York Times*, January 4, 1998.

4. Marrack Goulding, "The UN Will Work If We Let It," *The New Statesman*, May 8, 1998.

5. Angus Reid/*Economist* poll, *The Economist*, January 2, 1999.

6. Rudi Dornbusch, quoted in "Top CEOs Are Upbeat about Business," *International Herald Tribune*, January 29, 1999.

7. For a wider discussion, see "The New Cambridge Mafia," *Institutional Investor*, September 1998.

8. "Bitter Medicine: South Korea Played the Reluctant Patient to IMF's Rescue Team," *The Wall Street Journal*, March 2, 1998.

9. One nice example of what might have happened is shown in Paul Krugman, "Let's Not Panic—Yet," *The New York Times*, August 30, 1998.

10. Michael Mussa, "The IMF: Responsive and Accountable," *Brookings Review*, fall 1998.

11. "Global Finance: Time for a Redesign," *The Economist*, January 30, 1999.

12. Barry Eichengreen, "Capital Mobility," *The Milken Institute Review* 1:1 (first quarter 1999).

13. Allan Metzer of Carnegie Mellon University.

14. Cited in "The Bailout Backlash," *U.S. News and World Report*, February 2, 1998.

15. Stanley Fischer, "On the Need for an International Lender of Last Resort," speech delivered at the joint luncheon of the American Economic Association and the American Finance Association, New York, January 3, 1999 (posted at www.imf.org/external/np/speeches/1999/010399.htm).

16. Martin Woolf, "Pegging Out," *Financial Times*, January 20, 1999.

17. Quoted in Judy Shelton, "Time for a New Bretton Woods," *The Wall Street Journal*, October 15, 1998.

18. Charles Kindleberger, *Manias, Panics, and Crashes: A History of Financial Crises* (New York: John Wiley and Sons, 1996).

19. "White Man's Shame," *The Economist*, September 25, 1999.

20. Quoted in "U.S. Has to Lead in Market Reform," *International Herald Tribune*, February 6, 1999.

Chapter 10

1. The story of the rise of French cinema—and its subsequent defeat at the hands of Hollywood—is well told in Bill Grantham, *Some Big Bourgeois Brothel: Contexts for France's Culture Wars with Hollywood* (Luton: University of Luton Press, 1999).

2. Figures quoted in "Schools Brief: A World View," *The Economist*, November 29, 1997.

3. "The Mixed Feelings of Europeans," *The Economist*, April 17, 1999.

4. Paul Lewis, "Too Late to Say 'Extinct' in Ubykh, Eyak, or Ona," *The New York Times*, August 15, 1998.

5. Quoted in Benjamin Barber, *Jihad vs. McWorld* (New York: Times Books, 1995), p. 90.

6. Paul Farhi and Megan Rosenfeld, "American Pop Penetrates Worldwide," *The Washington Post*, October 25, 1998.

7. Alessandra Stanley, "Italy Can't Believe Its Ears: Movies Lose Their Voices," *The New York Times*, September 16, 1998.

8. Hal Lipper, "Will 'Mr. Cat Poop' Clean Up at the Box Office in Hong Kong?" *The Wall Street Journal*, April 13, 1998. This article sparked off something of a craze for alleged Chinese titles for Western movies, some of them even funnier but most of them fictitious.

9. Michael Medved, *Hollywood versus America* (New York: HarperPerennial, 1993).

10. Douglas Blackmon, "Forget the Stereotype: America Is Becoming a Nation of Culture," *The Wall Street Journal*, September 17, 1998.

11. William F. Baker and George Dessart, *Down the Tube: An Inside Account of the Failure of American Television* (New York: Basic Books, 1998), pp. 206–7.

12. Rana Dogar, "Changing Channels," *Newsweek*, June 7, 1999.

13. Richard Covington, "Local Bands Leapfrog Global Stars on the Charts," *International Herald Tribune*, February 4, 1998.

14. Paulette Thomas, "Minority Businesses Increase Cross-Ethnic Marketing," *The Wall Street Journal*, April 21, 1998.

15. Nathan Gardels, ed., *The Changing Global Order* (Oxford: Blackwell, 1997).

16. Michael Elliott, "Killing Off Kipling," *Newsweek*, December 29, 1997.

17. Robert Hershey, "Americans Abroad Learn Studies Can Be a Bargain," *The New York Times*, March 1, 1998.

18. John Seabrook, "The Big Sell Out," *The New Yorker*, October 20, 1997.

19. Farhi and Rosenfeld, "American Pop Penetrates Worldwide."

20. "Coming to Hillingdon," *The Economist*, February 17, 1996.

Chapter 11

1. Robert Frank and Philip Cook, *The Winner-Take-All Society* (New York: Free Press, 1995), p. 2.

2. These statistics, like many subsequent ones about Silicon Valley, come from Joint Venture: Silicon Valley Network's 2002 Index.

3. AnnaLee Saxenian, *Regional Advantage: Culture and Competition in Silicon Valley and Route 128* (Cambridge, Mass.: Harvard University Press, 1994).

4. Homa Bahrami and Stuart Evans, "Flexible Recycling and High Technology Entrepreneurship," *California Management Review* 37:3 (spring 1995).

5. Stan Liebowitz and Stephen Margolis, "The Fable of the Keys," *Journal of Law and Economics*, October 1990.

6. Stan Liebowitz and Stephen Margolis, *Winners, Losers, and Microsoft: Competition and Antitrust in High Technology* (Oakland: Independent Institute, 1999).

7. The number of millionaires comes from a speech by John Heilemann, October 7, 1999.

8. Andrea Adelson, "After a Computer Age Windfall, Workers Reinvent Their Lives," *The New York Times*, May 30, 1999.

9. David Case, "High Tech Embraces 'Offshore' Employees," *Wired*, March 1998.

10. Andrew Tanzer, "Silicon Island," *Forbes Global Business and Finance*, June 1, 1998.

11. Krishna Guha, "India's On-line Meritocracy," *Financial Times*, October 25, 1999.

12. Visit by Lucy Jones on behalf of authors, spring 1999.

13. Candice Goodwin, "Orkney, Where a Software Developer May Safely Graze," *Daily Telegraph*, June 2, 1998.

14. Such a man was David Filo, cofounder of Yahoo! See Po Bronson, *The Nudist on the Late Shift* (New York: Random House, 1999).

15. Tamara Jacoby, "The African-American Absence in High Tech," *The New Republic*, March 29, 1999.

Chapter 12

1. Quoted in Rosabeth Moss Kanter, *World Class: Thriving Locally in the Global Economy* (New York: Simon and Schuster, 1995), p. 45.

2. Anthony Sampson, *Company Man: The Rise and Fall of Corporate Life* (London: HarperCollins, 1995).

3. Joann Lublin, "More Toasts, Less Sleep," *The Wall Street Journal*, November 19, 1998.

4. Trinh Quang Do, "A Letter from Vietnam," *Stanford Business*, March 1998.

5. Paschal Zachary, "Yanks in Vogue," *The Wall Street Journal*, June 8, 1998.

6. Anthony Spaeth, "Get Rich Quick," *Time*, April 13, 1998.

7. James Bates, "Watch the Money," *Los Angeles Times Magazine*, January 31, 1999, p. 33.

8. Samuel P. Huntington, *The Clash of Civilizations and the Remaking of World Order* (New York: Simon and Schuster, 1996), p. 57.

9. Manuel Castells, *The Rise of the Network Society*, vol. 1 (Malden, Mass.: Blackwell, 1996), p. 232.

10. David Ewing, *Inside the Harvard Business School: Strategies and Lessons of America's Leading School of Business* (New York: Times Books, 1990), p. 30.

11. "The Hottest Campus on the Internet," *BusinessWeek*, October 20, 1997.

12. "The New Stars of Finance," *BusinessWeek*, October 27, 1997.

13. Nina Munk, "The New Organization Man," *Fortune*, March 16, 1998.

14. Nancy Ann Jeffrey, "Sleep: The New Status Symbol," *The Wall Street Journal*, April 2, 1999.

15. Sue Shellenbarger, "Families Are Facing New Strains as Work Expands across the Globe," *The Wall Street Journal*, November 12, 1997.

16. McKinsey and Company, "The War for Talent: Report to Participating Companies. March 1998," p. 17.

17. Robert Reich, *The Work of Nations: Preparing Ourselves for the Twenty-first Century* (New York: Alfred A. Knopf, 1991).

18. Castells, *Rise of the Network Society*, p. 415.

19. Kanter, *World Class*, p. 219.
20. Joel Kotkin, "Business Leadership in the New Economy: Southern California at a Crossroad," La Jolla Institute Report, July 1998, p. 8.
21. Kanter, *World Class*, p. 161.
22. Christopher Lasch, *The Revolt of the Elites and the Betrayal of Democracy* (New York: W. W. Norton, 1995), pp. 33, 47.

Chapter 13

1. Louis Uchtelle, "The Middle Class: Winning in Politics, Losing in Life," *The New York Times*, July 19, 1998.
2. Clay Chandler, "Bull Market Bypasses Many Americans," *International Herald Tribune*, April 8, 1999.
3. Bethany McLean, "Wretched Excess," *Fortune*, September 7, 1998.
4. Celestine Bohlen, "After Moscow Elite's Binge, Hangover Time Has Come," *The New York Times*, September 8, 1998.
5. Michael Reid, "Disorders of Progress: A Survey of Brazil," *The Economist*, March 1999.
6. Michael Phillips, "Dhaka on the Potomac," *The Wall Street Journal*, August 24, 1998.
7. Maggie O'Kane, "She Is Just Three and Suffers from a Plague That Kills Millions—The Plague of Debt," *The Guardian*, May 11, 1998.
8. Robert Fogel, cited in Ron Suskind, "Misery Amongst Plenty," *The Wall Street Journal*, special millennium section, January 11, 1999.
9. The prime resource for poverty statistics is the UNDP's *Human Development Report* (Oxford: Oxford University Press for the UNDP, 1999).
10. Raymond Baker and Jennifer Nordin, "A 150:1 Ratio Is Far Too Lopsided for Comfort," *International Herald Tribune*, February 5, 1999.
11. Larry Elliott, "Why the Poor Are Picking Up the Tab," *The Guardian*, May 11, 1998.
12. Michael Cox and Richard Alm, *Myths of Rich and Poor* (New York: Basic Books, 1999).
13. Jim Rohwer, *Asia Rising* (London: Nicholas Brealey, 1995), p. 127.
14. Maria Carmen de Mello Lemos, "The Cubatao Pollution Control Project: Popular Participation and Public Accountability," *Journal of Environment and Development* 7:1 (March 1998).
15. David Malin Roodman, *The Natural Wealth of Nations: Harnessing the Market for the Environment* (New York: W. W. Norton/Worldwatch, 1998), p. 19.

Chapter 14

1. Quoted in "U.S. Has to Lead in Market Reform," *International Herald Tribune*, February 6, 1999.

2. Quoted in Alan Cowell, "Annan Fears Backlash over Global Crisis," *The New York Times*, February 1, 1999.

3. Frances Williams, "Globalization Bad for Your Health, say UN Agencies," *Financial Times*, June 10, 1999.

4. Emma Rothschild, "Globalization and Democracy in Historical Perspective" (Working Paper, February 1999), p. 6.

5. Keynes, *Economic Consequences of the Peace*, p. 11.

6. "Letter from Nantahala," *The New Yorker*, March 15, 1999.

7. Ian Buruma, *Anglomania: A European Love Affair* (New York: Random House, 1999), p. 190.

8. Julia Preston, "Unrest in Mexico Breeds Resentment of Outsiders," *The New York Times*, February 14, 1998.

9. Research by Peter Bergen for his book *Holy War Inc.*

10. Ibid.

11. Peter Beinart, "Greens Flip over Turtles," *Time*, April 27, 1998.

12. Reuters Forum on Globalization at Columbia University, New York, April 1, 1998.

13. Nadine Gordimer, "Dare to Dream of Eradicating Poverty," *The New York Times*, August 1, 1998.

14. Edward Luttwak, *Turbo-Capitalism* (New York: HarperCollins, 1999), pp. 235–37.

15. Richard Rorty, "The American Road to Fascism," *New Statesman*, May 8, 1998.

16. Patrick Buchanan, *The Great Betrayal: How American Sovereignty and Social Justice Are Being Sacrificed to the Gods of the Global Economy* (New York: Little, Brown, 1998), p. 285.

17. Quoted in Roger Cohen, "Redrawing the Free Market," *The New York Times*, November 14, 1998.

18. William Pfaff, "Marx's Plan Did Not Work but He Did Understand Capitalism," *International Herald Tribune*, May 21, 1998.

19. Quoted in Robert Reich, "Trading Insecurities," *Financial Times*, May 20, 1999.

20. Ibid.

21. *International Herald Tribune*, February 17, 1998.

22. "Sunday," *The New York Times Magazine*, August 23, 1998.

23. "Europe's Burden," *The Economist*, May 22, 1999.

Chapter 15

1. Thomas Babington Macaulay, "Essay on Milton," in *Critical and Historical Essays* (London: Dent and Sons, 1966).
2. Ron Chernow, *Titan: The Life of John D. Rockefeller, Sr.* (New York: Random House, 1998).
3. The best guide to this subject is the World Bank's 1997 World Development Report, *The State in a Changing World*.
4. Landes, *Wealth and Poverty of Nations*, pp. 213–30.
5. Peter Brimelow, "The Cost of Castro," *Forbes*, March 23, 1998.
6. Roger Cohen, "Argentina Sees Other Face of Globalization," *The New York Times*, February 6, 1998.
7. Nicholas Timmins, "Another Inspector Calls," *Financial Times*, August 12, 1999.
8. Richard Perez-Pena, "A Riddle at the Tax Register," *The New York Times*, April 3, 1999.
9. Michael Phillips, "Taking Shelter," *The Wall Street Journal*, August 4, 1999.
10. Lester Thurow, "Building Wealth," *The Atlantic*, June 1999. His figures were derived by averaging the results of eight studies.
11. "Helping the Poorest of the Poor," *The Economist*, August 14, 1999.
12. "Education and the Wealth of Nations," *The Economist*, March 29, 1997.

Chapter 16

1. We should disclose that one of us has shares in one of Bank Sarasin's global funds.
2. See *1999 Global Entrepreneurship Monitor*.
3. Kim Clark, "Why It Pays to Quit," *U.S. News and World Report*, November 1, 1999.
4. Charles Handy, *The Hungry Spirit: Beyond Capitalism: A Quest for Purpose in the Modern World* (New York: Broadway, 1997), pp. 55–56.
5. William Whyte, *The Organization Man* (New York: Penguin, 1965).
6. Tom Peters, *The Brand You 50: 50 Ways to Transform Yourself from an "Employee" into a Brand That Shouts Distinction, Commitment, and Passion* (New York: Alfred A. Knopf, 1999), p. 12.
7. Ethan Kapstein, *Sharing the Wealth: Workers and the World Economy* (New York: W. W. Norton, 1999).
8. The debate about how much job tenure is changing is a long one. One good place to start is David Neumark, Daniel Polsky, and Daniel Hansen, "Has Job Stability Declined Yet? New Evidence for the 1990s," National Bureau of Economic Research, Working Paper 6330, December 1997.

9. According to the Economic Policy Institute, the average middle-class American family now works 3,335 hours a year—around eight workweeks more than in 1979.

10. For a comprehensive demolition of Al Dunlap, see John Byrne, *Chainsaw: The Notorious Career of Al Dunlap in the Era of Profit at Any Price* (New York: HarperCollins, 1999).

11. Peter Drucker, "Managing Oneself," *Harvard Business Review,* March–April 1999.

Conclusion

1. For any skeptics, the date was May 13, 1998.

2. Karl Marx and Friedrich Engels, *The Communist Manifesto* (London: Penguin Classics, 1985), pp. 83–84.

3. Ibid., p. 83.

4. "A Capital of Haves and Have Nots," *International Herald Tribune,* May 7, 1998.

5. Ibid.

6. Alexis de Tocqueville, *Democracy in America* (1835–1840), vol. 2, p. 99.

7. Marx and Engels, *The Communist Manifesto,* p. 83.

Bibliography

As should be obvious from many of the notes in this book, it would have been extremely difficult to write this without all the many reports from the multilateral organizations: the International Monetary Fund, the World Bank, the UN Development Program, the United Nations Conference on Trade and Development, the United Nations Children's Fund, the International Labor Organization, and so on. Listing all of them would swamp this bibliography. The websites of these organizations should be the first stop for anybody wanting to delve deeper into individual fields of globalization. Similarly, listing all the newspaper articles that we have read would amount to a deluge. This, then, is a list of the main books and papers that we have found useful.

Aggarwal, Vinod. *Institutional Designs for a Complex World* (Ithaca, N.Y.: Cornell University Press, 1998)

Aghion, Philippe, and Jeffrey Williamson. *Growth Inequality and Globalization* (Cambridge: Cambridge University Press, 1998)

Aharoni, Yari. *The Evolution and Management of State-Owned Enterprises* (Cambridge, Mass.: Ballinger Publishing, 1986)

Anderson, Malcolm. *Frontiers: Territory and State Formation in the Modern World* (London: Polity Press, 1996)

Applebaum, Anne. *Between East and West* (London: Pantheon, 1994)

Bahrami, Homa, and Stuart Evans. "Flexible Recycling and High Technology Entrepreneurship," *California Management Review* 37:3 (spring 1995)

Baker, William, and George Dessart. *Down the Tube: An Inside Account of the Failure of American Television* (New York: Basic Books, 1998)

Barber, Benjamin. *Jihad vs. McWorld* (New York: Times Books, 1995)

Barnet, Richard, and John Cavanagh. *Global Dreams: Imperial Corporations and the New World Order* (New York: Simon and Schuster, 1994)

Bhagwati, Jagdish. *A Stream of Windows: Unsettling Reflections on Trade, Immigration, and Democracy* (Cambridge, Mass.: MIT Press, 1998)

Bhagwati, Jagdish, ed. *Trading Blocs: Alternative Approaches to Analyzing Preferential Trade Agreements* (Cambridge, Mass.: MIT Press, 1999)

Bordo, Michael, Barry Eichengreen, and Douglas Irwin. "Is Globalization Really Different Than Globalization a Hundred Years Ago?" National Bureau of Economic Research, Working Paper 7195, June 1999

Bronson, Po. *The Nudist on the Late Shift* (New York: Random House, 1999)

Bryan, Lowell, and Diana Farrell. *Market Unbound: Unleashing Global Capitalism* (New York: John Wiley and Sons, 1996)

Bryan, Lowell, et al. *Race for the World: Strategies to Build a Great Global Firm* (Boston: Harvard Business School Press, 1999)

Buchanan, Patrick. *The Great Betrayal: How American Sovereignty and Social Justice Are Being Sacrificed to the Gods of the Global Economy* (New York: Little, Brown, 1998)

Buckingham, Marcus, and Curt Coffman. *First, Break All the Rules: What the World's Greatest Managers Do Differently* (New York: Simon and Schuster, 1999)

Burnham, James. *The Managerial Revolution* (London, 1941)

Burtless, Gary, et al. *Globaphobia: Confronting Fears about Open Trade* (Washington, D.C.: Brookings Institution Press, 1998)

Buruma, Ian. *Anglomania: A European Love Affair* (New York: Random House, 1999)

Byrne, John. *Chainsaw: The Notorious Career of Al Dunlap in the Era of Profit at Any Price* (New York: HarperCollins, 1999)

Cairncross, Frances. *The Death of Distance: How the Communications Revolution Will Change Our Lives* (Boston: Harvard Business School Press, 1997)

Castells, Manuel. *The Rise of the Network Society*, vol. 1 (Malden, Mass.: Blackwell, 1996)

———. *The Power of Identity* (Malden, Mass.: Blackwell, 1997)

———. *End of the Millennium* (Malden, Mass.: Blackwell, 1998)

Chernow, Ron. *Titan: The Life of John D. Rockefeller, Sr.* (New York: Random House, 1998)

Cooper, Robert. *The Post-Modern State and the World Order* (London: Demos, 1996)

Courchene, Thomas. *Room to Maneuver? Globalization and Policy Convergence* (Kingston, Ont.: McGill-Queen's University Press, 1999)

Crainer, Stuart, and Des Dearlove. *Gravy Training: Inside the Business of Business Schools* (San Francisco: Jossey-Bass, 1999)

Davis, Bob, and David Wessel. *Prosperity: The Coming Twenty-Year Boom and What It Means to You* (New York: Times Books, 1998)

Dobbin, Murray. *The Myth of the Good Corporate Citizen: Democracy under the Rule of Big Business* (Toronto: Stoddart, 1998)

Doremus, Paul, et al. *The Myth of the Global Corporation* (Princeton: Princeton University Press, 1998)

Drucker, Peter. *The Concept of the Corporation* (New York: Mentor, 1983)

———. *Post-Capitalist Society* (New York: HarperBusiness, 1983)

———. *Managing in a Time of Great Change* (New York: Truman Talley, 1996)

———. "The Global Economy and the Nation State," *Foreign Affairs*, September/October 1997.

———. "Managing Oneself," *Harvard Business Review*, March–April 1999

Dudley-Edwards, Ruth. *The Pursuit of Reason: The Economist 1843–1993* (London: Hamish Hamilton, 1993)

Eichengreen, Barry. "Capital Mobility," *The Milken Institute Review* 1:1 (first quarter 1999)

Ewing, David. *Inside the Harvard Business School: Strategies and Lessons of America's Leading School of Business* (New York: Times Books, 1990)

Fairbanks, Michael, and Stace Lindsay. *Plowing the Sea: Nurturing the Hidden Sources of Growth in the Developing World* (Boston: Harvard Business School Press, 1997)

Ferguson, Niall. *The House of Rothschild: Money's Prophets 1798–1848* (New York: Viking, 1998)

Frank, Robert. *Luxury Fever: Why Money Fails to Satisfy in an Era of Excess* (New York: Free Press, 1999)

Frank, Robert, and Philip Cook. *The Winner-Take-All Society* (New York: Free Press, 1995)

Freeman, Richard. *The New Inequality: Creating Solutions for Poor America* (Boston: Beacon Press/New Democracy Forum, 1998)

Freidheim, Cyrus. *The Trillion-Dollar Enterprise: How the Alliance Revolution Will Transform Global Business* (Reading, Mass.: Perseus Books, 1998)

Friedman, Thomas. *The Lexus and the Olive Tree* (New York: Farrar, Straus and Giroux, 1999)

Fukuyama, Francis. *The End of History* (New York: Free Press, 1992)

Galbraith, James. *Created Unequal: The Hidden Forces behind the Crisis in American Pay* (New York: Free Press, 1998)

Galbraith, John Kenneth. *The Good Society: The Human Agenda* (Boston: Houghton Mifflin, 1996)

Gardels, Nathan, ed. *The Changing Global Order* (Oxford: Blackwell, 1997)

Gates, Bill. *Business @ the Speed of Thought* (New York: Warner, 1999)

Gay, Peter. *The Enlightenment* (New York: Norton Library, 1977)

Ghoshal, Sumantra, and Christopher Bartlett. *The Individualized Corporation* (New York: HarperBusiness, 1997)

Goldie, Mark, ed. *Locke: Political Essays* (Cambridge: Cambridge University Press, 1997)

Grantham, Bill. *Some Big Bourgeois Brothel: Contexts for France's Culture Wars with Hollywood* (Luton: University of Luton Press, 1999)

Gray, John. *Against the New Liberalism* (London: Routledge, 1995)

———. *False Dawn: The Delusions of Global Capitalism* (London: Granta Books, 1998)

———. *John Stuart Mill: On Liberty and Other Essays* (Oxford: Oxford University Press, 1998)

Greider, William. *One World, Ready or Not: The Manic Logic of Global Capitalism* (New York: Touchstone, 1998)

Greising, David. *I'd Like the World to Buy a Coke: The Life and Leadership of Roberto Goizueta* (New York: John Wiley and Sons, 1998)

Handy, Charles. *The Hungry Spirit: Beyond Capitalism: A Quest for Purpose in the Modern World* (New York: Broadway, 1997)

Hardy, Henry, ed. *Isaiah Berlin: The Proper Study of Mankind: An Anthology of Essays* (New York: Farrar, Straus and Giroux, 1998)

Helliwell, John. *How Much Do National Borders Matter?* (Washington, D.C.: Brookings Institution Press, 1997)

Hobsbawm, E. J. *Nations and Nationalism since 1780: Programme, Myth, Reality* (Cambridge: Cambridge University Press, 1990)

———. *The Age of Extremes: A History of the World, 1914–1991* (New York: Vintage, 1994)

Howard, Michael, and William Roger Louis, eds. *The Oxford History of the Twentieth Century* (Oxford: Oxford University Press, 1998)

Huntington, Samuel P. *The Clash of Civilizations and the Remaking of World Order* (New York: Simon and Schuster, 1996)

Ignatieff, Michael. *Isaiah Berlin* (London: Chatto and Windus, 1998)

Irwin, Douglas. *Against the Tide: An Intellectual History of Free Trade* (Princeton: Princeton University Press, 1996)

Jenkins, Simon. *Accountable to None: The Tory Nationalization of Britain* (London: Hamish Hamilton, 1995)

Kahler, Miles, ed. *Capital Flows and Financial Crises* (Ithaca, N.Y.: Cornell University Press, 1998)

Kanter, Rosabeth Moss. *World Class: Thriving Locally in the Global Economy* (New York: Simon and Schuster, 1995)

———. *Frontiers of Management* (Boston: Harvard Business School Press, 1997)

Kaplan, Edward. *American Trade Policy, 1923–1995* (Westport, Conn.: Greenwood, 1996)

Kaplan, Robert. *The Ends of the Earth: A Journey at the Dawn of the Twenty-first Century* (New York: Random House, 1996)

Kapstein, Ethan. *Sharing the Wealth: Workers and the World Economy* (New York: W. W. Norton, 1999)

Kaul, Inge, Isabelle Grunberg, and Marc Stern. *Global Public Goods* (Oxford: Oxford University Press, 1999)

Keynes, John Maynard. *The Economic Consequences of the Peace* (London: Macmillan, 1919)

Kindleberger, Charles. *The World in Depression, 1929–1939*, rev. ed. (Berkeley and Los Angeles: University of California Press, 1986)

———. *Manias, Panics, and Crashes: A History of Financial Crises* (New York: John Wiley and Sons, 1996)

Kissinger, Henry. *Diplomacy* (London: Simon and Schuster, 1994)

Korey, William. *NGOs and the Universal Declaration of Human Rights* (New York: St. Martin's Press, 1998)

Kotkin, Joel. *Tribes: How Race, Religion, and Identity Determine Success in the New Global Economy* (New York: Random House, 1992)

———. "Business Leadership in the New Economy: Southern California at a Crossroad," La Jolla Institute Report, July 1998

Krugman, Paul. *Pop Internationalism* (Cambridge, Mass.: MIT Press, 1996)

———. *The Accidental Theorist* (New York: W. W. Norton, 1998)

———. *The Return of Depression Economics* (New York: W. W. Norton, 1999)

Landes, David. *The Wealth and Poverty of Nations: Why Some Are So Rich and Others Are So Poor* (New York: W. W. Norton, 1998)

Lasch, Christopher. *The Revolt of the Elites and the Betrayal of Democracy* (New York: W. W. Norton, 1995)

Lewis, Michael. *The New New Thing: A Silicon Valley Story* (New York: W. W. Norton, 1999)

Liebowitz, Stan, and Stephen Margolis. "The Fable of the Keys," *Journal of Law and Economics*, October 1990

———. *Winners, Losers, and Microsoft: Competition and Antitrust in High Technology* (Oakland: Independent Institute, 1999)

Luck, Edward. *Mixed Messages: American Politics and International Organization, 1919–1999* (Washington, D.C.: Brookings Institution Press, 1999)

Luttwak, Edward. *Turbo-Capitalism* (New York: HarperCollins, 1999)

Macaulay, Thomas Babington. "Essay on Milton," in *Critical and Historical Essays* (London: Dent and Sons, 1966)

MacKenzie, Norman, and Jeanne MacKenzie, eds. *The Diary of Beatrice Webb*, vol. 2, *1895–1905* (London: Virago, 1983)

McKinsey and Company. "The War for Talent: Report to Participating Companies. March 1998"

Mander, Jerry, and Edward Goldsmith, eds. *The Case Against the Global Economy* (San Francisco: Sierra Club Books, 1996)

Marx, Karl. *Capital: A Critique of Political Economy* (New York: Penguin, 1992)

Marx, Karl, and Friedrich Engels. *The Communist Manifesto* (London: Penguin Classics, 1985)

Millman, Gregory. *The Vandal's Crown: How Rebel Currency Traders Overthrew the World's Central Banks* (New York: Free Press, 1995)

Mintzberg, Henry. *Mintzberg on Management* (New York: Free Press, 1989)

Mitford, Jessica. *The American Way of Death Revisited* (New York: Alfred A. Knopf, 1998)

National Research Council. *The Changing Nature of Work: Implications for Occupational Analysis* (Washington, D.C.: National Academy Press, 1999)

Neumark, David, Daniel Polsky, and Daniel Hansen. "Has Job Stability Declined Yet? New Evidence for the 1990s," National Bureau of Economic Research, Working Paper 6330, December 1997

Ohmae, Kenichi. *Triad Power* (New York: Free Press, 1985)

———. *The Borderless World* (New York: HarperBusiness, 1990)

———. *The End of the Nation-State: The Rise of Regional Economics* (New York: Free Press, 1995)

Ohmae, Kenichi, ed. *The Evolving Global Economy: Making Sense of the New World Order* (Boston: Harvard Business School Press, 1985)

Oliver, Richard. *The Shape of Things to Come* (New York: Business Week Books, 1998)

Patten, Christopher. *East and West: China, Power, and the Future of Asia* (New York: Times Books, 1998)

Peters, Tom. *The Brand You 50: 50 Ways to Transform Yourself from an "Employee" into a Brand That Shouts Distinction, Commitment, and Passion* (New York: Alfred A. Knopf, 1999)

Picco, Giandomenico. *Man without a Gun: One Diplomat's Secret Struggle to Free the Hostages, Fight Terrorism, and End a War* (New York: Random House, 1999)

Porter, Michael. *Competitive Advantage* (New York: Free Press, 1985)

———. *Competitive Strategy* (New York: Free Press, 1985)

———. *Competitive Advantage of Nations* (London: Macmillan, 1989)

———. *Competitive Advantage of Massachusetts* (1991)

———. "Competitive Advantage of the Inner City," *Harvard Business Review*, May 1995

———. *On Competition* (Boston: Harvard Business School Press, 1998)

Puttnam, David. *Movies and Money* (New York: Alfred A. Knopf, 1998)

Reich, Robert. *The Work of Nations: Preparing Ourselves for the Twenty-first Century* (New York: Alfred A. Knopf, 1991)

Rifkin, Jeremy. *The End of Work: The Decline of the Global Labor Force and the Dawn of the Post-Market Era* (New York: Putnam, 1995)

Rodrik, Dani. "The Debate over Globalization," paper presented at Harvard University, April 1998

Rohwer, Jim. *Asia Rising* (London: Nicholas Brealey, 1995)

Roodman, David Malin. *The Natural Wealth of Nations: Harnessing the Market for the Environment* (New York: W. W. Norton/Worldwatch, 1998)

Ruigrok, Winfried, and Rob van Tulder. *The Logic of International Restructuring* (London: Routledge, 1995)

Russell, Bertrand. *Autobiography, 1872–1914* (London, 1967)

Sachs, Jeffrey. "Globalization and Employment," speech given at the International Institute for Labor Studies, Geneva, March 1996

Sampson, Anthony. *The Sovereign State of ITT* (New York: Stein and Day, 1973)

———. *Company Man: The Rise and Fall of Corporate Life* (London: HarperCollins, 1995)

Samuel, Raphael. *Island Stories: Unravelling Britain* (London: Verso, 1998)

Saxenian, AnnaLee. *Regional Advantage: Culture and Competition in Silicon Valley and Route 128* (Cambridge, Mass.: Harvard University Press, 1994)

———. *Silicon Valley's New Immigrant Entrepreneurs* (San Francisco: Public Policy Institute of California, 1999)

Skidelsky, Robert. *John Maynard Keynes: Hopes Betrayed, 1883–1920* (London: Macmillan, 1983)

———. *John Maynard Keynes: The Economist as Savior, 1920–1937* (London: Macmillan, 1992)

———. *The Road from Serfdom* (New York: Penguin, 1996)

Skinner, Quentin. *Liberty before Liberalism* (Cambridge: Cambridge University Press, 1998)

Slaughter, Ann-Marie. "The Real New World Order," *Foreign Affairs*, September/October 1997

Smith, Adam. *The Wealth of Nations: An Inquiry into the Nature and Causes* (New York: Modern Library, 1994)

———. *The Theory of Moral Sentiments* (New York: Regnery, 1999)

Stewart, Thomas. *Intellectual Capital: The New Wealth of Organizations* (New York: Doubleday/Currency, 1997)

Strouse, Jean. *Morgan: American Financier* (New York: Random House, 1999)

Thurow, Lester. *The Future of Capitalism: How Today's Economic Forces Shape Tomorrow's World* (London: Nicholas Brealey, 1996)

———. *Building Wealth: The New Rules for Individuals, Companies, and Nations in a Knowledge-Based Economy* (New York: HarperCollins, 1999)

Tichy, Noel, and Eli Cohen. *The Leadership Engine* (New York: HarperCollins, 1997)

Tichy, Noel, and Stratford Sherman. *Control Your Destiny or Somebody Else Will* (New York: Doubleday, 1993)

Tocqueville, Alexis de. *Democracy in America* (1835–1840)

United States Commission on National Security/Twenty-first Century, *New World Coming: American Security in the Twenty-first Century* (1999)

United States Department of Labor. *Report on the American Workforce* (Washington, D.C., 1999)

Van der Pijl, Kees. *Transnational Classes and International Relations* (London: Routledge, 1998)

Vernon, Raymond. *Sovereignty at Bay* (New York: Basic Books, 1971)

Watson, James, ed. *Golden Arches East: McDonald's in East Asia* (Stanford: Stanford University Press, 1998)

Weiss, Linda. *The Myth of the Powerless State* (Ithaca, N.Y.: Cornell University Press, 1998)

Whyte, William. *The Organization Man* (New York, Penguin, 1965)

Wilms, Wellford. *Restoring Prosperity: How Workers and Managers Are Forging a New Culture of Cooperation* (New York: Times Books, 1996)

Winchester, Simon. *The Fracture Zone: A Return to the Balkans* (New York: HarperCollins, 1999)

Yergin, Daniel, and Joseph Stanislaw. *The Commanding Heights: The Battle Between Government and the Marketplace That Is Remaking the Modern World* (New York: Simon and Schuster, 1998)

Zakaria, Fareed. *From Wealth to Power: The Unusual Origins of America's World Power* (Princeton: Princeton University Press, 1998)

Index